BEASTARS
Volume 15

Story & Art by
Paru Itagaki

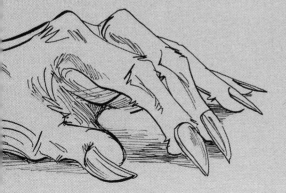

STORY & CAST OF CHARACTERS

Legoshi has been designated a registered meat offender after consensually eating his friend Louis's leg to give him the strength to defeat Riz, the bear who murdered their friend Tem. Now Legoshi has dropped out of school and is working at Bebebe, an udon noodle shop. While delivering takeout to a marine animal for the first time, Legoshi is rescued from a miscommunication with a hungry customer by Sagwan, a spotted seal. Sagwan is a half-marine, half-land animal who speaks both realms' languages. It turns out he lives in the same apartment complex as Legoshi. Through conversations with his new friend, Legoshi learns about the philosophies of the marine world, which are radically different from those on land.

Beastar Yahya has a grudge against Legoshi's grandfather Gosha and takes his revenge on Legoshi. Legoshi is horrified when he learns the source of Yahya's power—turning evil beasts he captures into fertilizer to grow his food. Then Legoshi goes on a date with Haru, who insists they visit the black market. Meanwhile, Yahya investigates elephant-tusk poaching and confronts Melon, a crazed beast who is half-carnivore, half-herbivore...

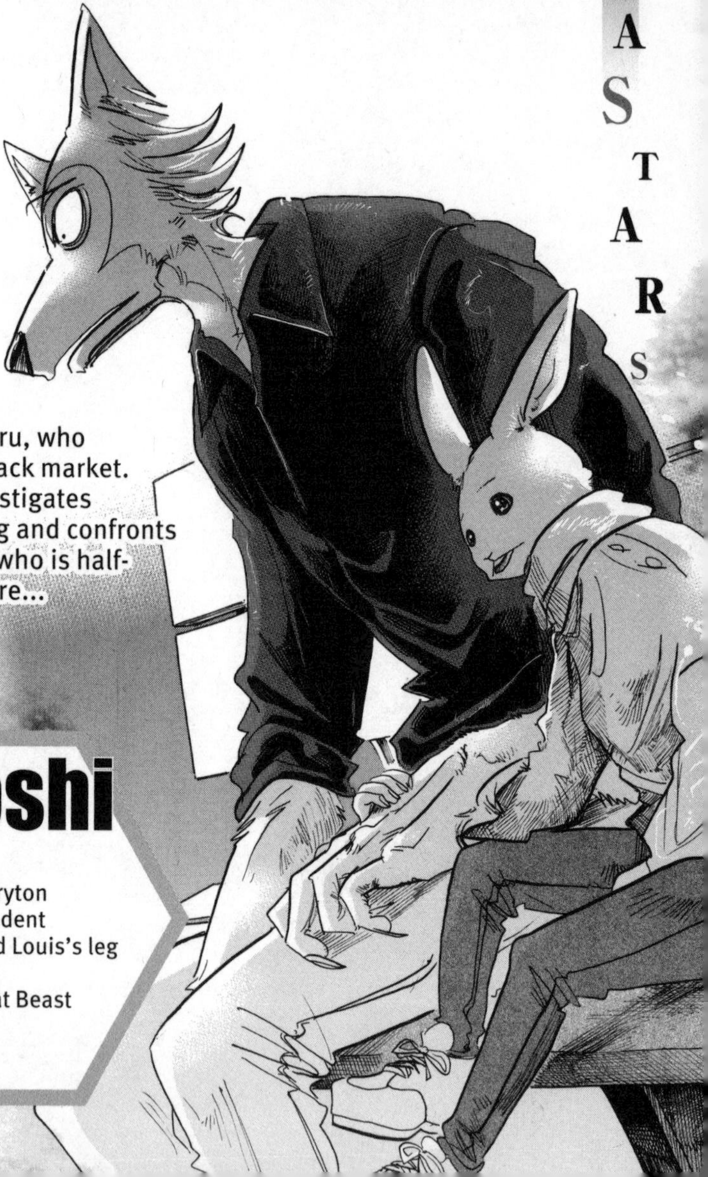

Legoshi

- ★Gray wolf ♂
- ★Former Cherryton Academy student
- ★Ate his friend Louis's leg to defeat Riz
- ★Lives alone at Beast Apartments

Louis

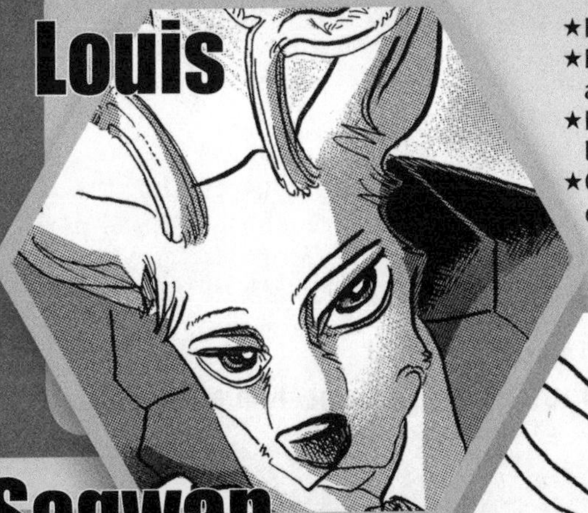

- ★Red deer ♂
- ★Former leader of the Drama Club actors pool
- ★Former leader of the Shishi-gumi lion gang
- ★Offered his leg to Legoshi so he could defeat Riz

Haru

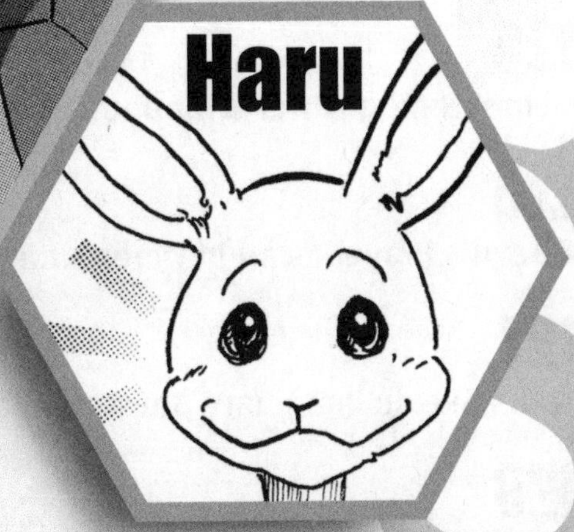

- ★Netherland dwarf rabbit ♀
- ★University student

Sagwan

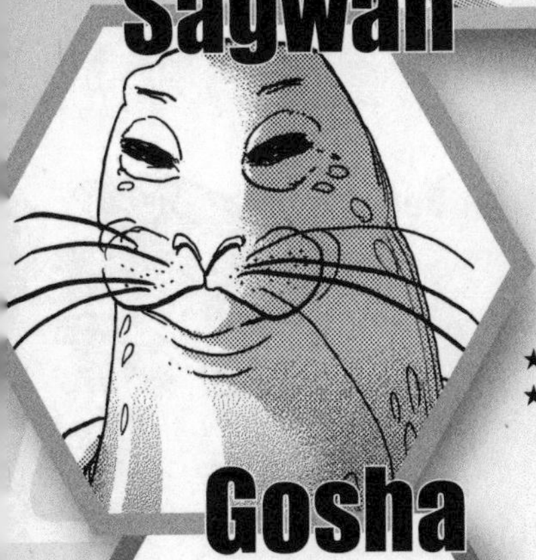

- ★Spotted seal ♂
- ★A half-marine, half-land animal and resident of Beast Apartments

Gosha

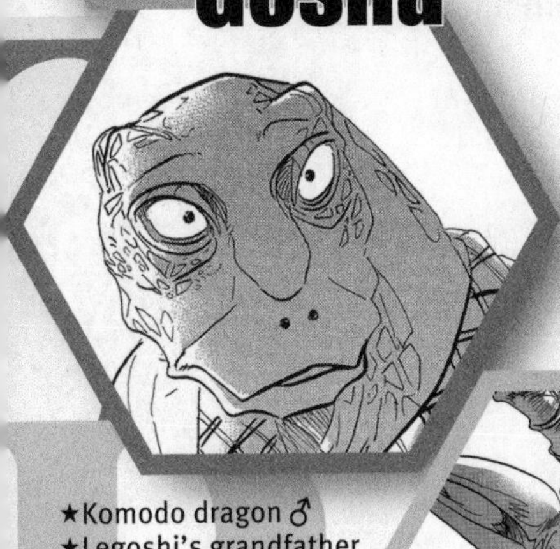

- ★Komodo dragon ♂
- ★Legoshi's grandfather
- ★Has a history with Beastar Yahya

Yahya

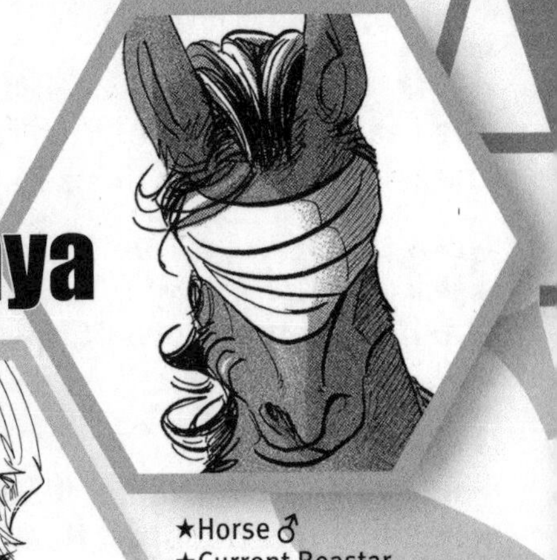

- ★Horse ♂
- ★Current Beastar
- ★Powerful combatant

Melon

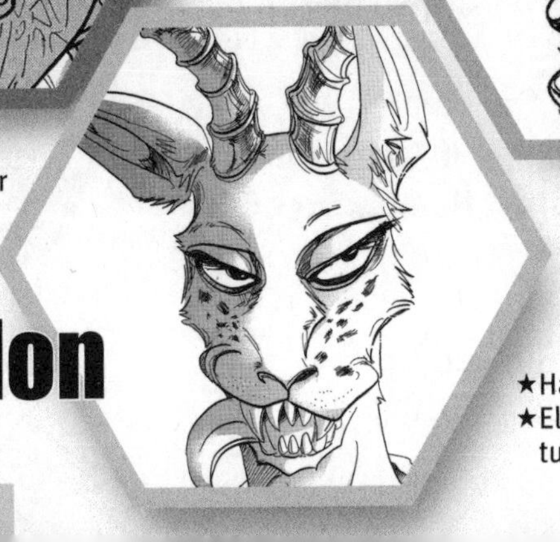

- ★Half-leopard, half-gazelle ♂
- ★Elephant poacher who sells tusks on the black market

BEASTARS

Volume 15

CONTENTS

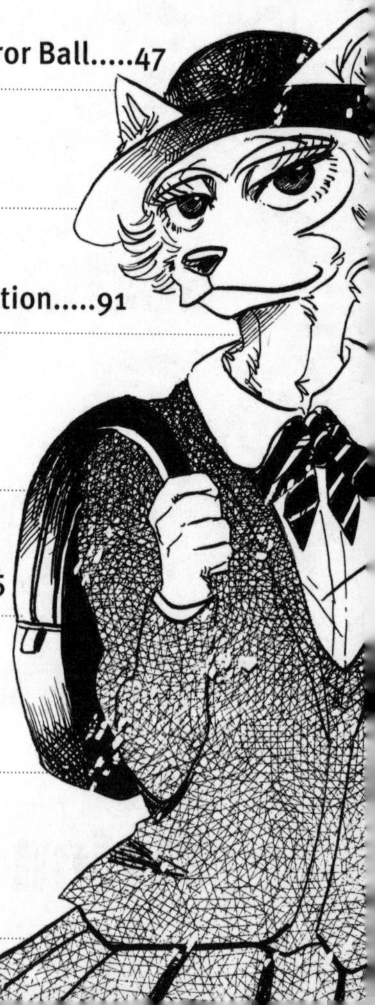

Chapter 125: A Threatening Letter Wrapped like a Gift Sent by a Monster

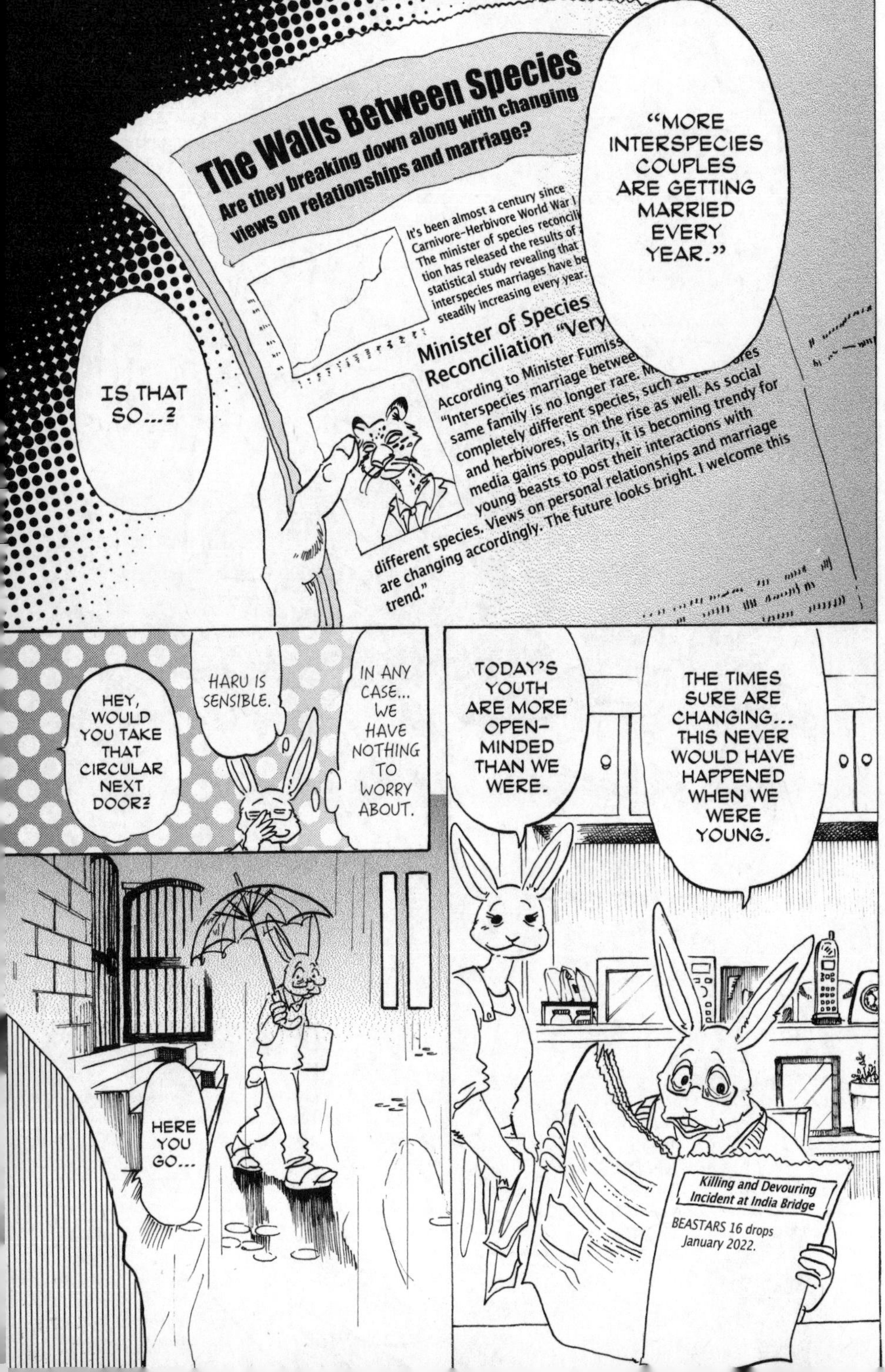
"MORE INTERSPECIES COUPLES ARE GETTING MARRIED EVERY YEAR."
The Walls Between Species
Are they breaking down along with changing views on relationships and marriage?
It's been almost a century since Carnivore-Herbivore World War I
The minister of species reconcili
tion has released the results of
statistical study revealing that
interspecies marriages have be
steadily increasing every year.
Minister of Species Reconciliation "Very
According to Minister Fumiss
"Interspecies marriage betwee
same family is no longer rare. M
completely different species, such as
and herbivores, is on the rise as well. As social media gains popularity, it is becoming trendy for young beasts to post their interactions with different species. Views on personal relationships and marriage are changing accordingly. The future looks bright. I welcome this trend."
IS THAT SO...?
THE TIMES SURE ARE CHANGING... THIS NEVER WOULD HAVE HAPPENED WHEN WE WERE YOUNG.
TODAY'S YOUTH ARE MORE OPEN-MINDED THAN WE WERE.
Killing and Devouring Incident at India Bridge
BEASTARS 16 drops January 2022.
IN ANY CASE... WE HAVE NOTHING TO WORRY ABOUT.
HARU IS SENSIBLE.
HEY, WOULD YOU TAKE THAT CIRCULAR NEXT DOOR?
HERE YOU GO...

Chapter 125: A Threatening Letter Wrapped like a Gift Sent by a Monster

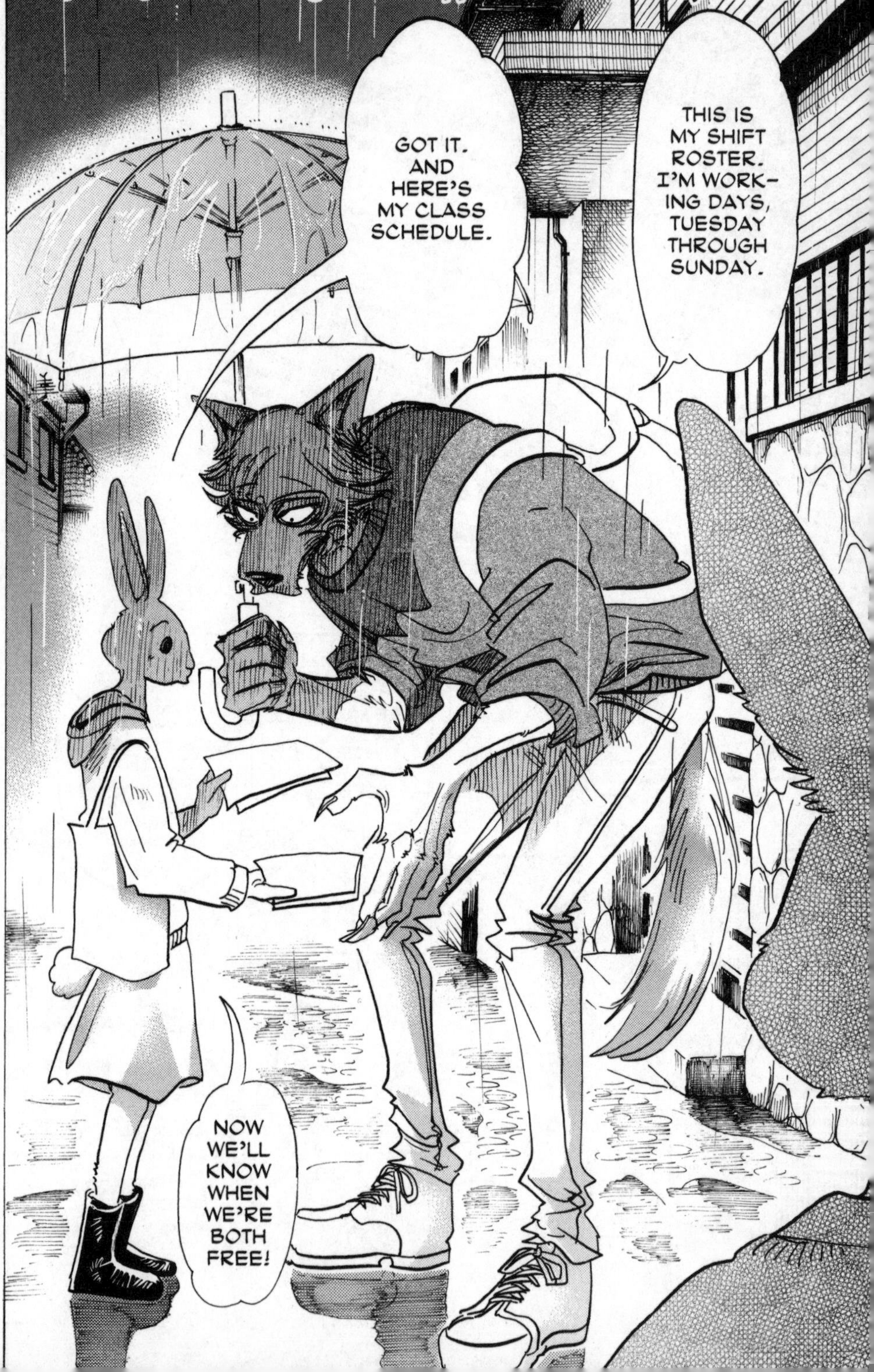
THIS IS MY SHIFT ROSTER. I'M WORKING DAYS, TUESDAY THROUGH SUNDAY.
GOT IT. AND HERE'S MY CLASS SCHEDULE.
NOW WE'LL KNOW WHEN WE'RE BOTH FREE!

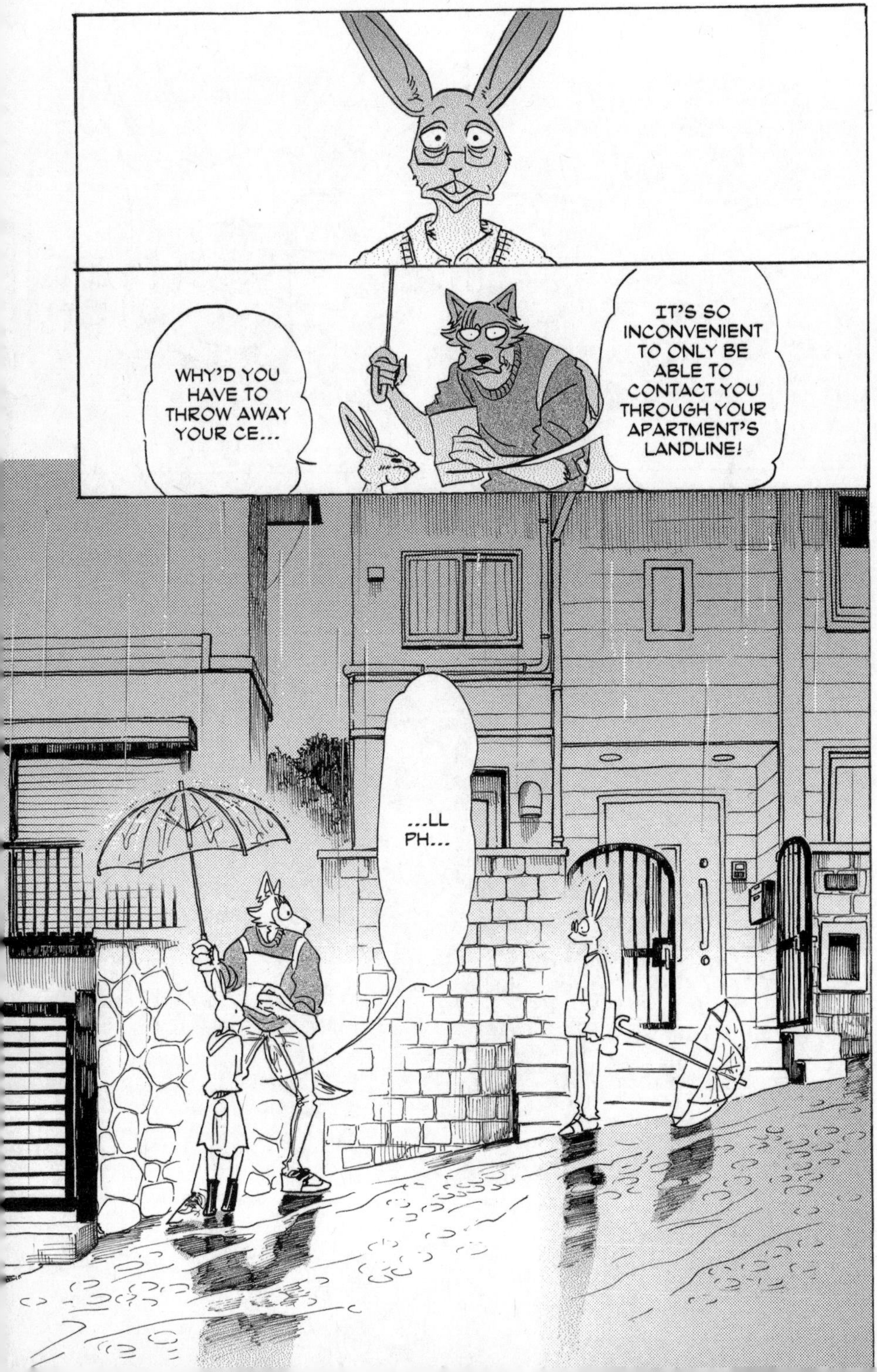
IT'S SO INCONVENIENT TO ONLY BE ABLE TO CONTACT YOU THROUGH YOUR APARTMENT'S LANDLINE!
WHY'D YOU HAVE TO THROW AWAY YOUR CE...
...LL PH...

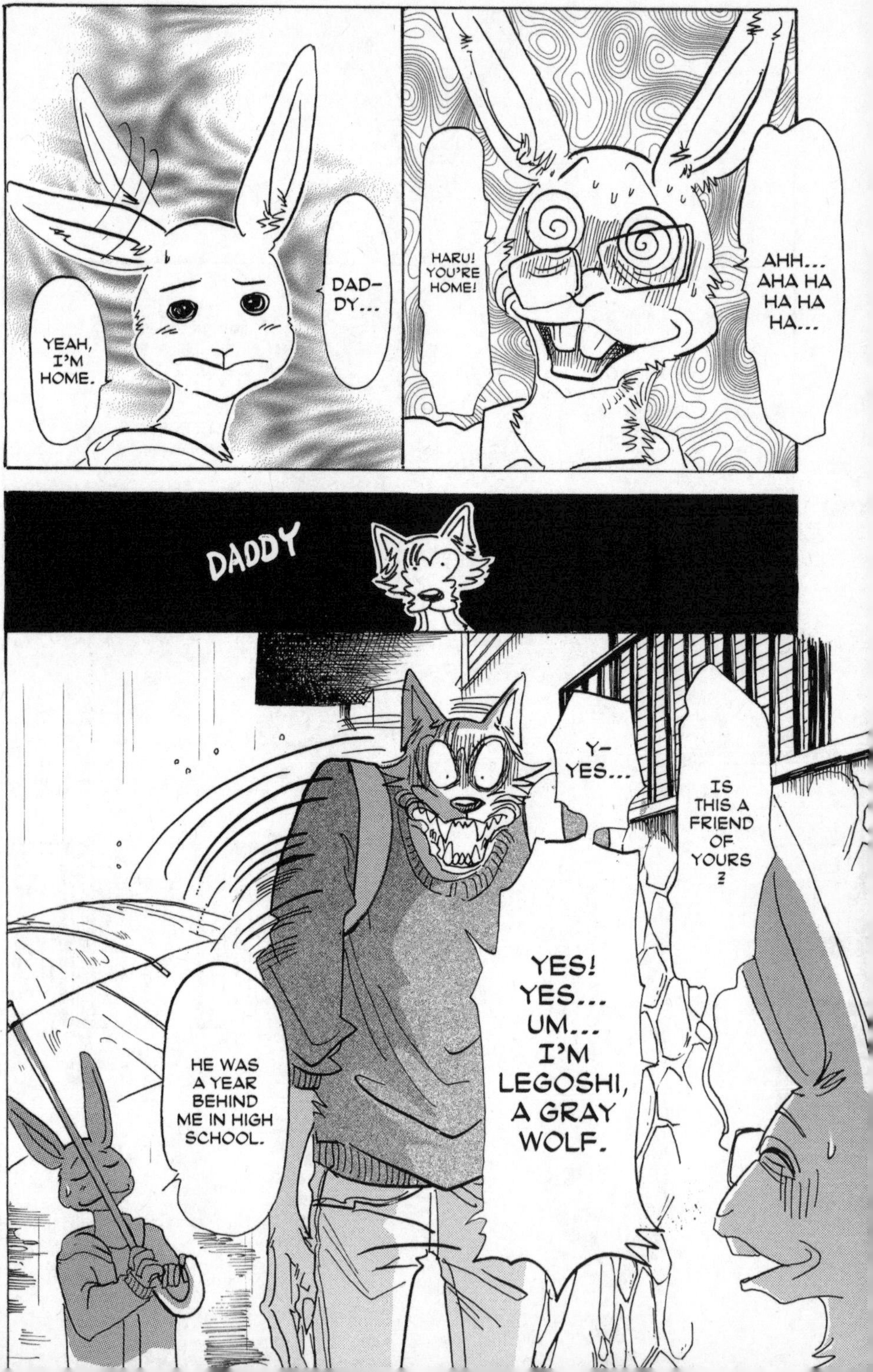
AHH... AHA HA HA HA HA...
HARU! YOU'RE HOME!
DADDY...
YEAH, I'M HOME.
DADDY
IS THIS A FRIEND OF YOURS?
Y-YES...
YES! YES... UM... I'M LEGOSHI, A GRAY WOLF.
HE WAS A YEAR BEHIND ME IN HIGH SCHOOL.

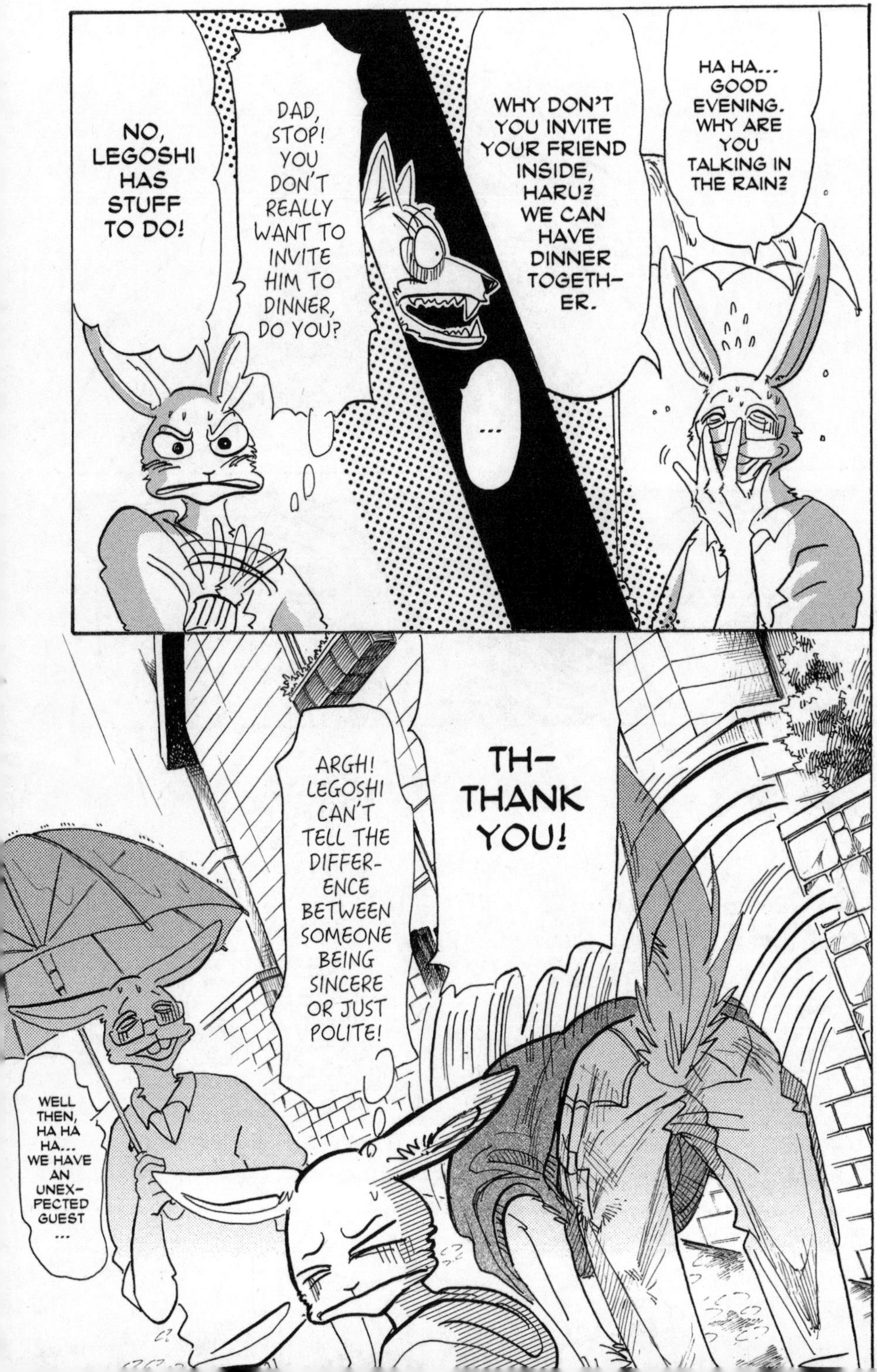
HA HA... GOOD EVENING. WHY ARE YOU TALKING IN THE RAIN?
WHY DON'T YOU INVITE YOUR FRIEND INSIDE, HARU? WE CAN HAVE DINNER TOGETH-ER.
...
DAD, STOP! YOU DON'T REALLY WANT TO INVITE HIM TO DINNER, DO YOU?
NO, LEGOSHI HAS STUFF TO DO!
TH-THANK YOU!
ARGH! LEGOSHI CAN'T TELL THE DIFFER-ENCE BETWEEN SOMEONE BEING SINCERE OR JUST POLITE!
WELL THEN, HA HA HA... WE HAVE AN UNEX-PECTED GUEST ...

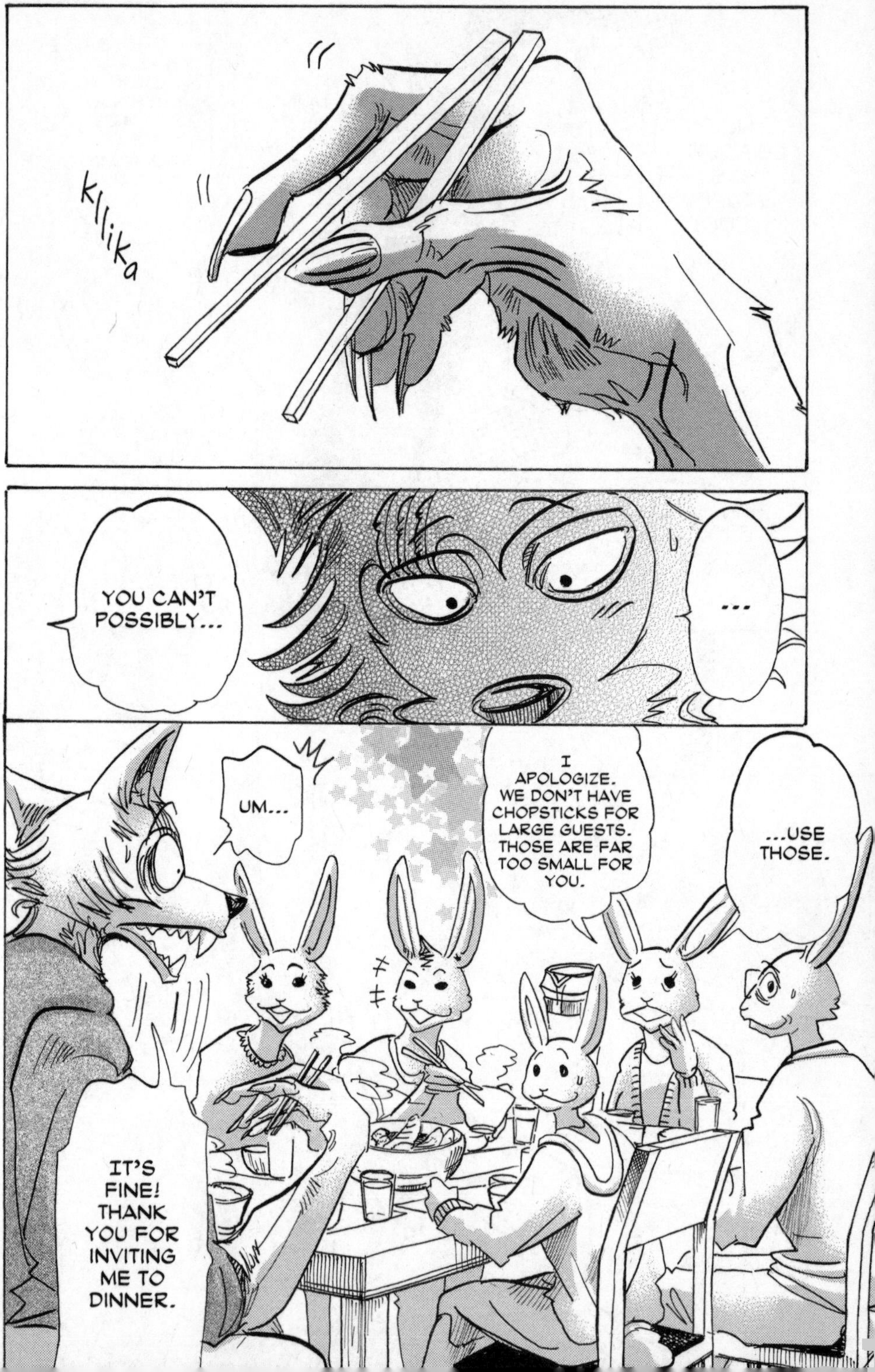
Kllika
...
YOU CAN'T POSSIBLY...
...USE THOSE.
I APOLOGIZE. WE DON'T HAVE CHOPSTICKS FOR LARGE GUESTS. THOSE ARE FAR TOO SMALL FOR YOU.
UM...
IT'S FINE! THANK YOU FOR INVITING ME TO DINNER.

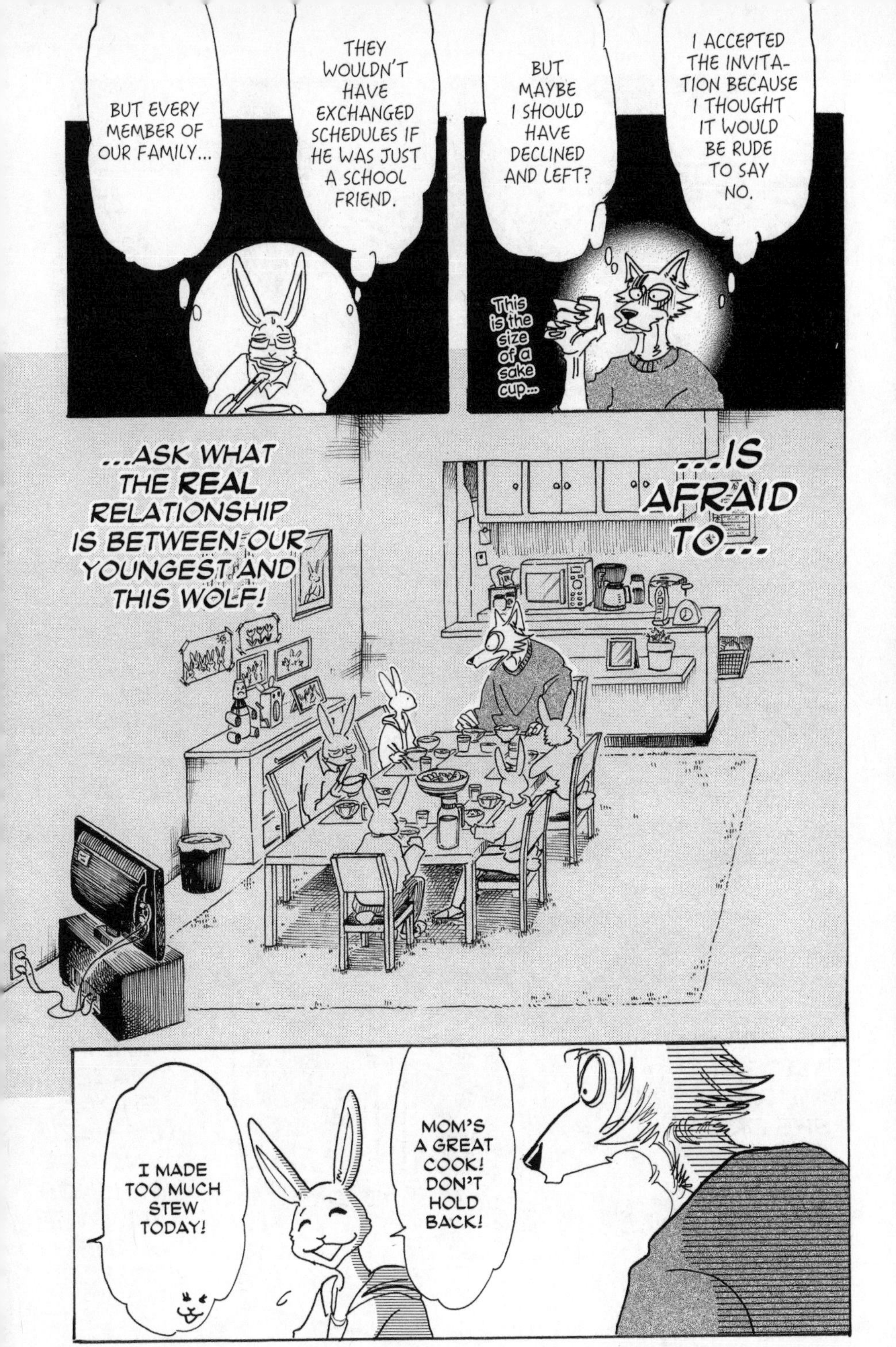
I ACCEPTED THE INVITATION BECAUSE I THOUGHT IT WOULD BE RUDE TO SAY NO.
BUT MAYBE I SHOULD HAVE DECLINED AND LEFT?
This is the size of a sake cup...
THEY WOULDN'T HAVE EXCHANGED SCHEDULES IF HE WAS JUST A SCHOOL FRIEND.
BUT EVERY MEMBER OF OUR FAMILY...
...IS AFRAID TO...
...ASK WHAT THE REAL RELATIONSHIP IS BETWEEN OUR YOUNGEST AND THIS WOLF!
MOM'S A GREAT COOK! DON'T HOLD BACK!
I MADE TOO MUCH STEW TODAY!

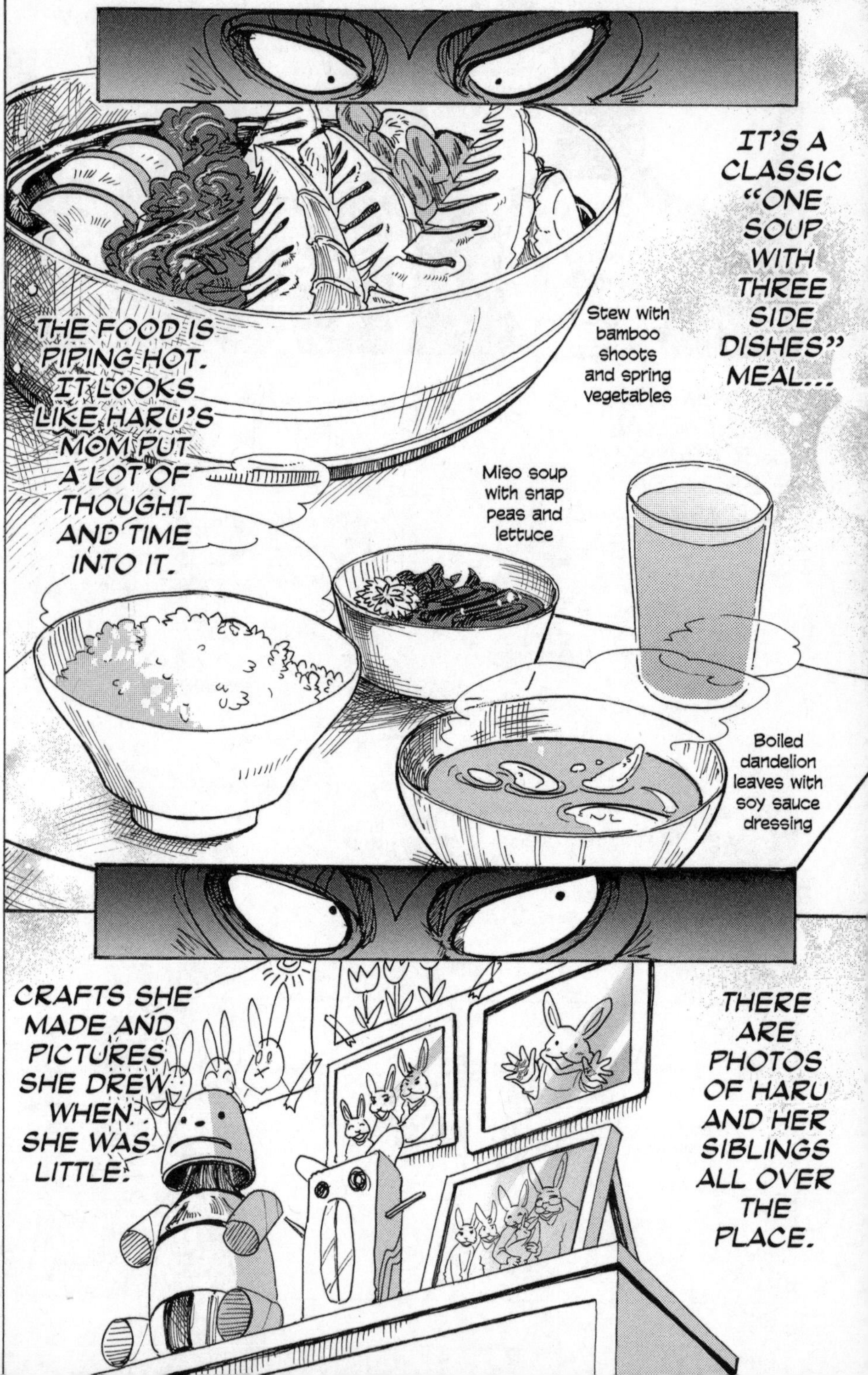
IT'S A CLASSIC "ONE SOUP WITH THREE SIDE DISHES" MEAL...
Stew with bamboo shoots and spring vegetables
THE FOOD IS PIPING HOT. IT LOOKS LIKE HARU'S MOM PUT A LOT OF THOUGHT AND TIME INTO IT.
Miso soup with snap peas and lettuce
Boiled dandelion leaves with soy sauce dressing
THERE ARE PHOTOS OF HARU AND HER SIBLINGS ALL OVER THE PLACE.
CRAFTS SHE MADE AND PICTURES SHE DREW WHEN SHE WAS LITTLE.

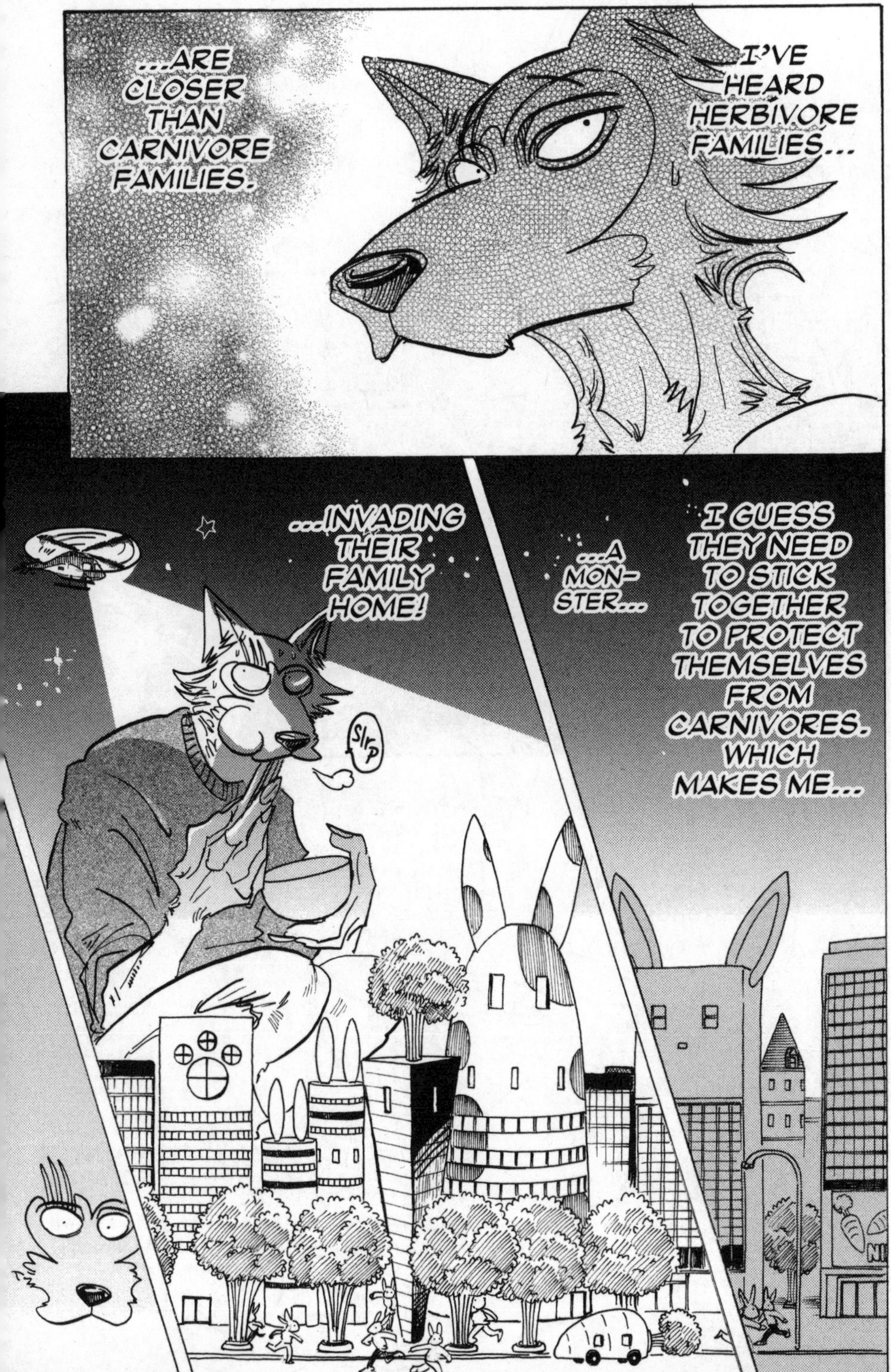
I'VE HEARD HERBIVORE FAMILIES...
...ARE CLOSER THAN CARNIVORE FAMILIES.
I GUESS THEY NEED TO STICK TOGETHER TO PROTECT THEMSELVES FROM CARNIVORES. WHICH MAKES ME...
...A MON-STER...
...INVADING THEIR FAMILY HOME!
Slrp

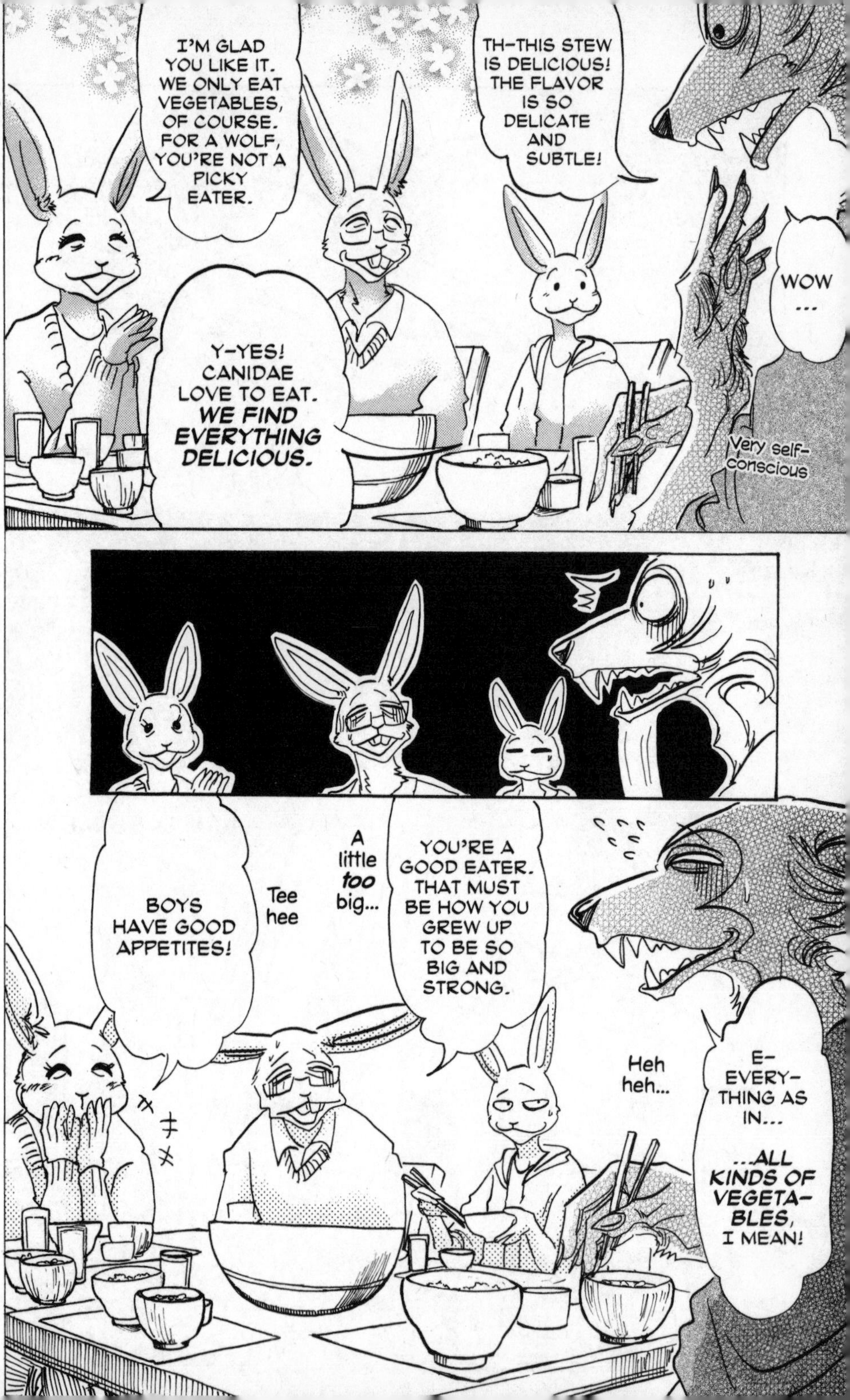
TH-THIS STEW IS DELICIOUS! THE FLAVOR IS SO DELICATE AND SUBTLE!
WOW ...
Very self-conscious
I'M GLAD YOU LIKE IT. WE ONLY EAT VEGETABLES, OF COURSE. FOR A WOLF, YOU'RE NOT A PICKY EATER.
Y-YES! CANIDAE LOVE TO EAT. *WE FIND EVERYTHING DELICIOUS.*
E-EVERY-THING AS IN...
...ALL KINDS OF VEGETA-BLES, I MEAN!
Heh heh...
YOU'RE A GOOD EATER. THAT MUST BE HOW YOU GREW UP TO BE SO BIG AND STRONG.
A little *too* big...
Tee hee
BOYS HAVE GOOD APPETITES!

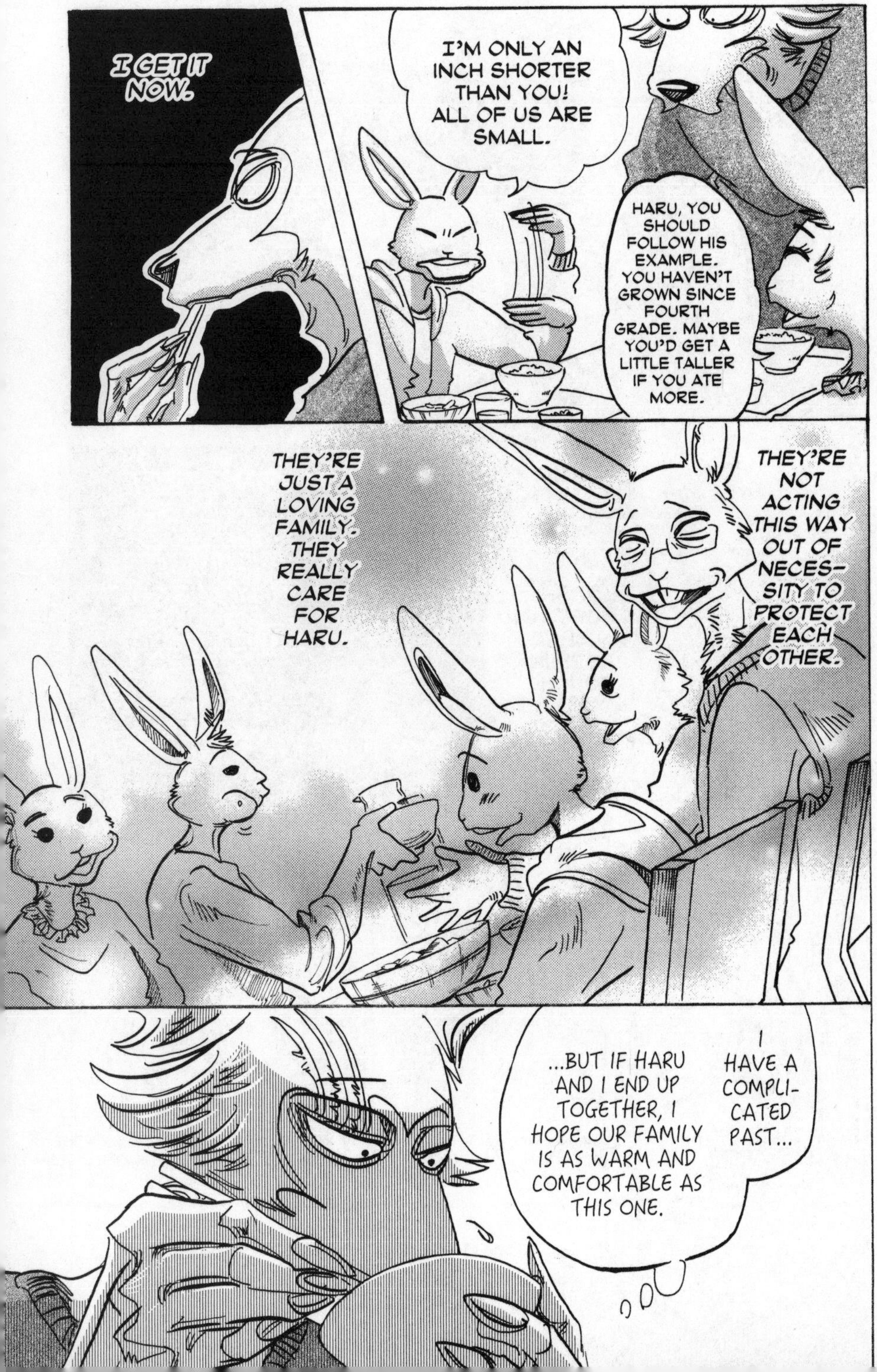
HARU, YOU SHOULD FOLLOW HIS EXAMPLE. YOU HAVEN'T GROWN SINCE FOURTH GRADE. MAYBE YOU'D GET A LITTLE TALLER IF YOU ATE MORE.
I'M ONLY AN INCH SHORTER THAN YOU! ALL OF US ARE SMALL.
I GET IT NOW.
THEY'RE NOT ACTING THIS WAY OUT OF NECES-SITY TO PROTECT EACH OTHER.
THEY'RE JUST A LOVING FAMILY. THEY REALLY CARE FOR HARU.
I HAVE A COMPLI-CATED PAST...
...BUT IF HARU AND I END UP TOGETHER, I HOPE OUR FAMILY IS AS WARM AND COMFORTABLE AS THIS ONE.

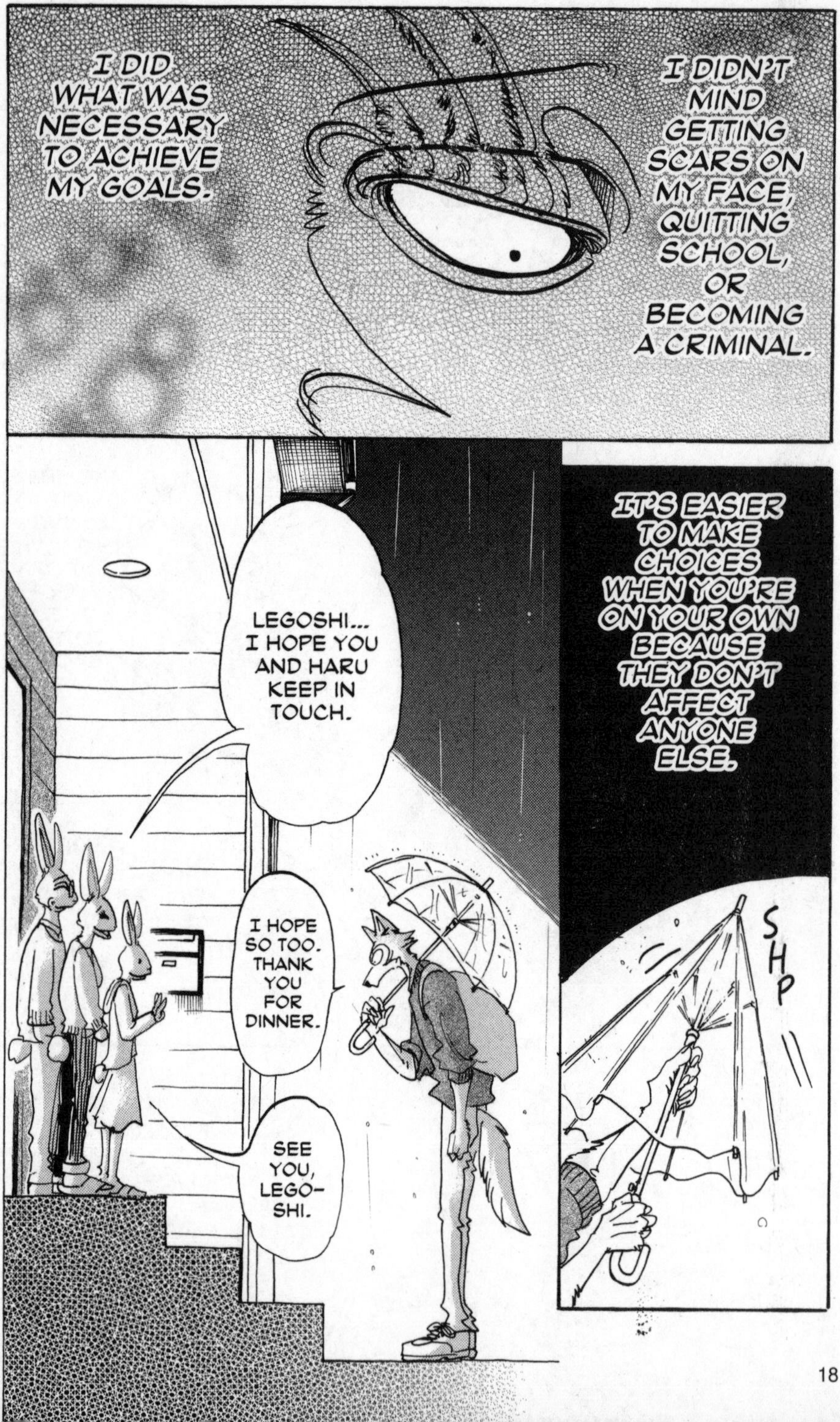
I DIDN'T MIND GETTING SCARS ON MY FACE, QUITTING SCHOOL, OR BECOMING A CRIMINAL.
I DID WHAT WAS NECESSARY TO ACHIEVE MY GOALS.
IT'S EASIER TO MAKE CHOICES WHEN YOU'RE ON YOUR OWN BECAUSE THEY DON'T AFFECT ANYONE ELSE.
SHP
LEGOSHI... I HOPE YOU AND HARU KEEP IN TOUCH.
I HOPE SO TOO. THANK YOU FOR DINNER.
SEE YOU, LEGO-SHI.

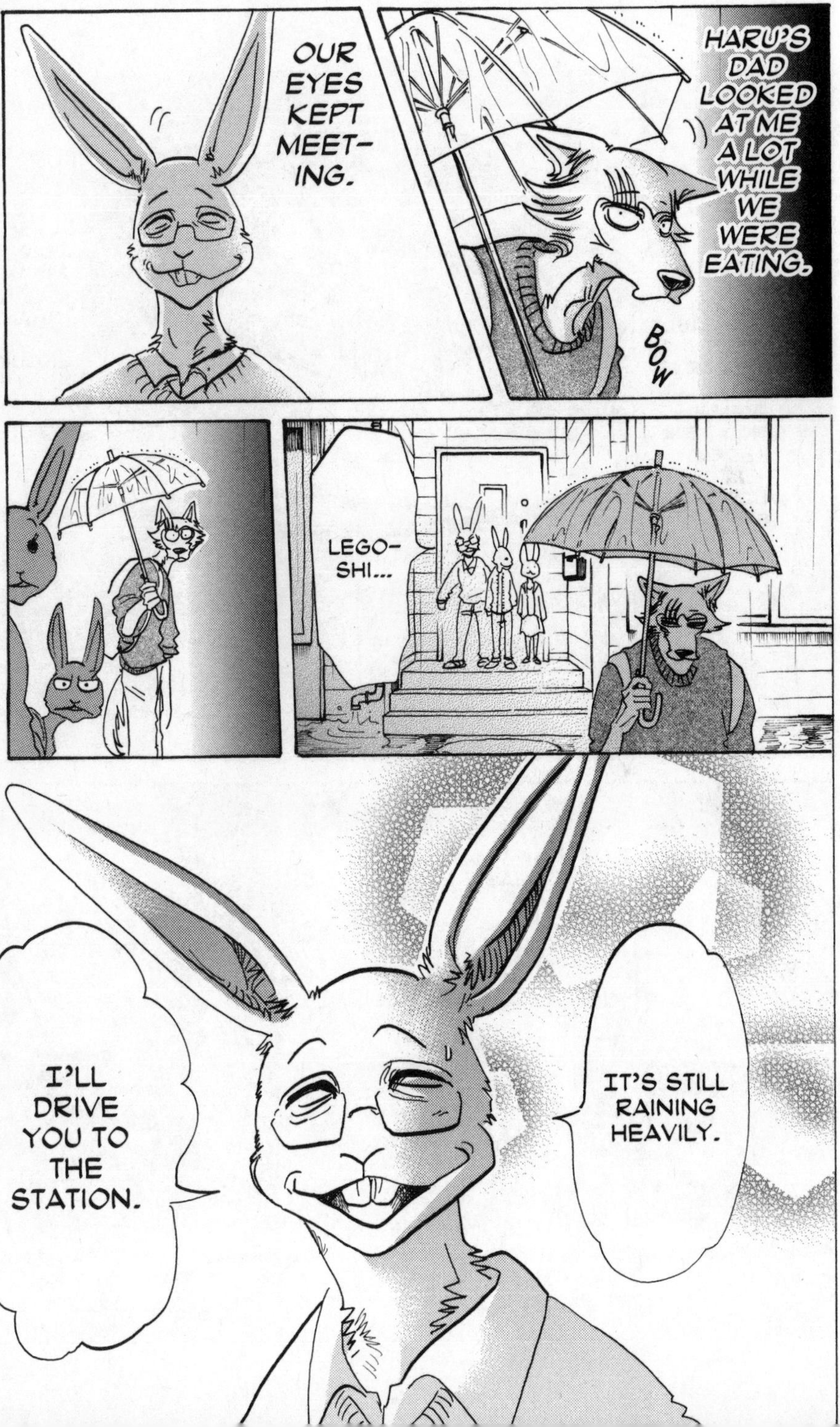
HARU'S DAD LOOKED AT ME A LOT WHILE WE WERE EATING.
BOW
OUR EYES KEPT MEET-ING.
LEGO-SHI...
IT'S STILL RAINING HEAVILY.
I'LL DRIVE YOU TO THE STATION.

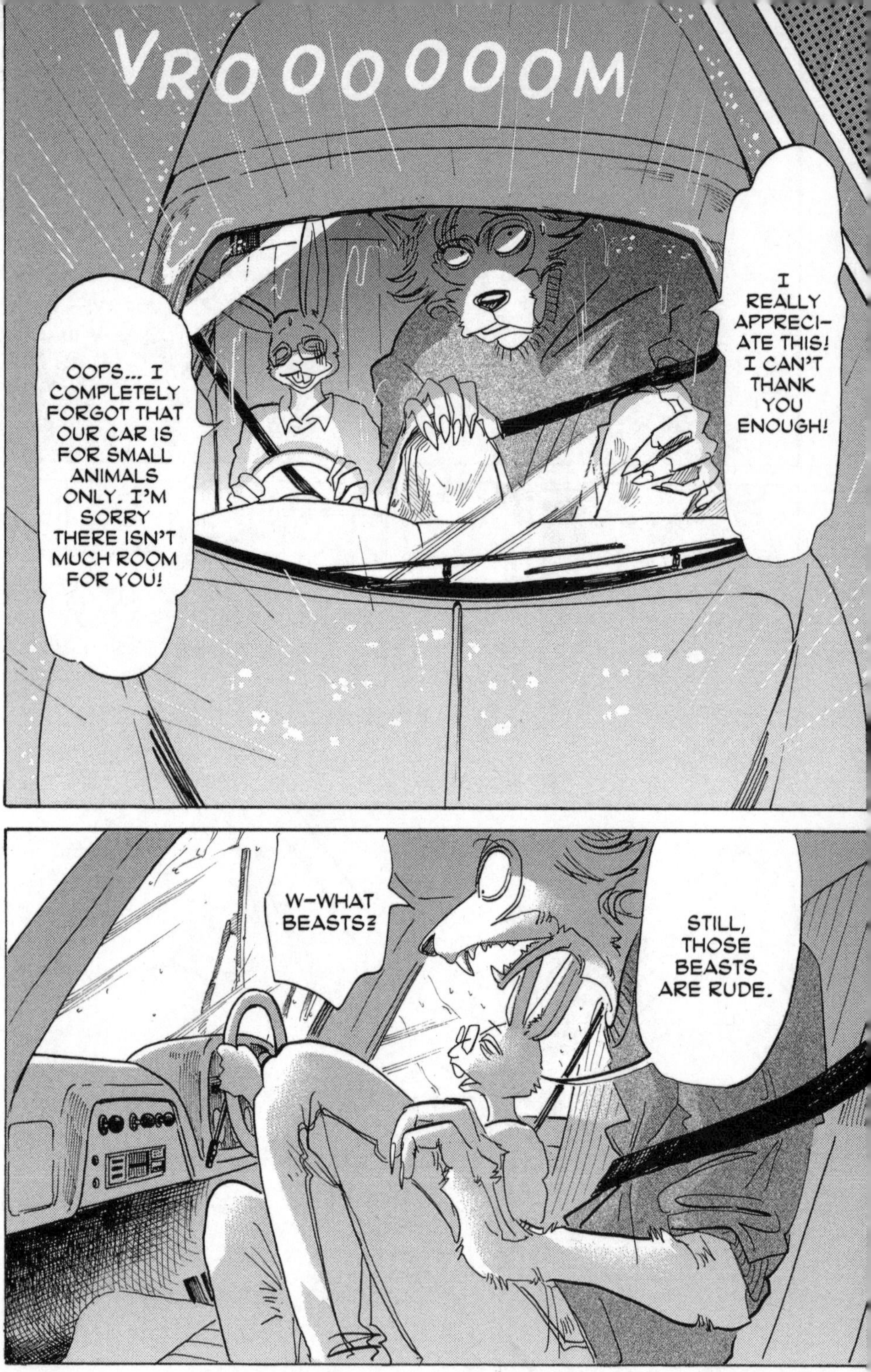
VROOOOOOM
I REALLY APPRECIATE THIS! I CAN'T THANK YOU ENOUGH!
OOPS... I COMPLETELY FORGOT THAT OUR CAR IS FOR SMALL ANIMALS ONLY. I'M SORRY THERE ISN'T MUCH ROOM FOR YOU!
STILL, THOSE BEASTS ARE RUDE.
W-WHAT BEASTS?

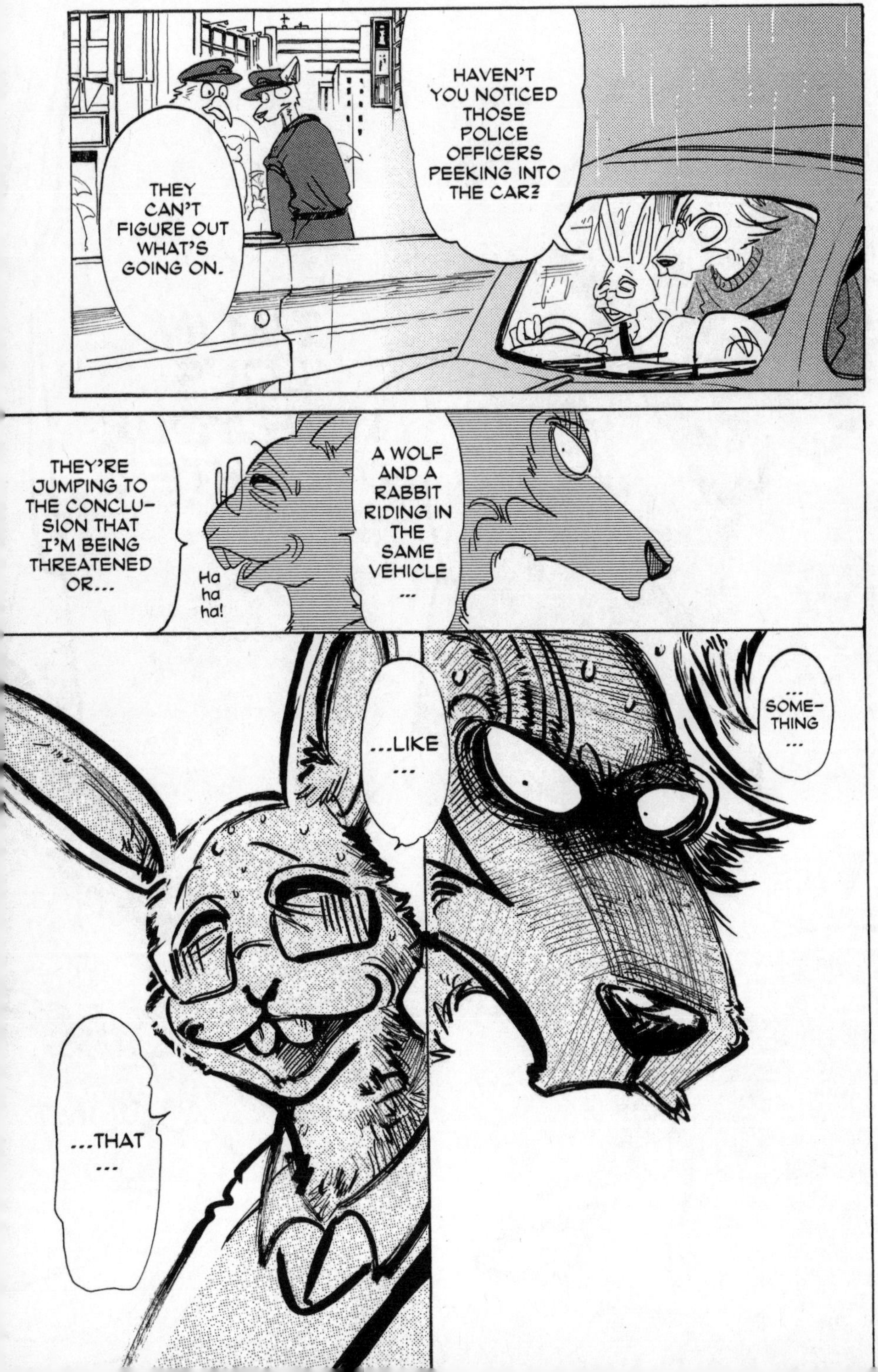
HAVEN'T YOU NOTICED THOSE POLICE OFFICERS PEEKING INTO THE CAR?
THEY CAN'T FIGURE OUT WHAT'S GOING ON.
A WOLF AND A RABBIT RIDING IN THE SAME VEHICLE ...
Ha ha ha!
THEY'RE JUMPING TO THE CONCLUSION THAT I'M BEING THREATENED OR...
...SOMETHING...
...LIKE...
...THAT...

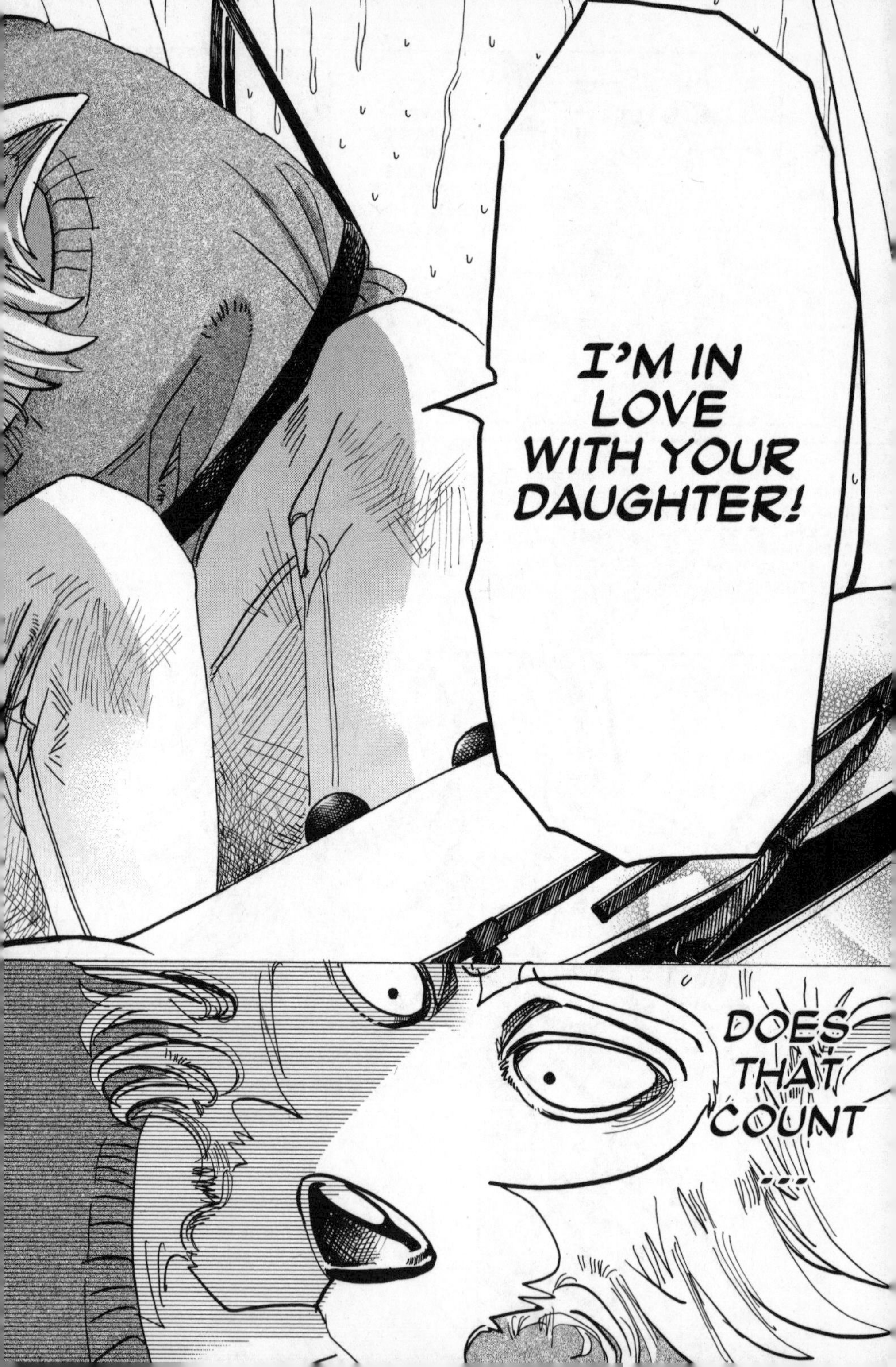
I'M IN LOVE WITH YOUR DAUGHTER!
DOES THAT COUNT ...

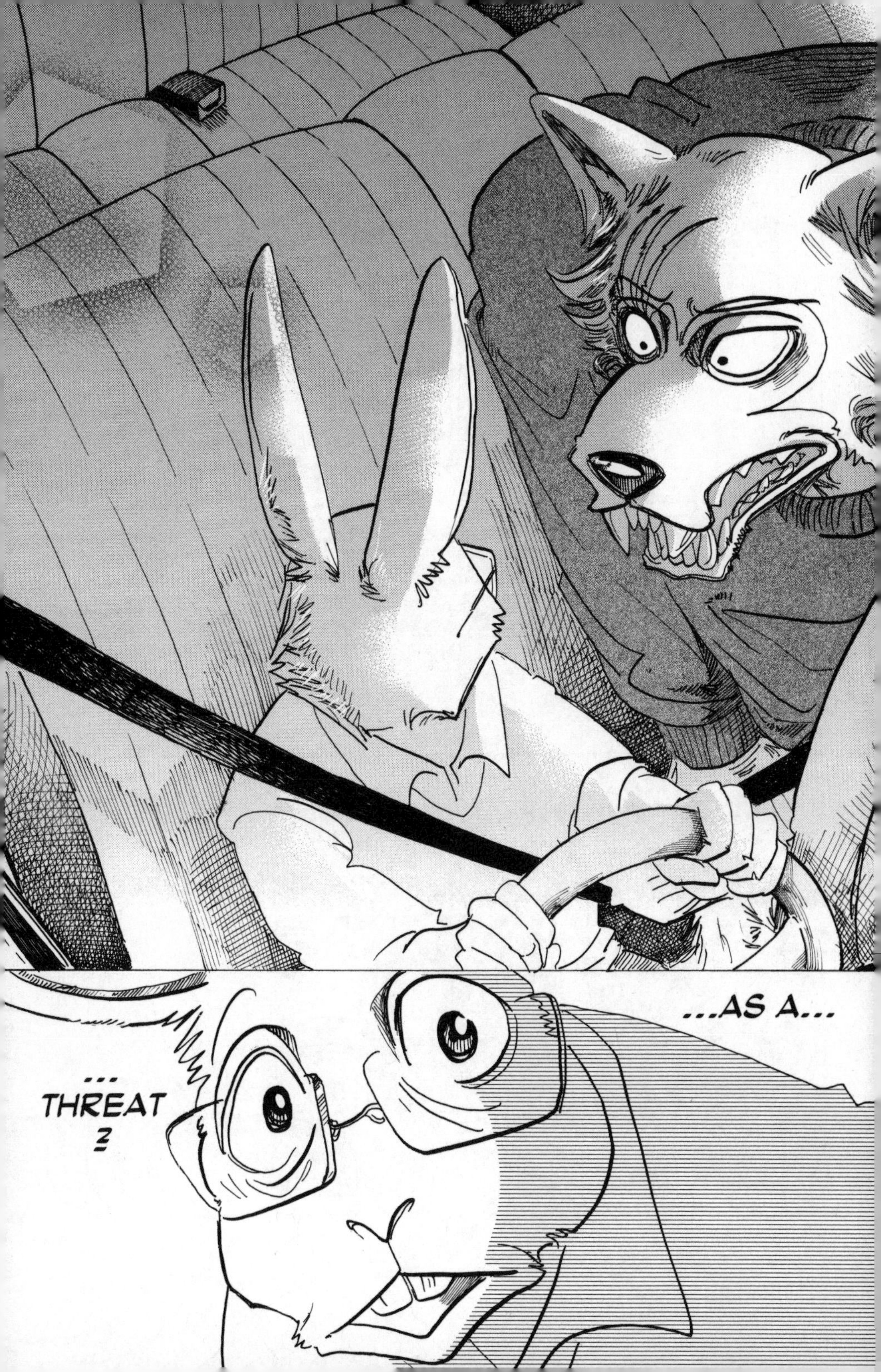
...AS A...
...THREAT?

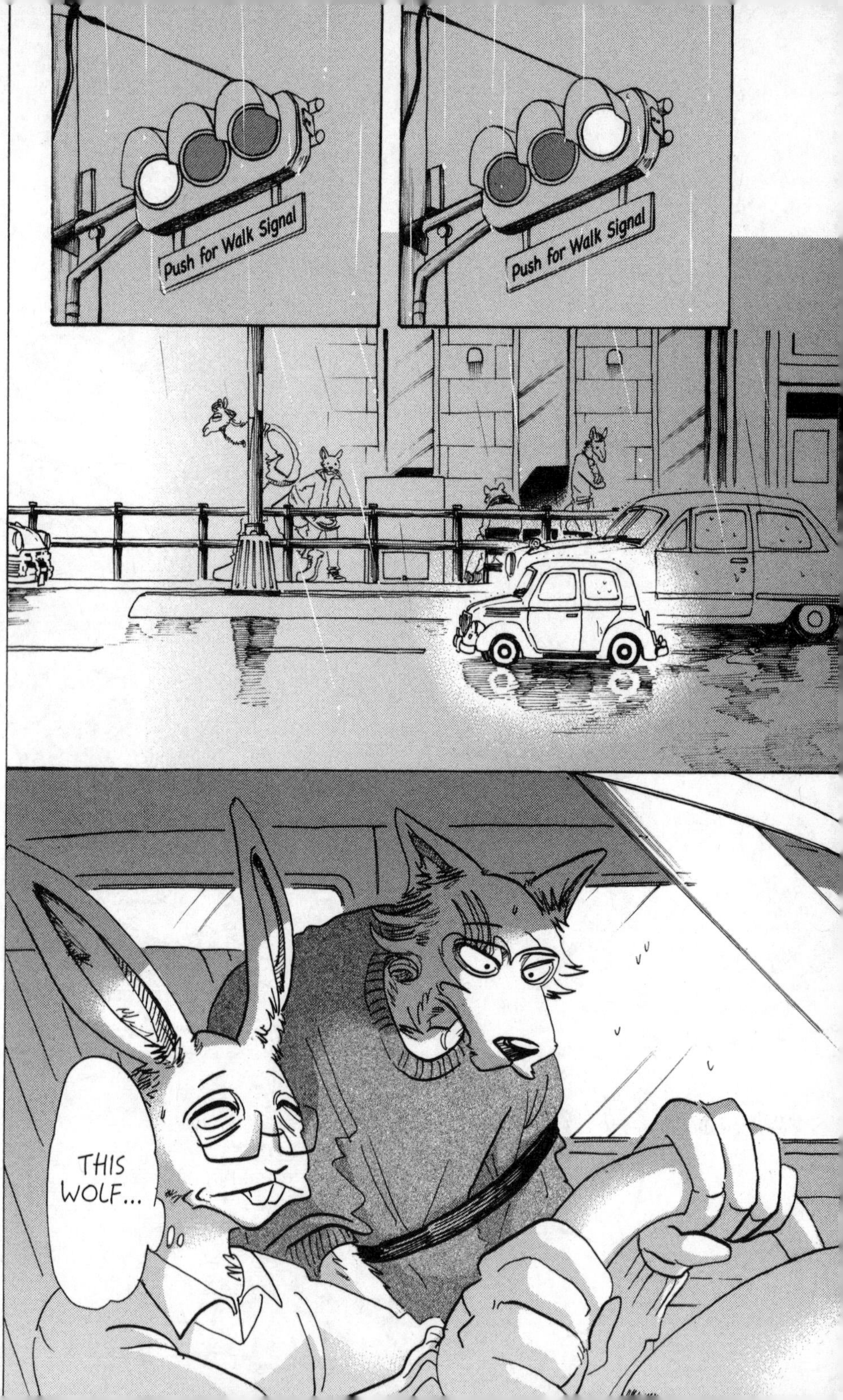
Push for Walk Signal
Push for Walk Signal
THIS WOLF...

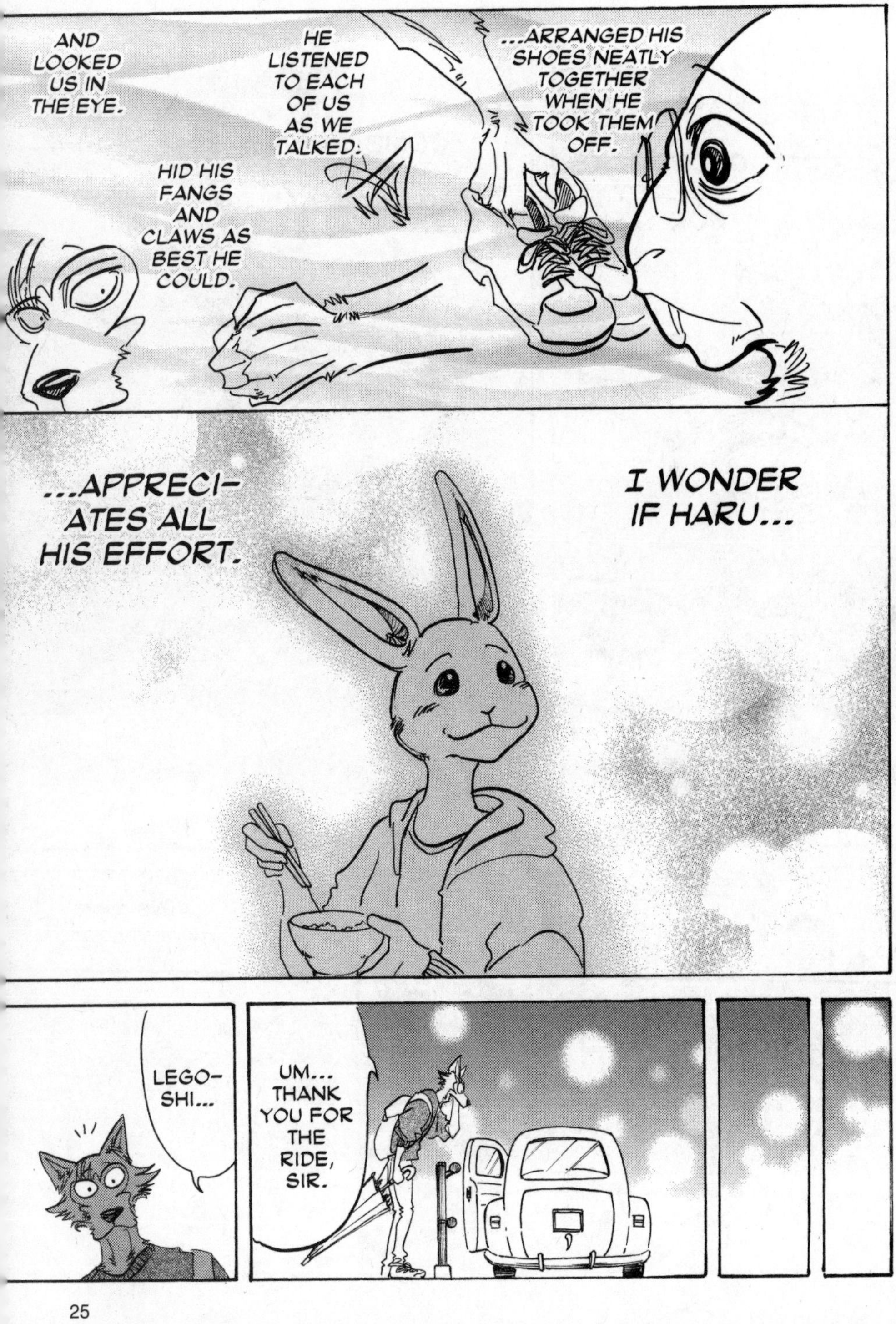
...ARRANGED HIS SHOES NEATLY TOGETHER WHEN HE TOOK THEM OFF.
HE LISTENED TO EACH OF US AS WE TALKED.
AND LOOKED US IN THE EYE.
HID HIS FANGS AND CLAWS AS BEST HE COULD.
I WONDER IF HARU...
...APPRECI-ATES ALL HIS EFFORT.
UM... THANK YOU FOR THE RIDE, SIR.
LEGO-SHI...

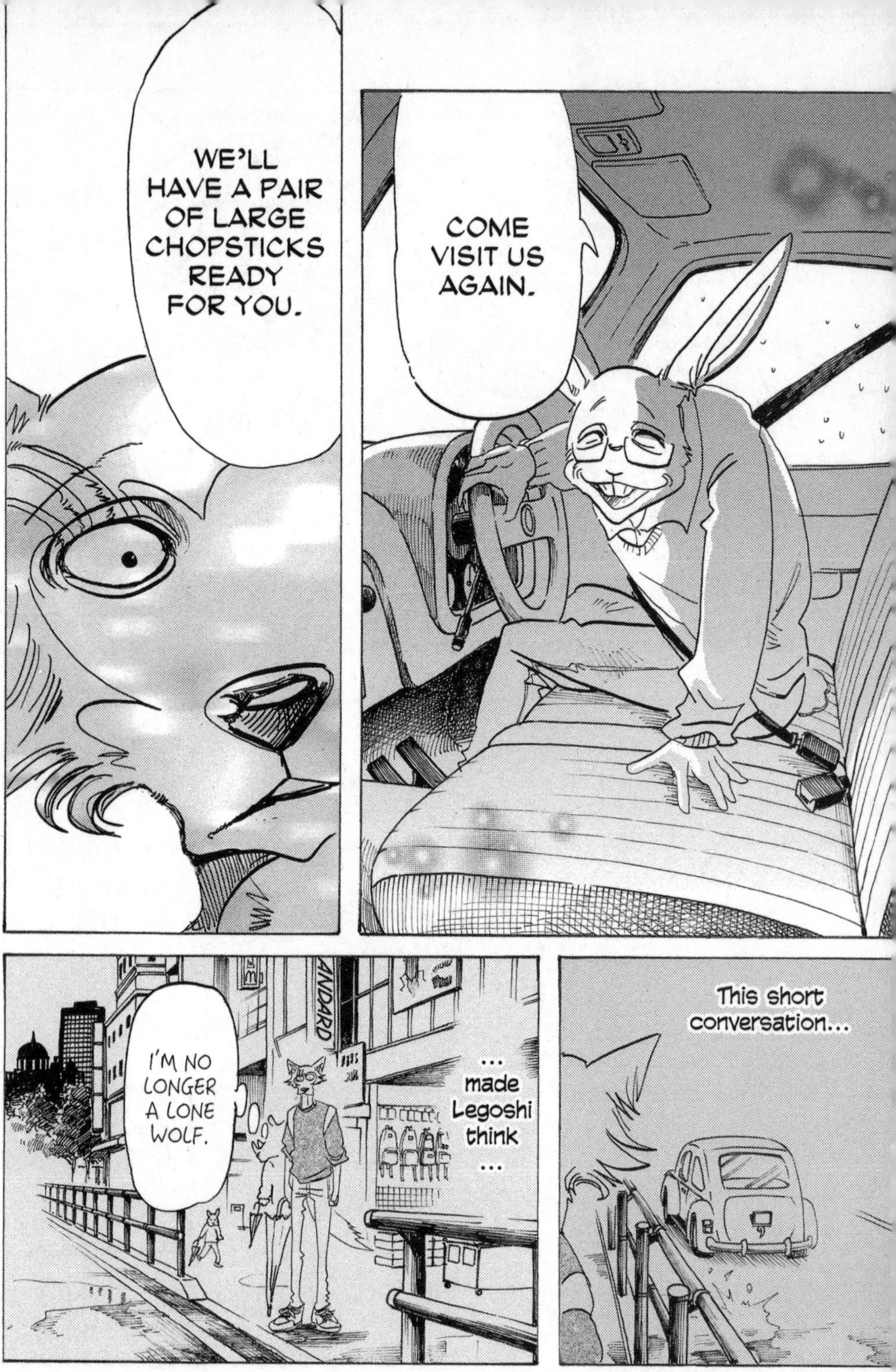
COME VISIT US AGAIN.
WE'LL HAVE A PAIR OF LARGE CHOPSTICKS READY FOR YOU.
This short conversation...
...made Legoshi think...
I'M NO LONGER A LONE WOLF.

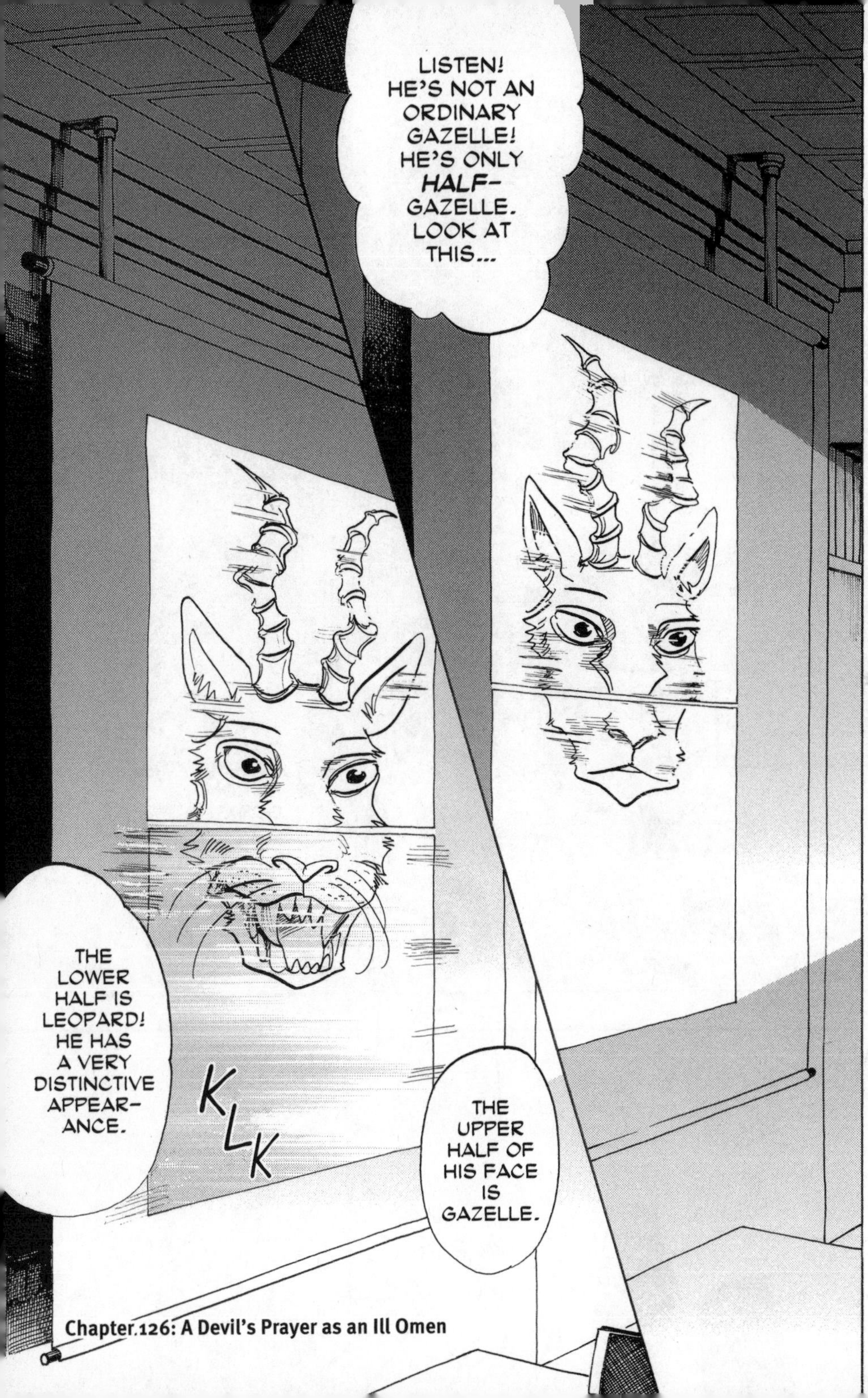
LISTEN! HE'S NOT AN ORDINARY GAZELLE! HE'S ONLY *HALF*-GAZELLE. LOOK AT THIS...
THE UPPER HALF OF HIS FACE IS GAZELLE.
THE LOWER HALF IS LEOPARD! HE HAS A VERY DISTINCTIVE APPEAR-ANCE.
KLK

Chapter.126: A Devil's Prayer as an Ill Omen

Chapter 126: A Devil's Prayer as an Ill Omen

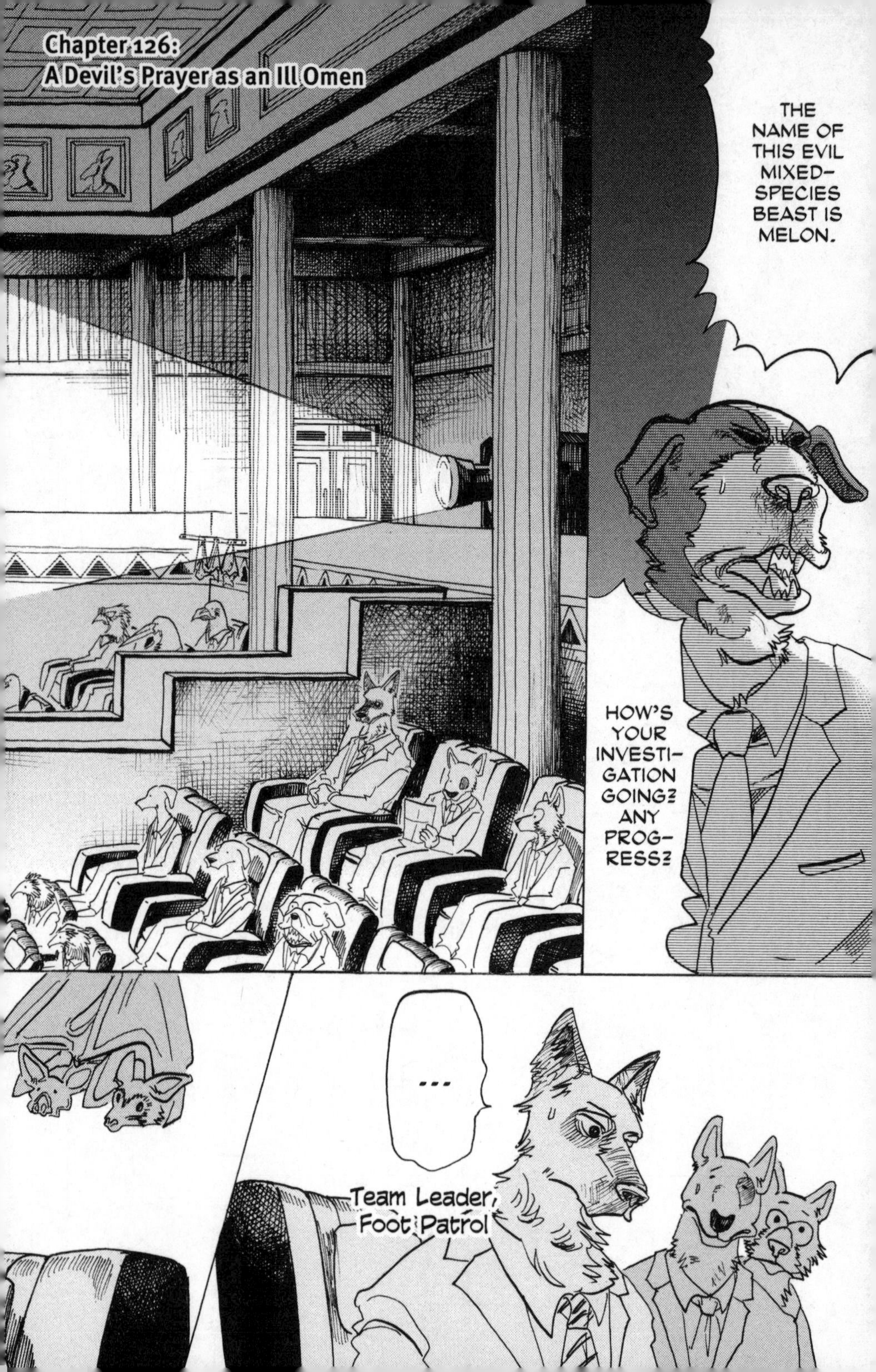

THE NAME OF THIS EVIL MIXED-SPECIES BEAST IS MELON.
HOW'S YOUR INVESTIGATION GOING? ANY PROGRESS?
...
Team Leader, Foot Patrol

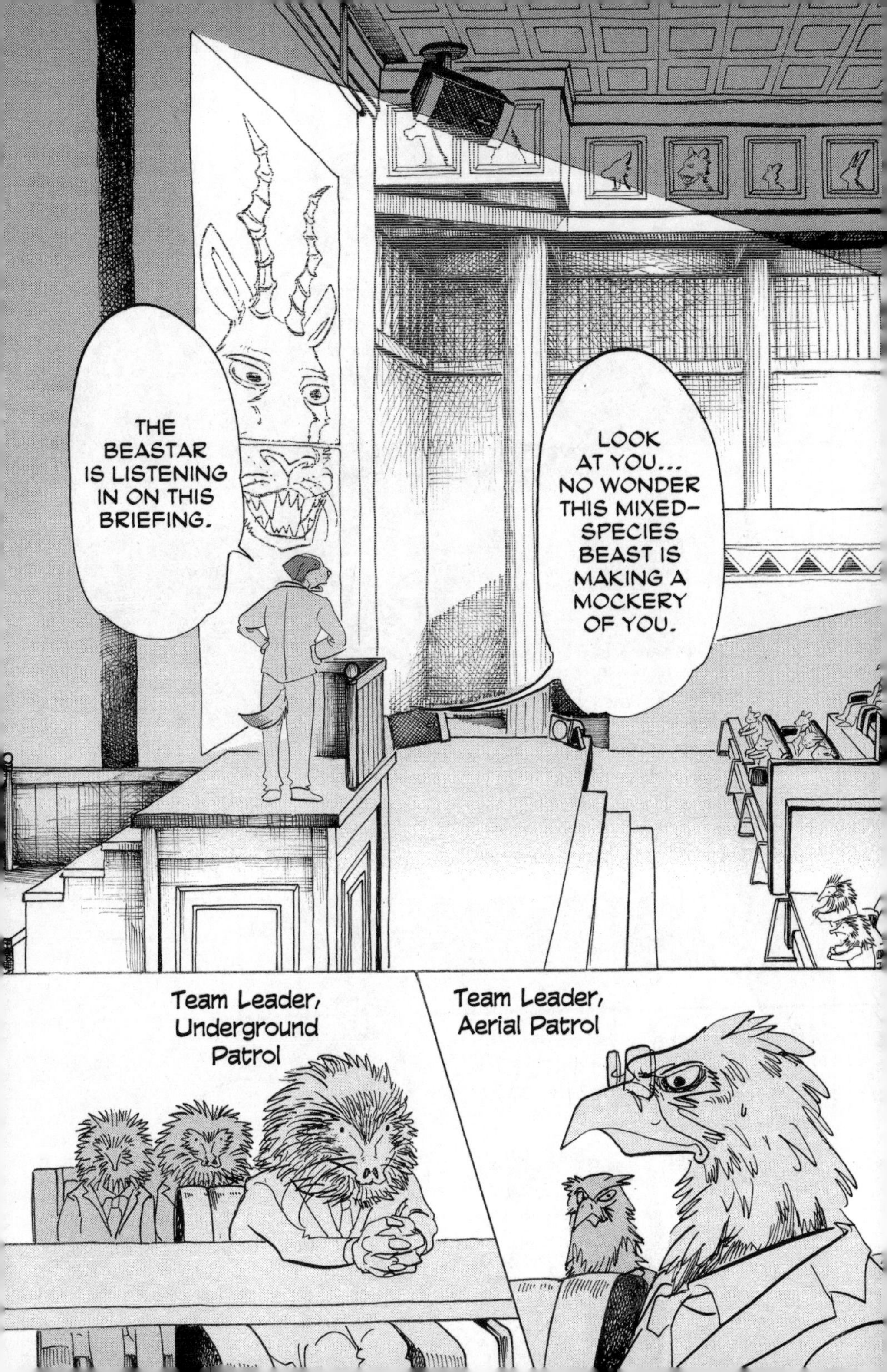
LOOK AT YOU... NO WONDER THIS MIXED-SPECIES BEAST IS MAKING A MOCKERY OF YOU.
THE BEASTAR IS LISTENING IN ON THIS BRIEFING.
Team Leader, Aerial Patrol
Team Leader, Underground Patrol

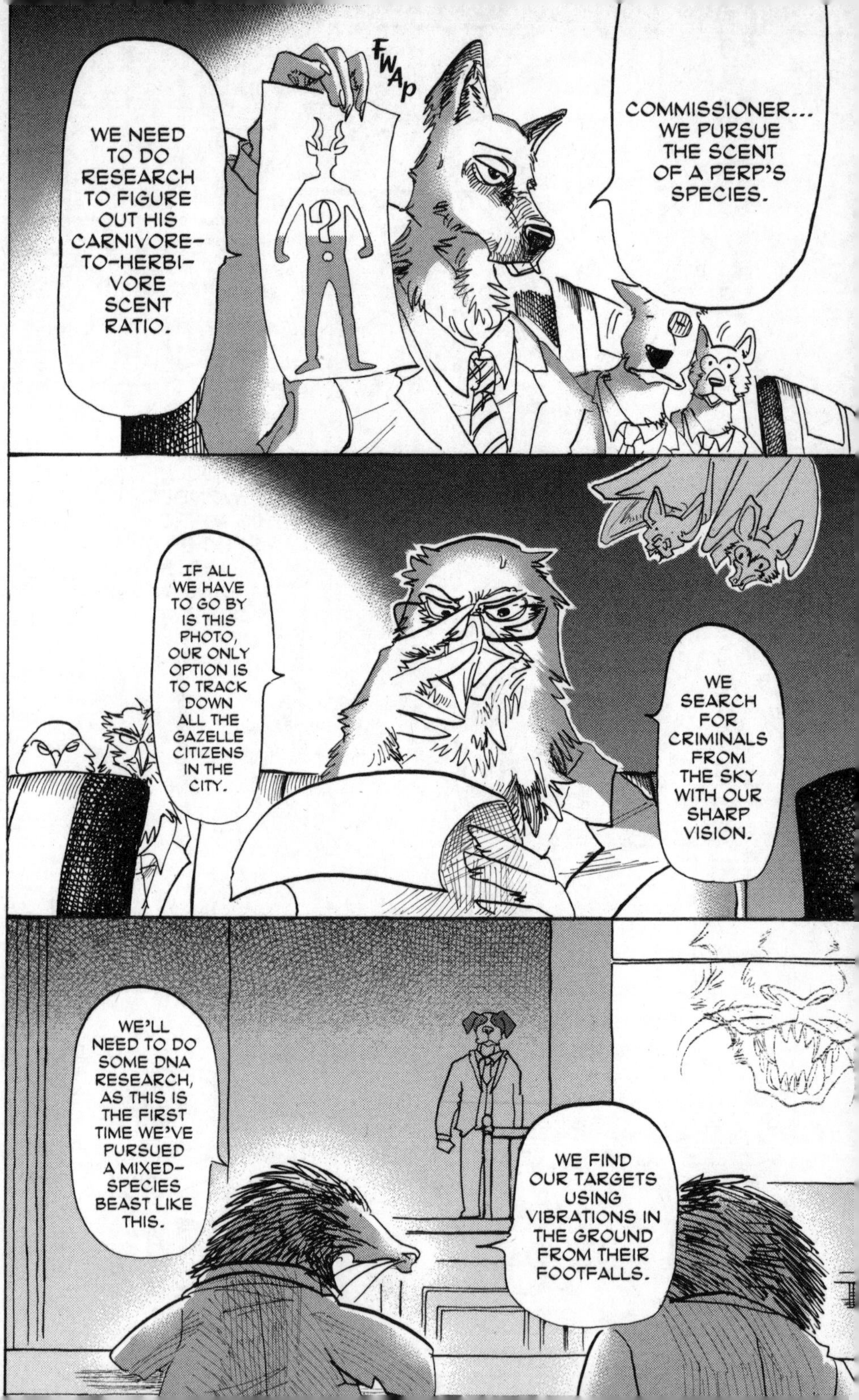
COMMISSIONER... WE PURSUE THE SCENT OF A PERP'S SPECIES.
FWAP
WE NEED TO DO RESEARCH TO FIGURE OUT HIS CARNIVORE-TO-HERBIVORE SCENT RATIO.
WE SEARCH FOR CRIMINALS FROM THE SKY WITH OUR SHARP VISION.
IF ALL WE HAVE TO GO BY IS THIS PHOTO, OUR ONLY OPTION IS TO TRACK DOWN ALL THE GAZELLE CITIZENS IN THE CITY.
WE FIND OUR TARGETS USING VIBRATIONS IN THE GROUND FROM THEIR FOOTFALLS.
WE'LL NEED TO DO SOME DNA RESEARCH, AS THIS IS THE FIRST TIME WE'VE PURSUED A MIXED-SPECIES BEAST LIKE THIS.

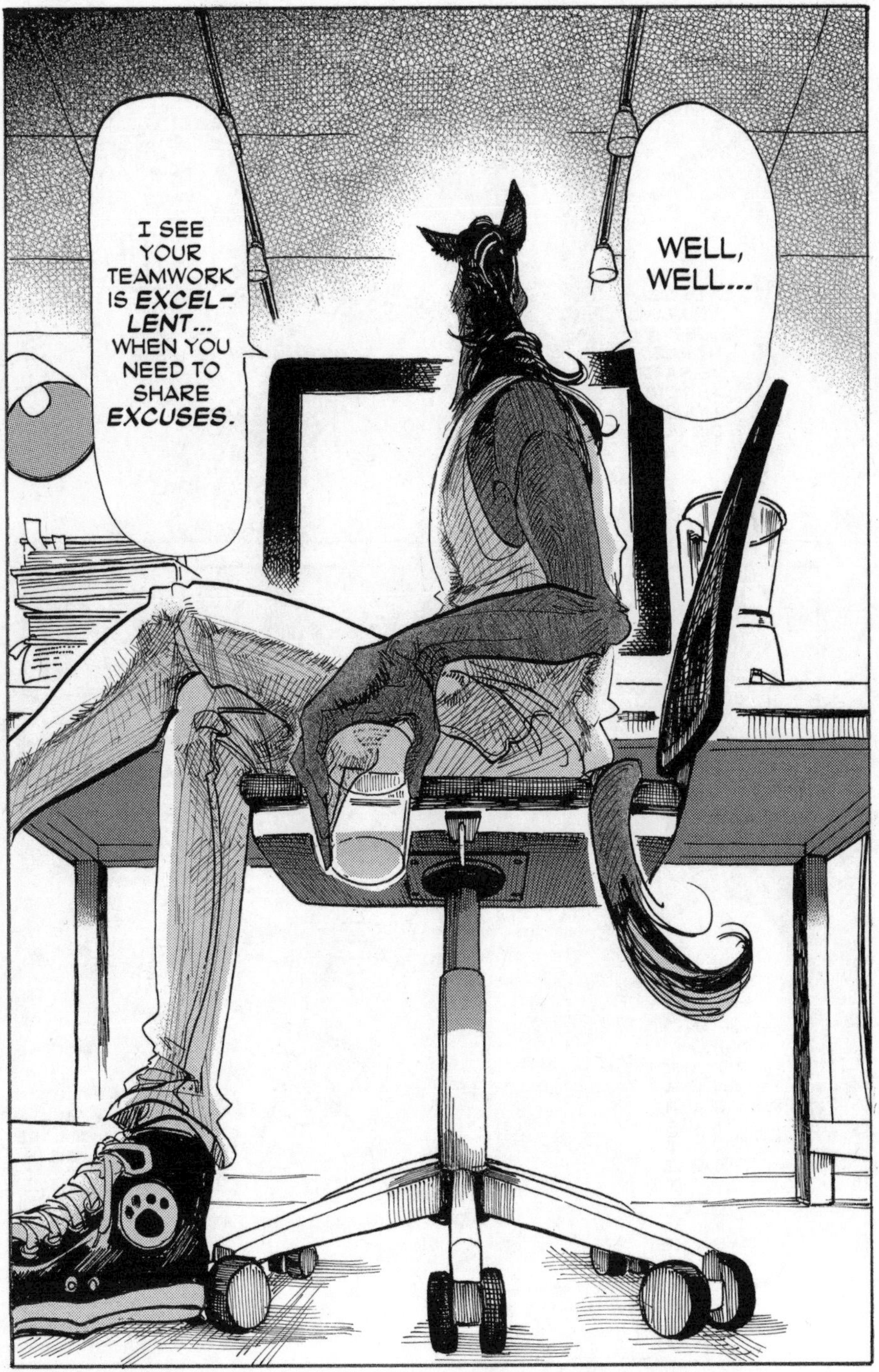
WELL, WELL...
I SEE YOUR TEAMWORK IS EXCEL-LENT... WHEN YOU NEED TO SHARE EXCUSES.

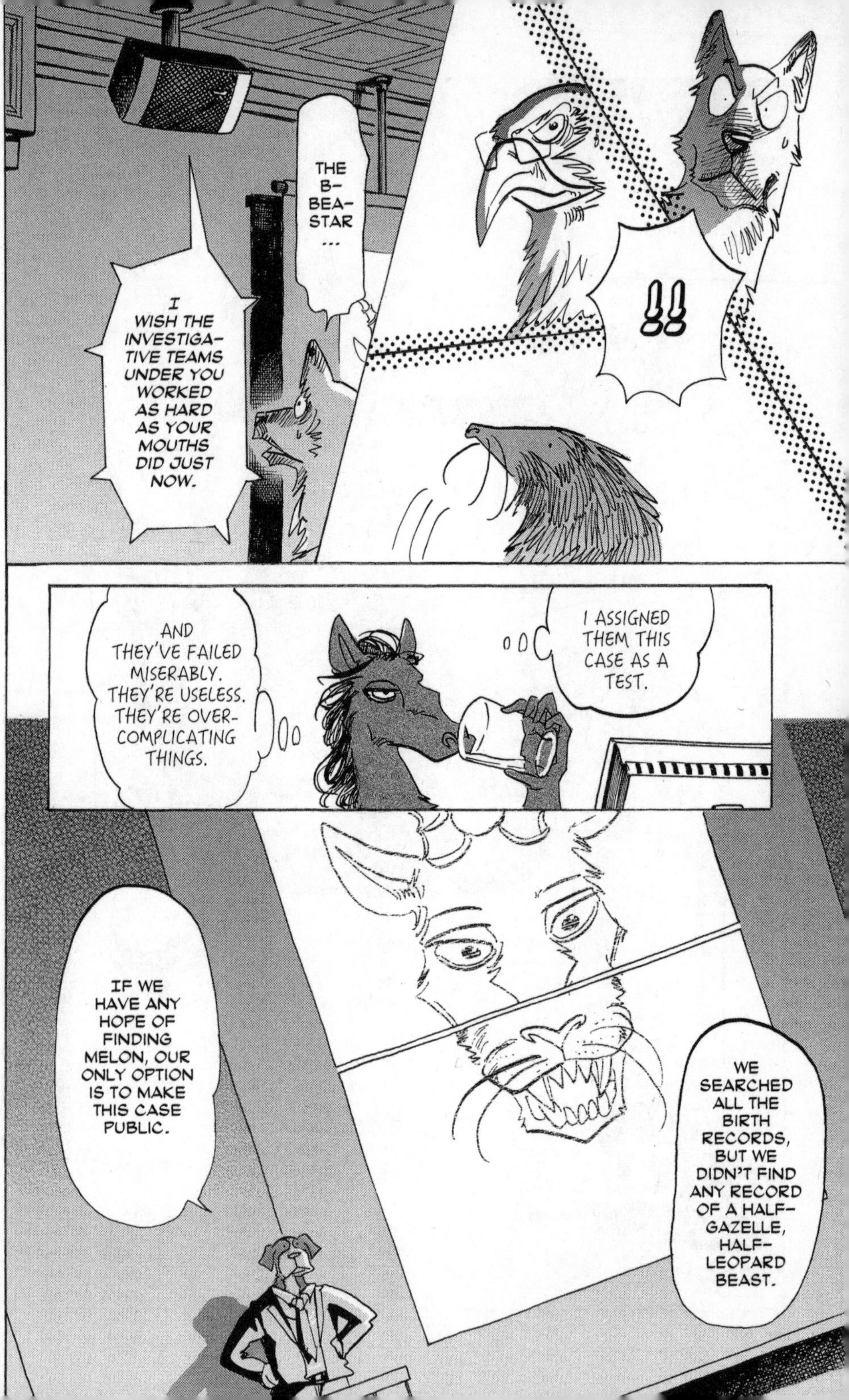
!!
THE B-BEASTAR ...
I WISH THE INVESTIGATIVE TEAMS UNDER YOU WORKED AS HARD AS YOUR MOUTHS DID JUST NOW.
I ASSIGNED THEM THIS CASE AS A TEST.
AND THEY'VE FAILED MISERABLY. THEY'RE USELESS. THEY'RE OVER-COMPLICATING THINGS.
WE SEARCHED ALL THE BIRTH RECORDS, BUT WE DIDN'T FIND ANY RECORD OF A HALF-GAZELLE, HALF-LEOPARD BEAST.
IF WE HAVE ANY HOPE OF FINDING MELON, OUR ONLY OPTION IS TO MAKE THIS CASE PUBLIC.

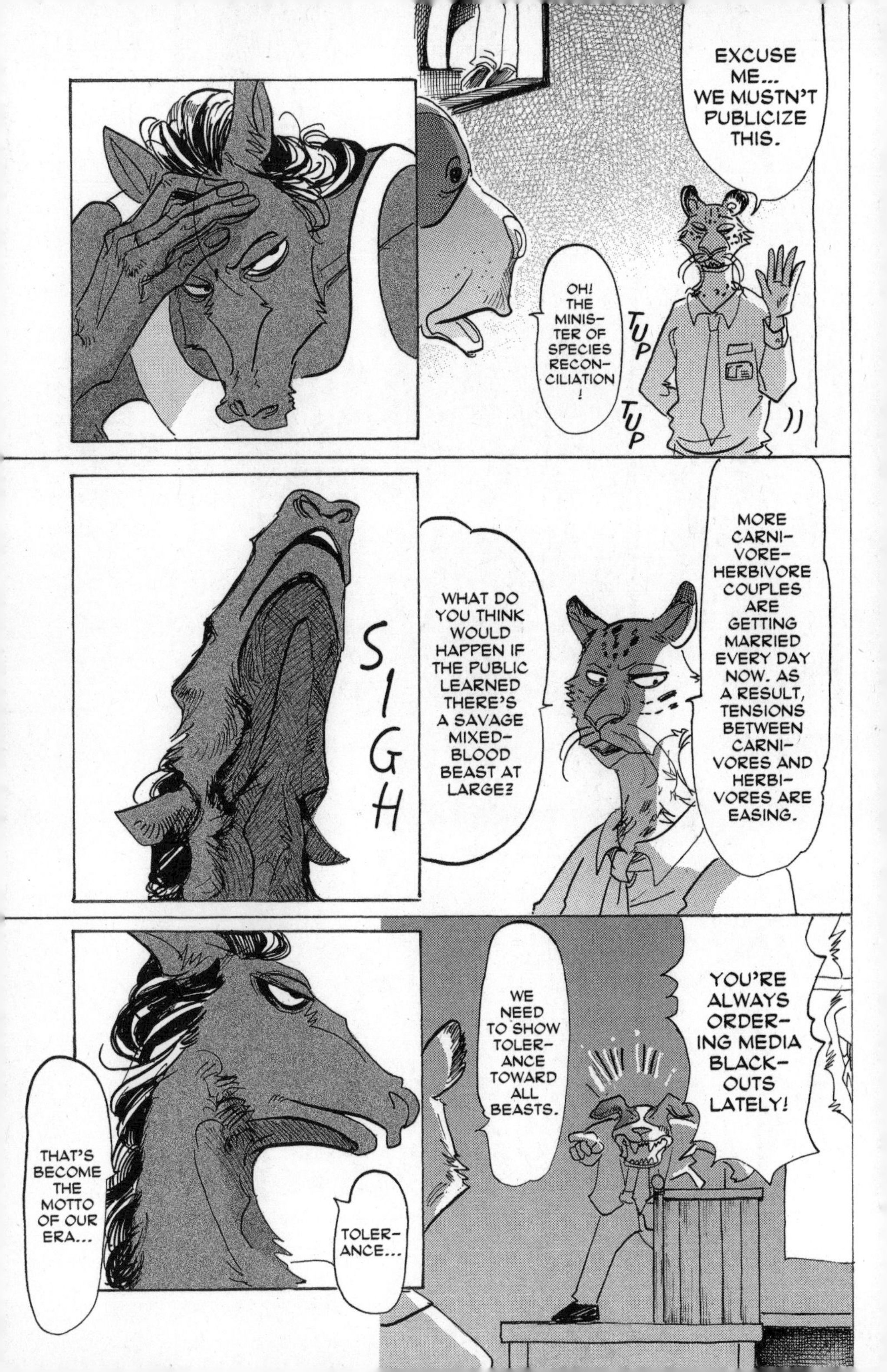
EXCUSE ME... WE MUSTN'T PUBLICIZE THIS.
OH! THE MINISTER OF SPECIES RECONCILIATION!
TUP TUP
MORE CARNIVORE-HERBIVORE COUPLES ARE GETTING MARRIED EVERY DAY NOW. AS A RESULT, TENSIONS BETWEEN CARNIVORES AND HERBIVORES ARE EASING.
WHAT DO YOU THINK WOULD HAPPEN IF THE PUBLIC LEARNED THERE'S A SAVAGE MIXED-BLOOD BEAST AT LARGE?
SIGH
YOU'RE ALWAYS ORDERING MEDIA BLACKOUTS LATELY!
WE NEED TO SHOW TOLERANCE TOWARD ALL BEASTS.
TOLERANCE...
THAT'S BECOME THE MOTTO OF OUR ERA...

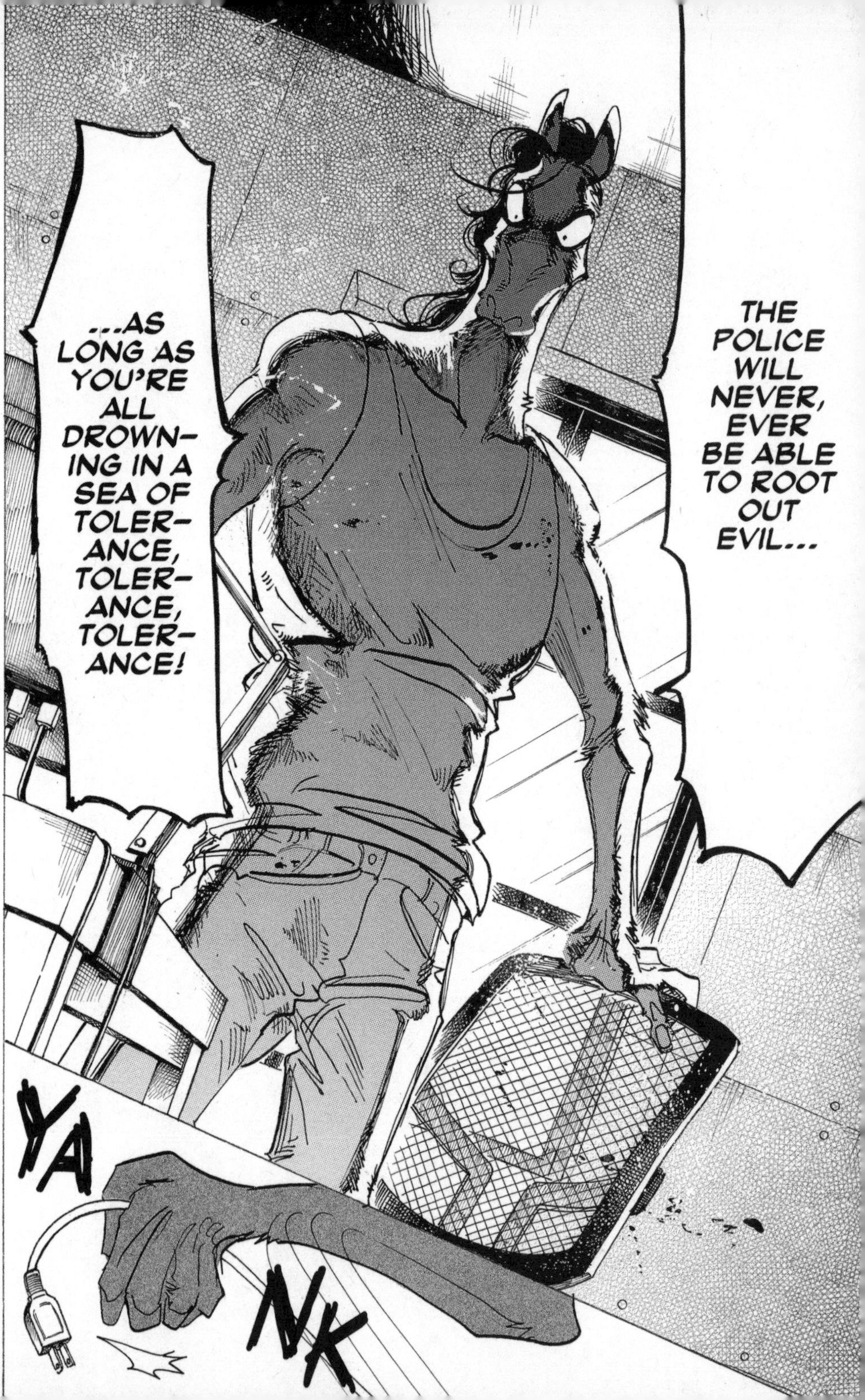
THE POLICE WILL NEVER, EVER BE ABLE TO ROOT OUT EVIL...
...AS LONG AS YOU'RE ALL DROWNING IN A SEA OF TOLERANCE, TOLERANCE, TOLERANCE!
YANK

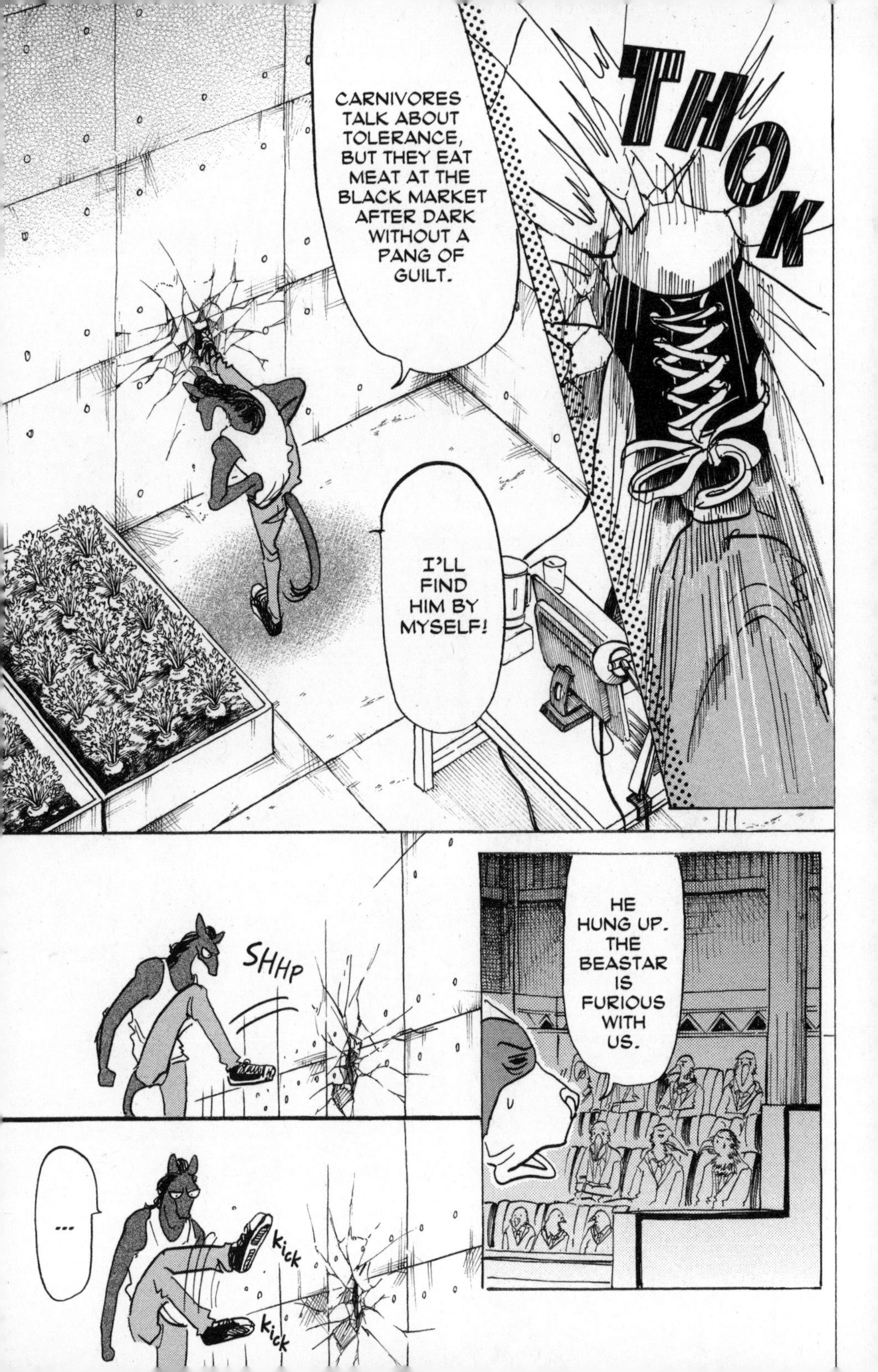
THOK
CARNIVORES TALK ABOUT TOLERANCE, BUT THEY EAT MEAT AT THE BLACK MARKET AFTER DARK WITHOUT A PANG OF GUILT.
I'LL FIND HIM BY MYSELF!
HE HUNG UP. THE BEASTAR IS FURIOUS WITH US.
SHHP
...
kick
kick

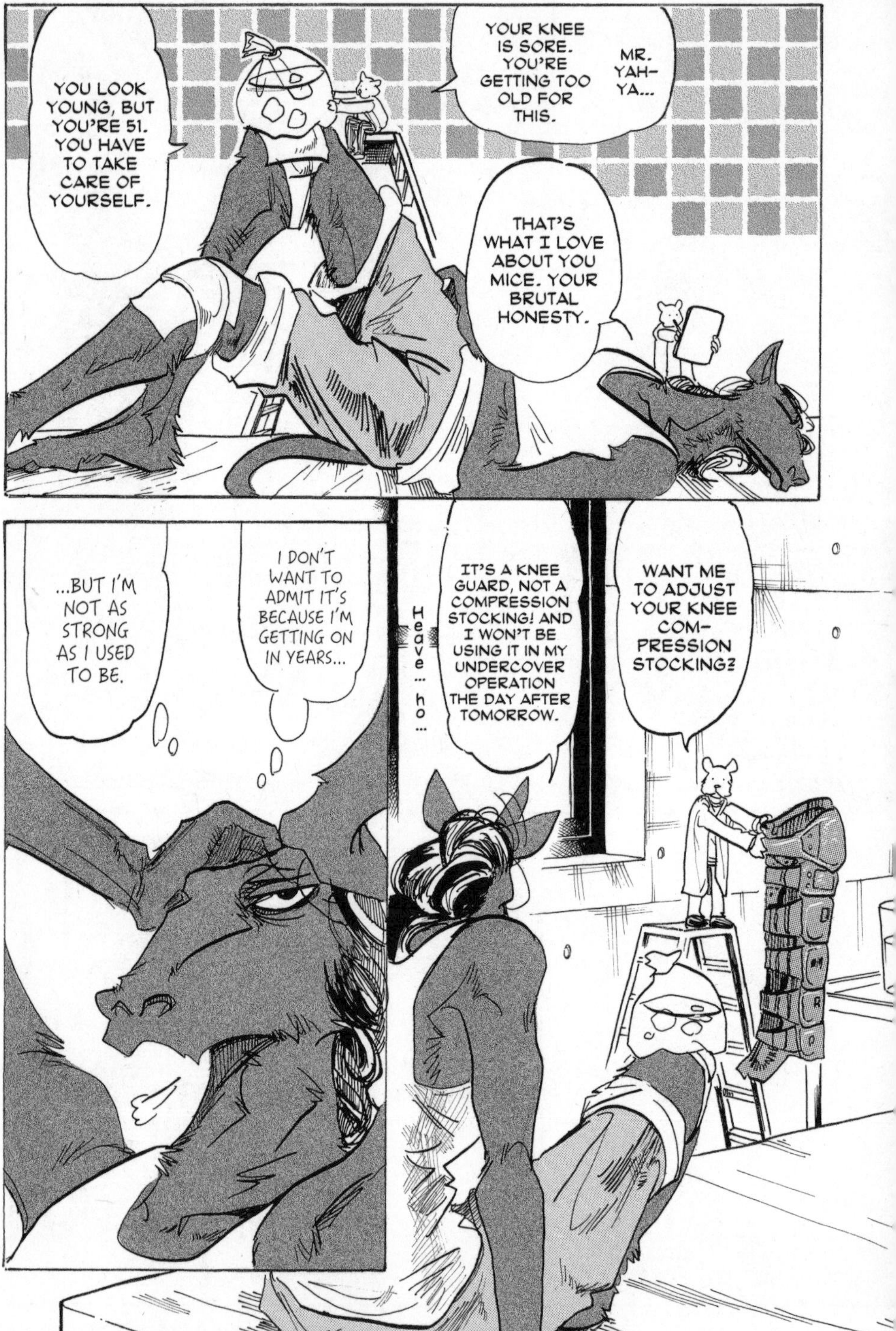
MR. YAH-YA...
YOUR KNEE IS SORE. YOU'RE GETTING TOO OLD FOR THIS.
YOU LOOK YOUNG, BUT YOU'RE 51. YOU HAVE TO TAKE CARE OF YOURSELF.
THAT'S WHAT I LOVE ABOUT YOU MICE. YOUR BRUTAL HONESTY.
WANT ME TO ADJUST YOUR KNEE COM-PRESSION STOCKING?
IT'S A KNEE GUARD, NOT A COMPRESSION STOCKING! AND I WON'T BE USING IT IN MY UNDERCOVER OPERATION THE DAY AFTER TOMORROW.
Heave... ho...
I DON'T WANT TO ADMIT IT'S BECAUSE I'M GETTING ON IN YEARS...
...BUT I'M NOT AS STRONG AS I USED TO BE.

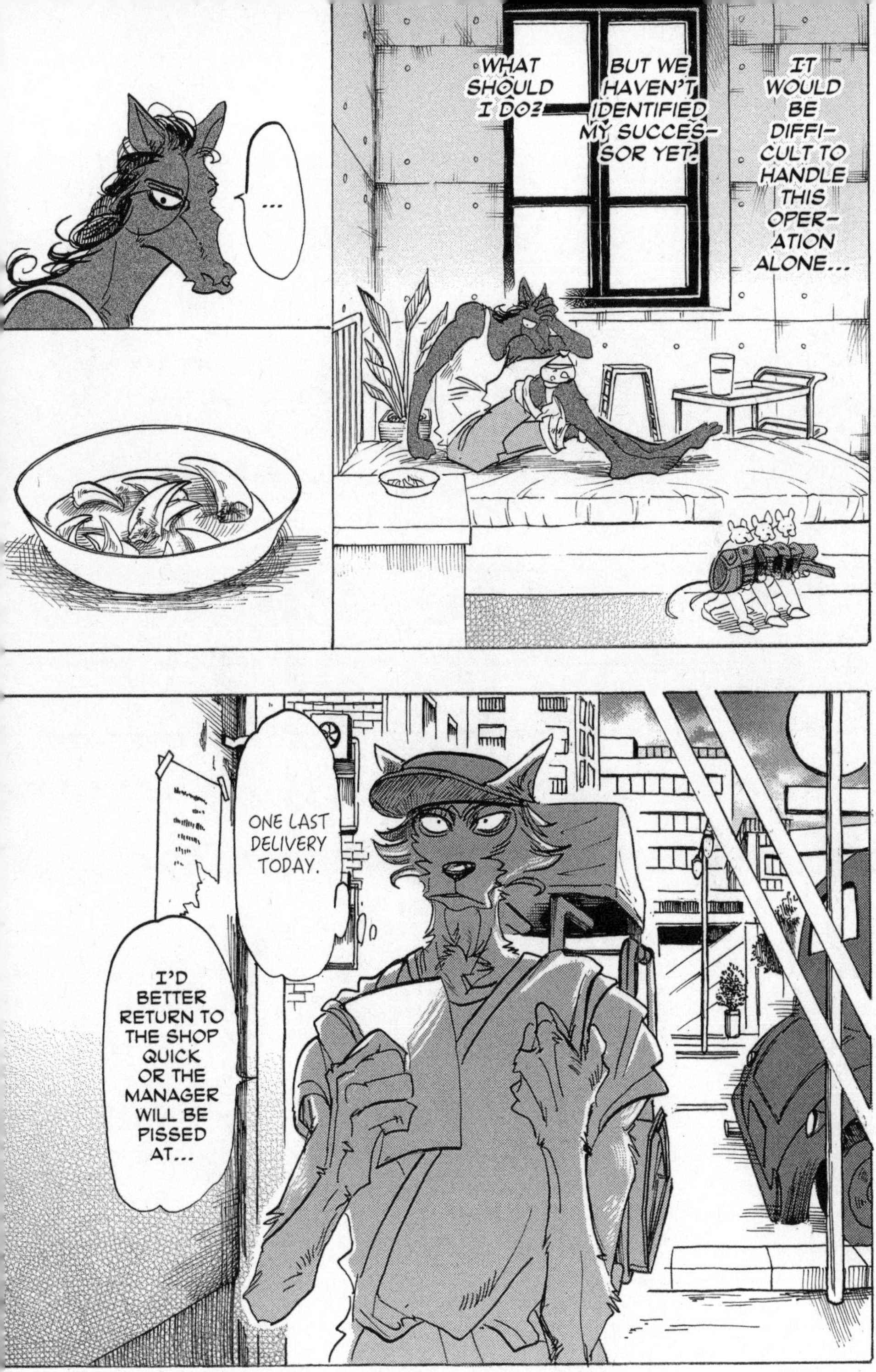
IT WOULD BE DIFFI-CULT TO HANDLE THIS OPER-ATION ALONE...
BUT WE HAVEN'T IDENTIFIED MY SUCCES-SOR YET.
WHAT SHOULD I DO?
...
ONE LAST DELIVERY TODAY.
I'D BETTER RETURN TO THE SHOP QUICK OR THE MANAGER WILL BE PISSED AT...

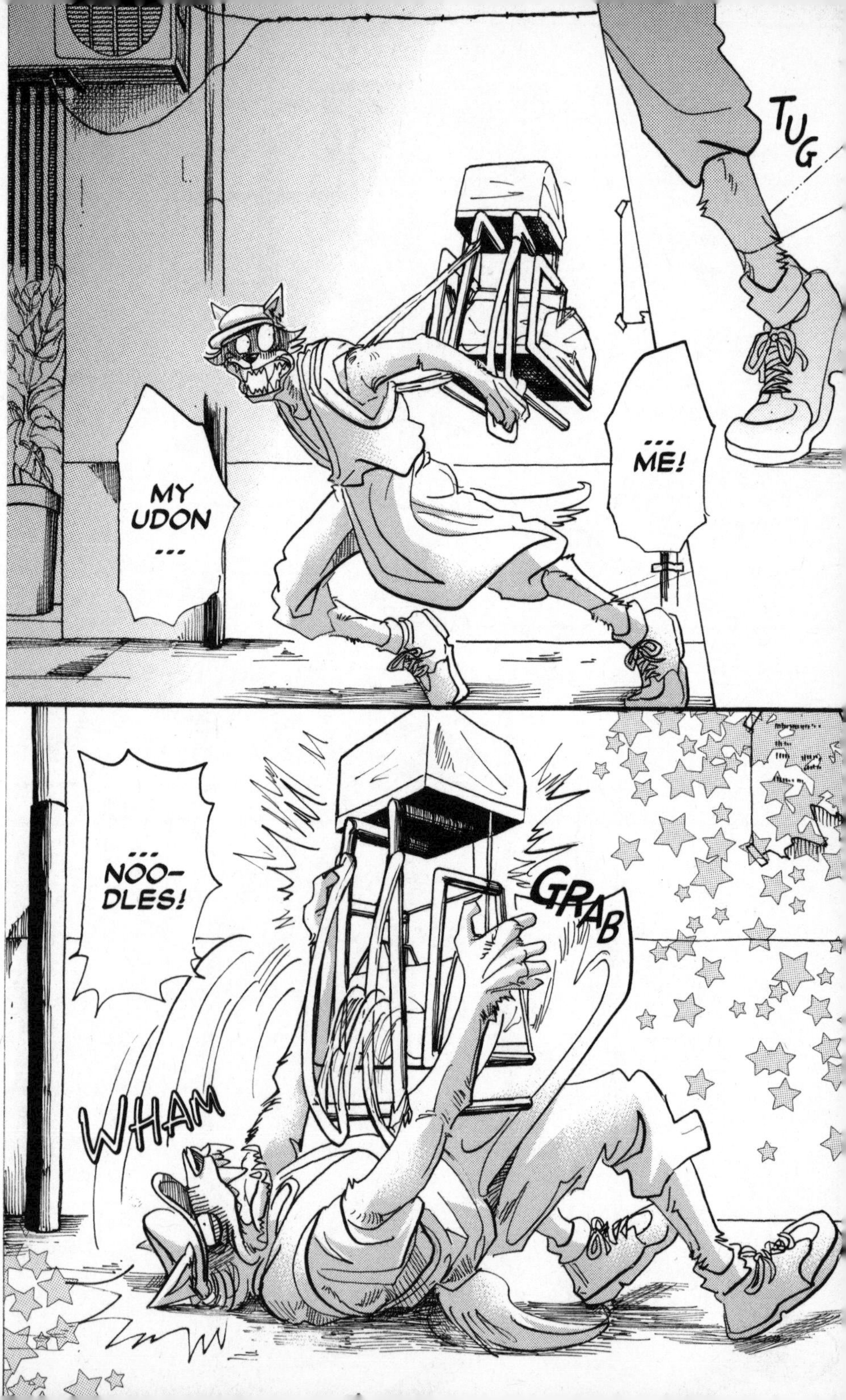
TUG
...ME!
MY UDON ...
GRAB
... NOO-DLES!
WHAM

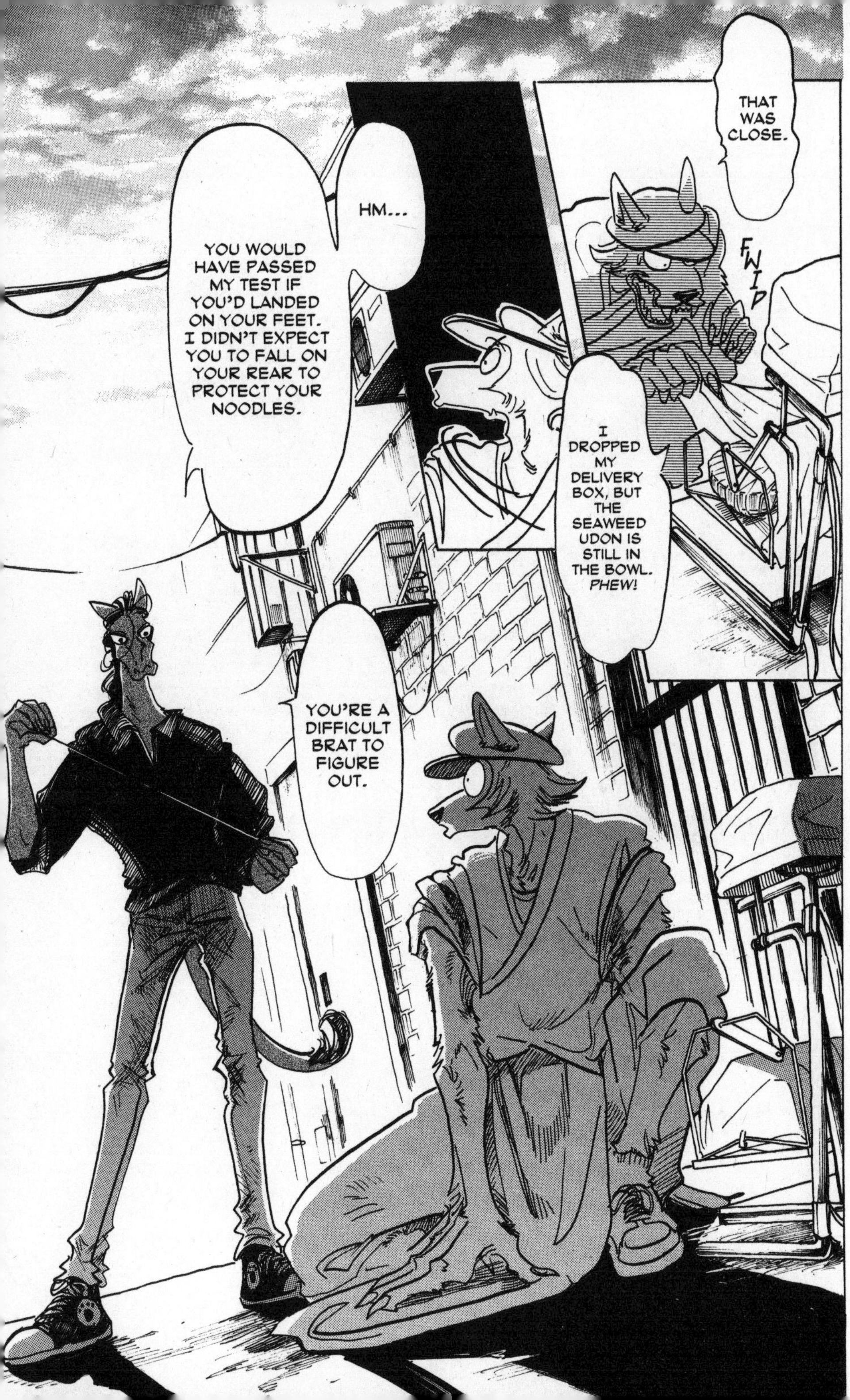
THAT WAS CLOSE.
FWIP
I DROPPED MY DELIVERY BOX, BUT THE SEAWEED UDON IS STILL IN THE BOWL. *PHEW!*
HM...
YOU WOULD HAVE PASSED MY TEST IF YOU'D LANDED ON YOUR FEET. I DIDN'T EXPECT YOU TO FALL ON YOUR REAR TO PROTECT YOUR NOODLES.
YOU'RE A DIFFICULT BRAT TO FIGURE OUT.

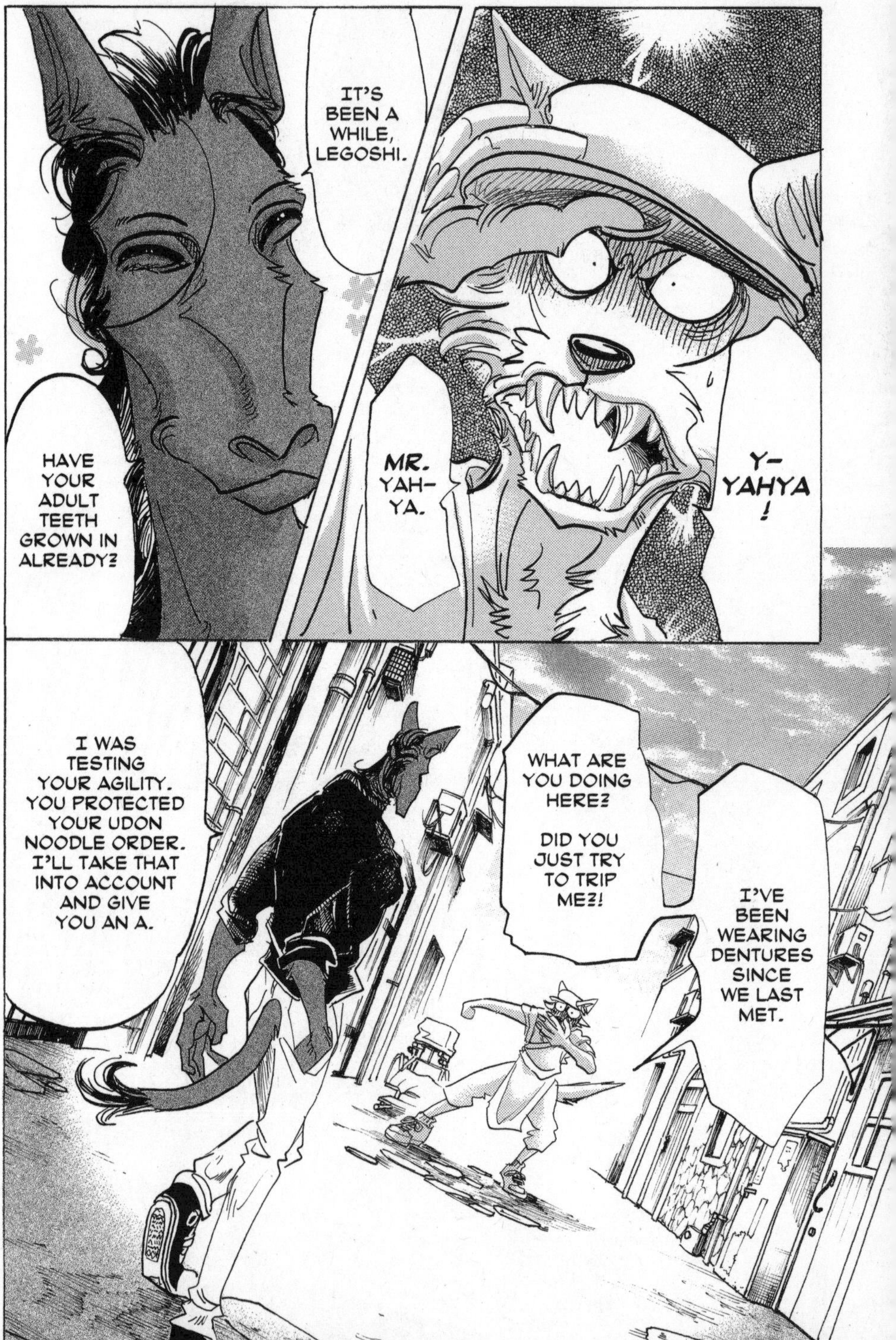
Y-YAHYA!
MR. YAH-YA.
IT'S BEEN A WHILE, LEGOSHI.
HAVE YOUR ADULT TEETH GROWN IN ALREADY?
WHAT ARE YOU DOING HERE?
DID YOU JUST TRY TO TRIP ME?!
I'VE BEEN WEARING DENTURES SINCE WE LAST MET.
I WAS TESTING YOUR AGILITY. YOU PROTECTED YOUR UDON NOODLE ORDER. I'LL TAKE THAT INTO ACCOUNT AND GIVE YOU AN A.

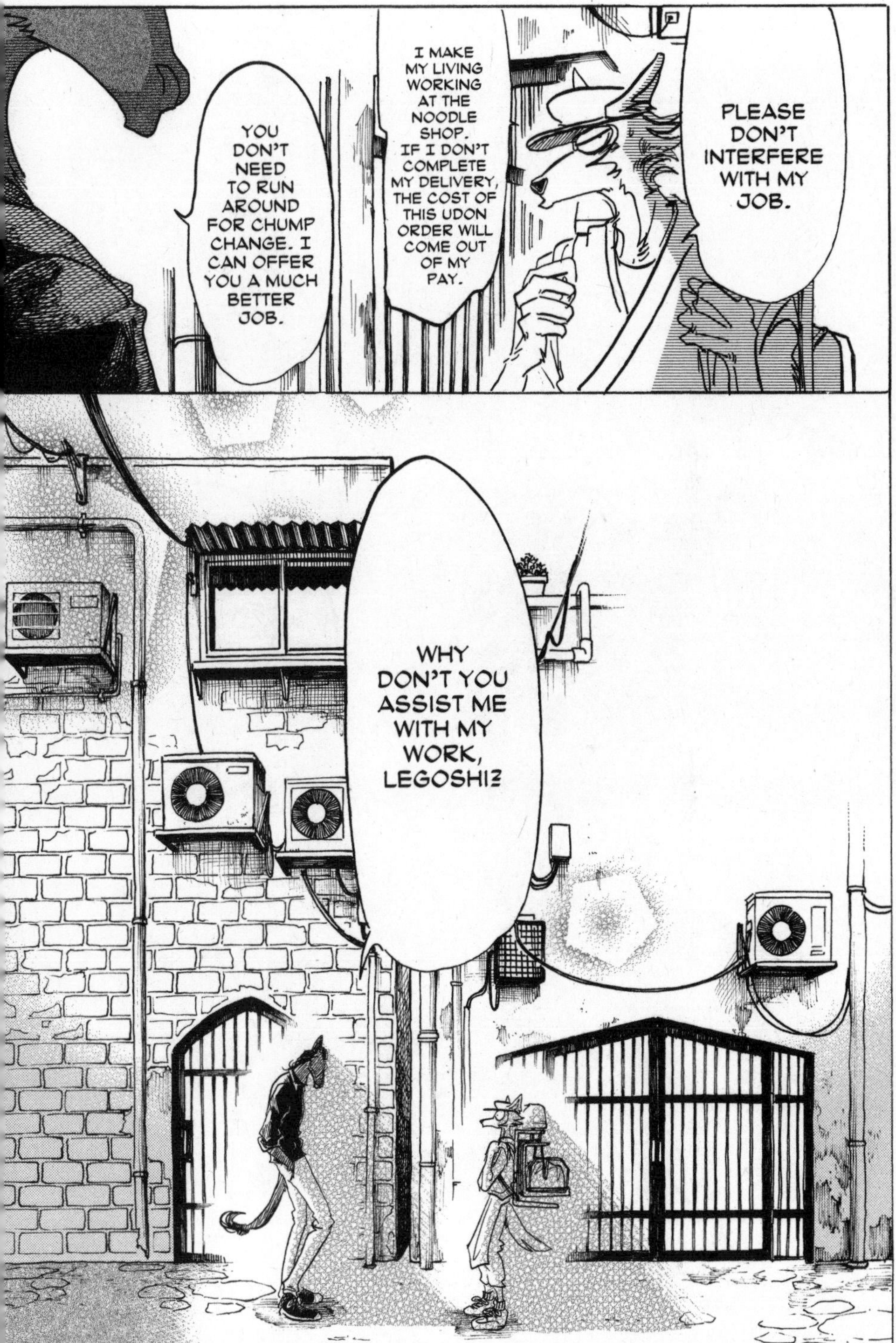
PLEASE DON'T INTERFERE WITH MY JOB.
I MAKE MY LIVING WORKING AT THE NOODLE SHOP. IF I DON'T COMPLETE MY DELIVERY, THE COST OF THIS UDON ORDER WILL COME OUT OF MY PAY.
YOU DON'T NEED TO RUN AROUND FOR CHUMP CHANGE. I CAN OFFER YOU A MUCH BETTER JOB.
WHY DON'T YOU ASSIST ME WITH MY WORK, LEGOSHI?

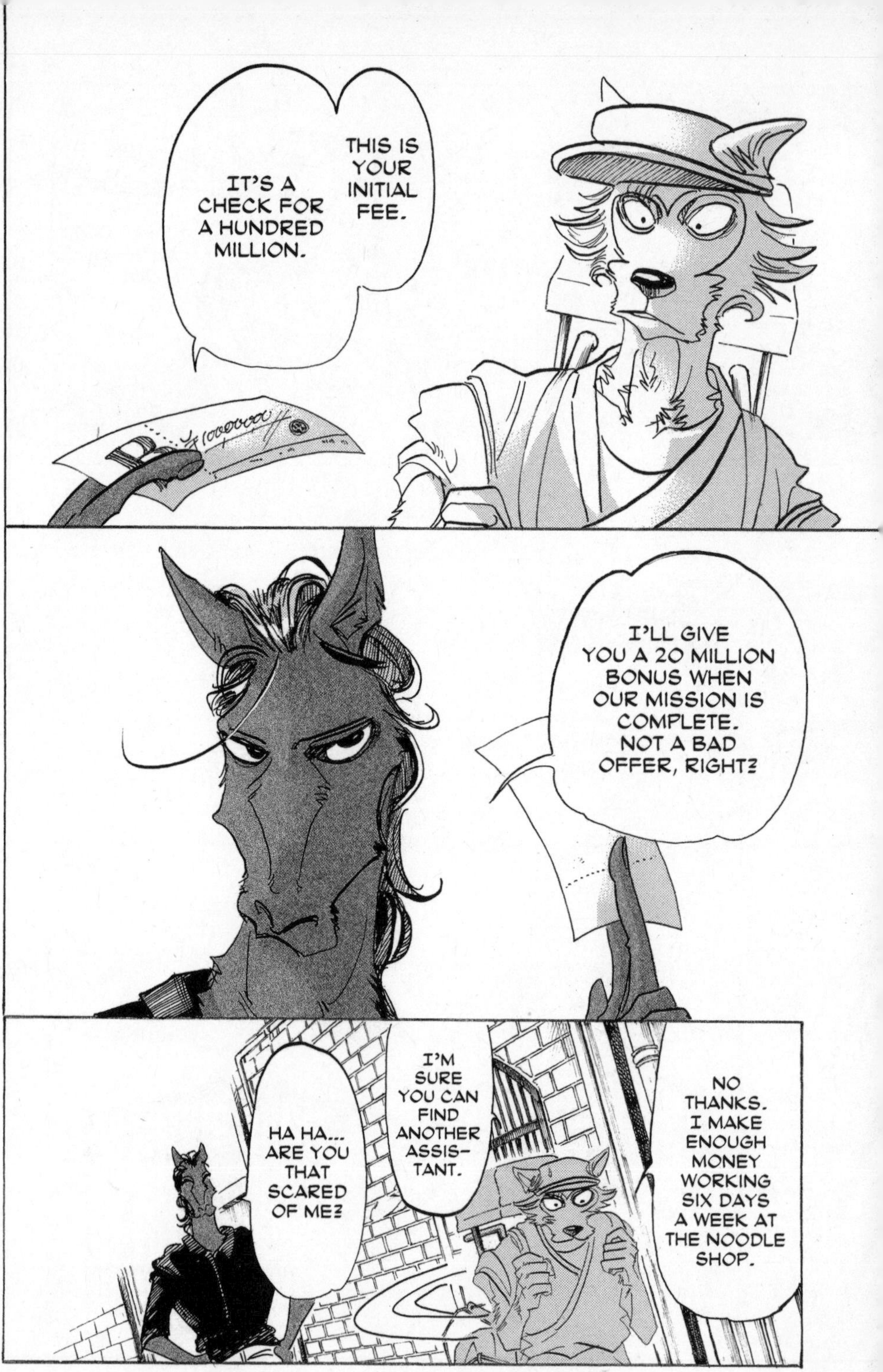
THIS IS YOUR INITIAL FEE.
IT'S A CHECK FOR A HUNDRED MILLION.
I'LL GIVE YOU A 20 MILLION BONUS WHEN OUR MISSION IS COMPLETE. NOT A BAD OFFER, RIGHT?
NO THANKS. I MAKE ENOUGH MONEY WORKING SIX DAYS A WEEK AT THE NOODLE SHOP.
I'M SURE YOU CAN FIND ANOTHER ASSIS-TANT.
HA HA... ARE YOU THAT SCARED OF ME?

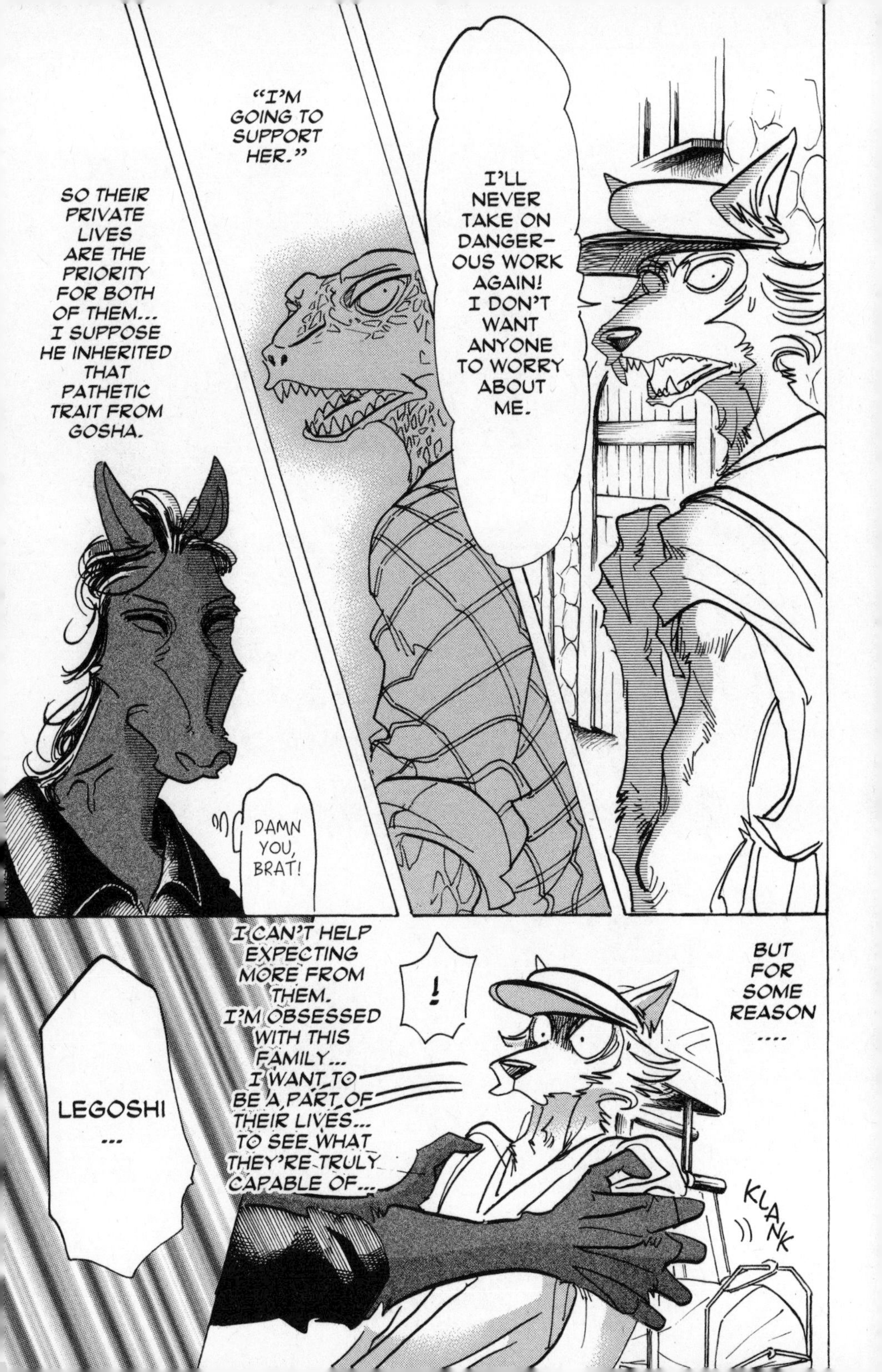
I'LL NEVER TAKE ON DANGER-OUS WORK AGAIN! I DON'T WANT ANYONE TO WORRY ABOUT ME.
"I'M GOING TO SUPPORT HER."
SO THEIR PRIVATE LIVES ARE THE PRIORITY FOR BOTH OF THEM... I SUPPOSE HE INHERITED THAT PATHETIC TRAIT FROM GOSHA.
DAMN YOU, BRAT!
BUT FOR SOME REASON....
!
I CAN'T HELP EXPECTING MORE FROM THEM. I'M OBSESSED WITH THIS FAMILY... I WANT TO BE A PART OF THEIR LIVES... TO SEE WHAT THEY'RE TRULY CAPABLE OF...
KLANK
LEGOSHI...

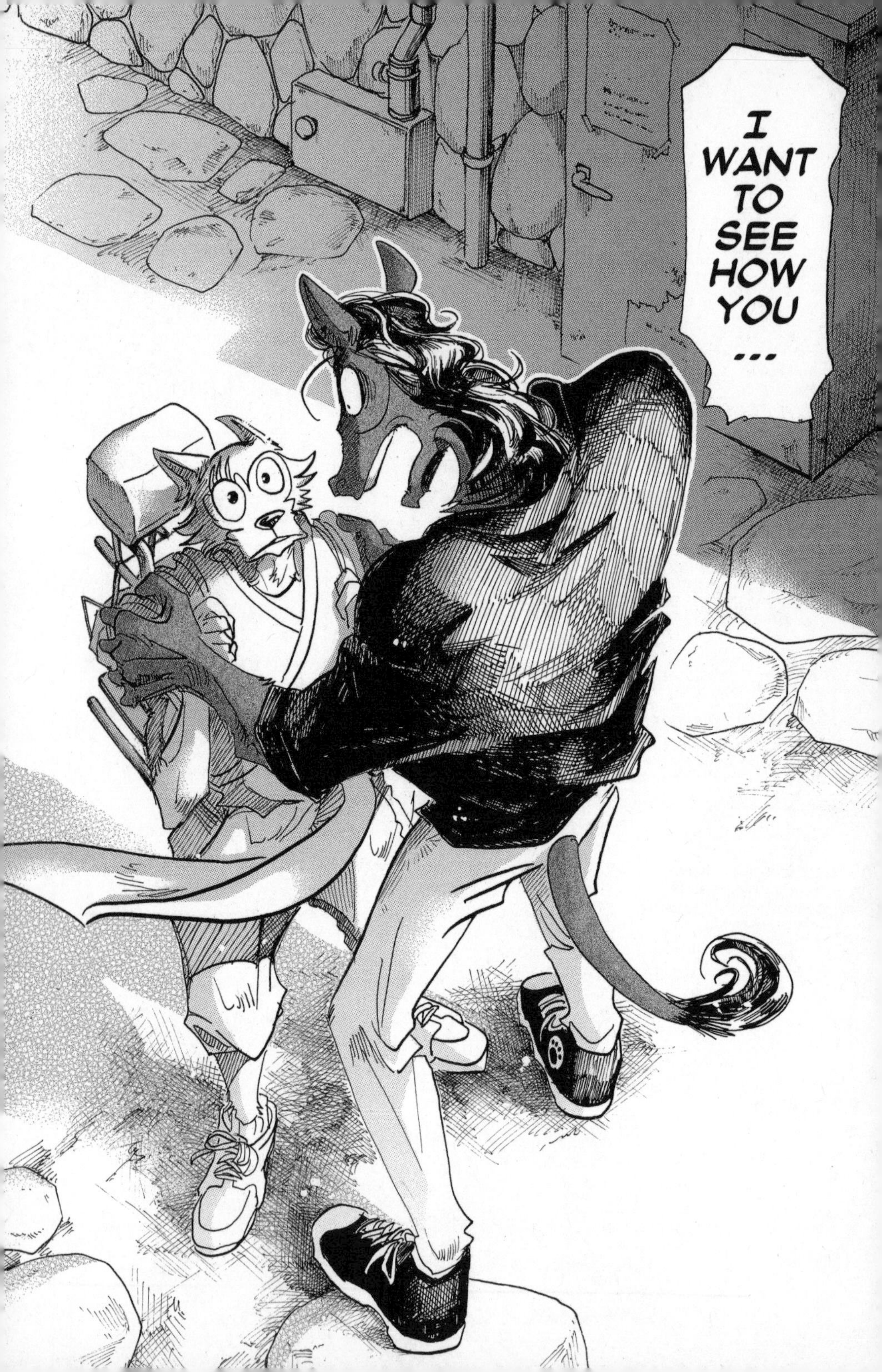
I WANT TO SEE HOW YOU ...

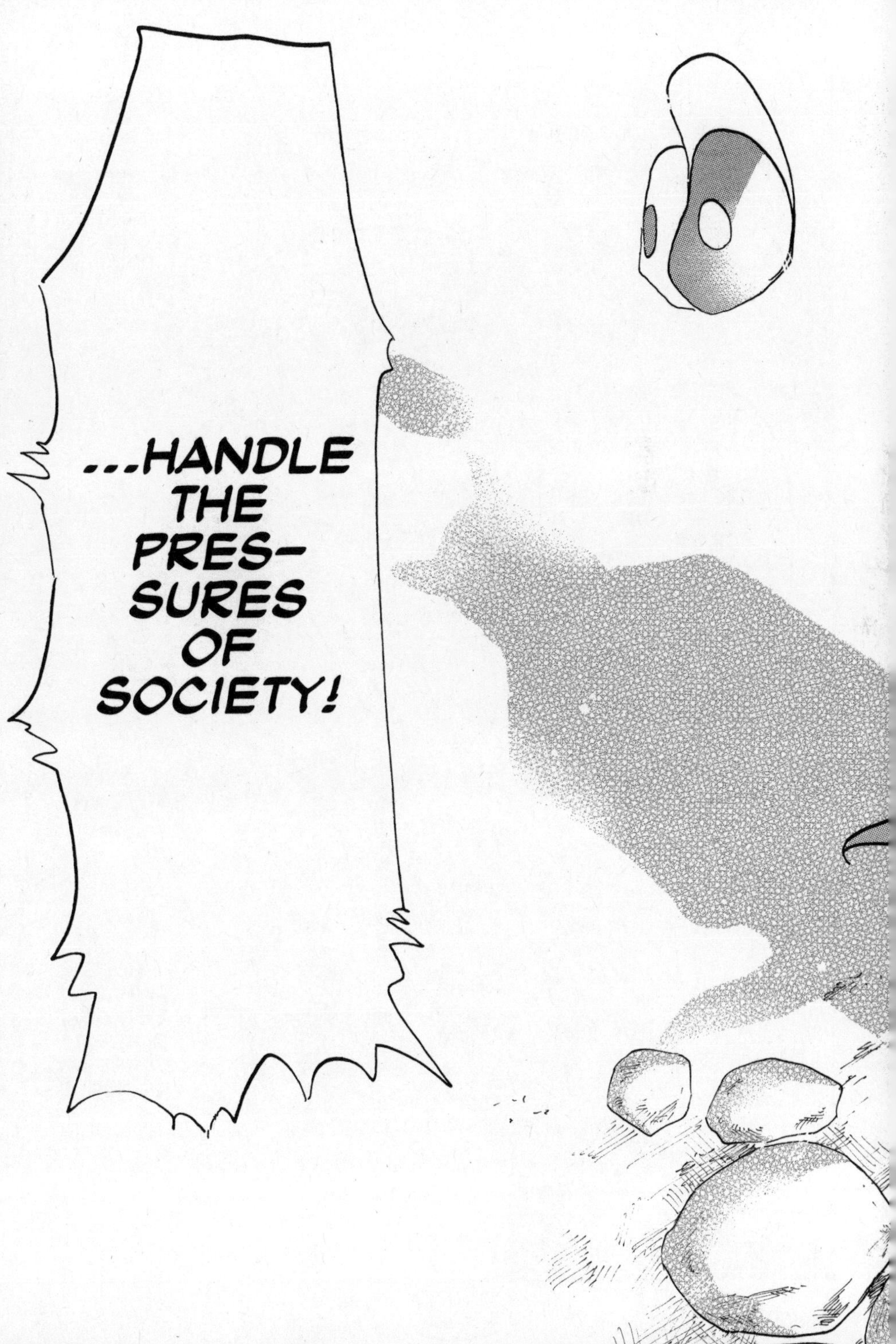
...HANDLE THE PRES-SURES OF SOCIETY!

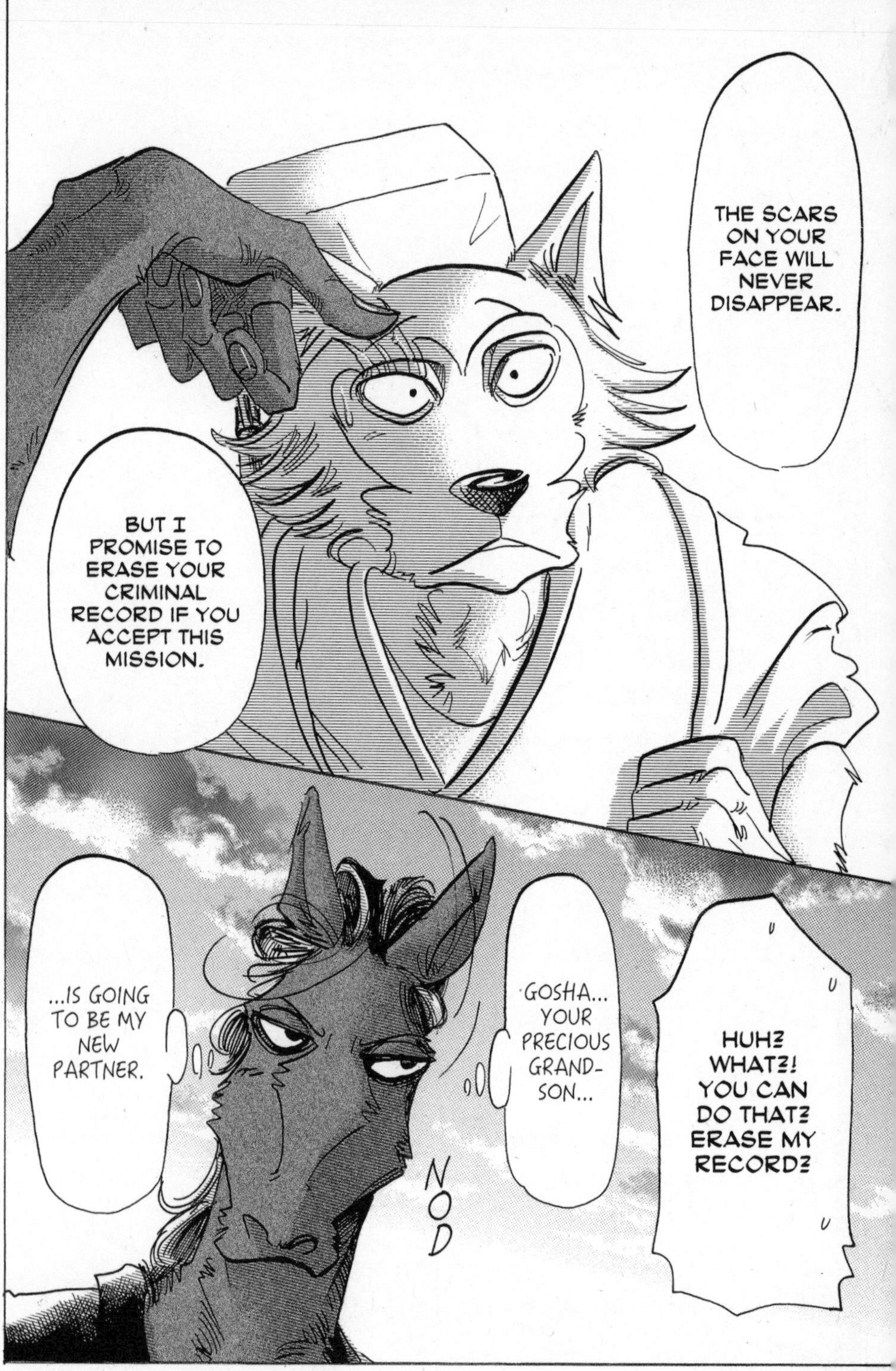
THE SCARS ON YOUR FACE WILL NEVER DISAPPEAR.
BUT I PROMISE TO ERASE YOUR CRIMINAL RECORD IF YOU ACCEPT THIS MISSION.
HUH? WHAT?! YOU CAN DO THAT? ERASE MY RECORD?
GOSHA... YOUR PRECIOUS GRAND-SON...
NOD
...IS GOING TO BE MY NEW PARTNER.

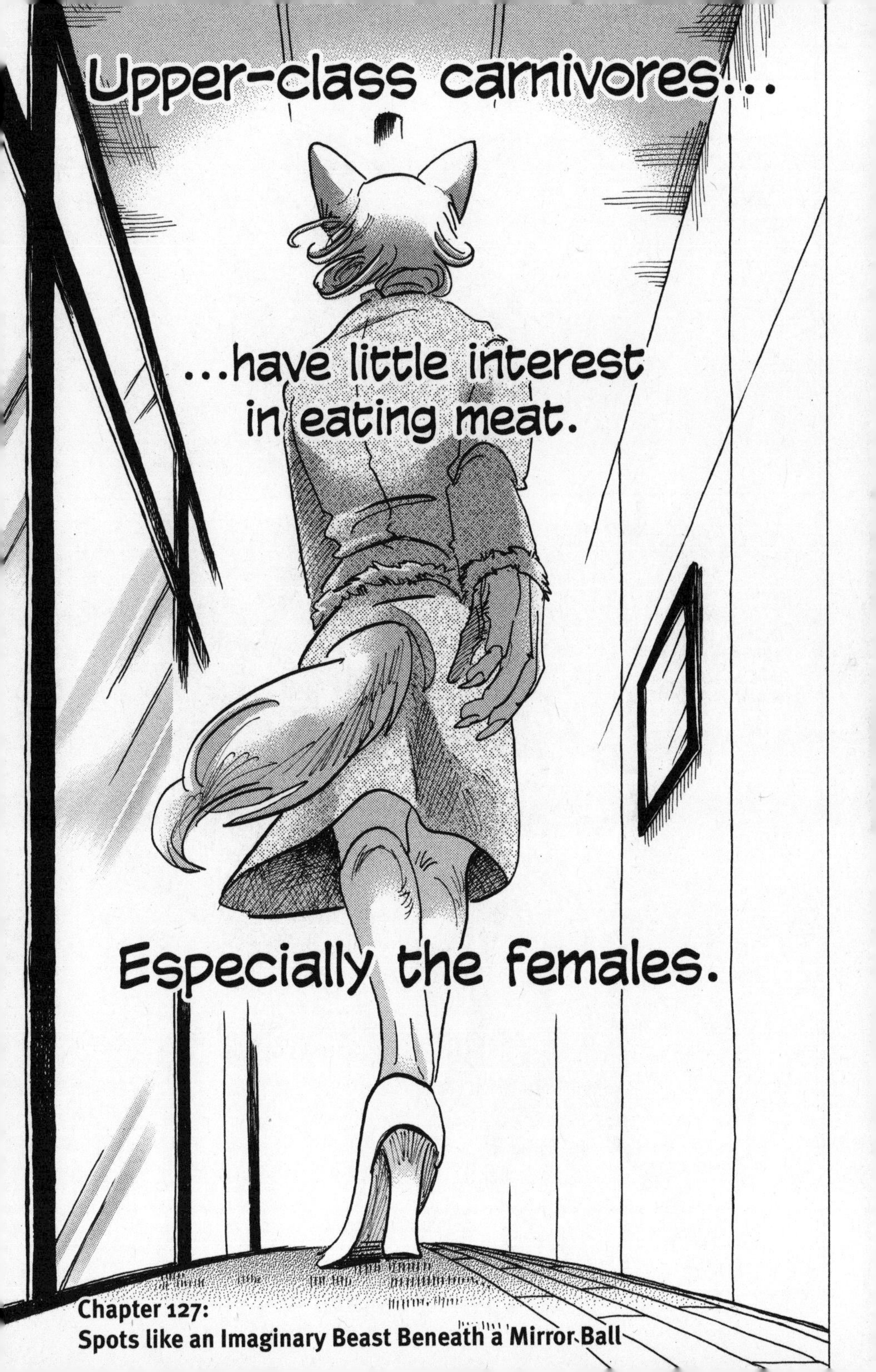
Upper-class carnivores...
...have little interest in eating meat.
Especially the females.

Chapter 127:
Spots like an Imaginary Beast Beneath a Mirror Ball

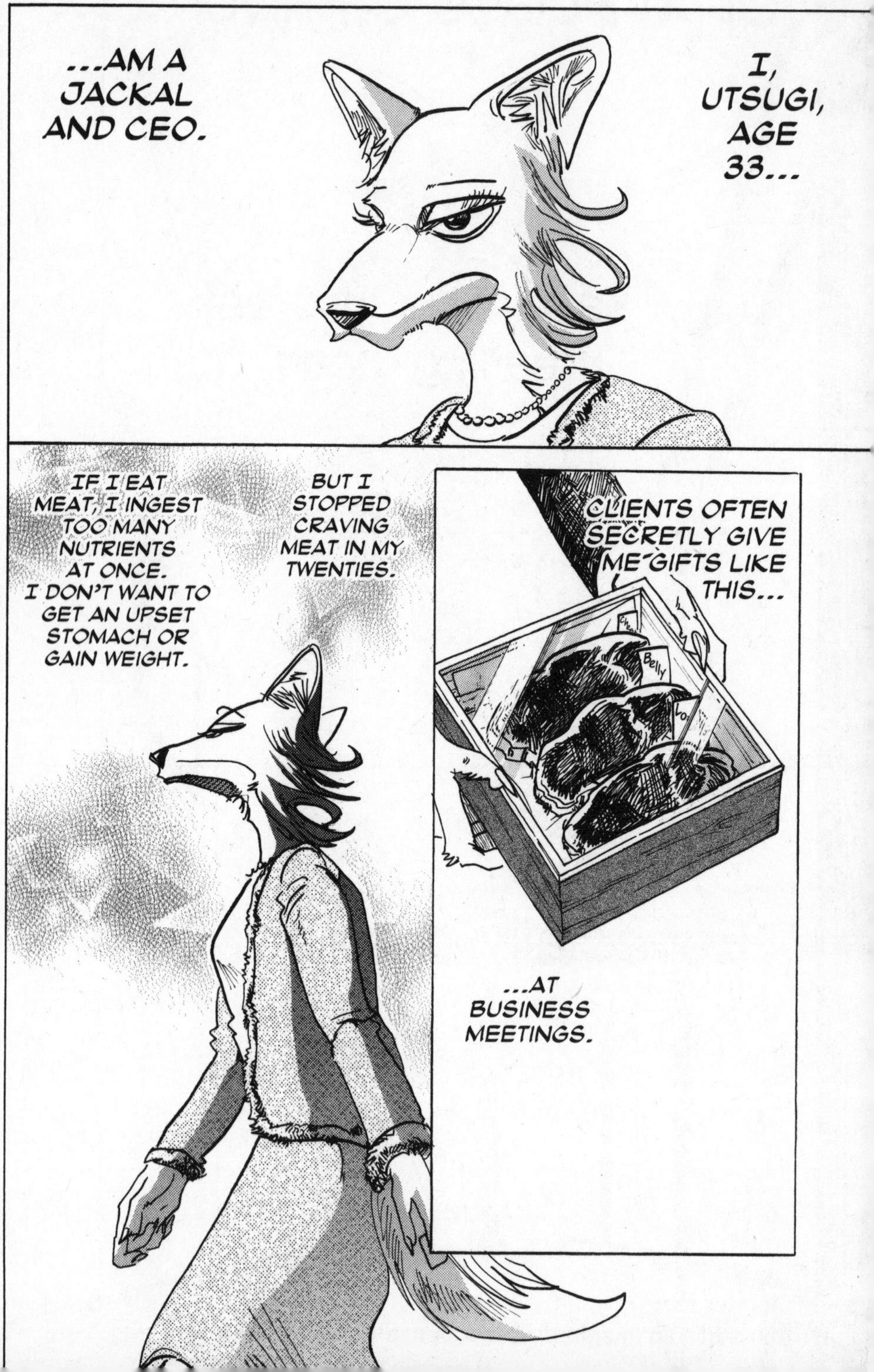
I, UTSUGI, AGE 33...
...AM A JACKAL AND CEO.
CLIENTS OFTEN SECRETLY GIVE ME GIFTS LIKE THIS...
Belly
...AT BUSINESS MEETINGS.
BUT I STOPPED CRAVING MEAT IN MY TWENTIES.
IF I EAT MEAT, I INGEST TOO MANY NUTRIENTS AT ONCE. I DON'T WANT TO GET AN UPSET STOMACH OR GAIN WEIGHT.

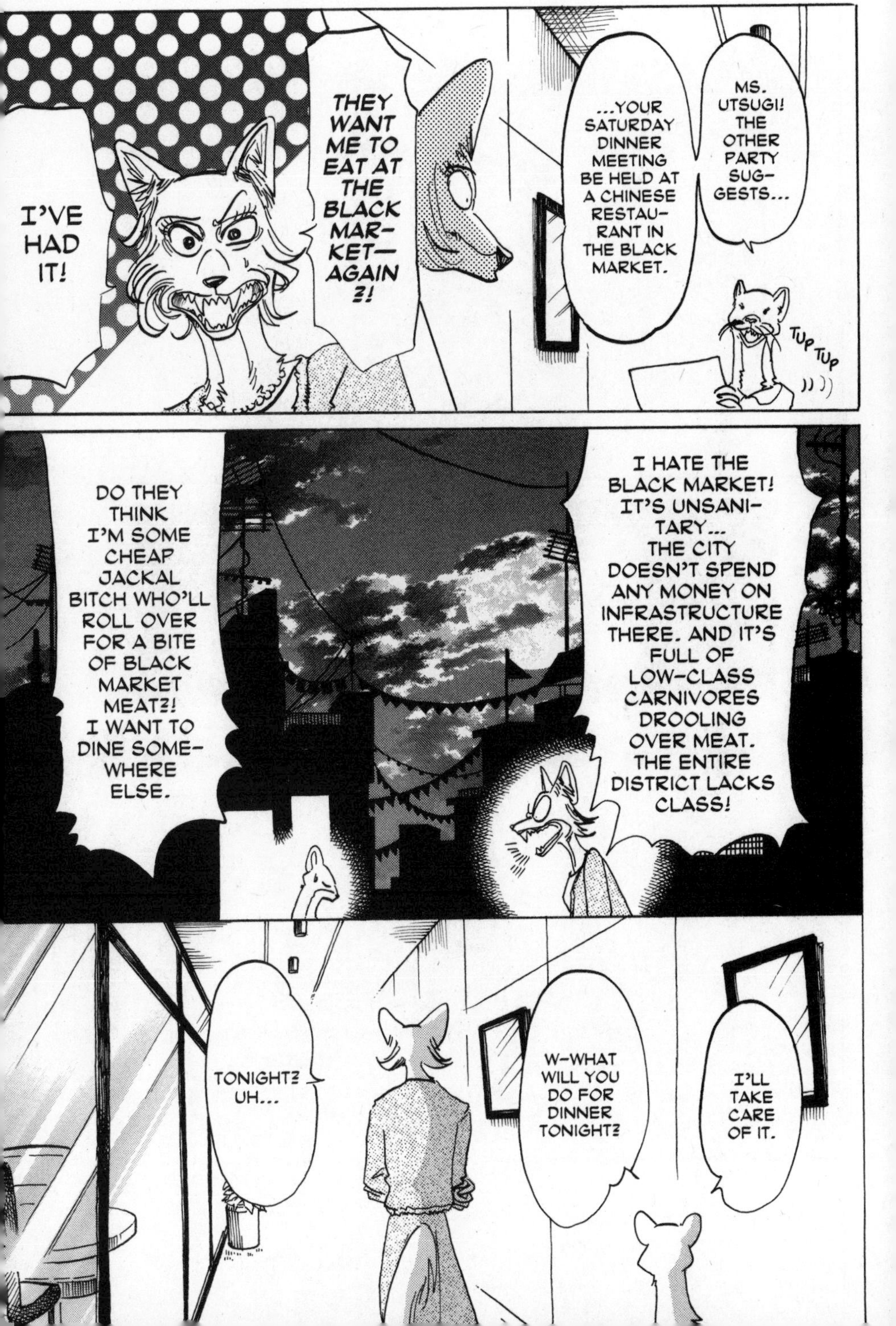
MS. UTSUGI! THE OTHER PARTY SUGGESTS...
...YOUR SATURDAY DINNER MEETING BE HELD AT A CHINESE RESTAURANT IN THE BLACK MARKET.
TUP TUP
THEY WANT ME TO EAT AT THE BLACK MARKET—AGAIN?!
I'VE HAD IT!
I HATE THE BLACK MARKET! IT'S UNSANITARY... THE CITY DOESN'T SPEND ANY MONEY ON INFRASTRUCTURE THERE. AND IT'S FULL OF LOW-CLASS CARNIVORES DROOLING OVER MEAT. THE ENTIRE DISTRICT LACKS CLASS!
DO THEY THINK I'M SOME CHEAP JACKAL BITCH WHO'LL ROLL OVER FOR A BITE OF BLACK MARKET MEAT?! I WANT TO DINE SOMEWHERE ELSE.
I'LL TAKE CARE OF IT.
W-WHAT WILL YOU DO FOR DINNER TONIGHT?
TONIGHT? UH...

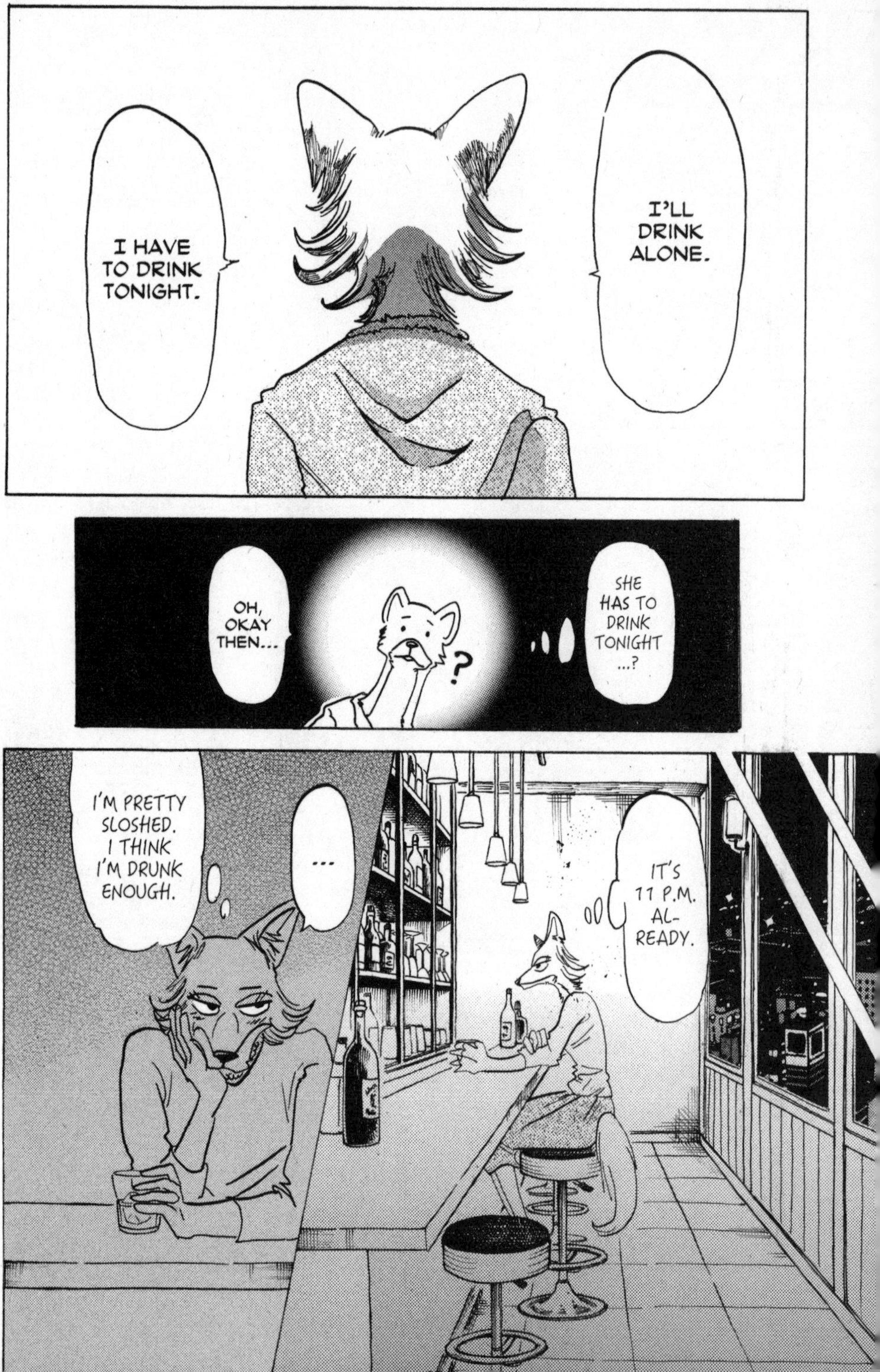
I'LL DRINK ALONE.
I HAVE TO DRINK TONIGHT.
SHE HAS TO DRINK TONIGHT ...?
OH, OKAY THEN...
?
IT'S 11 P.M. AL-READY.
...
I'M PRETTY SLOSHED. I THINK I'M DRUNK ENOUGH.

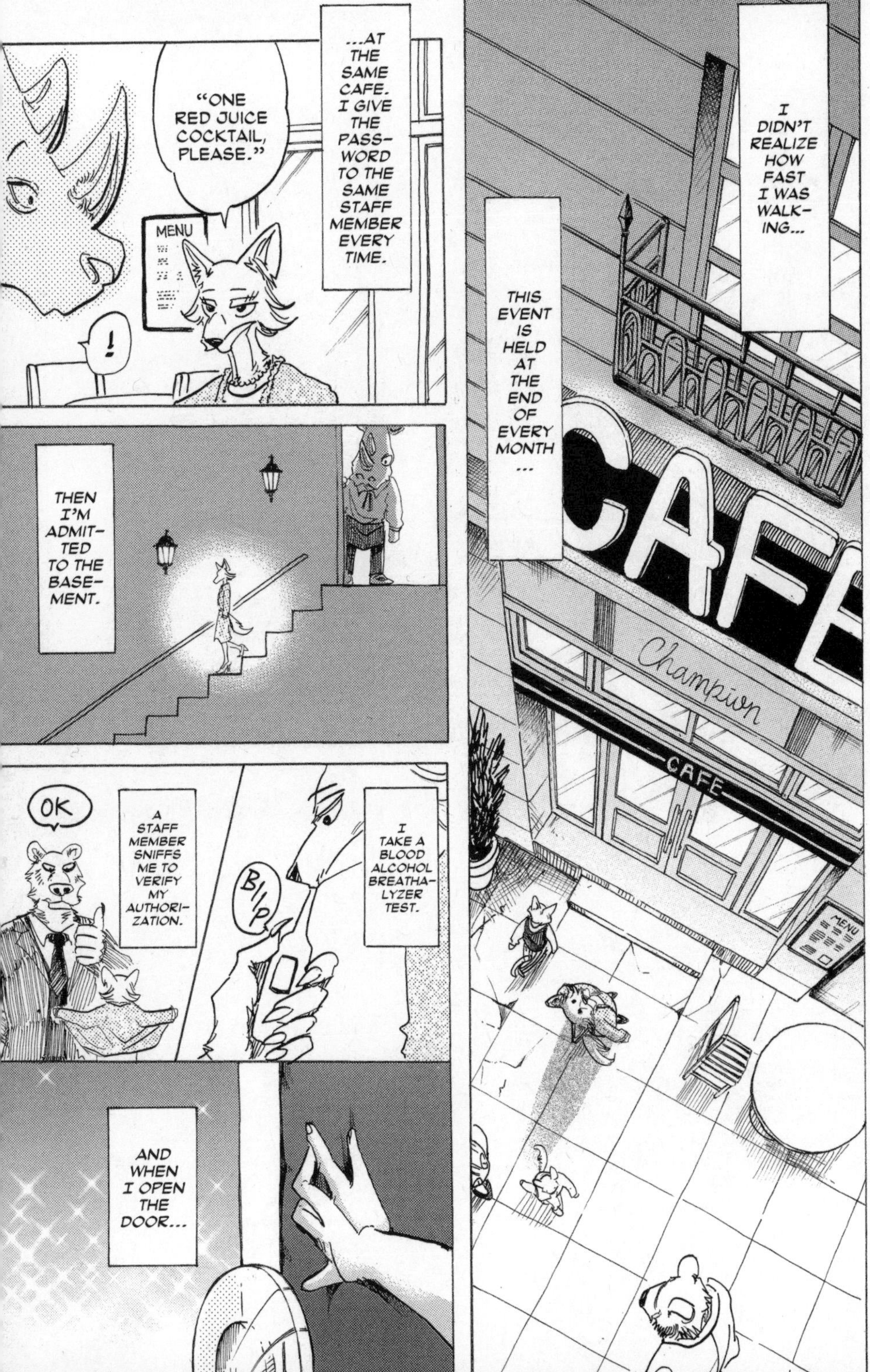
I DIDN'T REALIZE HOW FAST I WAS WALKING...
CAFE
Champion
CAFE
MENU
THIS EVENT IS HELD AT THE END OF EVERY MONTH...
...AT THE SAME CAFE. I GIVE THE PASSWORD TO THE SAME STAFF MEMBER EVERY TIME.
"ONE RED JUICE COCKTAIL, PLEASE."
MENU
!
THEN I'M ADMITTED TO THE BASEMENT.
I TAKE A BLOOD ALCOHOL BREATHALYZER TEST.
BLIP
A STAFF MEMBER SNIFFS ME TO VERIFY MY AUTHORIZATION.
OK
AND WHEN I OPEN THE DOOR...

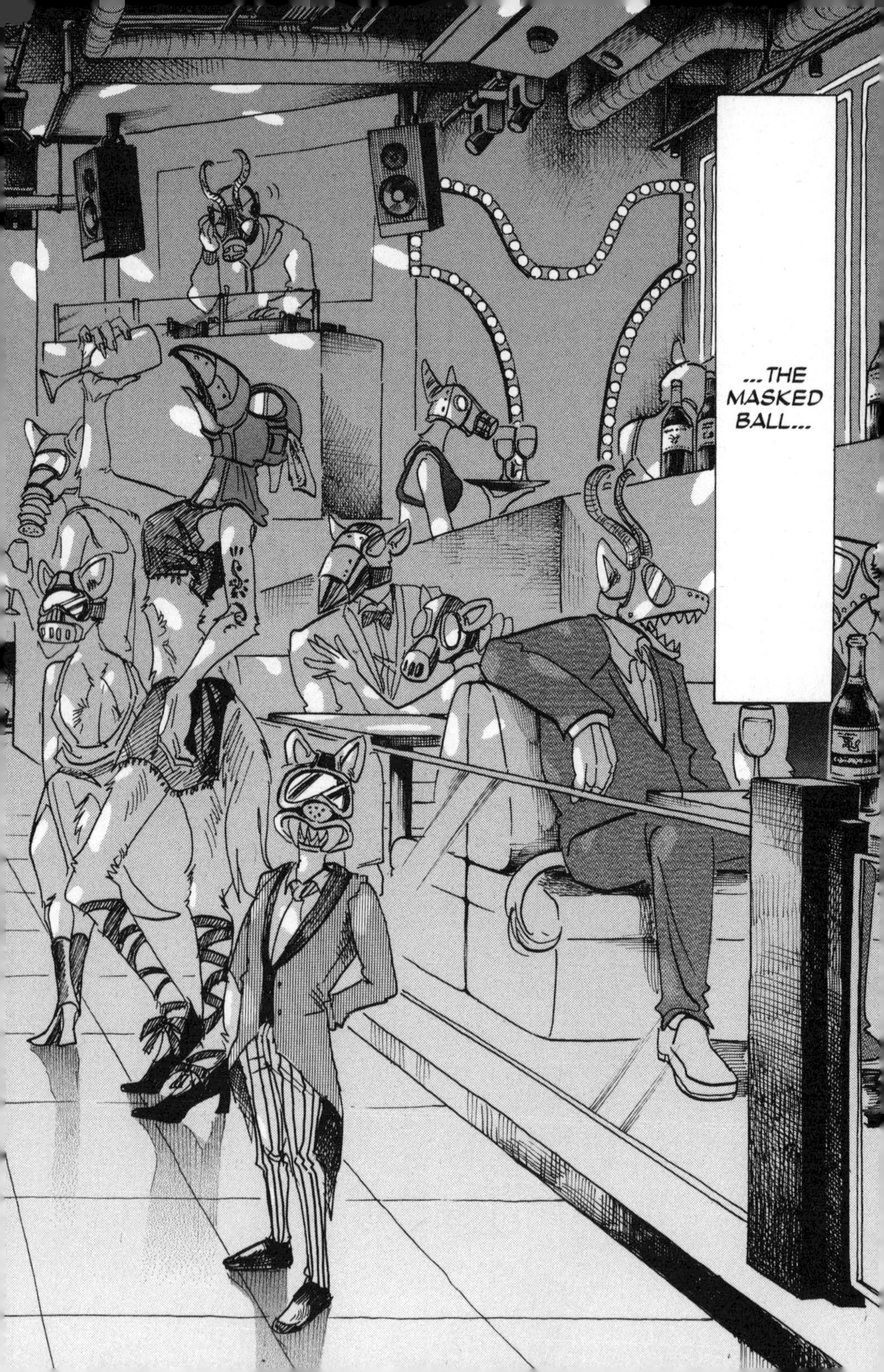
...THE MASKED BALL...

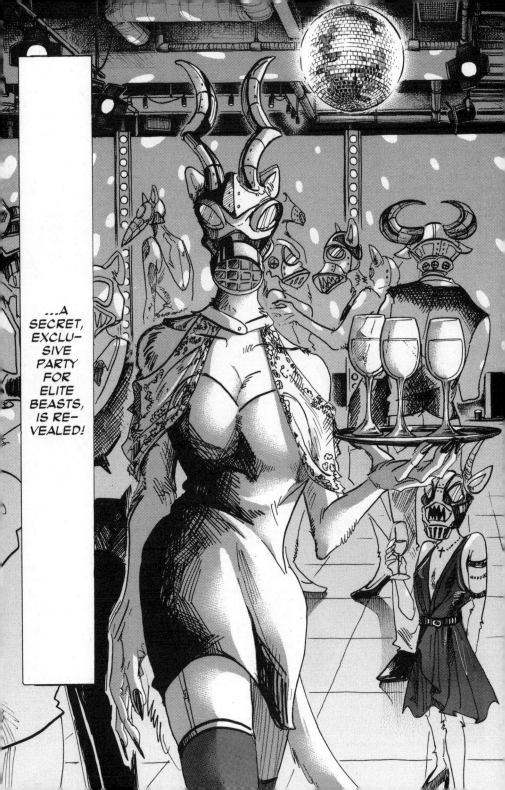

...A SECRET, EXCLUSIVE PARTY FOR ELITE BEASTS, IS REVEALED!

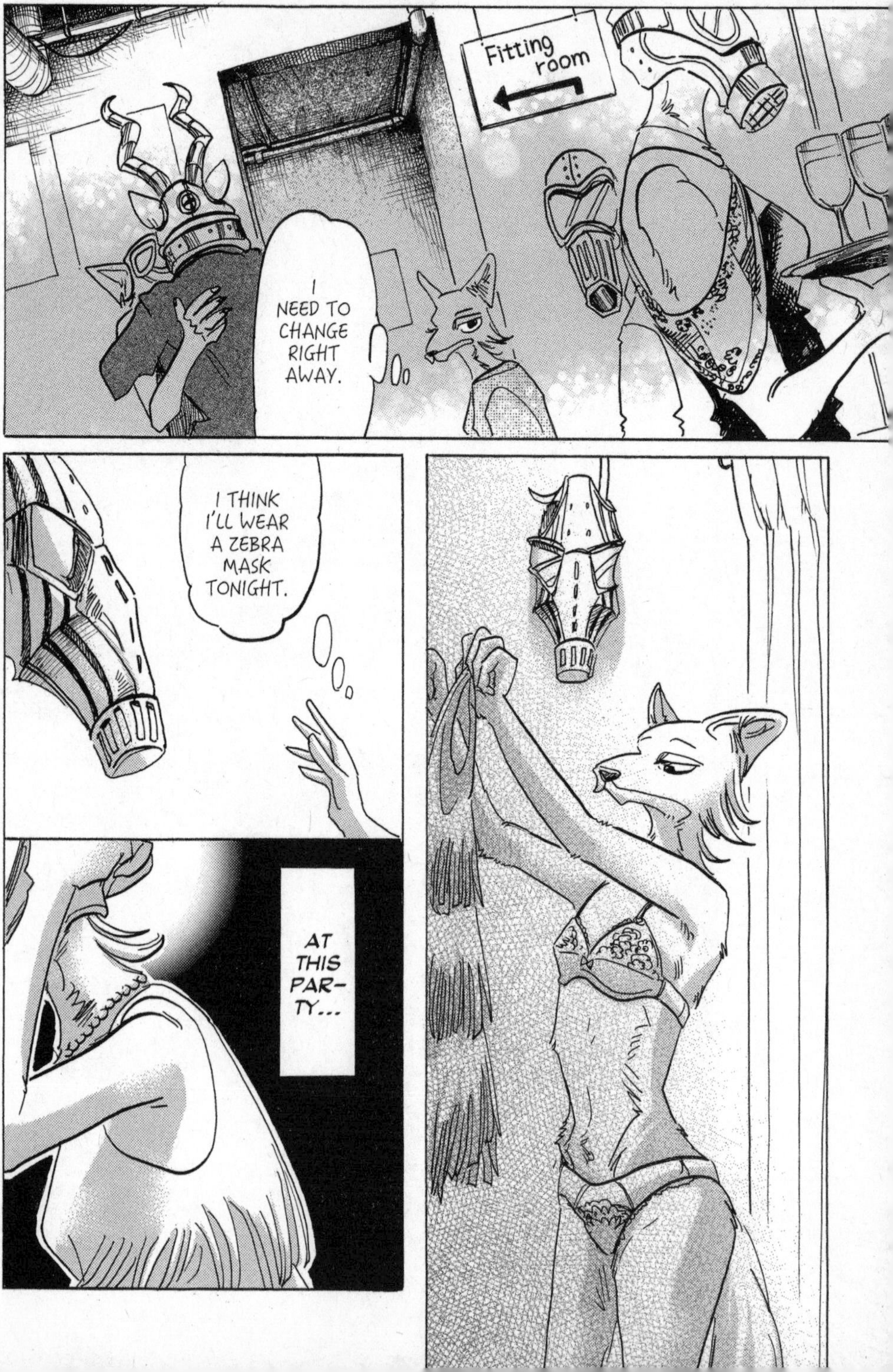
Fitting room
I NEED TO CHANGE RIGHT AWAY.
I THINK I'LL WEAR A ZEBRA MASK TONIGHT.
AT THIS PAR-TY...

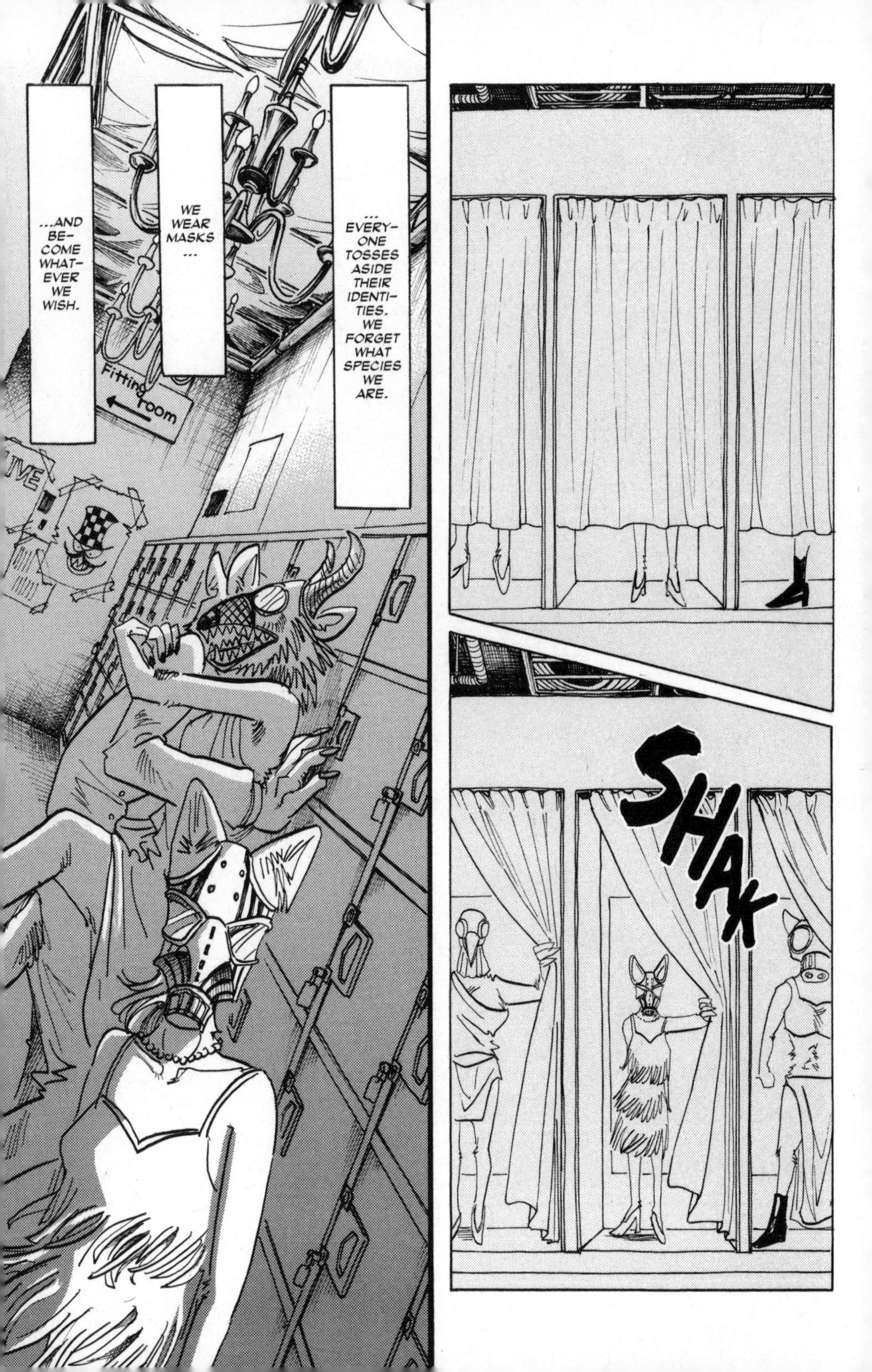
SHAK
...EVERYONE TOSSES ASIDE THEIR IDENTITIES. WE FORGET WHAT SPECIES WE ARE.
WE WEAR MASKS...
...AND BECOME WHATEVER WE WISH.
Fitting room

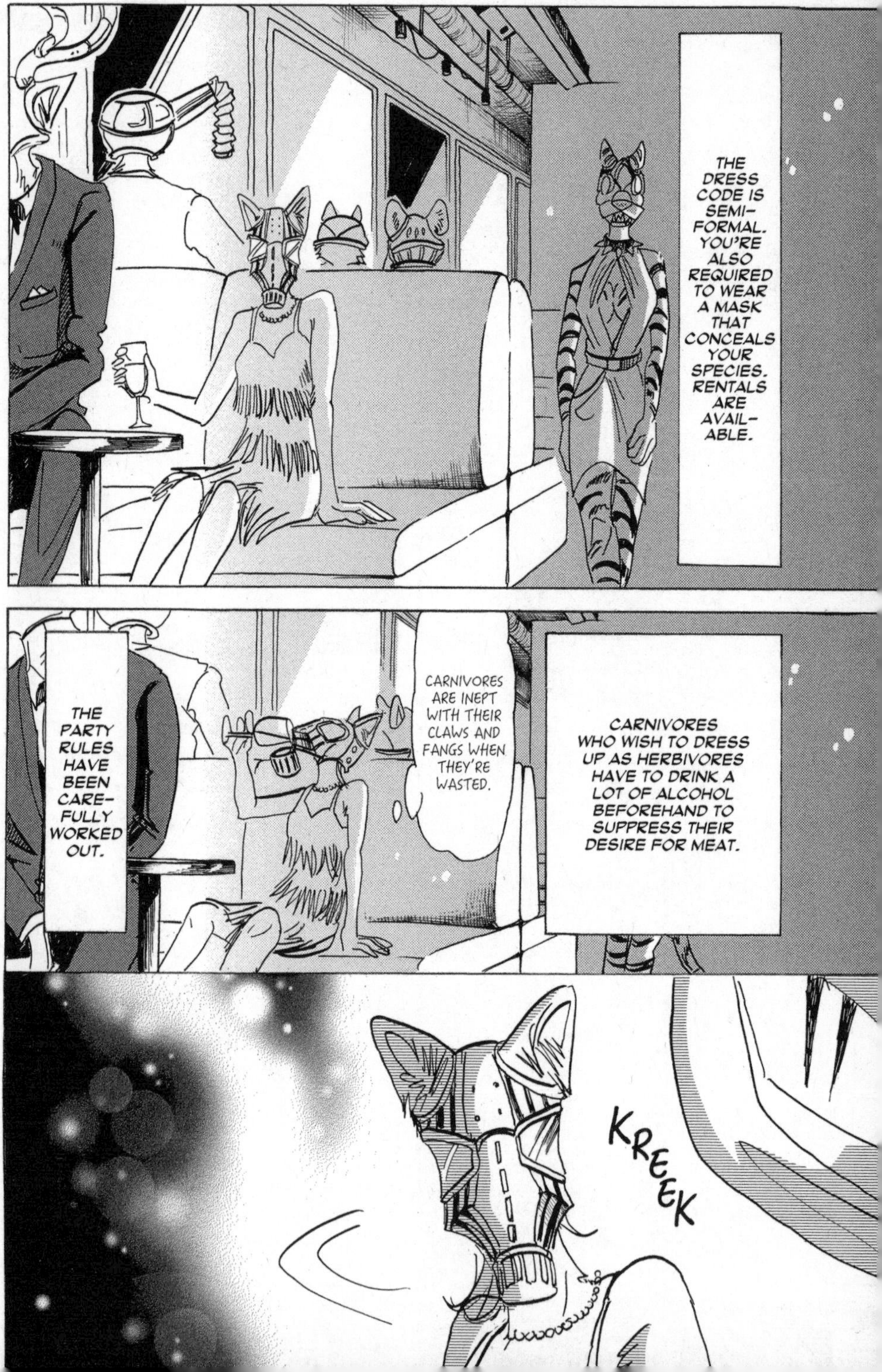
THE DRESS CODE IS SEMI-FORMAL. YOU'RE ALSO REQUIRED TO WEAR A MASK THAT CONCEALS YOUR SPECIES. RENTALS ARE AVAIL-ABLE.
CARNIVORES WHO WISH TO DRESS UP AS HERBIVORES HAVE TO DRINK A LOT OF ALCOHOL BEFOREHAND TO SUPPRESS THEIR DESIRE FOR MEAT.
CARNIVORES ARE INEPT WITH THEIR CLAWS AND FANGS WHEN THEY'RE WASTED.
THE PARTY RULES HAVE BEEN CARE-FULLY WORKED OUT.
KREEK

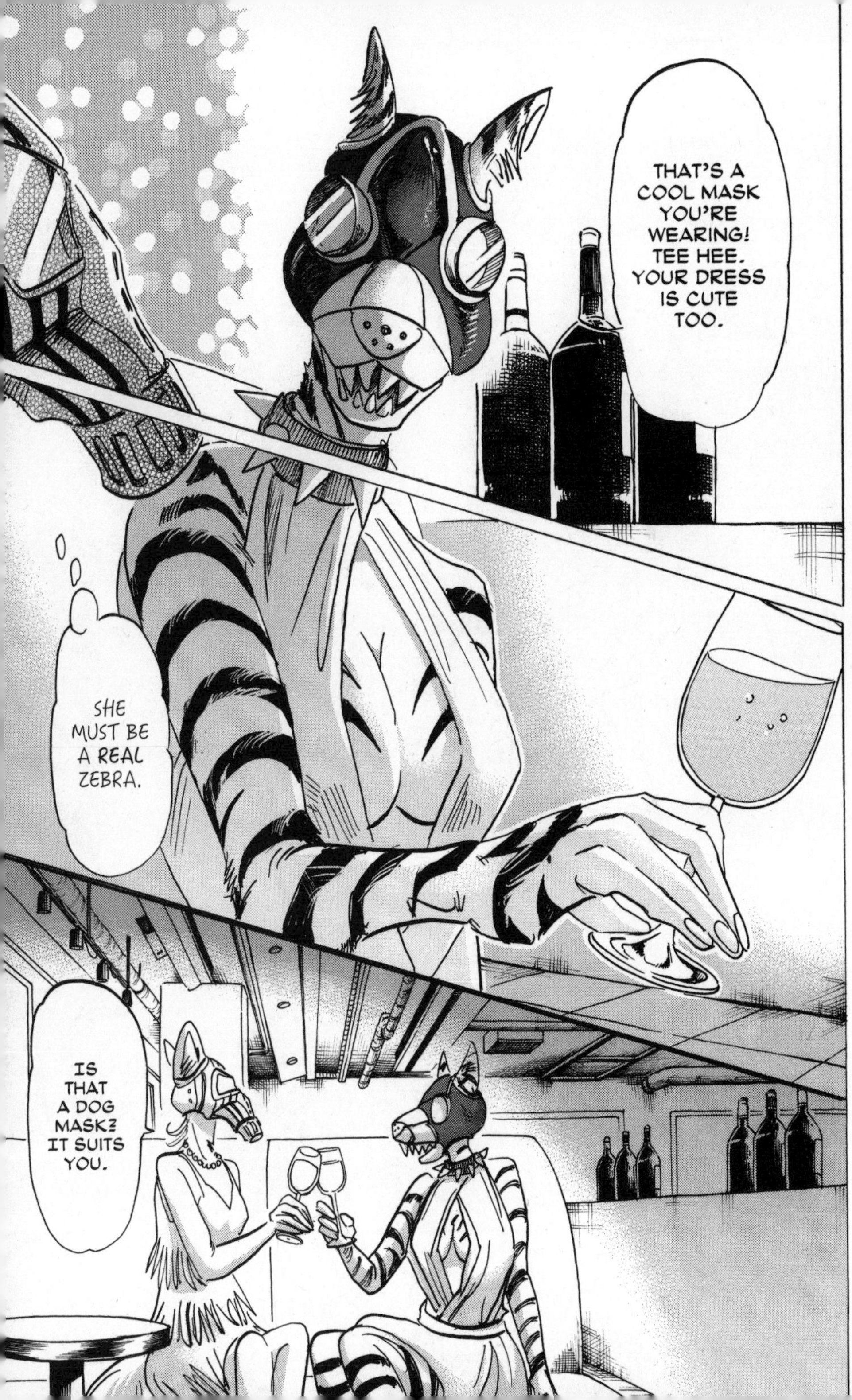
THAT'S A COOL MASK YOU'RE WEARING! TEE HEE. YOUR DRESS IS CUTE TOO.
SHE MUST BE A REAL ZEBRA.
IS THAT A DOG MASK? IT SUITS YOU.

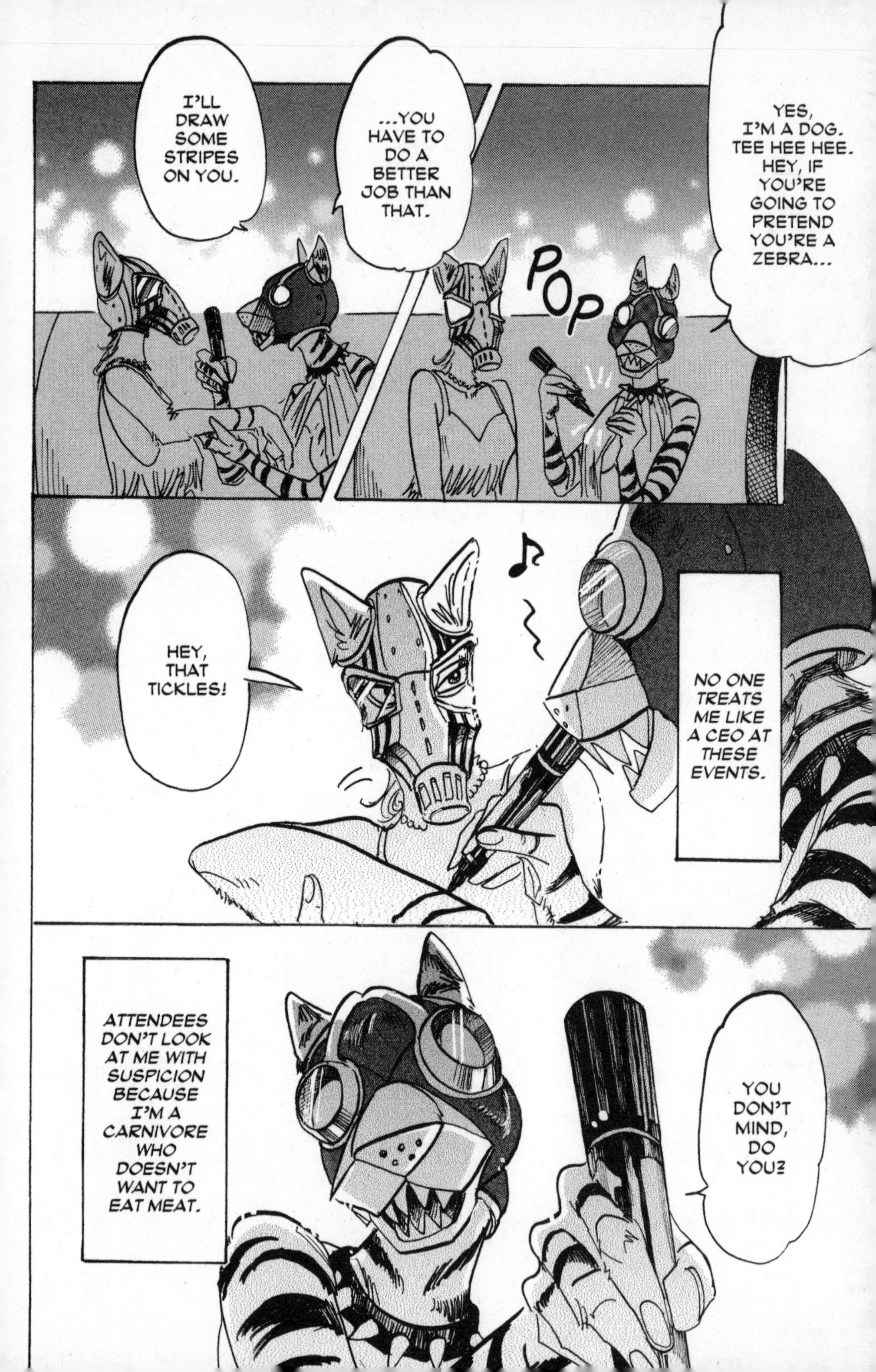
YES, I'M A DOG. TEE HEE HEE. HEY, IF YOU'RE GOING TO PRETEND YOU'RE A ZEBRA...
...YOU HAVE TO DO A BETTER JOB THAN THAT.
POP
I'LL DRAW SOME STRIPES ON YOU.
NO ONE TREATS ME LIKE A CEO AT THESE EVENTS.
HEY, THAT TICKLES!
YOU DON'T MIND, DO YOU?
ATTENDEES DON'T LOOK AT ME WITH SUSPICION BECAUSE I'M A CARNIVORE WHO DOESN'T WANT TO EAT MEAT.

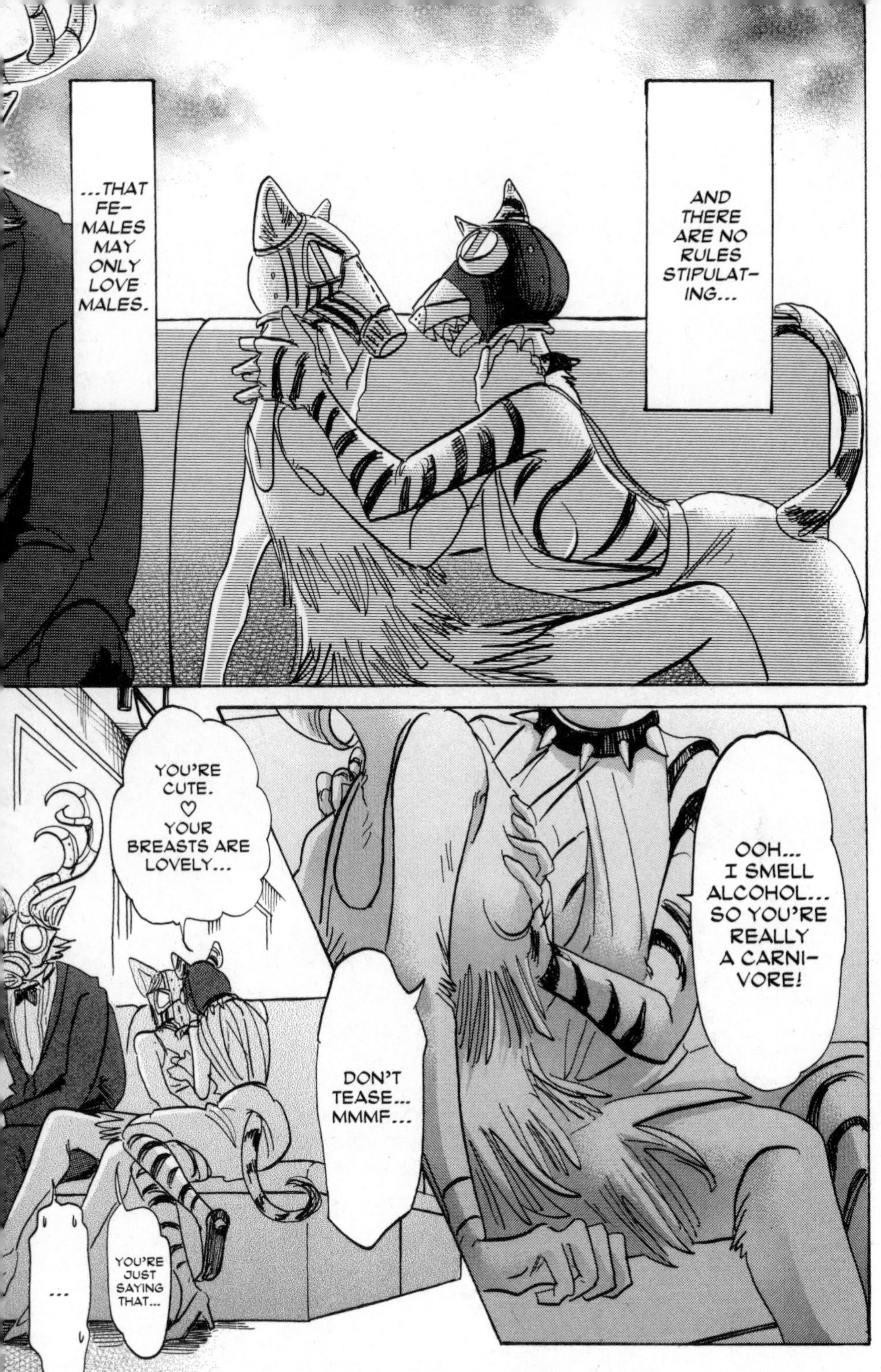
AND THERE ARE NO RULES STIPULATING...
...THAT FE-MALES MAY ONLY LOVE MALES.
OOH... I SMELL ALCOHOL... SO YOU'RE REALLY A CARNIVORE!
YOU'RE CUTE. ♡ YOUR BREASTS ARE LOVELY...
DON'T TEASE... MMMF...
YOU'RE JUST SAYING THAT...
...

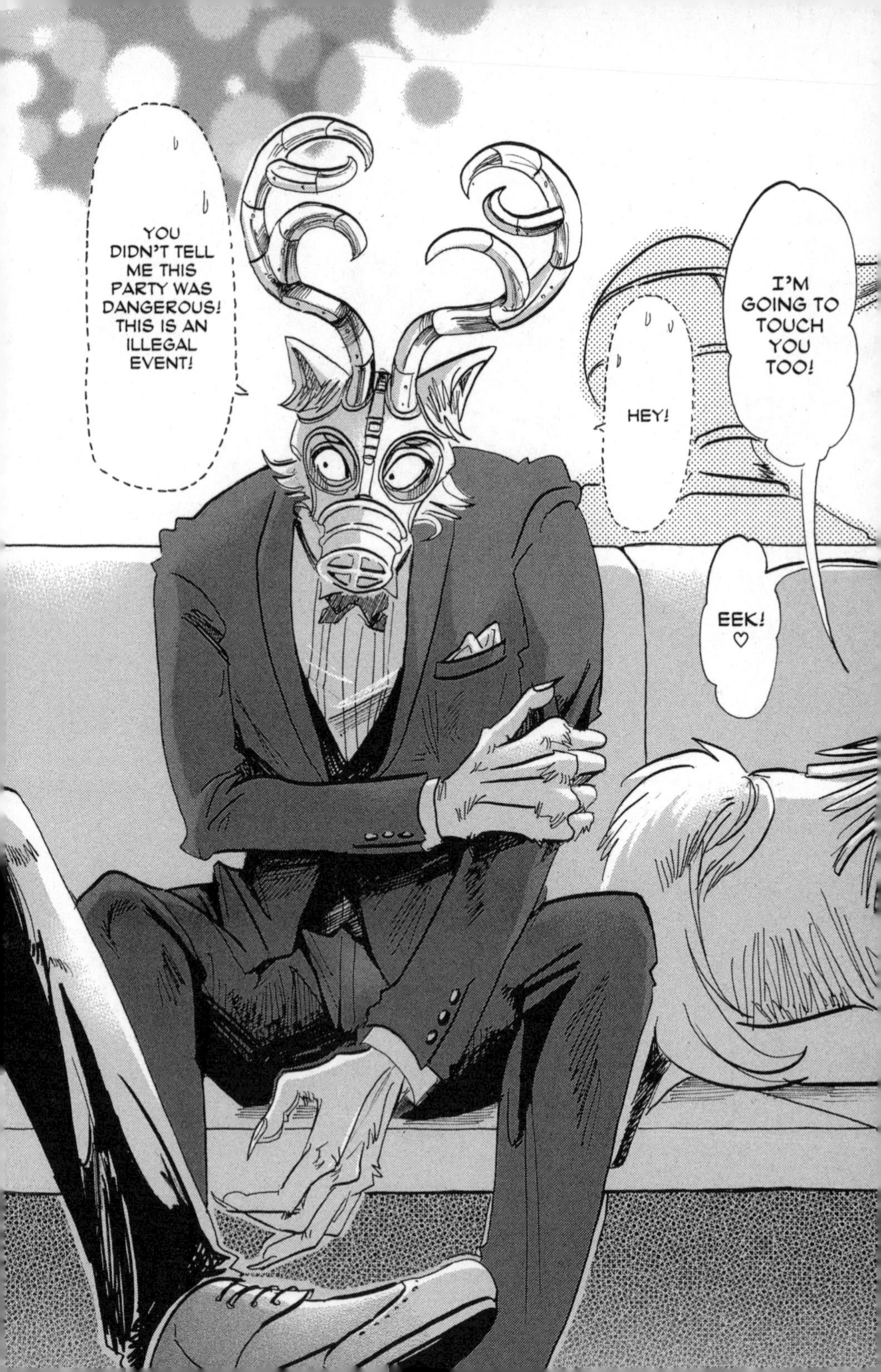
I'M GOING TO TOUCH YOU TOO!
EEK! ♡
HEY!
YOU DIDN'T TELL ME THIS PARTY WAS DANGEROUS! THIS IS AN ILLEGAL EVENT!

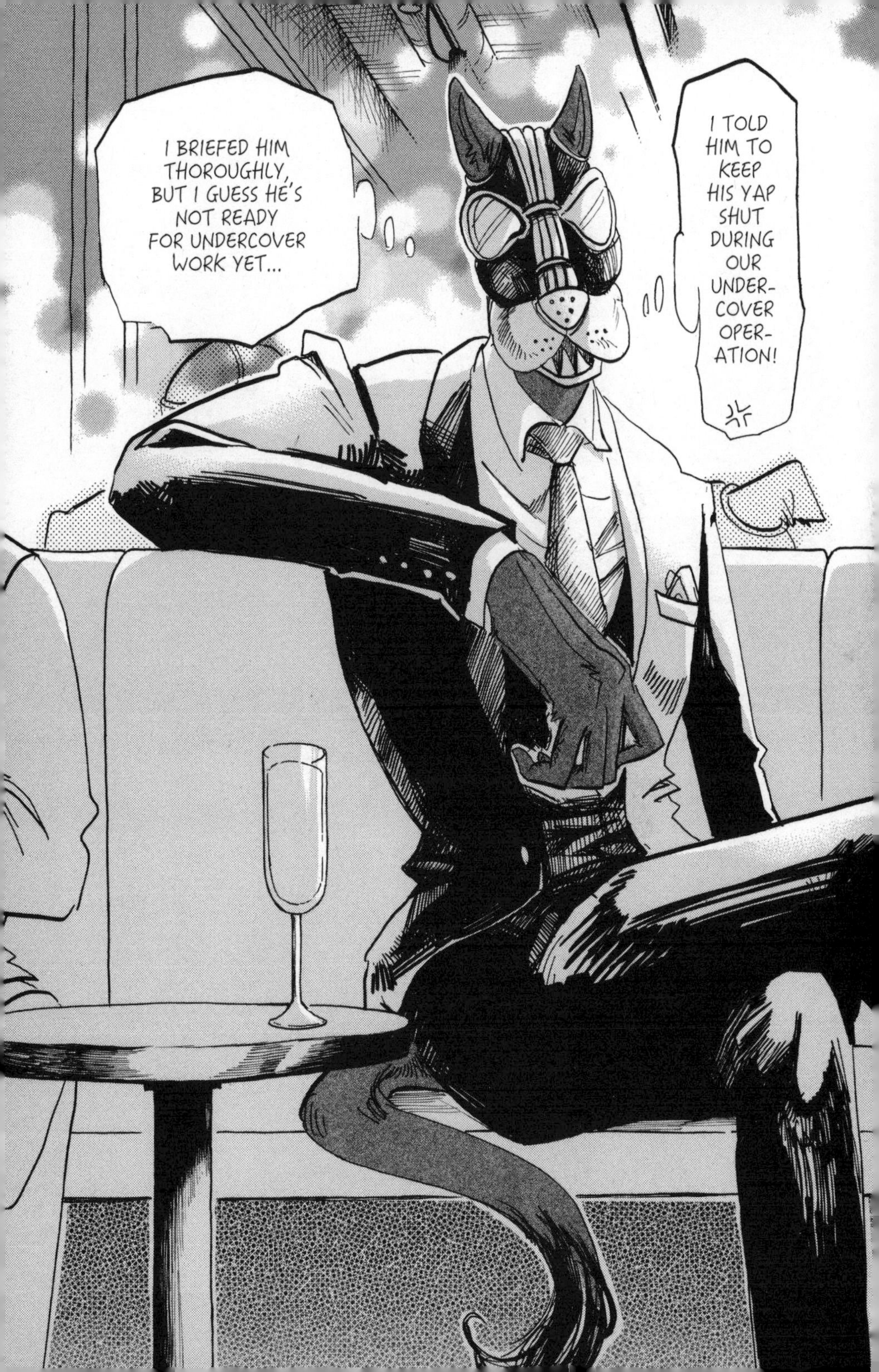
I TOLD HIM TO KEEP HIS YAP SHUT DURING OUR UNDER-COVER OPER-ATION!
I BRIEFED HIM THOROUGHLY, BUT I GUESS HE'S NOT READY FOR UNDERCOVER WORK YET...

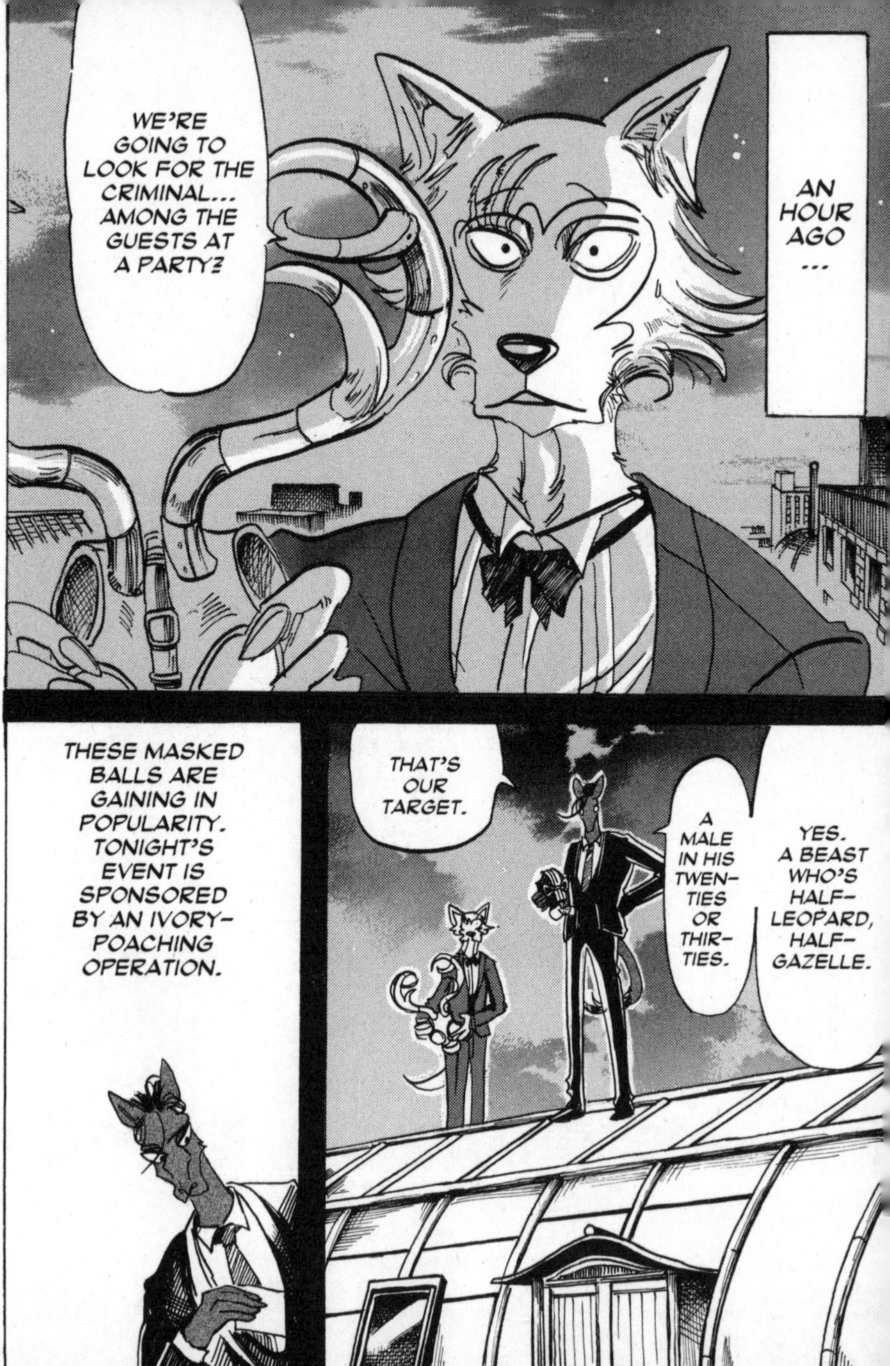
AN HOUR AGO ...
WE'RE GOING TO LOOK FOR THE CRIMINAL... AMONG THE GUESTS AT A PARTY?
YES. A BEAST WHO'S HALF-LEOPARD, HALF-GAZELLE.
A MALE IN HIS TWENTIES OR THIRTIES.
THAT'S OUR TARGET.
THESE MASKED BALLS ARE GAINING IN POPULARITY. TONIGHT'S EVENT IS SPONSORED BY AN IVORY-POACHING OPERATION.

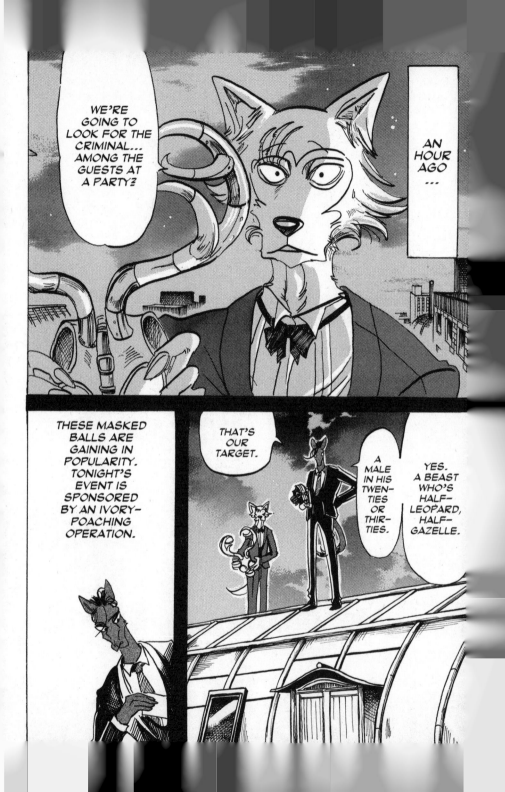

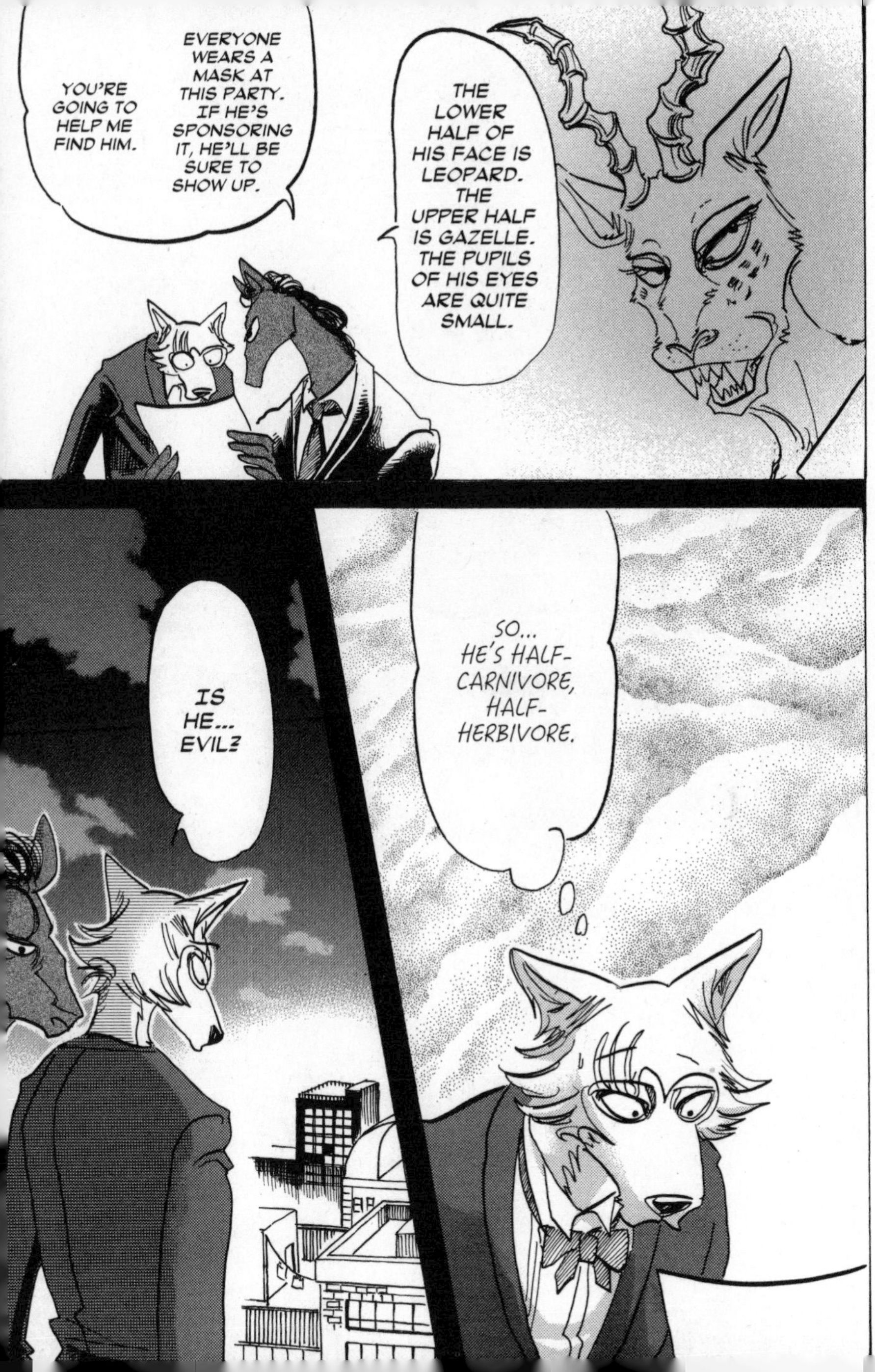
THE LOWER HALF OF HIS FACE IS LEOPARD. THE UPPER HALF IS GAZELLE. THE PUPILS OF HIS EYES ARE QUITE SMALL.
EVERYONE WEARS A MASK AT THIS PARTY. IF HE'S SPONSORING IT, HE'LL BE SURE TO SHOW UP.
YOU'RE GOING TO HELP ME FIND HIM.
SO... HE'S HALF-CARNIVORE, HALF-HERBIVORE.
IS HE... EVIL?

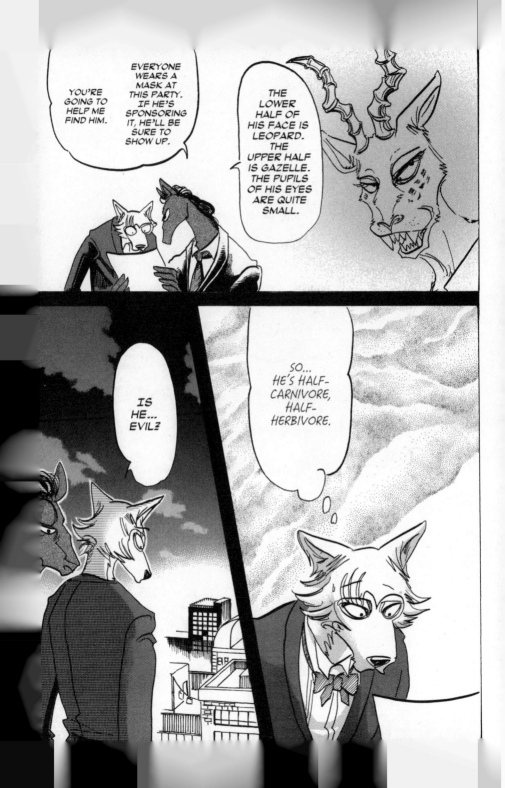

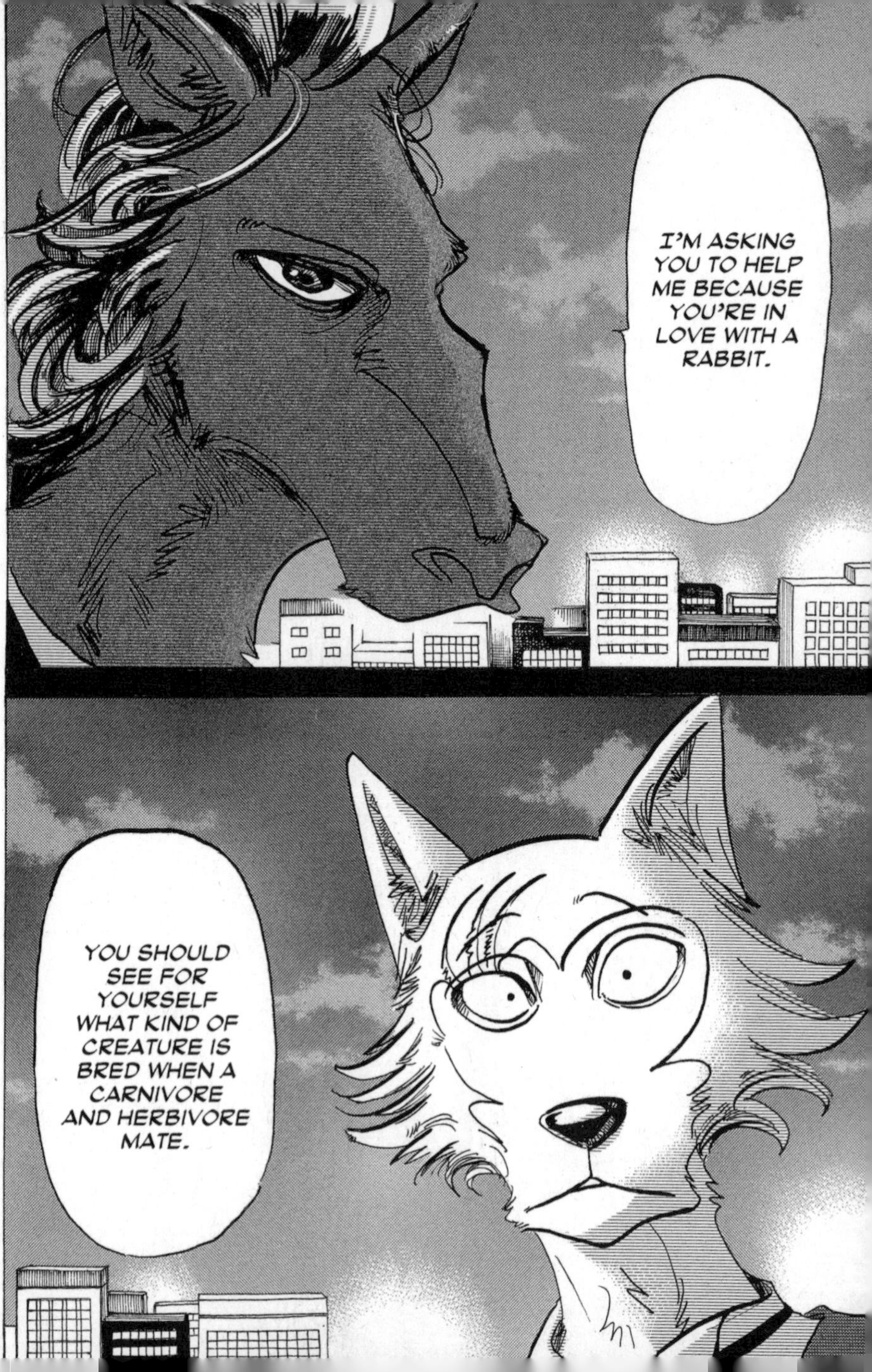
I'M ASKING YOU TO HELP ME BECAUSE YOU'RE IN LOVE WITH A RABBIT.
YOU SHOULD SEE FOR YOURSELF WHAT KIND OF CREATURE IS BRED WHEN A CARNIVORE AND HERBIVORE MATE.

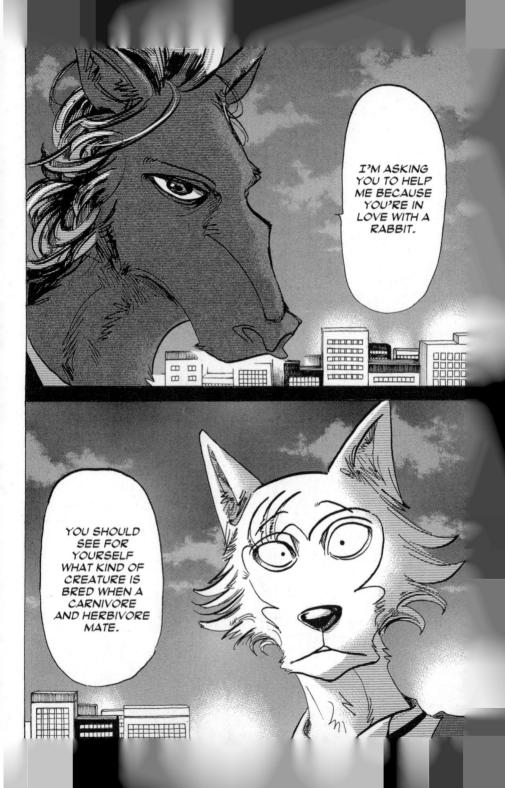

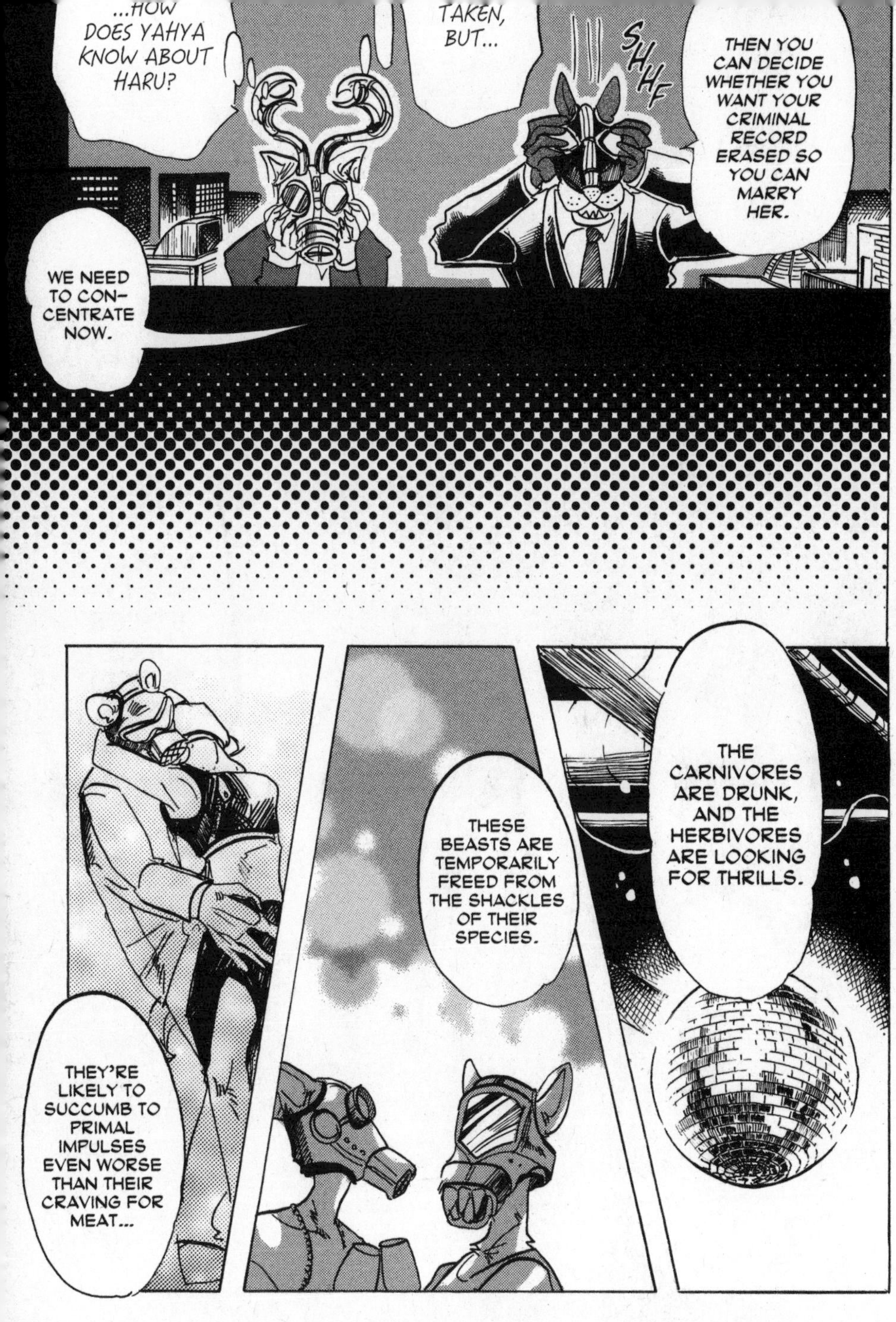
THEN YOU CAN DECIDE WHETHER YOU WANT YOUR CRIMINAL RECORD ERASED SO YOU CAN MARRY HER.
SHHF
TAKEN, BUT...
...HOW DOES YAHYA KNOW ABOUT HARU?
WE NEED TO CON-CENTRATE NOW.
THE CARNIVORES ARE DRUNK, AND THE HERBIVORES ARE LOOKING FOR THRILLS.
THESE BEASTS ARE TEMPORARILY FREED FROM THE SHACKLES OF THEIR SPECIES.
THEY'RE LIKELY TO SUCCUMB TO PRIMAL IMPULSES EVEN WORSE THAN THEIR CRAVING FOR MEAT...

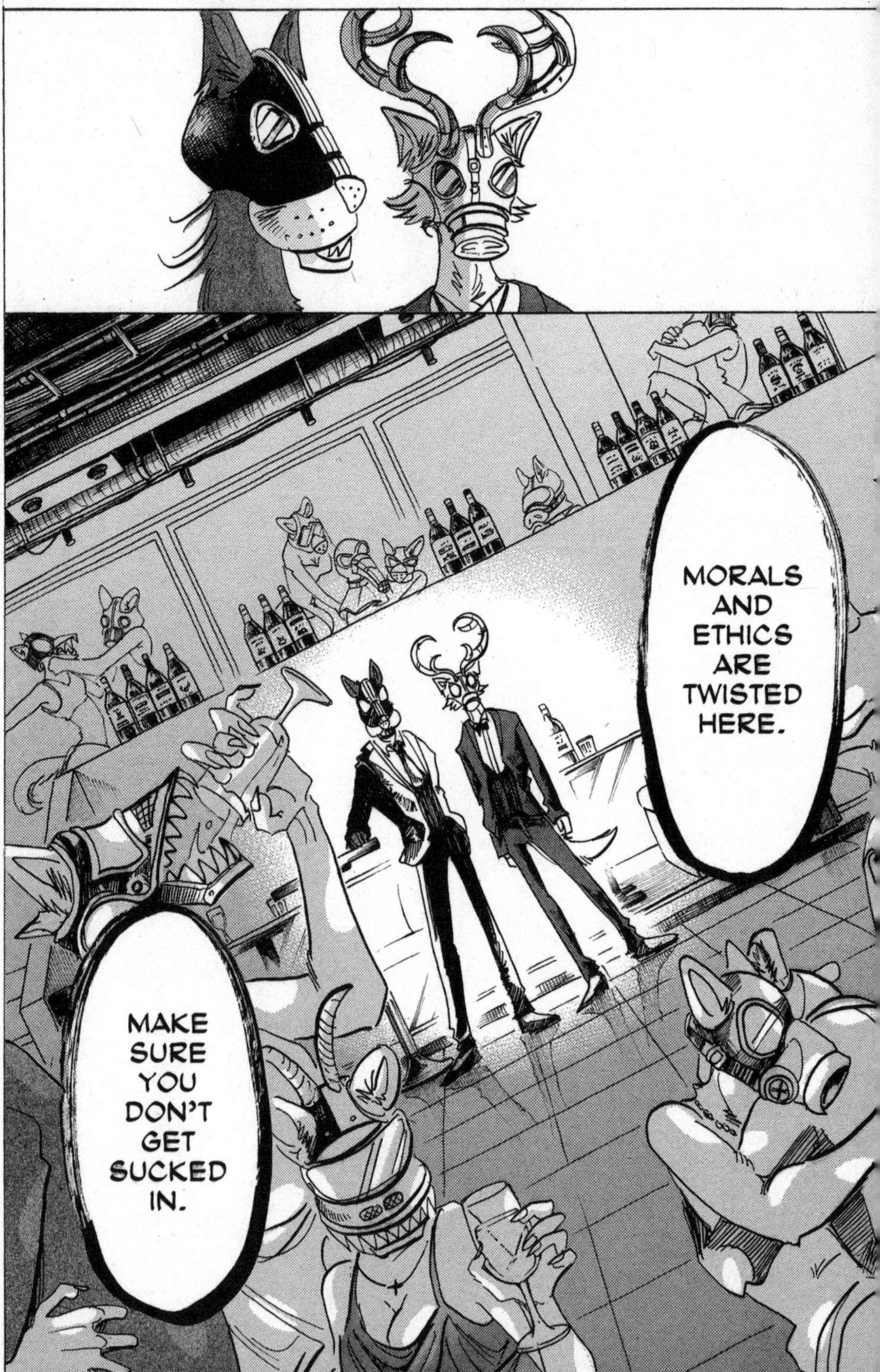
MORALS AND ETHICS ARE TWISTED HERE.
MAKE SURE YOU DON'T GET SUCKED IN.

BEASTARS
Vol. 15

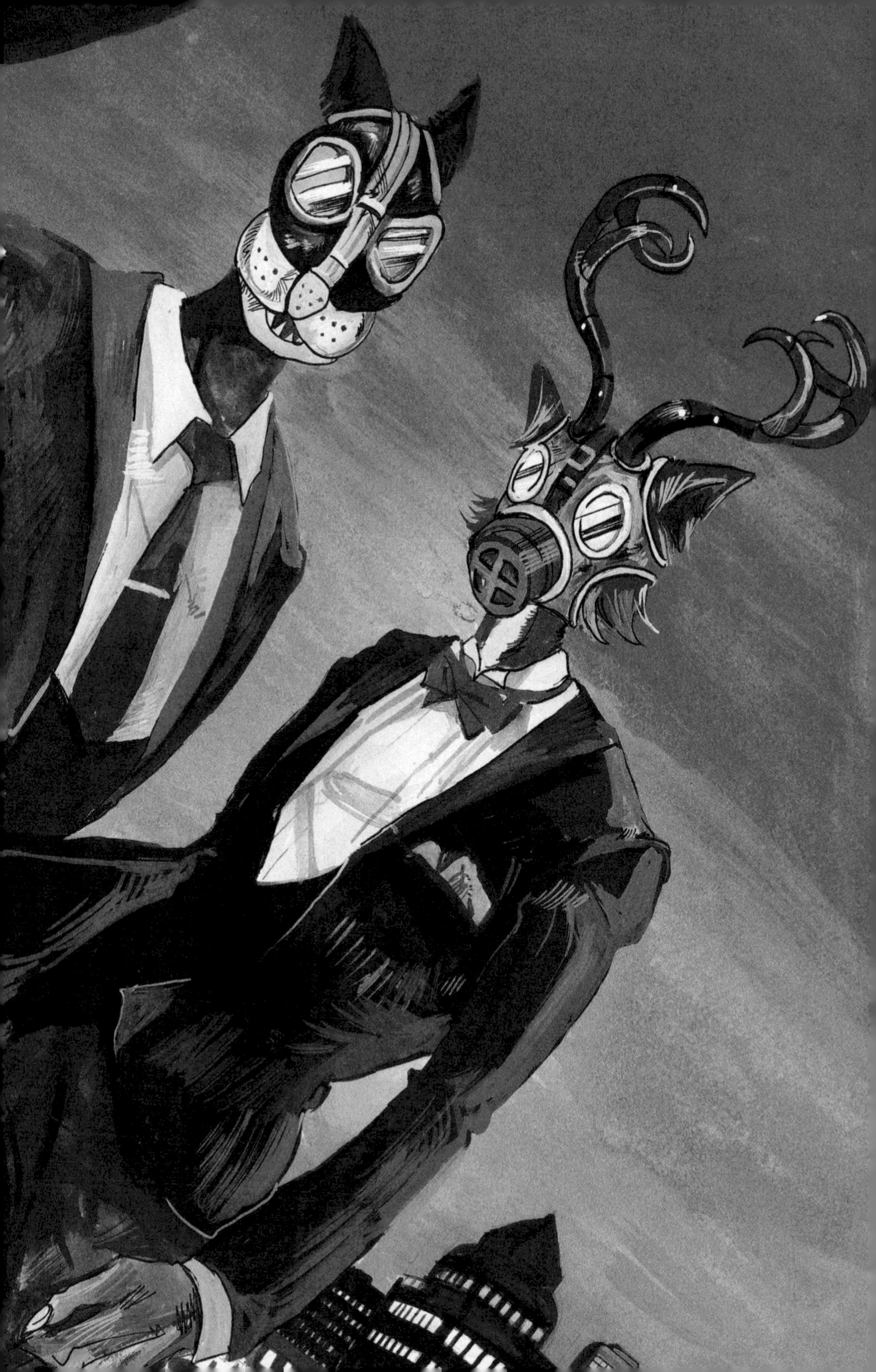

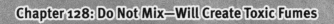

Chapter 128: Do Not Mix—Will Create Toxic Fumes

BEASTARS
Vol. 15

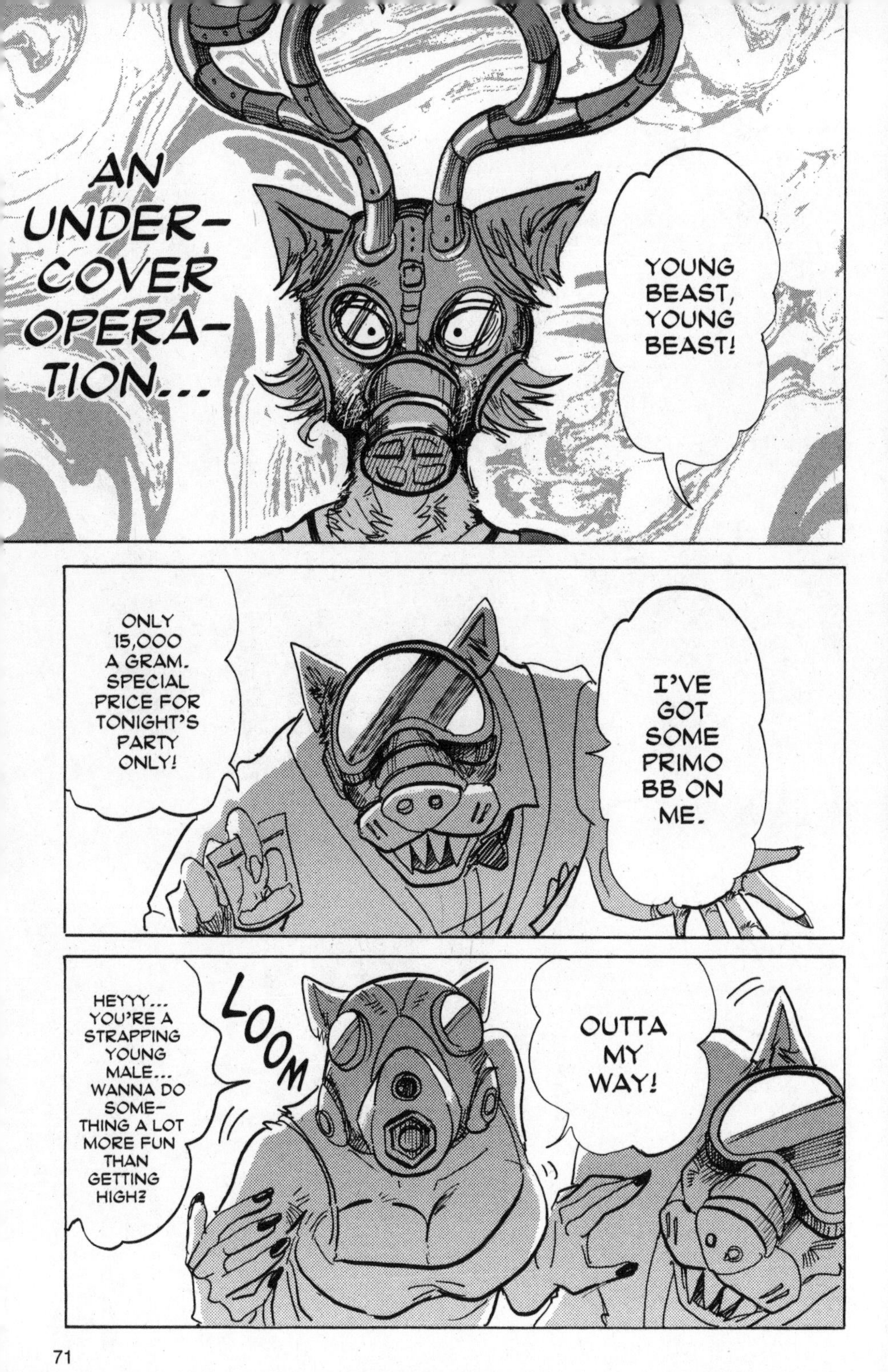
YOUNG BEAST, YOUNG BEAST!
AN UNDER-COVER OPERA-TION...
I'VE GOT SOME PRIMO BB ON ME.
ONLY 15,000 A GRAM. SPECIAL PRICE FOR TONIGHT'S PARTY ONLY!
OUTTA MY WAY!
LOOM
HEYYY... YOU'RE A STRAPPING YOUNG MALE... WANNA DO SOME-THING A LOT MORE FUN THAN GETTING HIGH?

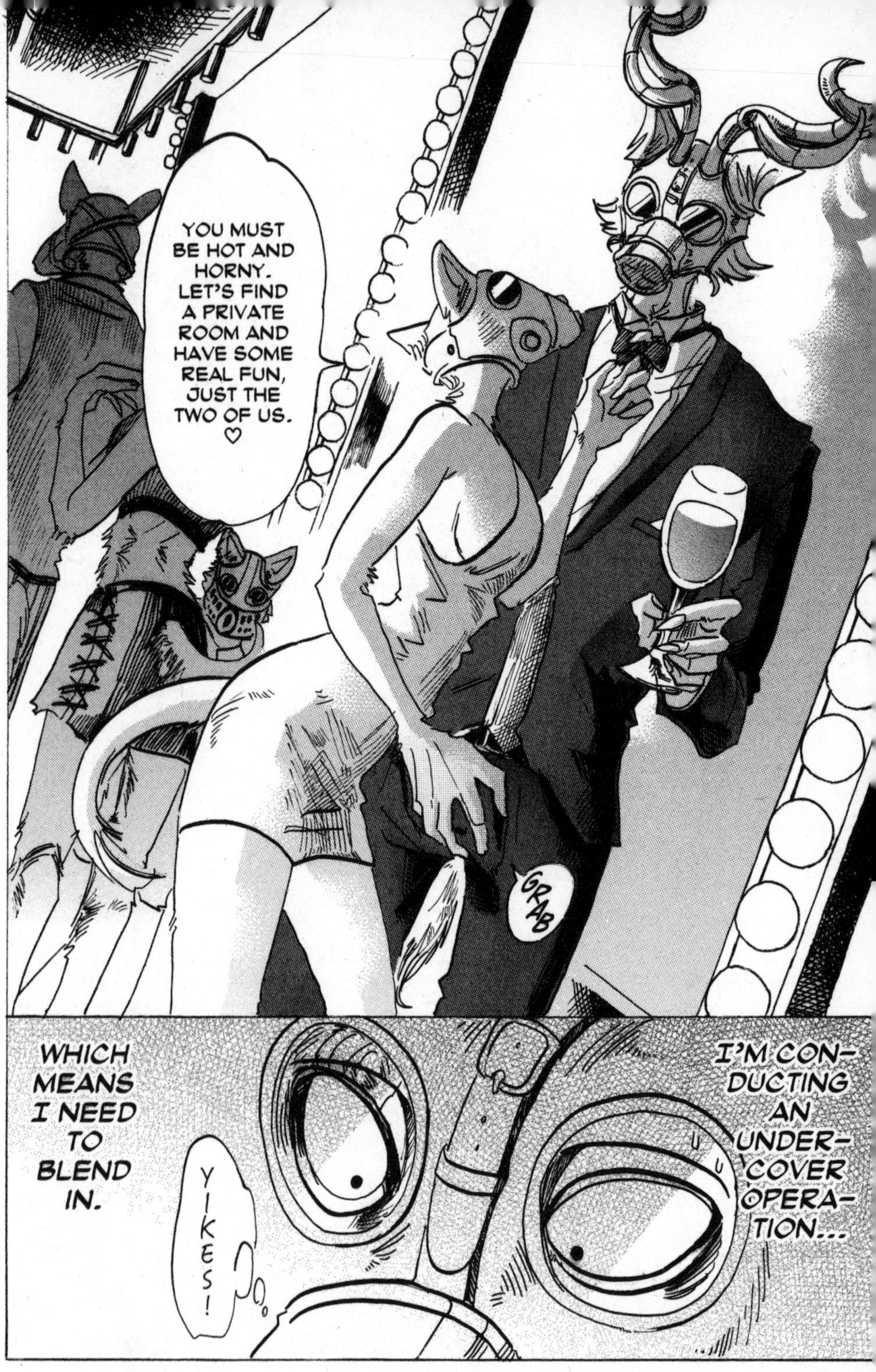
YOU MUST BE HOT AND HORNY. LET'S FIND A PRIVATE ROOM AND HAVE SOME REAL FUN, JUST THE TWO OF US. ♡
GRAB
I'M CONDUCTING AN UNDERCOVER OPERATION...
WHICH MEANS I NEED TO BLEND IN.
YIKES!

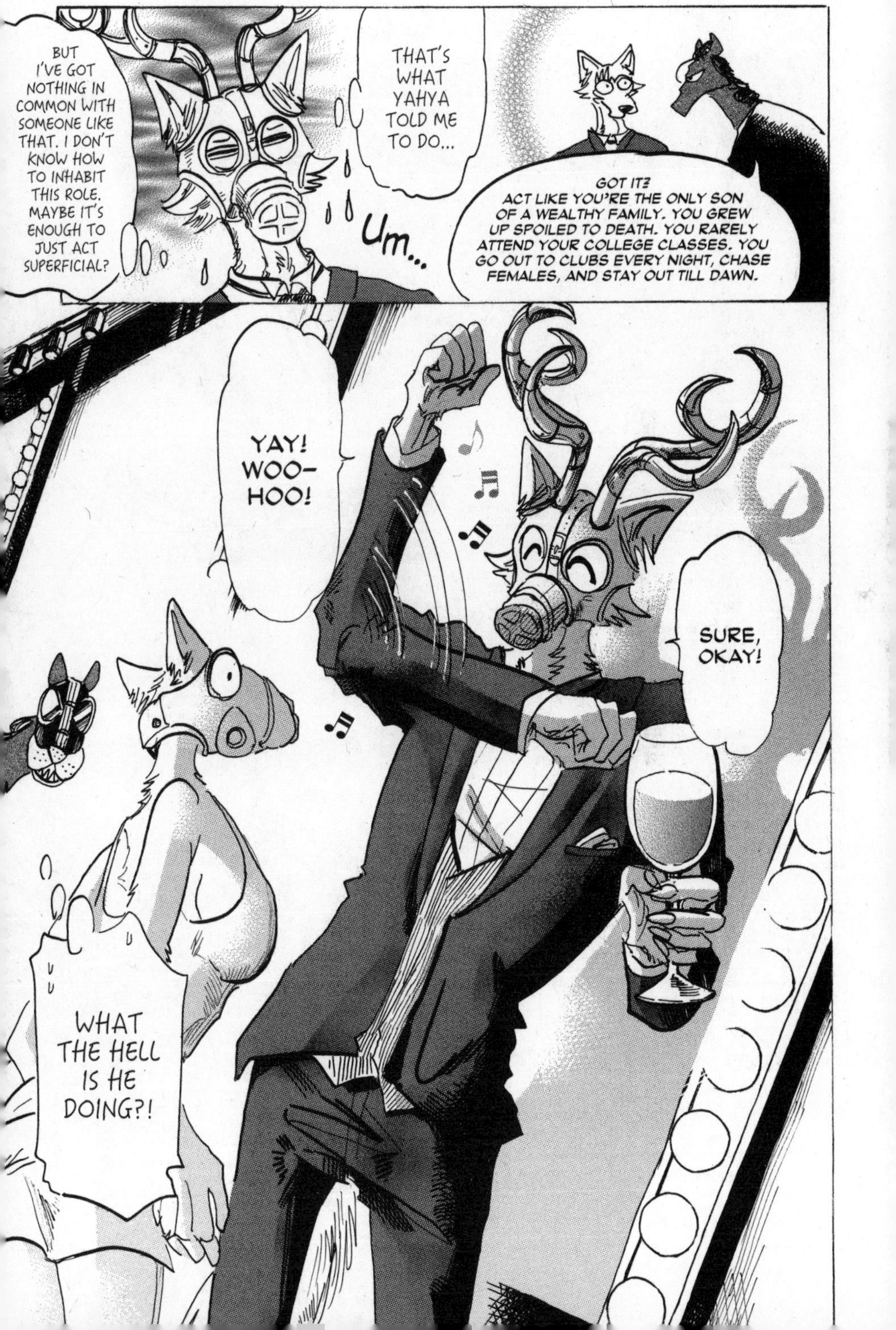
GOT IT? ACT LIKE YOU'RE THE ONLY SON OF A WEALTHY FAMILY. YOU GREW UP SPOILED TO DEATH. YOU RARELY ATTEND YOUR COLLEGE CLASSES. YOU GO OUT TO CLUBS EVERY NIGHT, CHASE FEMALES, AND STAY OUT TILL DAWN.
Um...
THAT'S WHAT YAHYA TOLD ME TO DO...
BUT I'VE GOT NOTHING IN COMMON WITH SOMEONE LIKE THAT. I DON'T KNOW HOW TO INHABIT THIS ROLE. MAYBE IT'S ENOUGH TO JUST ACT SUPERFICIAL?
SURE, OKAY!
YAY! WOO-HOO!
WHAT THE HELL IS HE DOING?!

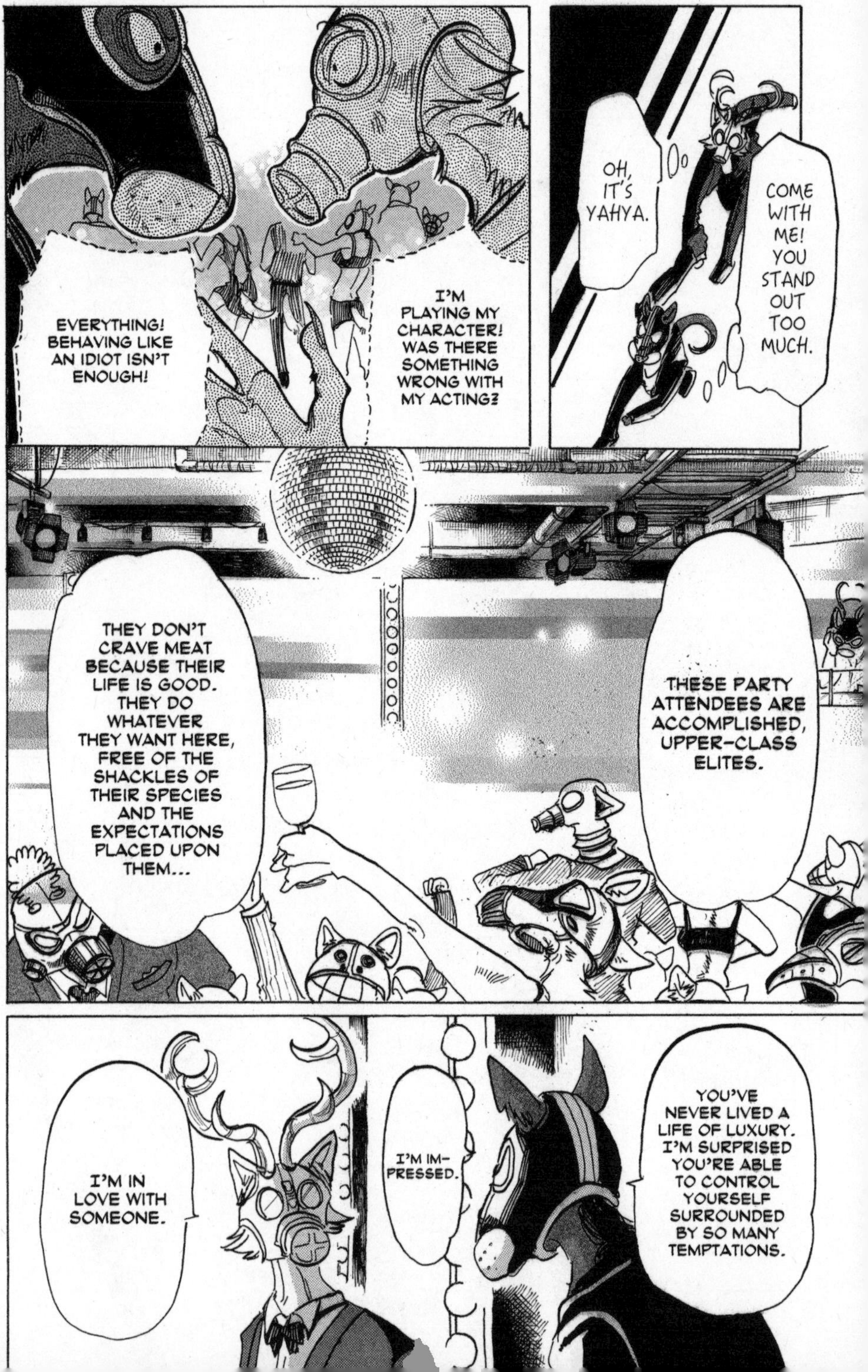
COME WITH ME! YOU STAND OUT TOO MUCH.
OH, IT'S YAHYA.
I'M PLAYING MY CHARACTER! WAS THERE SOMETHING WRONG WITH MY ACTING?
EVERYTHING! BEHAVING LIKE AN IDIOT ISN'T ENOUGH!
THESE PARTY ATTENDEES ARE ACCOMPLISHED, UPPER-CLASS ELITES.
THEY DON'T CRAVE MEAT BECAUSE THEIR LIFE IS GOOD. THEY DO WHATEVER THEY WANT HERE, FREE OF THE SHACKLES OF THEIR SPECIES AND THE EXPECTATIONS PLACED UPON THEM...
YOU'VE NEVER LIVED A LIFE OF LUXURY. I'M SURPRISED YOU'RE ABLE TO CONTROL YOURSELF SURROUNDED BY SO MANY TEMPTATIONS.
I'M IM-PRESSED.
I'M IN LOVE WITH SOMEONE.

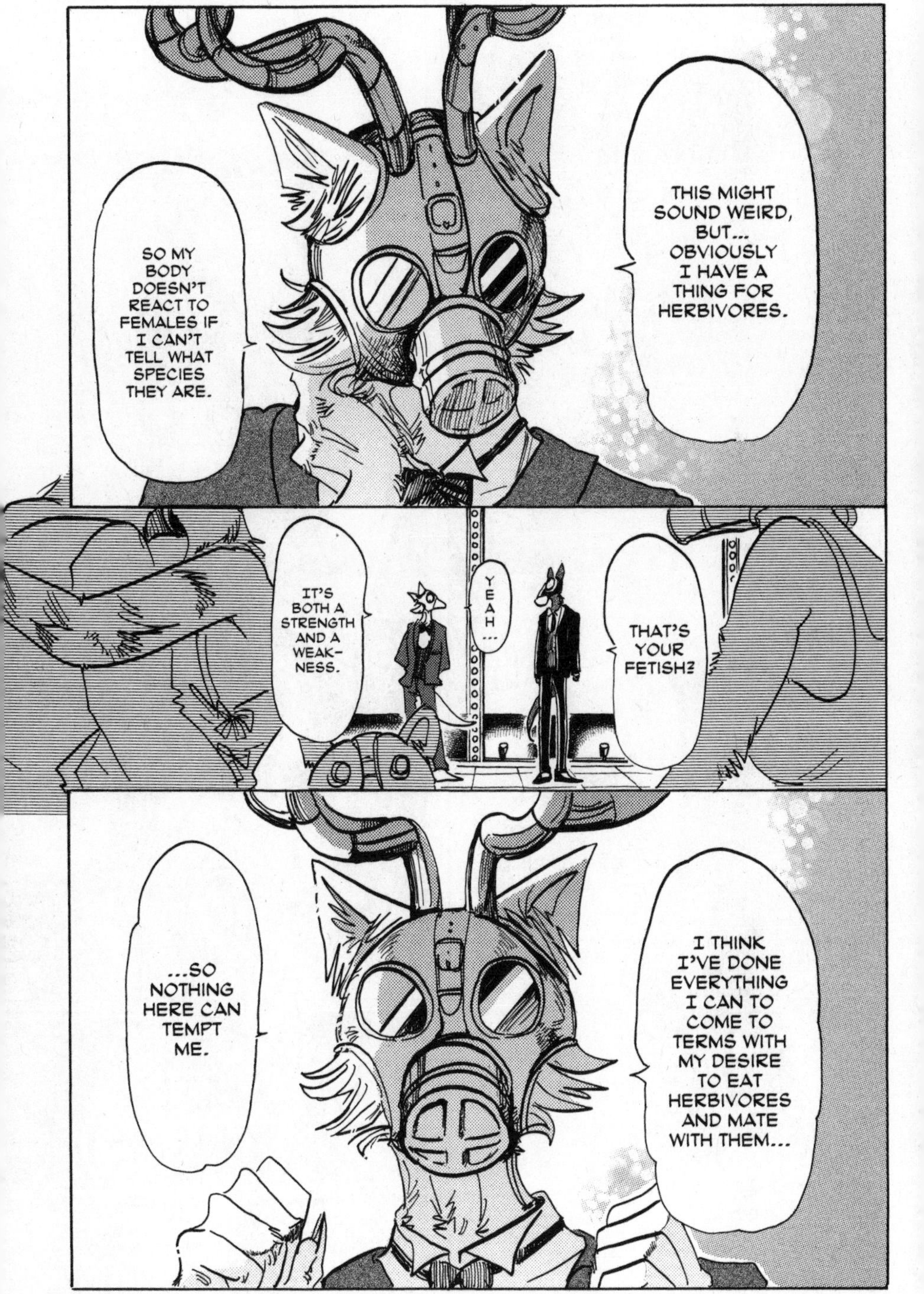
THIS MIGHT SOUND WEIRD, BUT... OBVIOUSLY I HAVE A THING FOR HERBIVORES.
SO MY BODY DOESN'T REACT TO FEMALES IF I CAN'T TELL WHAT SPECIES THEY ARE.
THAT'S YOUR FETISH?
YEAH...
IT'S BOTH A STRENGTH AND A WEAK-NESS.
I THINK I'VE DONE EVERYTHING I CAN TO COME TO TERMS WITH MY DESIRE TO EAT HERBIVORES AND MATE WITH THEM...
...SO NOTHING HERE CAN TEMPT ME.

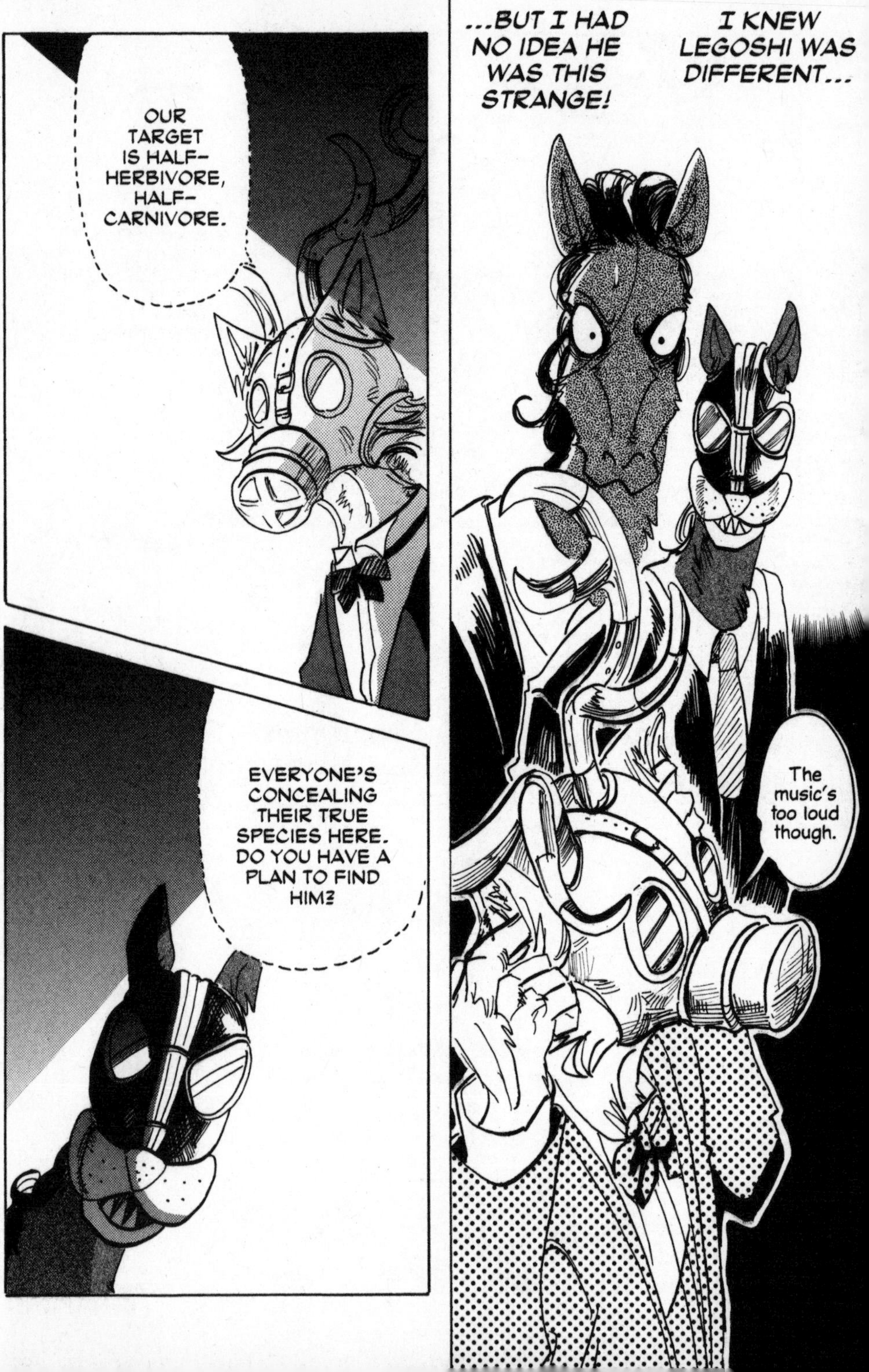
I KNEW LEGOSHI WAS DIFFERENT...
...BUT I HAD NO IDEA HE WAS THIS STRANGE!
The music's too loud though.
OUR TARGET IS HALF-HERBIVORE, HALF-CARNIVORE.
EVERYONE'S CONCEALING THEIR TRUE SPECIES HERE. DO YOU HAVE A PLAN TO FIND HIM?

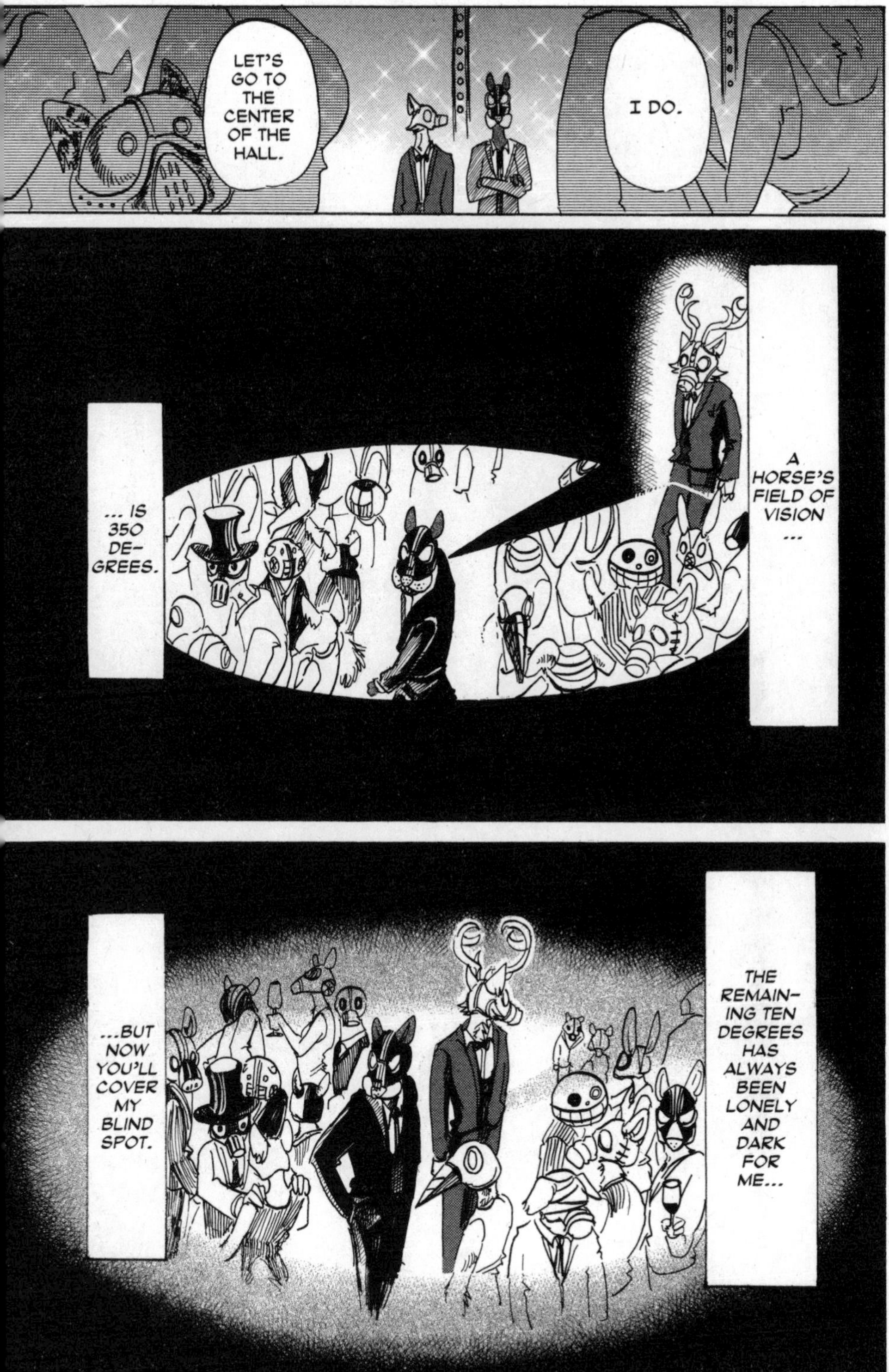
I DO.
LET'S GO TO THE CENTER OF THE HALL.
A HORSE'S FIELD OF VISION ...
... IS 350 DE-GREES.
THE REMAIN-ING TEN DEGREES HAS ALWAYS BEEN LONELY AND DARK FOR ME...
...BUT NOW YOU'LL COVER MY BLIND SPOT.

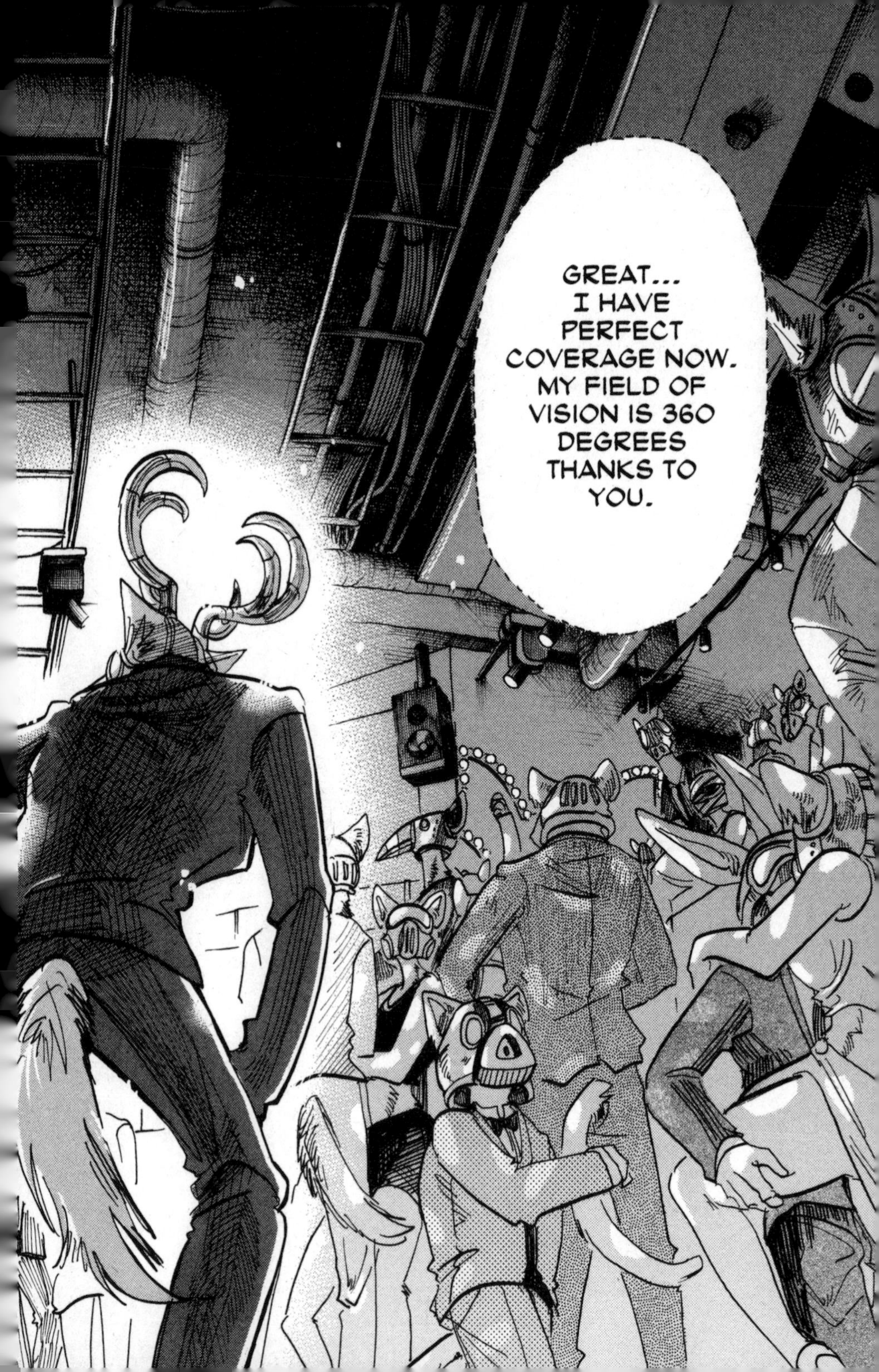
GREAT... I HAVE PERFECT COVERAGE NOW. MY FIELD OF VISION IS 360 DEGREES THANKS TO YOU.

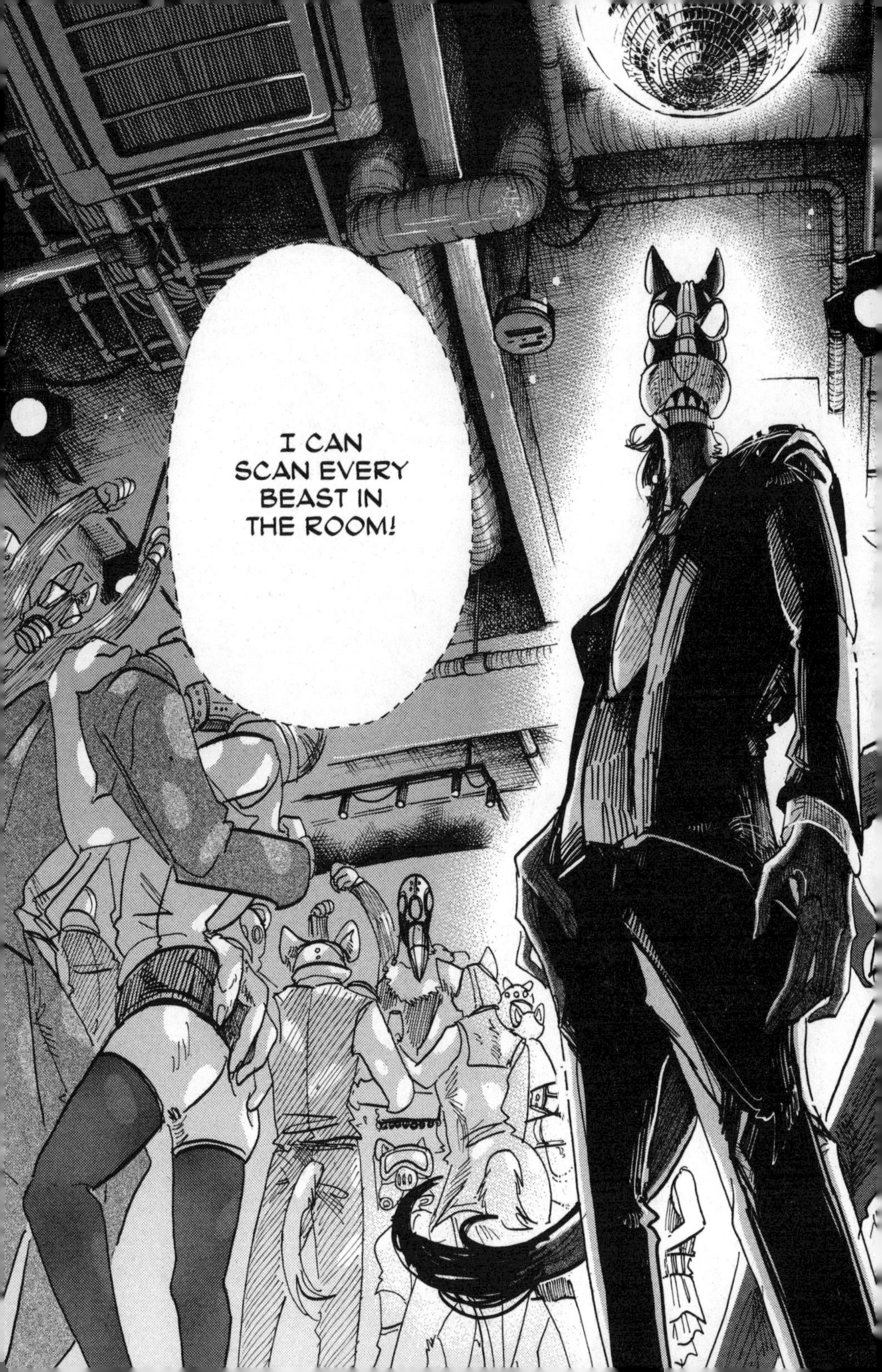
I CAN SCAN EVERY BEAST IN THE ROOM!

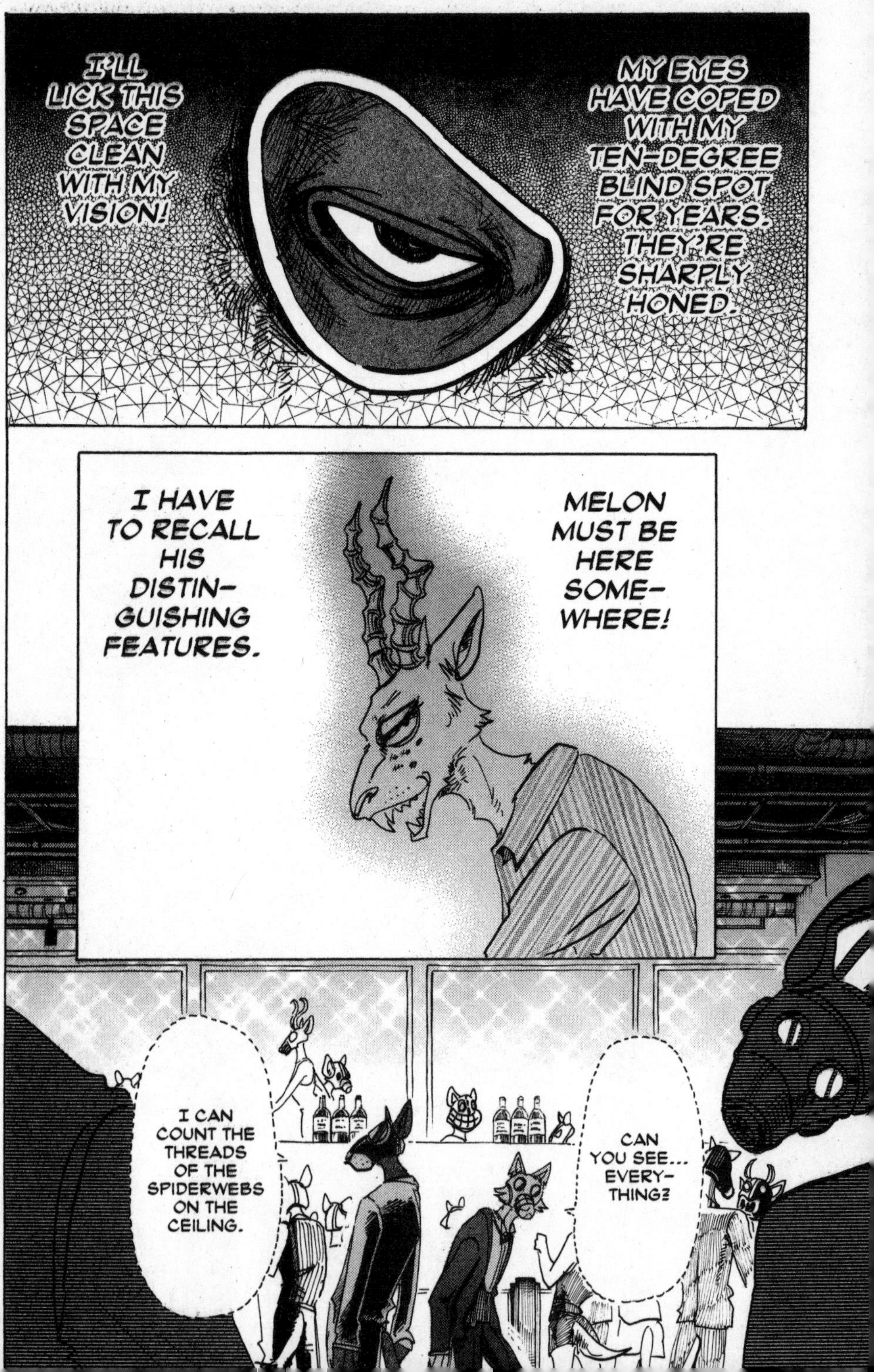
MY EYES HAVE COPED WITH MY TEN-DEGREE BLIND SPOT FOR YEARS. THEY'RE SHARPLY HONED.
I'LL LICK THIS SPACE CLEAN WITH MY VISION!
MELON MUST BE HERE SOME-WHERE!
I HAVE TO RECALL HIS DISTIN-GUISHING FEATURES.
CAN YOU SEE... EVERY-THING?
I CAN COUNT THE THREADS OF THE SPIDERWEBS ON THE CEILING.

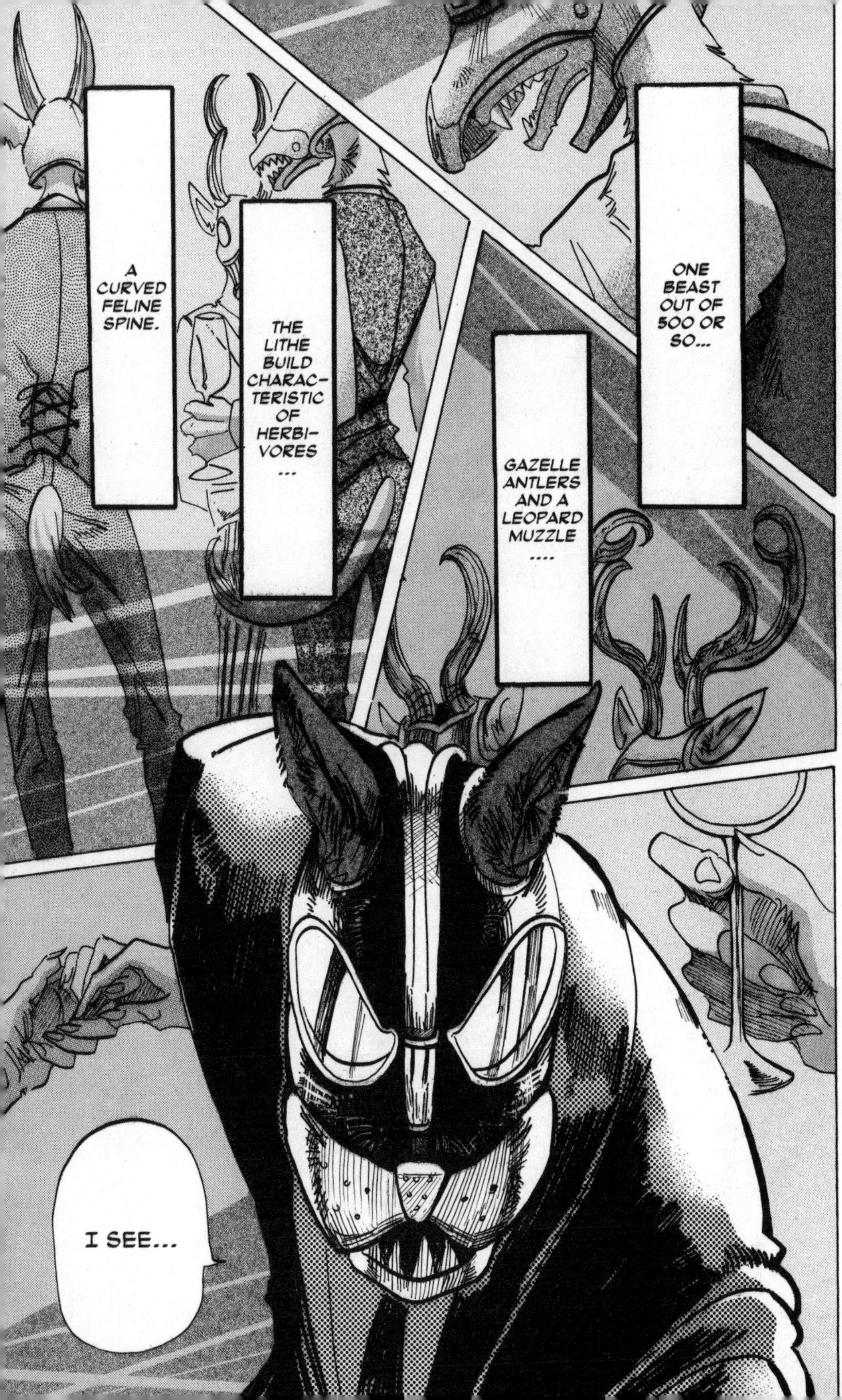
ONE BEAST OUT OF 500 OR SO...
GAZELLE ANTLERS AND A LEOPARD MUZZLE ....
THE LITHE BUILD CHARAC-TERISTIC OF HERBI-VORES ...
A CURVED FELINE SPINE.
I SEE...

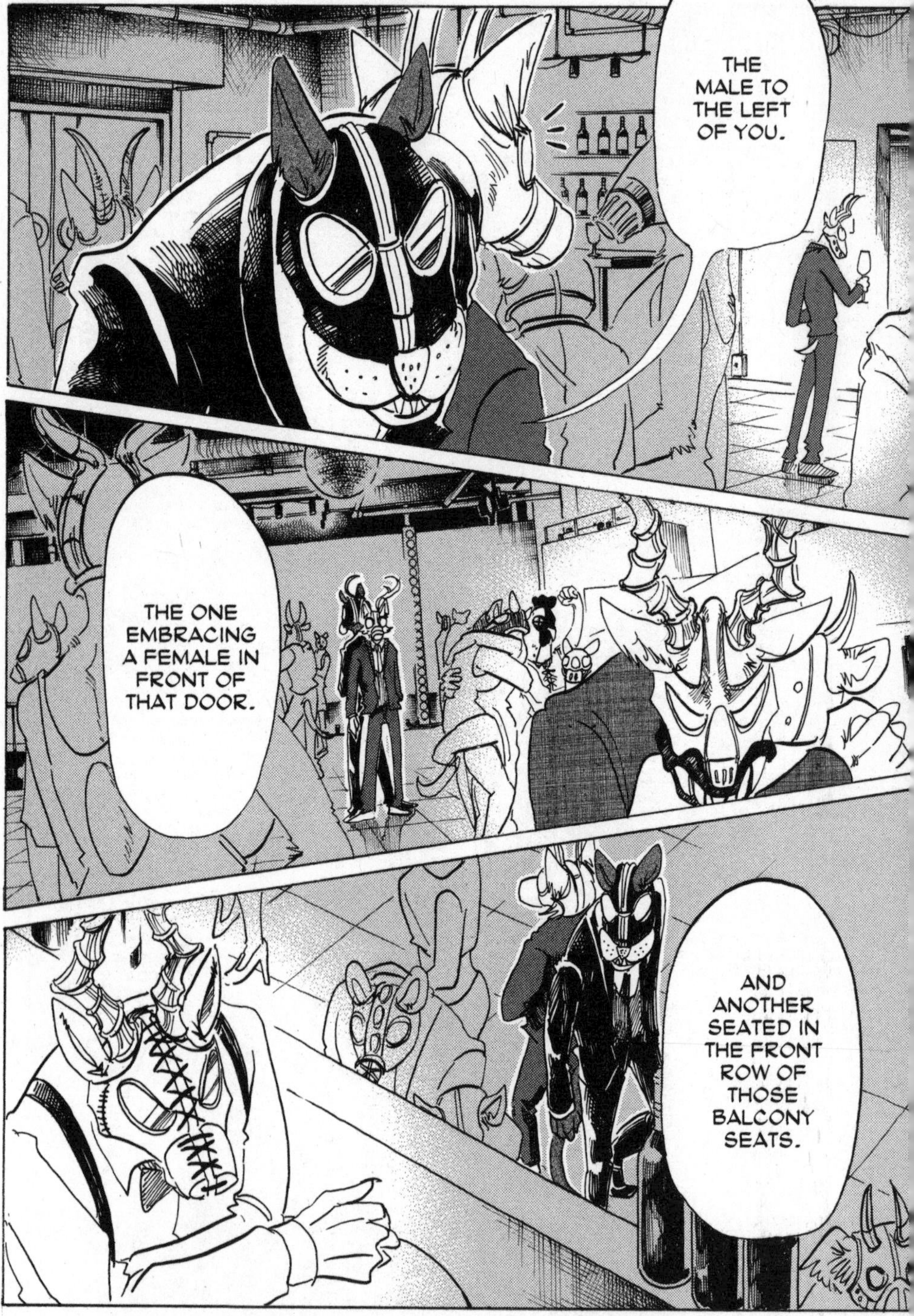
THE MALE TO THE LEFT OF YOU.
THE ONE EMBRACING A FEMALE IN FRONT OF THAT DOOR.
AND ANOTHER SEATED IN THE FRONT ROW OF THOSE BALCONY SEATS.

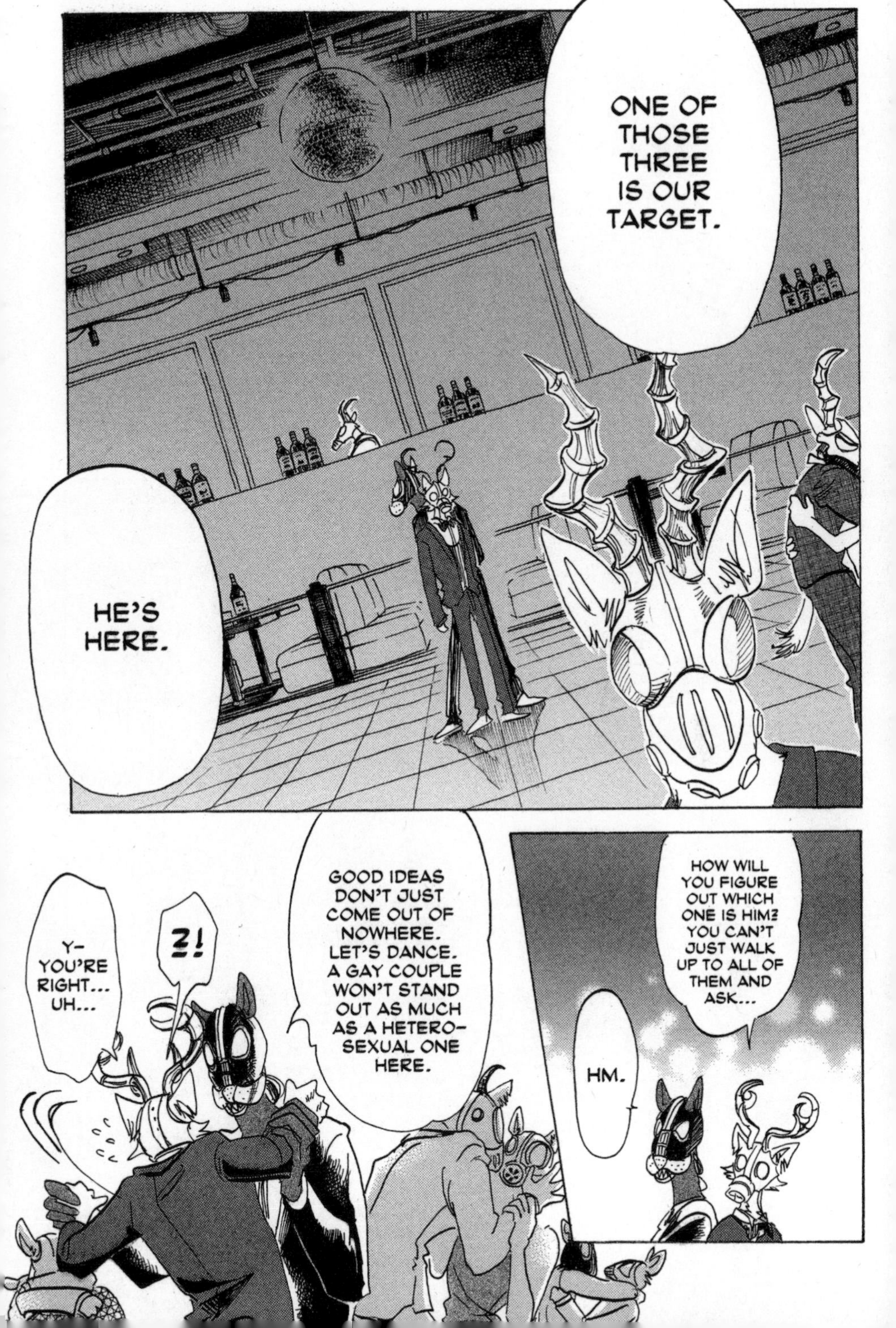
ONE OF THOSE THREE IS OUR TARGET.
HE'S HERE.
HOW WILL YOU FIGURE OUT WHICH ONE IS HIM? YOU CAN'T JUST WALK UP TO ALL OF THEM AND ASK...
HM.
GOOD IDEAS DON'T JUST COME OUT OF NOWHERE. LET'S DANCE. A GAY COUPLE WON'T STAND OUT AS MUCH AS A HETERO-SEXUAL ONE HERE.
?!
Y- YOU'RE RIGHT... UH...

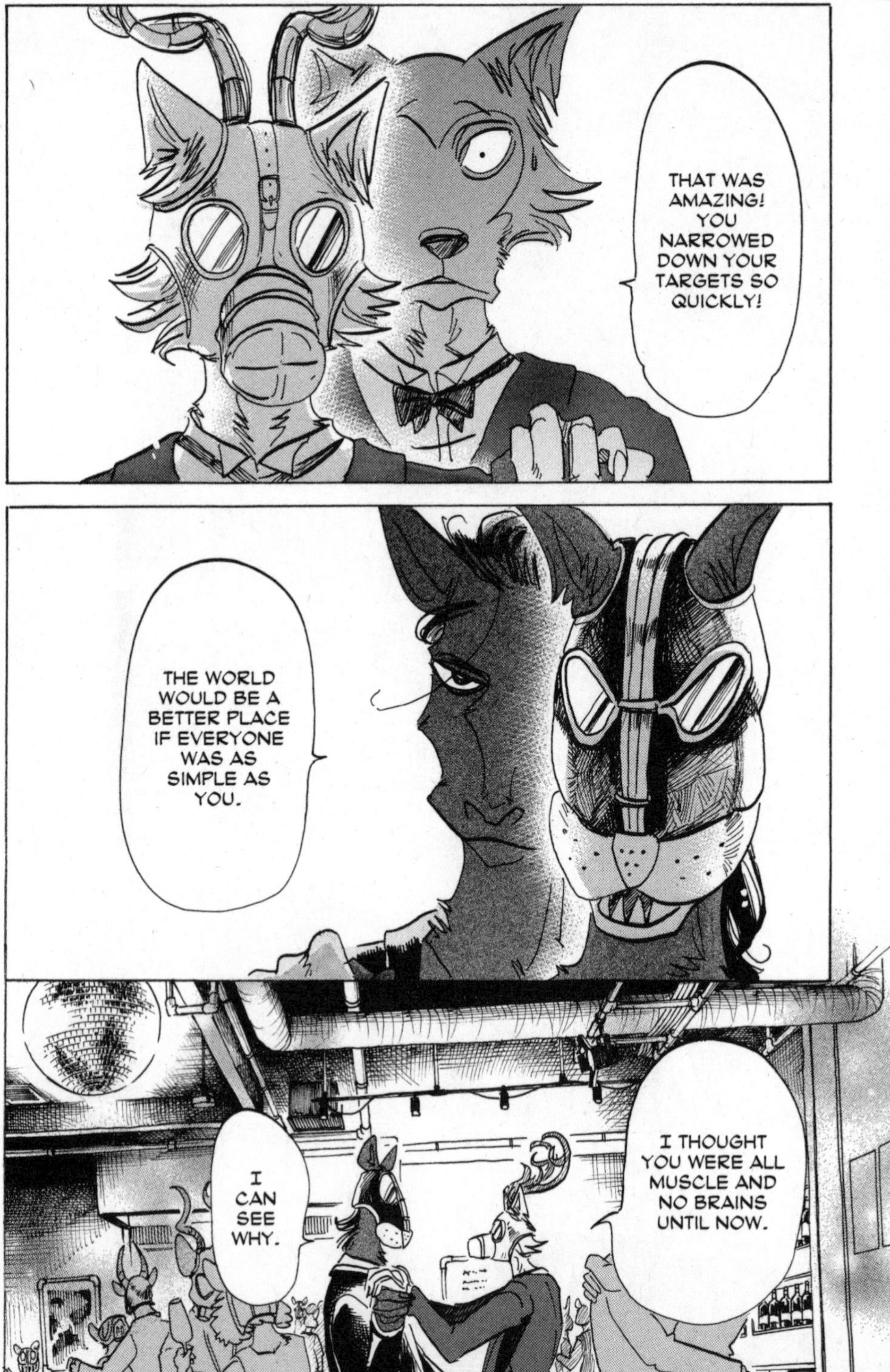
THAT WAS AMAZING! YOU NARROWED DOWN YOUR TARGETS SO QUICKLY!
THE WORLD WOULD BE A BETTER PLACE IF EVERYONE WAS AS SIMPLE AS YOU.
I THOUGHT YOU WERE ALL MUSCLE AND NO BRAINS UNTIL NOW.
I CAN SEE WHY.

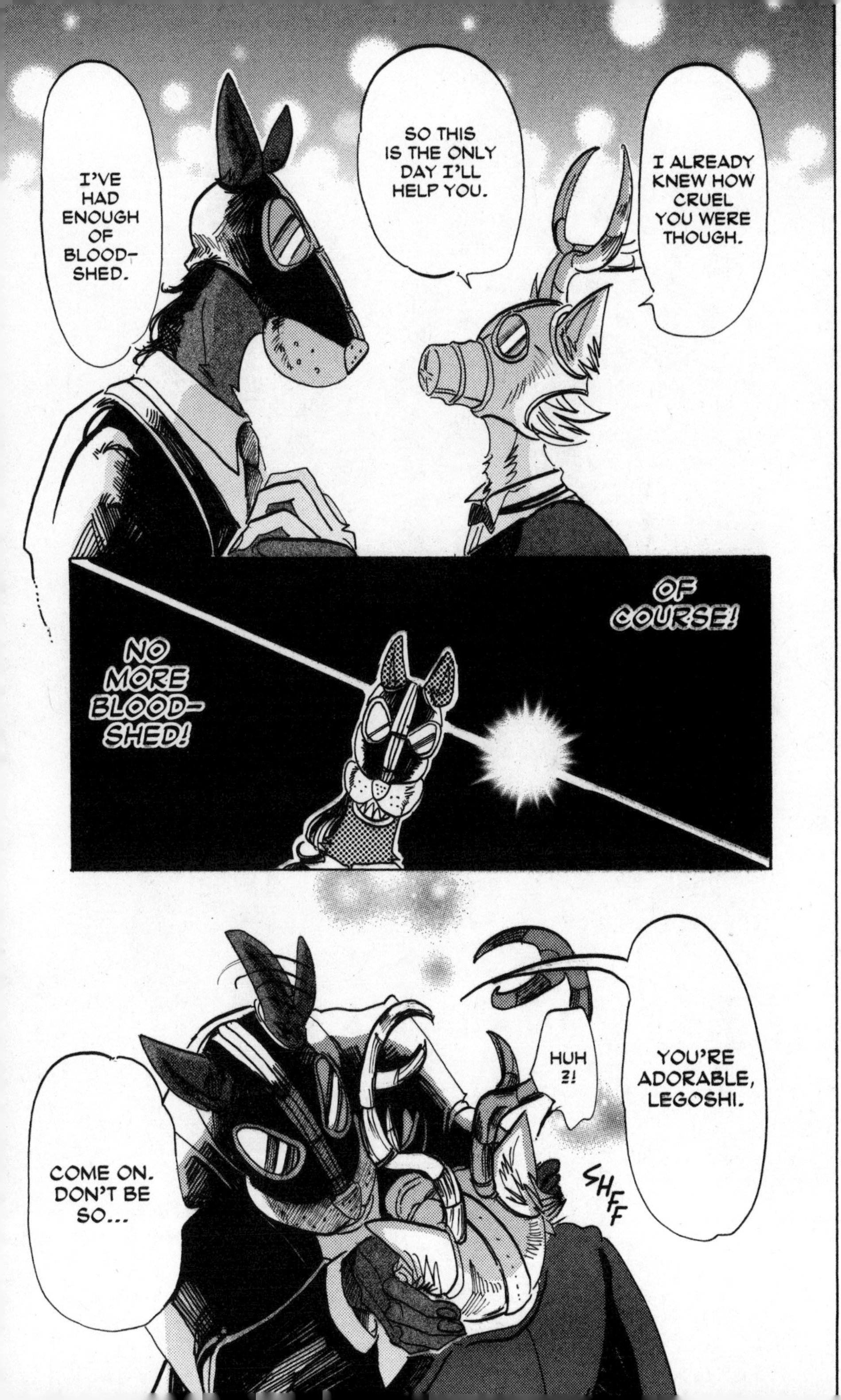
I ALREADY KNEW HOW CRUEL YOU WERE THOUGH.
SO THIS IS THE ONLY DAY I'LL HELP YOU.
I'VE HAD ENOUGH OF BLOOD-SHED.
OF COURSE!
NO MORE BLOOD-SHED!
YOU'RE ADORABLE, LEGOSHI.
HUH?!
SHFF
COME ON. DON'T BE SO...

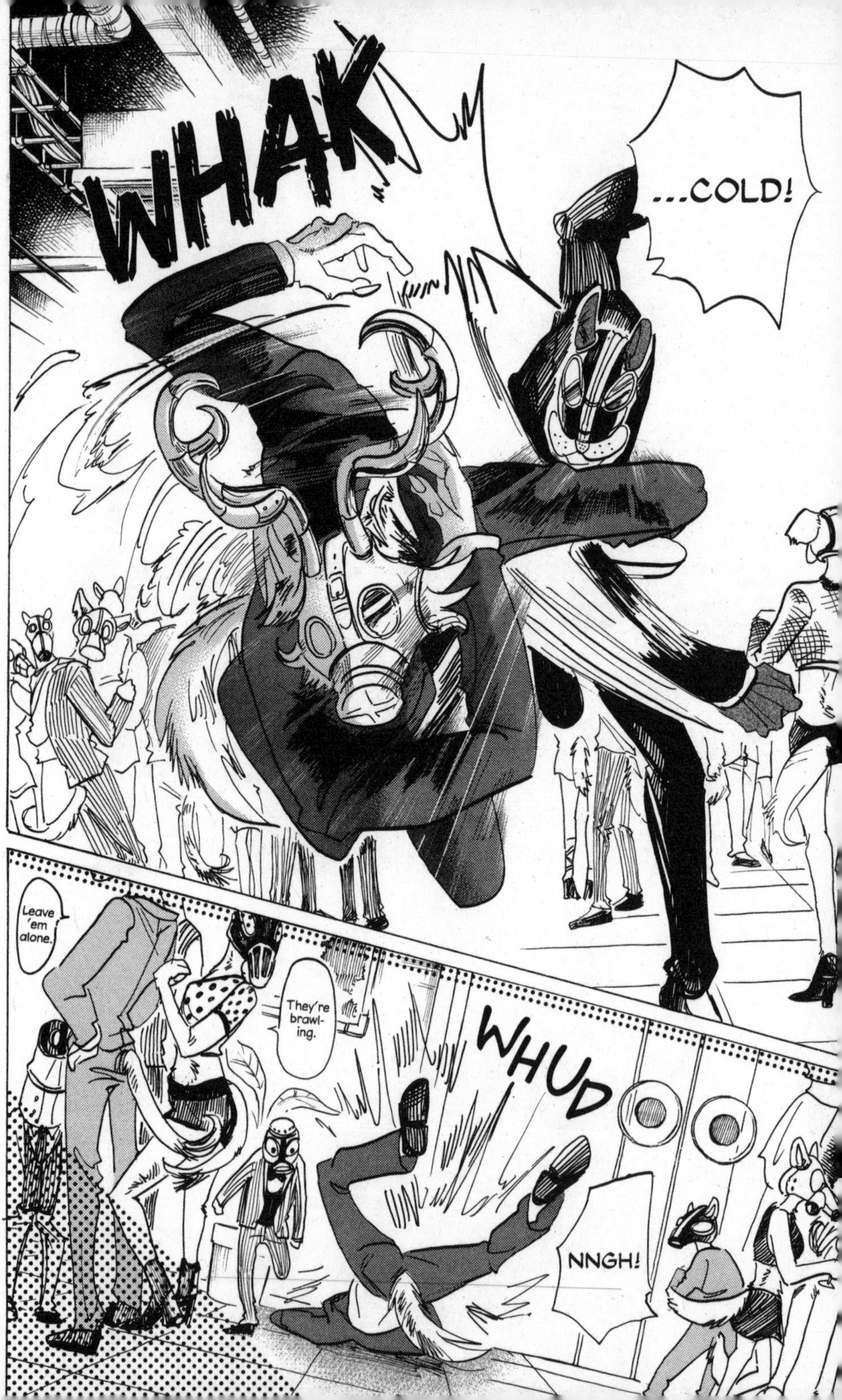
WHAK
...COLD!
WHUD
NNGH!
They're brawl-ing.
Leave 'em alone.

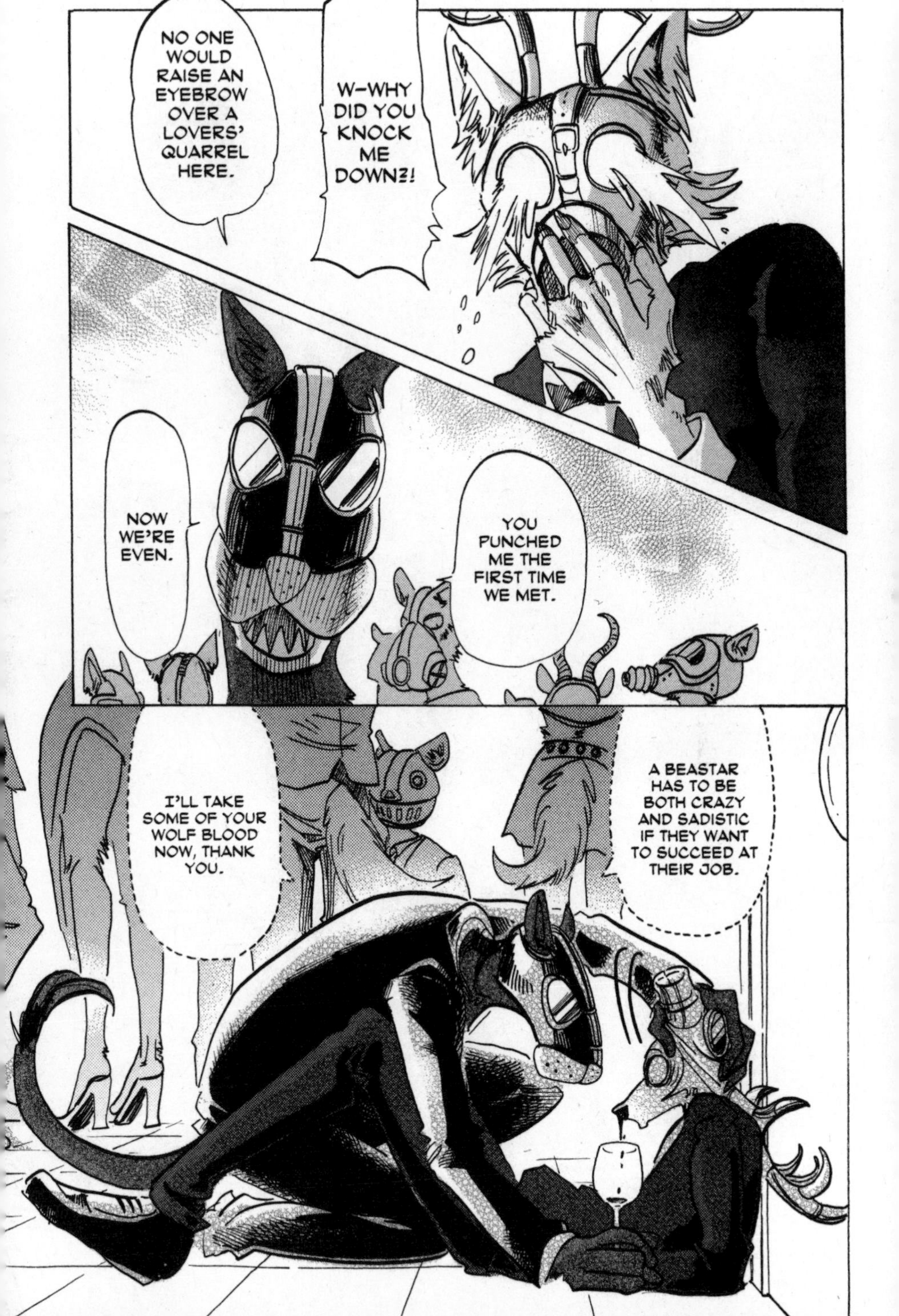
W-WHY DID YOU KNOCK ME DOWN?!
NO ONE WOULD RAISE AN EYEBROW OVER A LOVERS' QUARREL HERE.
YOU PUNCHED ME THE FIRST TIME WE MET.
NOW WE'RE EVEN.
A BEASTAR HAS TO BE BOTH CRAZY AND SADISTIC IF THEY WANT TO SUCCEED AT THEIR JOB.
I'LL TAKE SOME OF YOUR WOLF BLOOD NOW, THANK YOU.

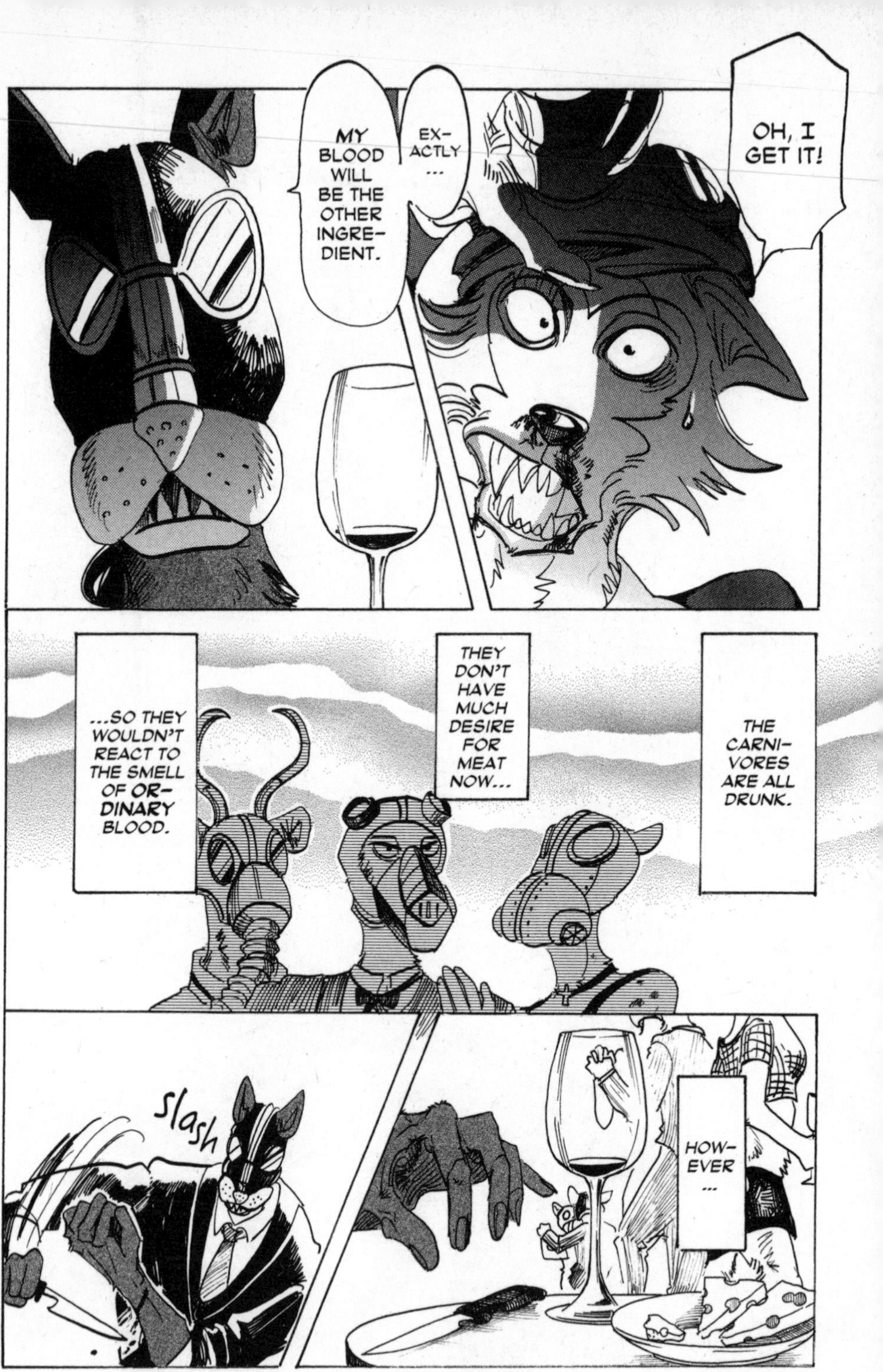

OH, I GET IT!
EX-ACTLY...
MY BLOOD WILL BE THE OTHER INGREDIENT.
THE CARNIVORES ARE ALL DRUNK.
THEY DON'T HAVE MUCH DESIRE FOR MEAT NOW...
...SO THEY WOULDN'T REACT TO THE SMELL OF ORDINARY BLOOD.
HOW-EVER...
slash

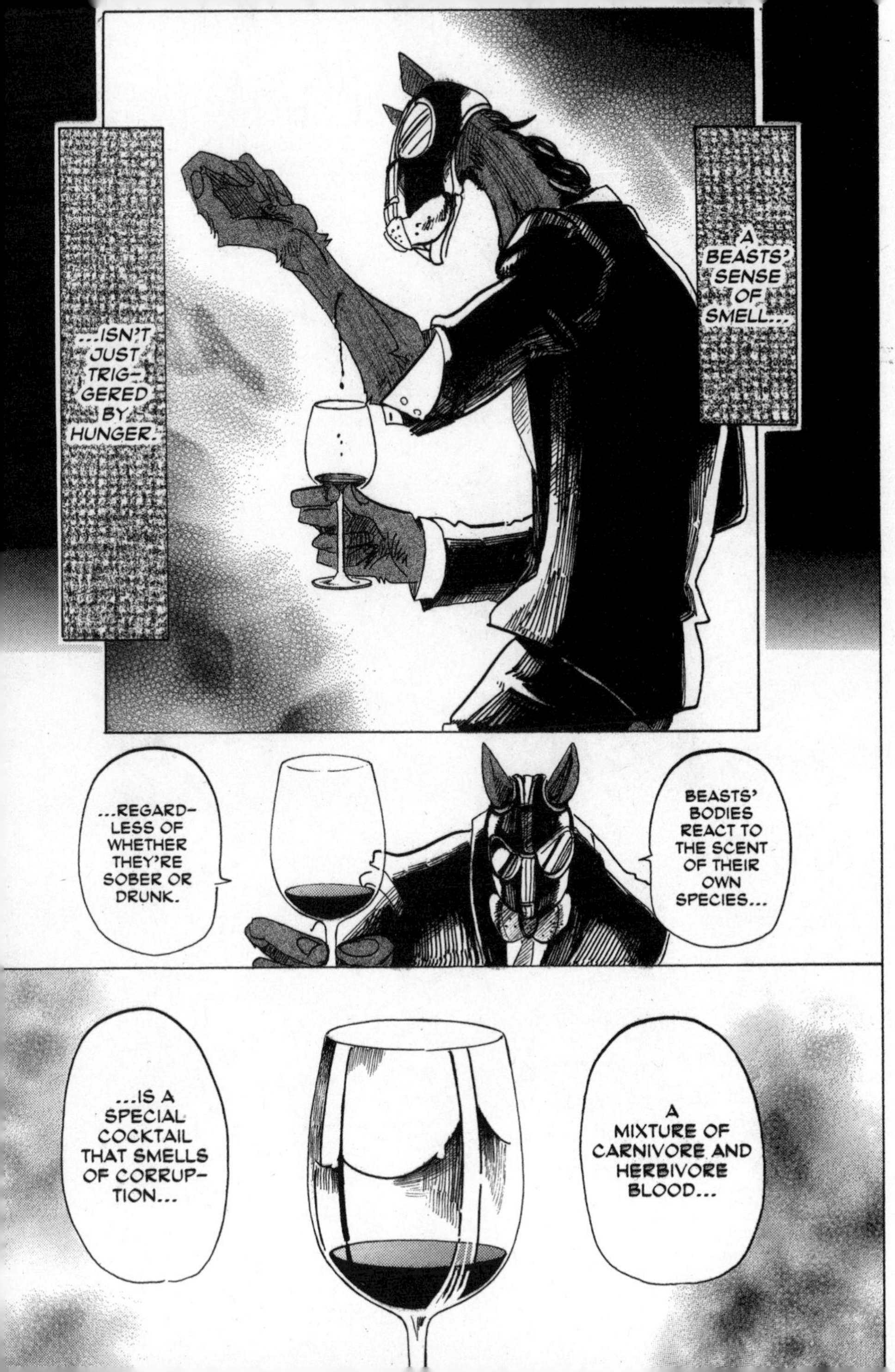
A BEASTS' SENSE OF SMELL...
...ISN'T JUST TRIGGERED BY HUNGER.
BEASTS' BODIES REACT TO THE SCENT OF THEIR OWN SPECIES...
...REGARDLESS OF WHETHER THEY'RE SOBER OR DRUNK.
A MIXTURE OF CARNIVORE AND HERBIVORE BLOOD...
...IS A SPECIAL COCKTAIL THAT SMELLS OF CORRUPTION...

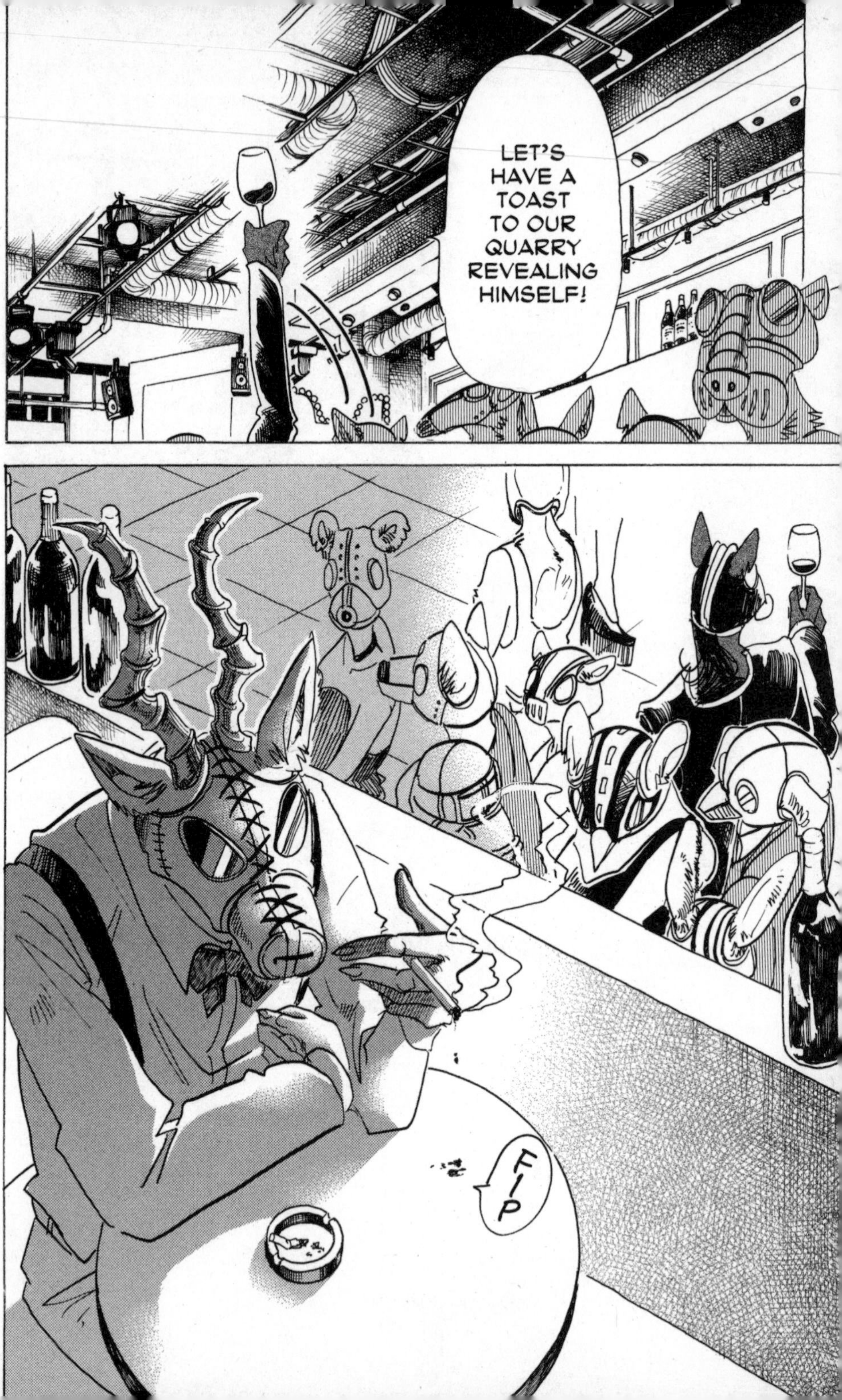
LET'S HAVE A TOAST TO OUR QUARRY REVEALING HIMSELF!
FLIP

Chapter 129: Jumping out of Bed from a Dream of Annunciation

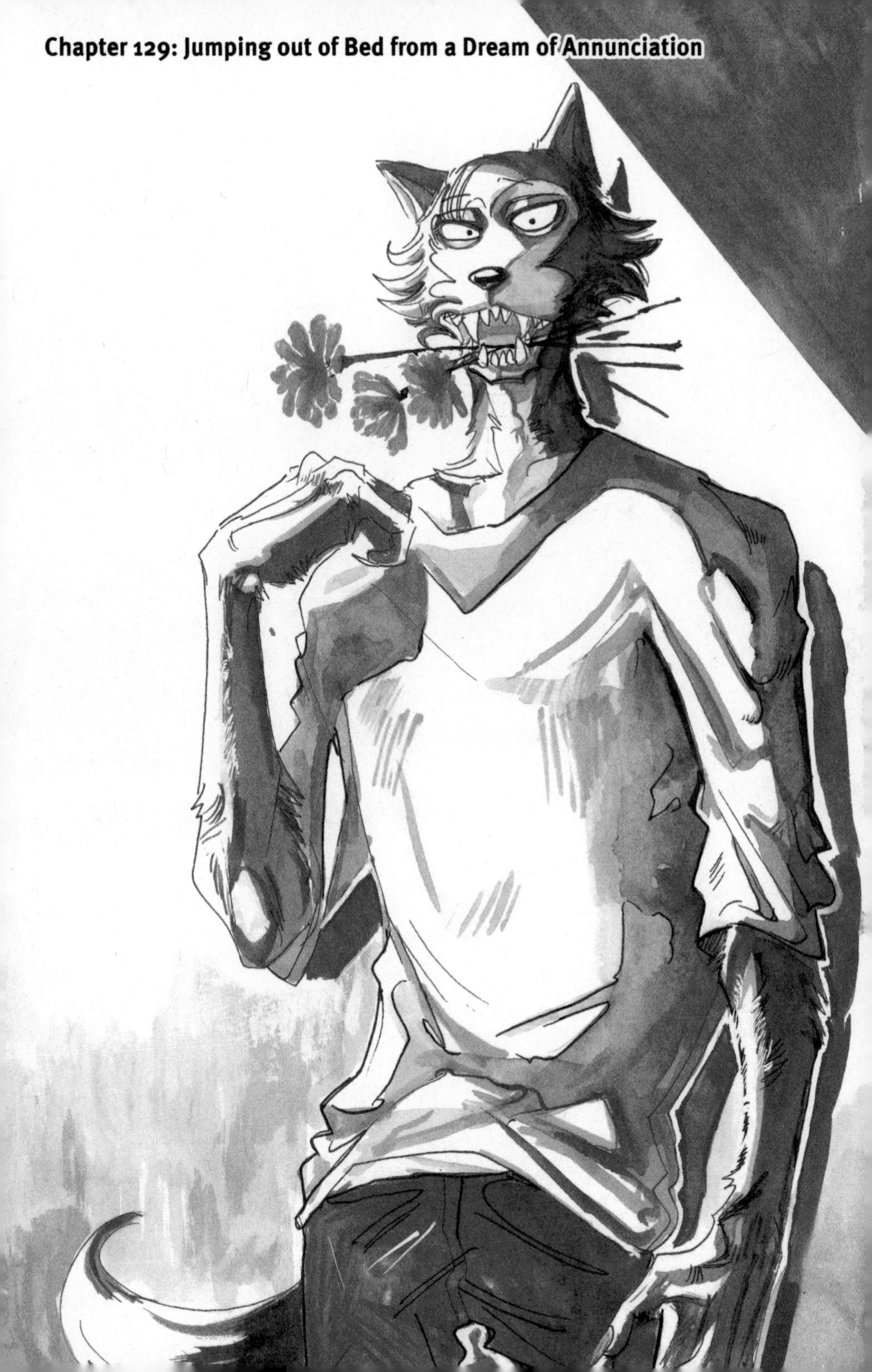

BEASTARS
Vol. 15

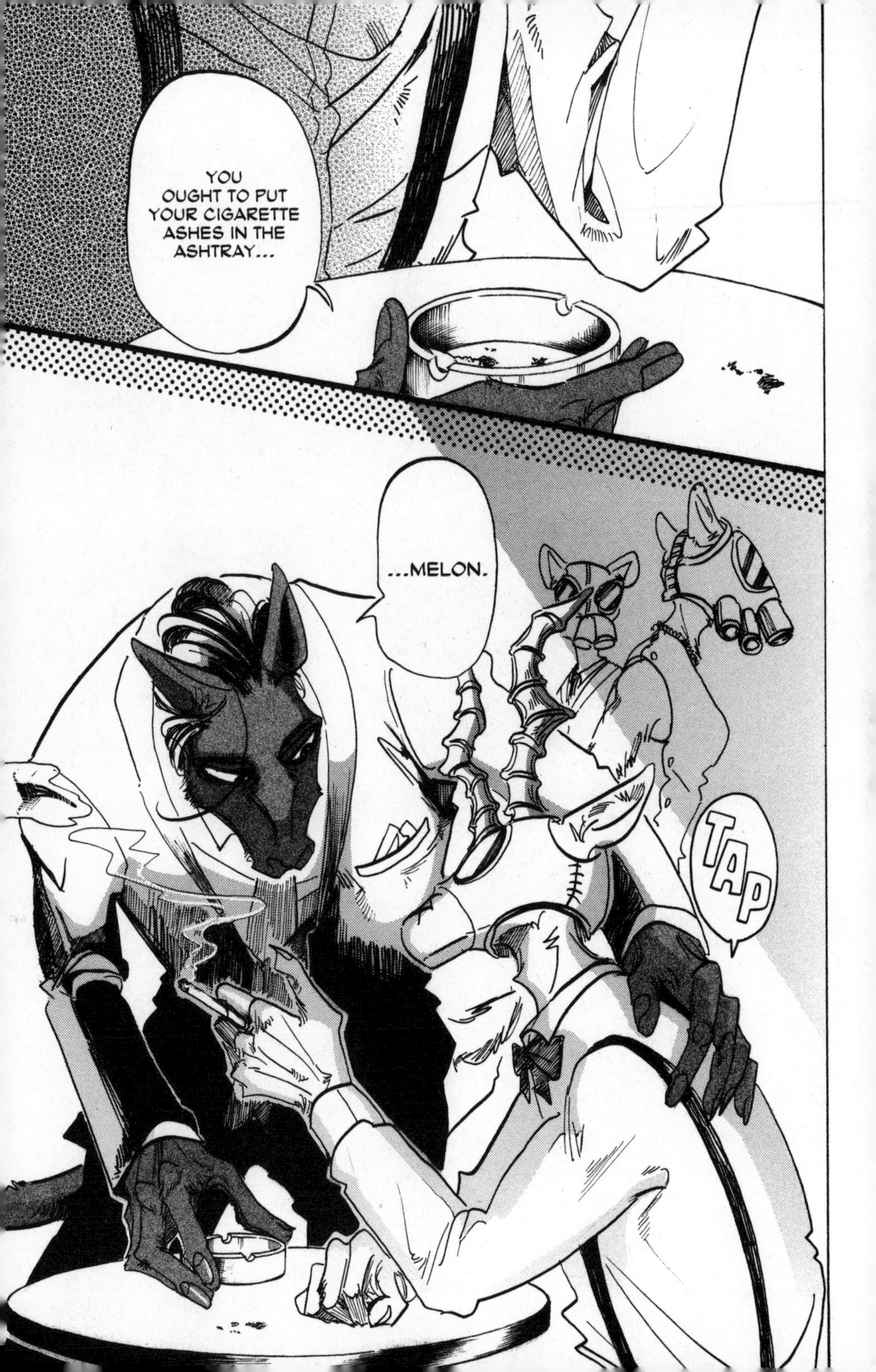
YOU OUGHT TO PUT YOUR CIGARETTE ASHES IN THE ASHTRAY...
...MELON.
TAP

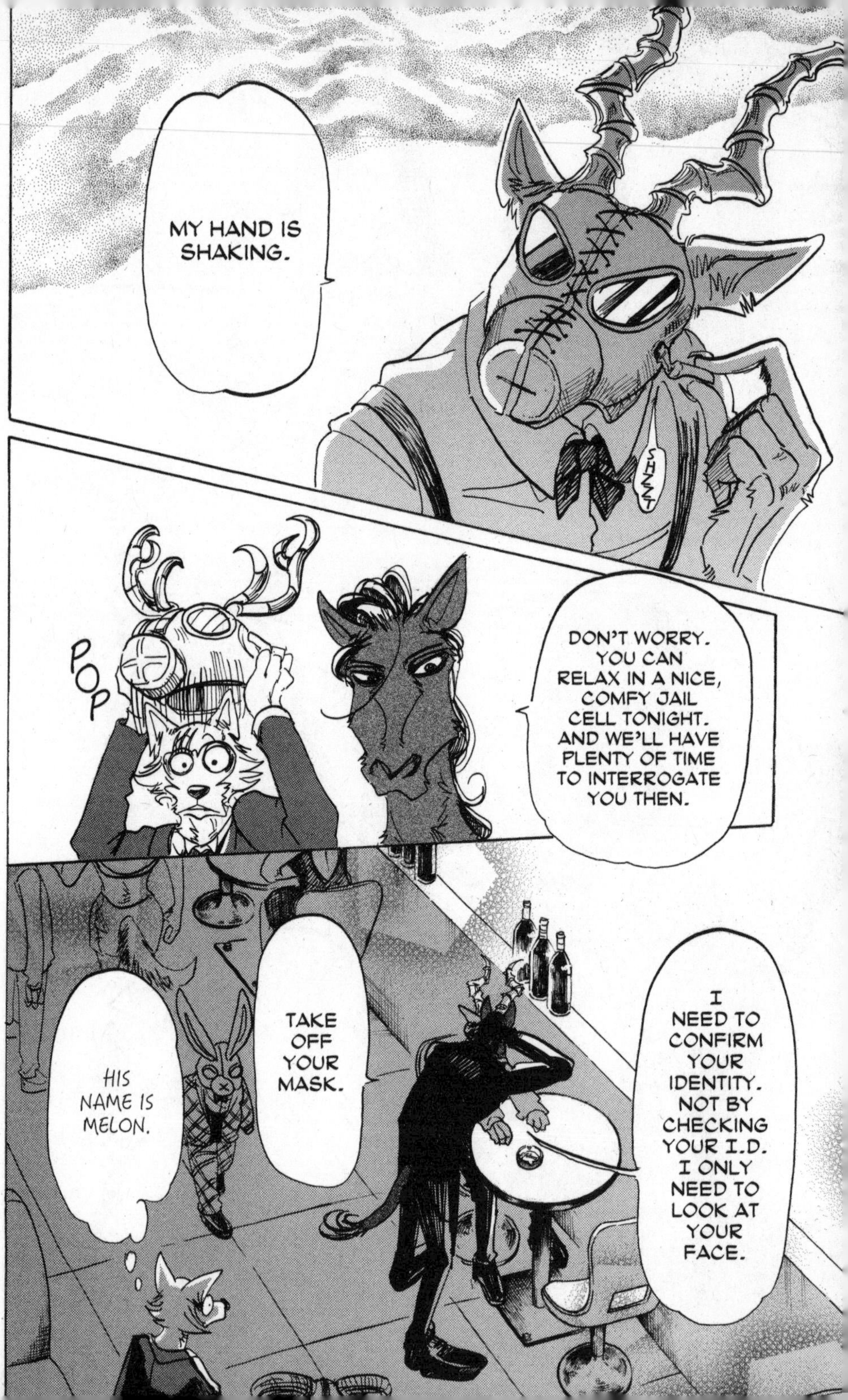
MY HAND IS SHAKING.
SHZZT
DON'T WORRY. YOU CAN RELAX IN A NICE, COMFY JAIL CELL TONIGHT. AND WE'LL HAVE PLENTY OF TIME TO INTERROGATE YOU THEN.
POP
I NEED TO CONFIRM YOUR IDENTITY. NOT BY CHECKING YOUR I.D. I ONLY NEED TO LOOK AT YOUR FACE.
TAKE OFF YOUR MASK.
HIS NAME IS MELON.

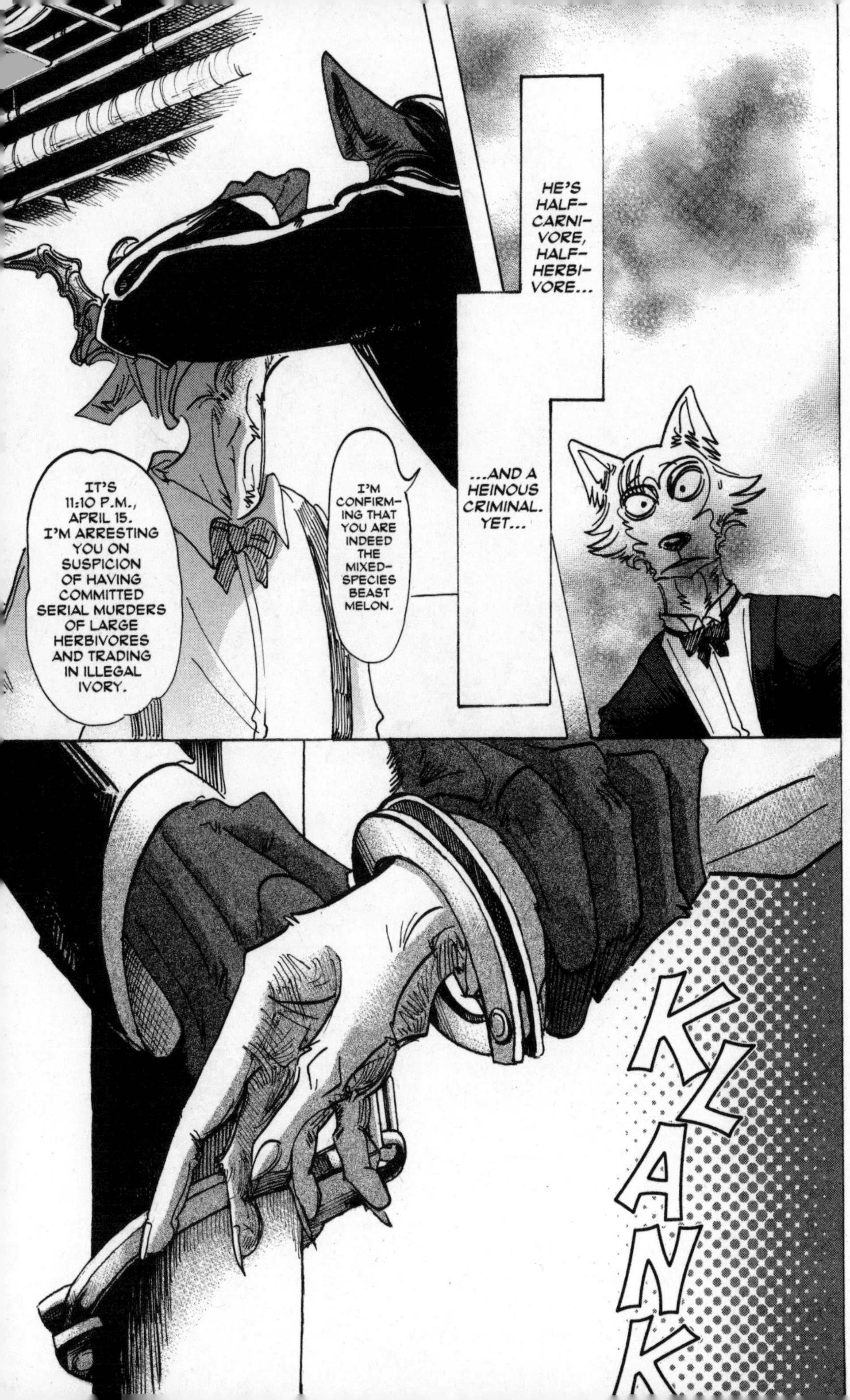
HE'S HALF-CARNIVORE, HALF-HERBIVORE...
...AND A HEINOUS CRIMINAL. YET...
I'M CONFIRMING THAT YOU ARE INDEED THE MIXED-SPECIES BEAST MELON.
IT'S 11:10 P.M., APRIL 15. I'M ARRESTING YOU ON SUSPICION OF HAVING COMMITTED SERIAL MURDERS OF LARGE HERBIVORES AND TRADING IN ILLEGAL IVORY.
KLANK

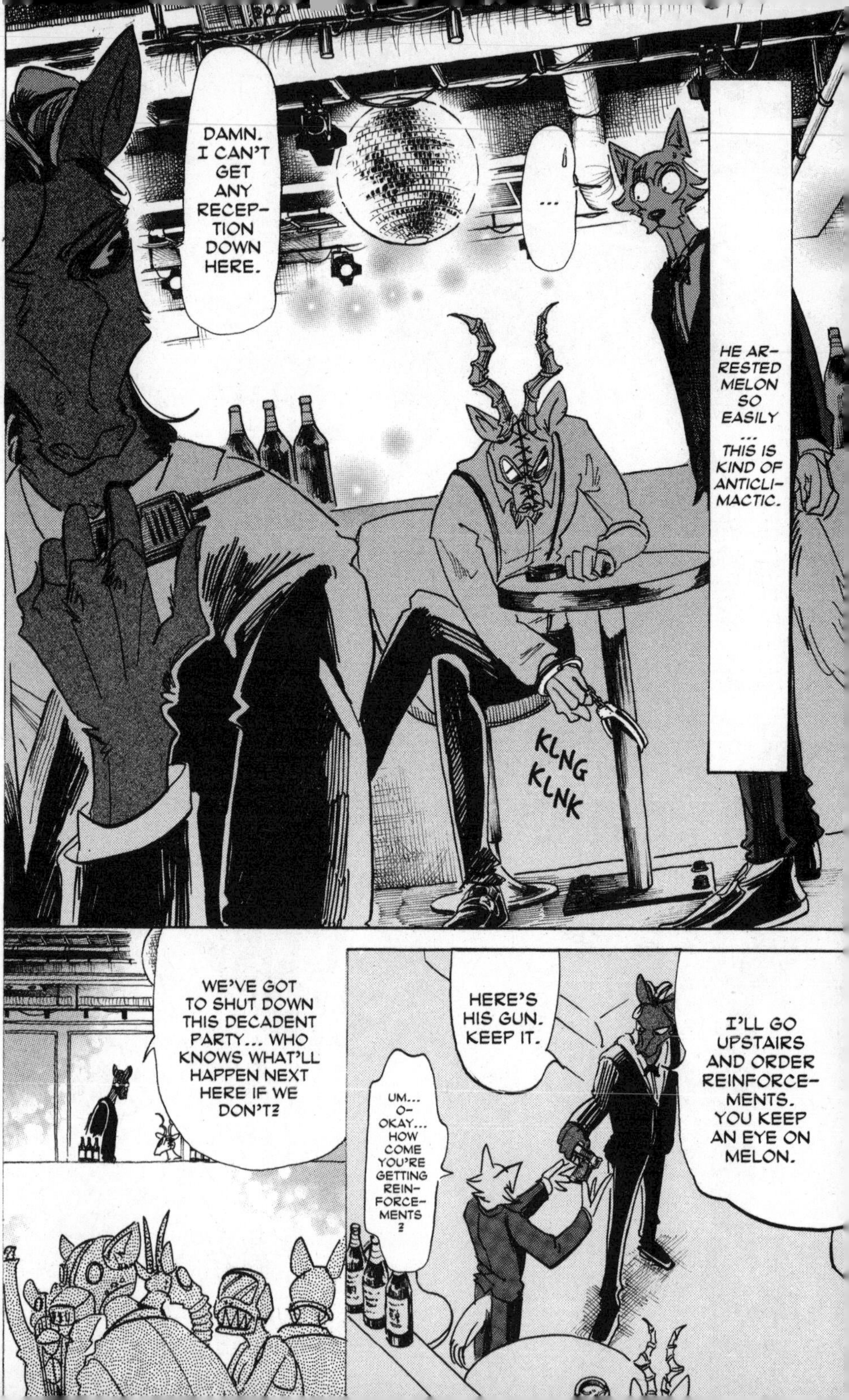
HE AR-RESTED MELON SO EASILY ... THIS IS KIND OF ANTICLI-MACTIC.
...
DAMN. I CAN'T GET ANY RECEP-TION DOWN HERE.
KLNG KLNK
HERE'S HIS GUN. KEEP IT.
I'LL GO UPSTAIRS AND ORDER REINFORCE-MENTS. YOU KEEP AN EYE ON MELON.
UM... O-OKAY... HOW COME YOU'RE GETTING REIN-FORCE-MENTS?
WE'VE GOT TO SHUT DOWN THIS DECADENT PARTY... WHO KNOWS WHAT'LL HAPPEN NEXT HERE IF WE DON'T?

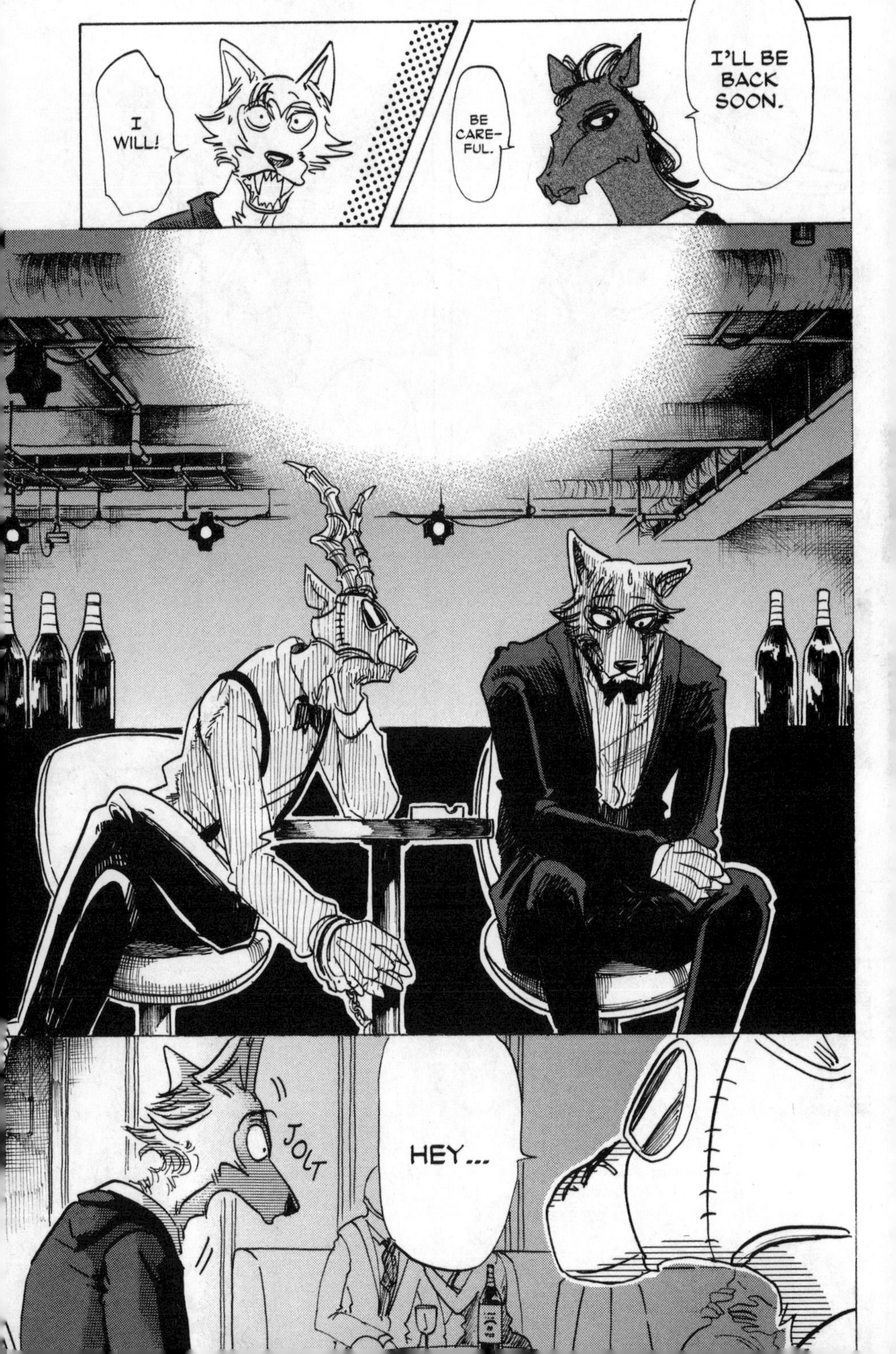
I'LL BE BACK SOON.
BE CARE-FUL.
I WILL!
HEY...
JOLT

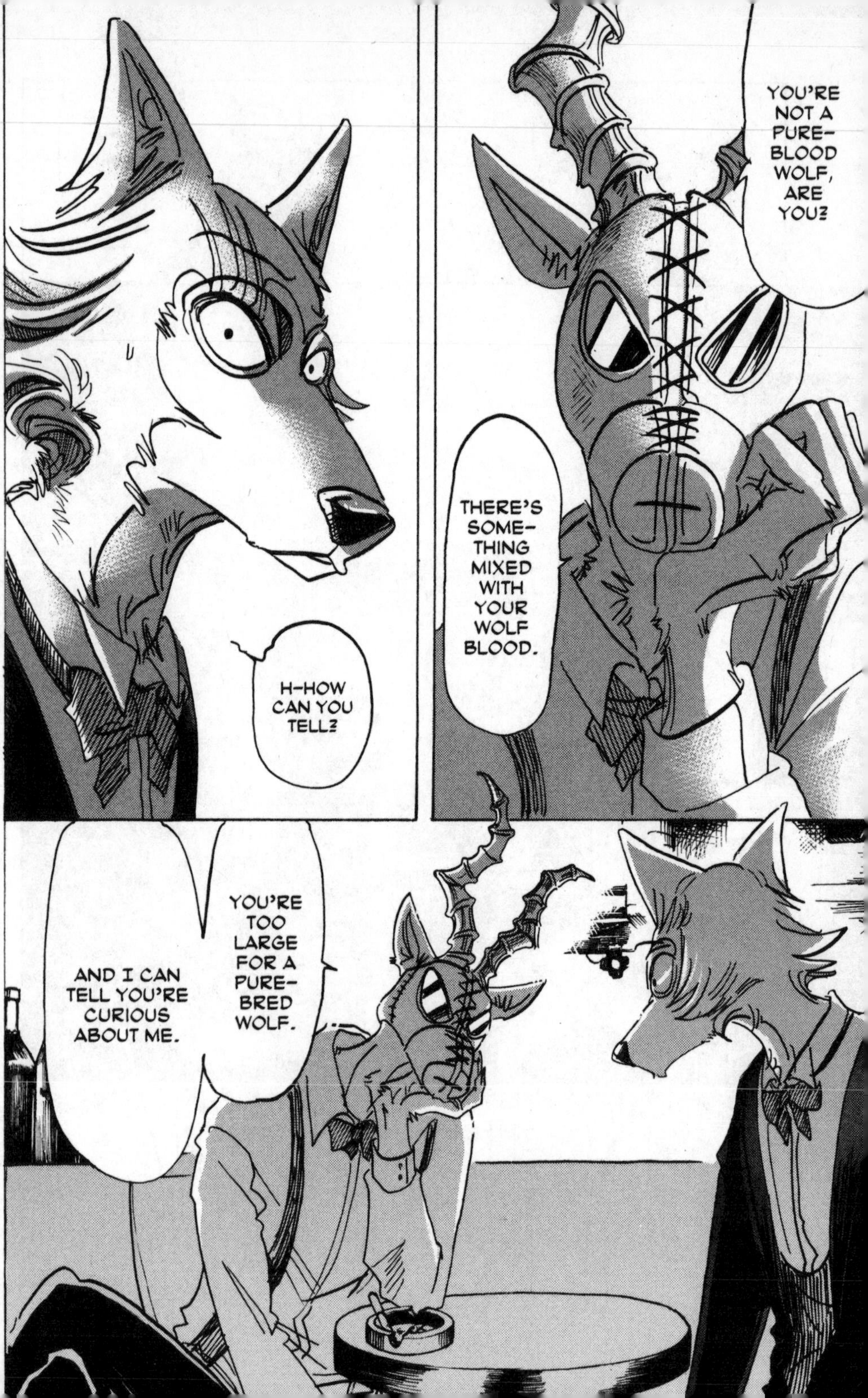
YOU'RE NOT A PURE-BLOOD WOLF, ARE YOU?
THERE'S SOME-THING MIXED WITH YOUR WOLF BLOOD.
H-HOW CAN YOU TELL?
YOU'RE TOO LARGE FOR A PURE-BRED WOLF.
AND I CAN TELL YOU'RE CURIOUS ABOUT ME.

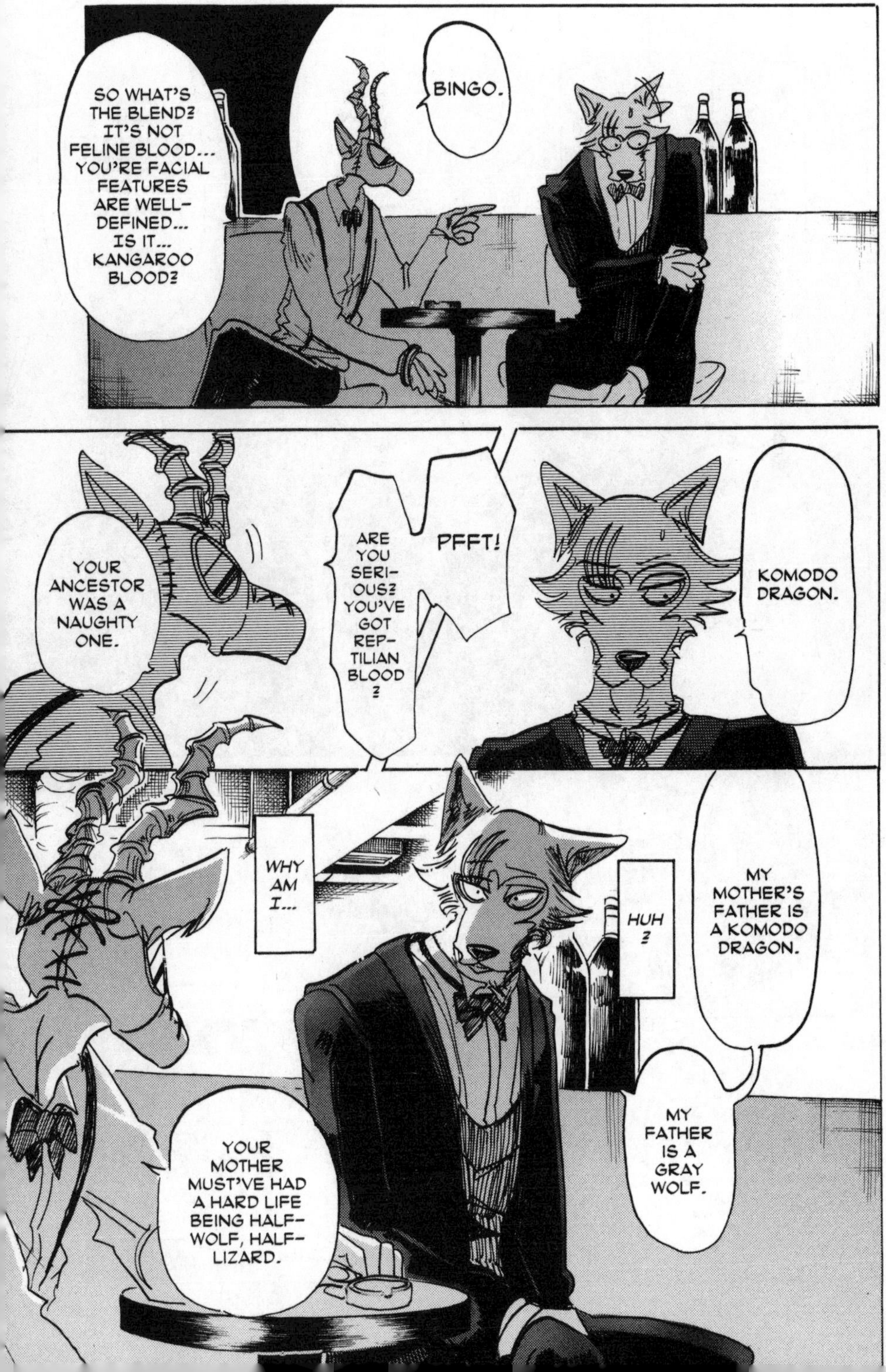
BINGO.
SO WHAT'S THE BLEND? IT'S NOT FELINE BLOOD... YOU'RE FACIAL FEATURES ARE WELL-DEFINED... IS IT... KANGAROO BLOOD?
KOMODO DRAGON.
PFFT!
ARE YOU SERIOUS? YOU'VE GOT REP-TILIAN BLOOD?
YOUR ANCESTOR WAS A NAUGHTY ONE.
MY MOTHER'S FATHER IS A KOMODO DRAGON.
HUH?
WHY AM I...
MY FATHER IS A GRAY WOLF.
YOUR MOTHER MUST'VE HAD A HARD LIFE BEING HALF-WOLF, HALF-LIZARD.

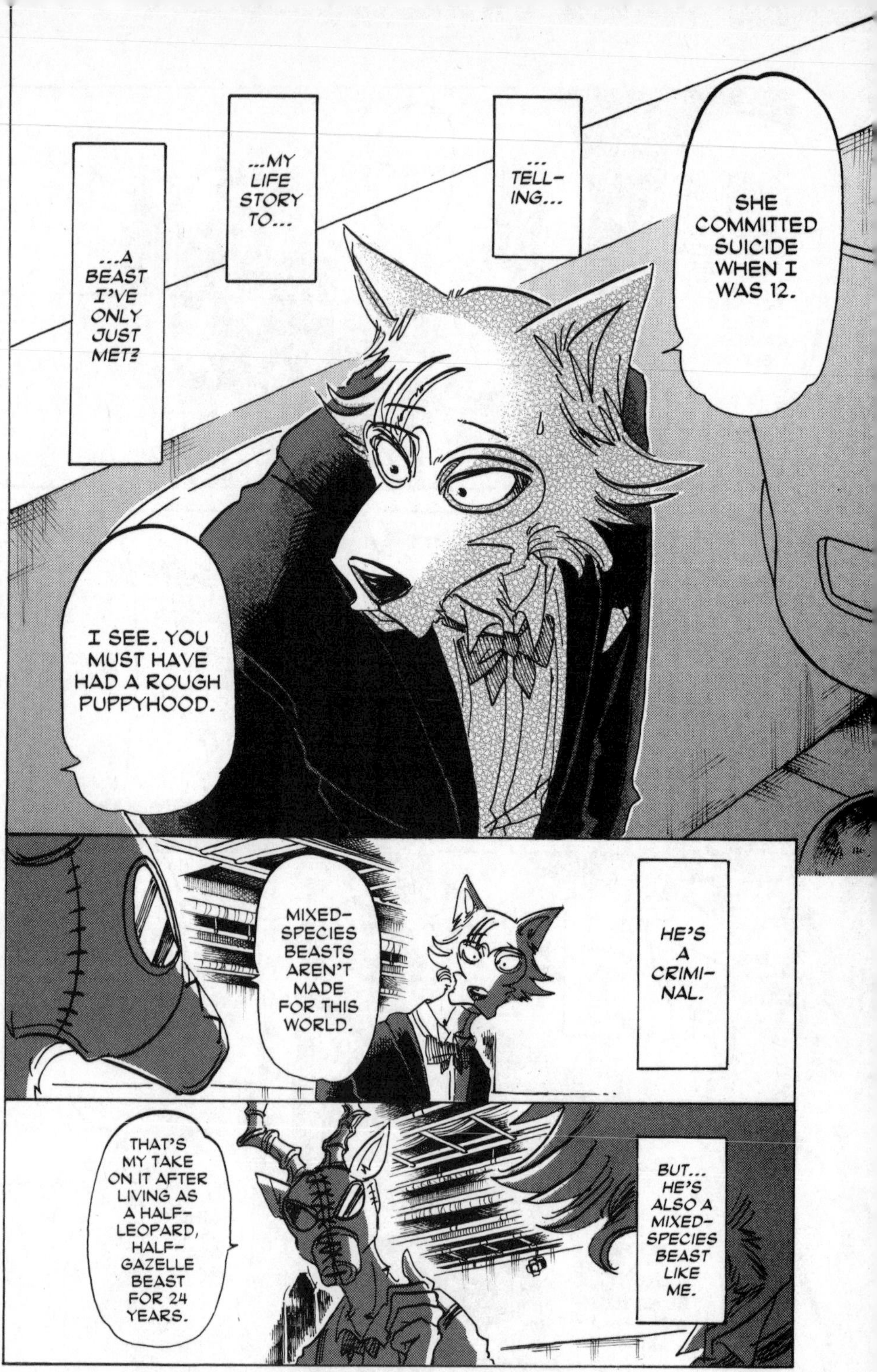
SHE COMMITTED SUICIDE WHEN I WAS 12.
...TELLING...
...MY LIFE STORY TO...
...A BEAST I'VE ONLY JUST MET?
I SEE. YOU MUST HAVE HAD A ROUGH PUPPYHOOD.
HE'S A CRIMINAL.
MIXED-SPECIES BEASTS AREN'T MADE FOR THIS WORLD.
BUT... HE'S ALSO A MIXED-SPECIES BEAST LIKE ME.
THAT'S MY TAKE ON IT AFTER LIVING AS A HALF-LEOPARD, HALF-GAZELLE BEAST FOR 24 YEARS.

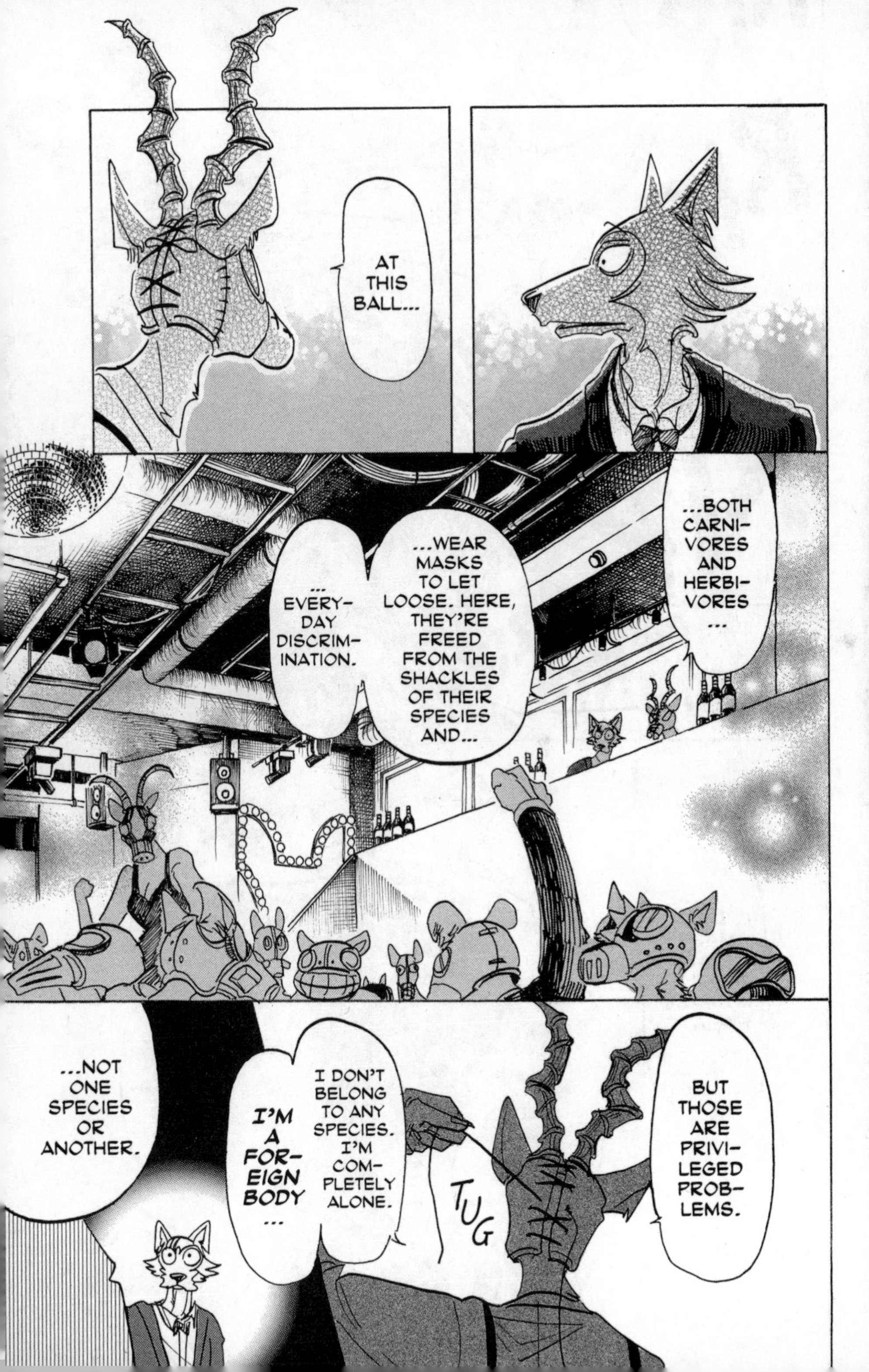
AT THIS BALL...
...BOTH CARNIVORES AND HERBIVORES ...
...WEAR MASKS TO LET LOOSE. HERE, THEY'RE FREED FROM THE SHACKLES OF THEIR SPECIES AND...
... EVERYDAY DISCRIMINATION.
BUT THOSE ARE PRIVILEGED PROBLEMS.
TUG
I DON'T BELONG TO ANY SPECIES. I'M COMPLETELY ALONE.
I'M A FOREIGN BODY ...
...NOT ONE SPECIES OR ANOTHER.

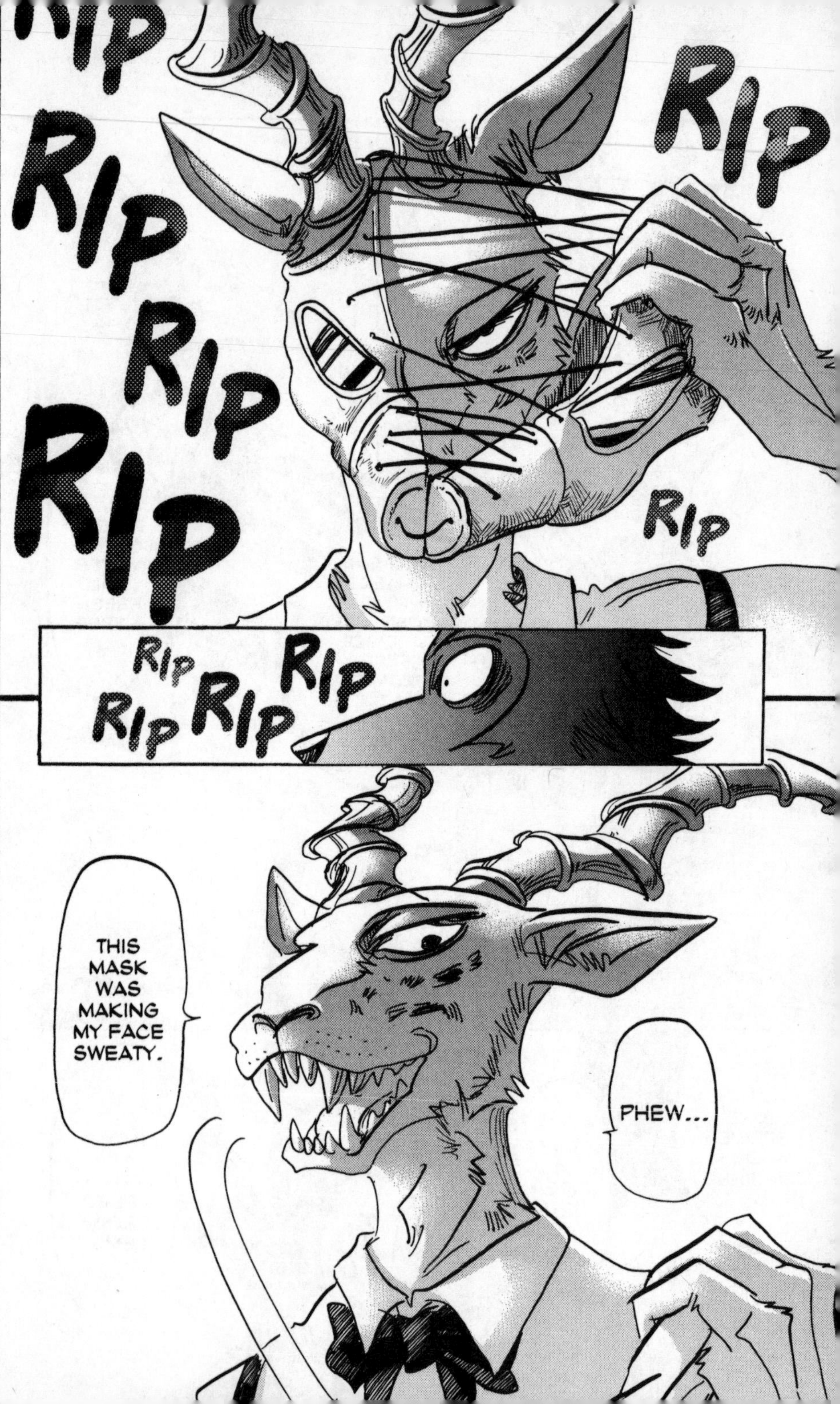
RIP
RIP
RIP
RIP
RIP
RIP
RIP
RIP
RIP
PHEW...
THIS MASK WAS MAKING MY FACE SWEATY.

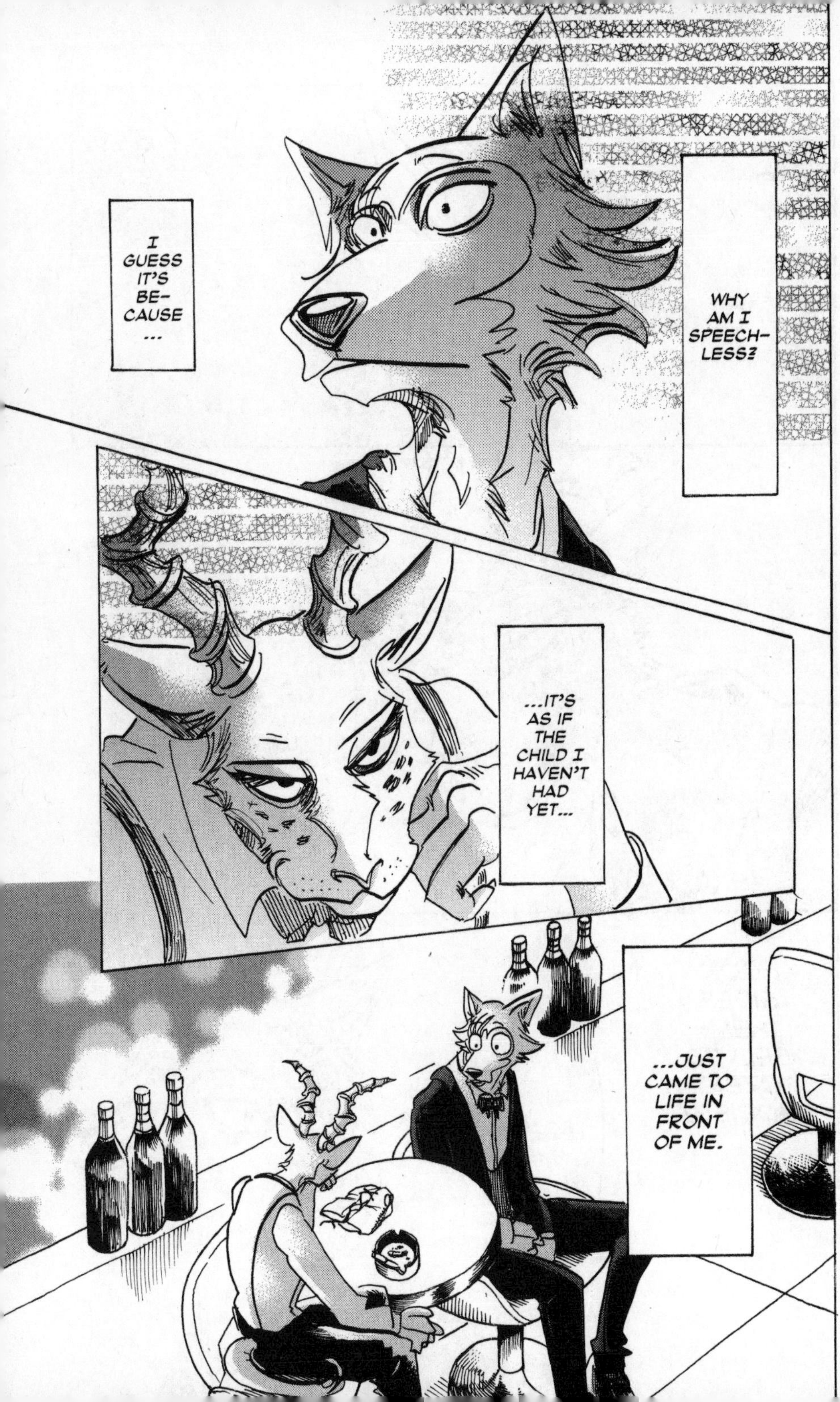
WHY AM I SPEECHLESS?
I GUESS IT'S BECAUSE...
...IT'S AS IF THE CHILD I HAVEN'T HAD YET...
...JUST CAME TO LIFE IN FRONT OF ME.

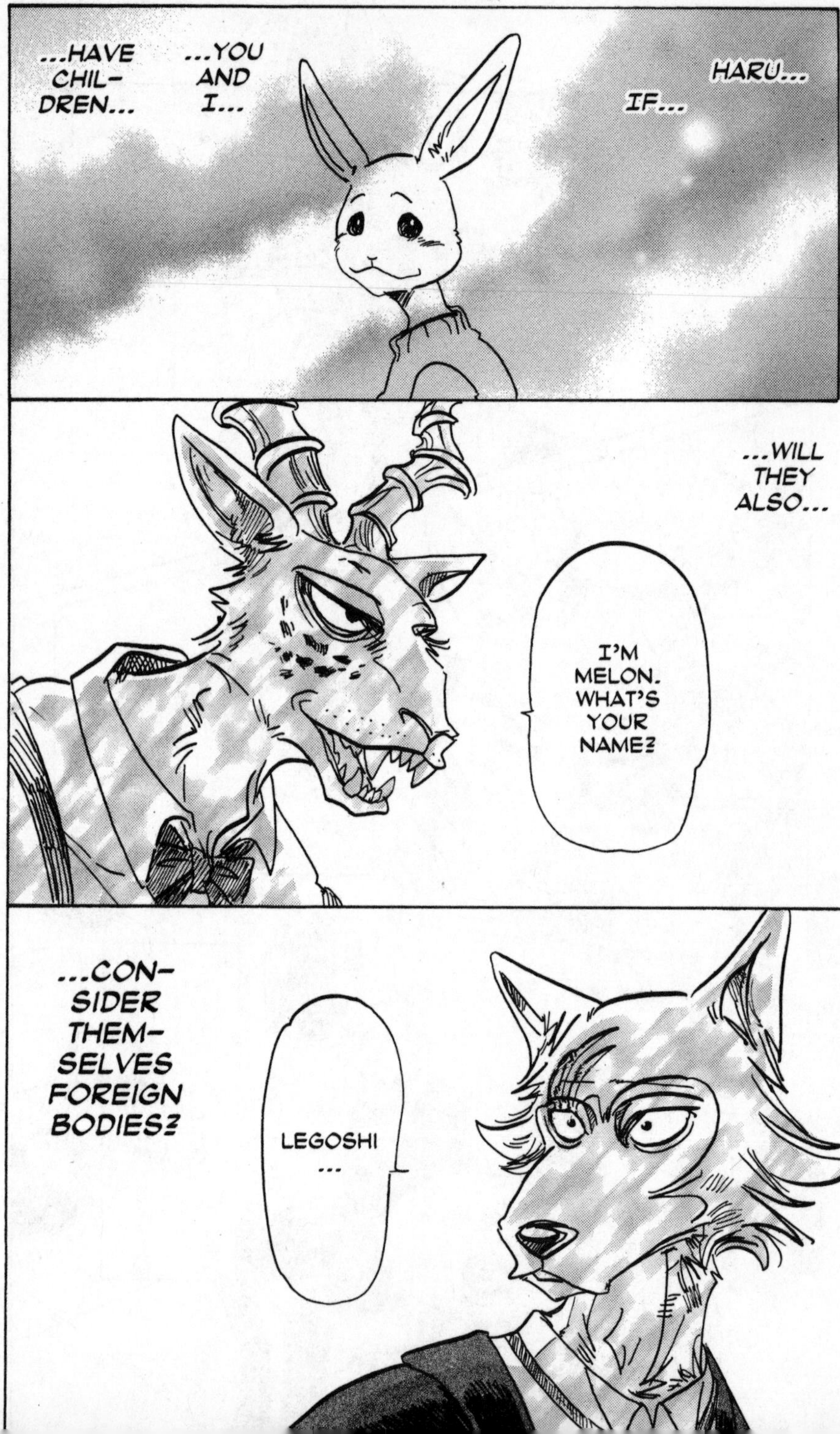
HARU...
IF...
...YOU AND I...
...HAVE CHIL-DREN...
...WILL THEY ALSO...
I'M MELON. WHAT'S YOUR NAME?
LEGOSHI ...
...CON-SIDER THEM-SELVES FOREIGN BODIES?

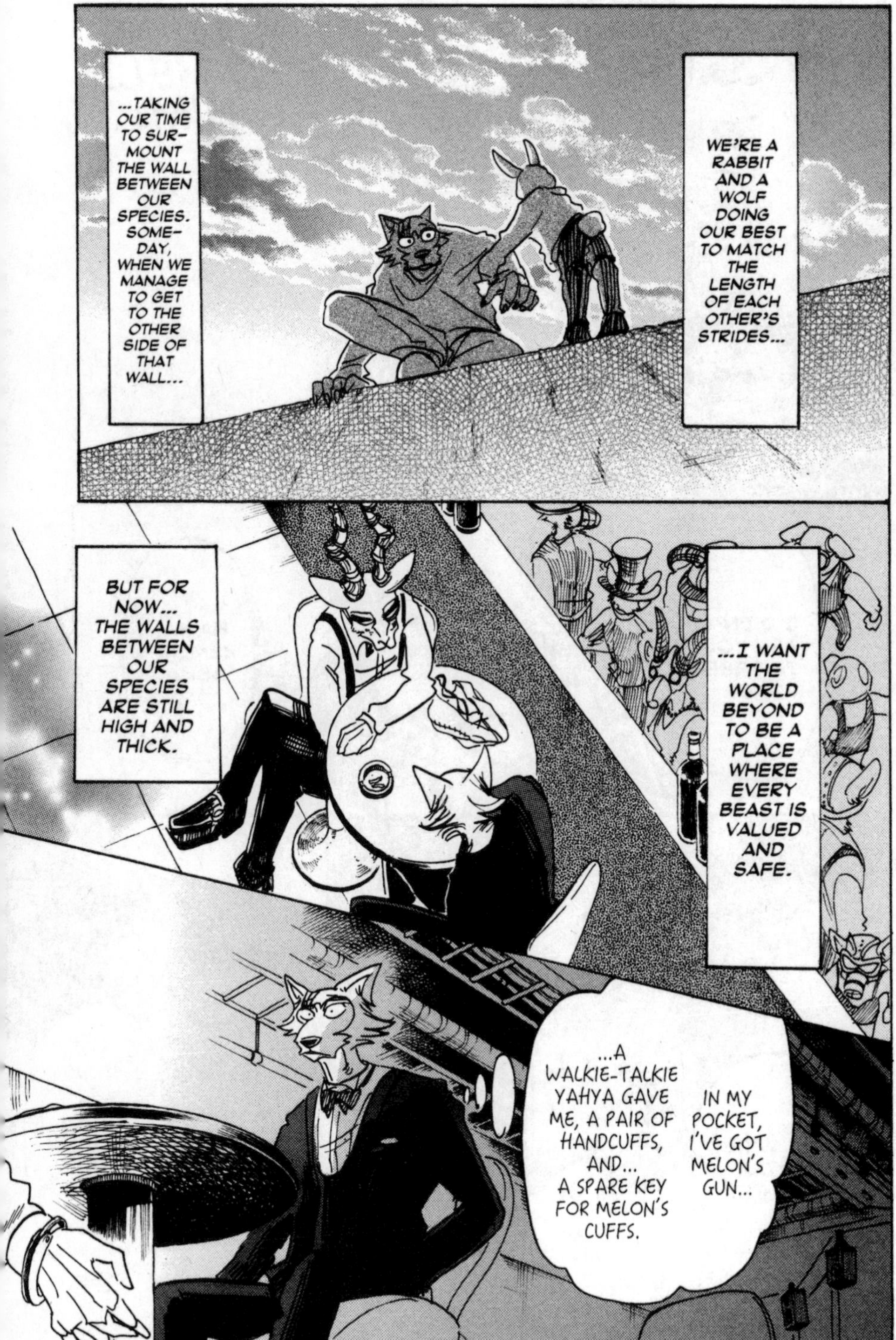
WE'RE A RABBIT AND A WOLF DOING OUR BEST TO MATCH THE LENGTH OF EACH OTHER'S STRIDES...
...TAKING OUR TIME TO SUR-MOUNT THE WALL BETWEEN OUR SPECIES. SOME-DAY, WHEN WE MANAGE TO GET TO THE OTHER SIDE OF THAT WALL...
...I WANT THE WORLD BEYOND TO BE A PLACE WHERE EVERY BEAST IS VALUED AND SAFE.
BUT FOR NOW... THE WALLS BETWEEN OUR SPECIES ARE STILL HIGH AND THICK.
IN MY POCKET, I'VE GOT MELON'S GUN...
...A WALKIE-TALKIE YAHYA GAVE ME, A PAIR OF HANDCUFFS, AND... A SPARE KEY FOR MELON'S CUFFS.

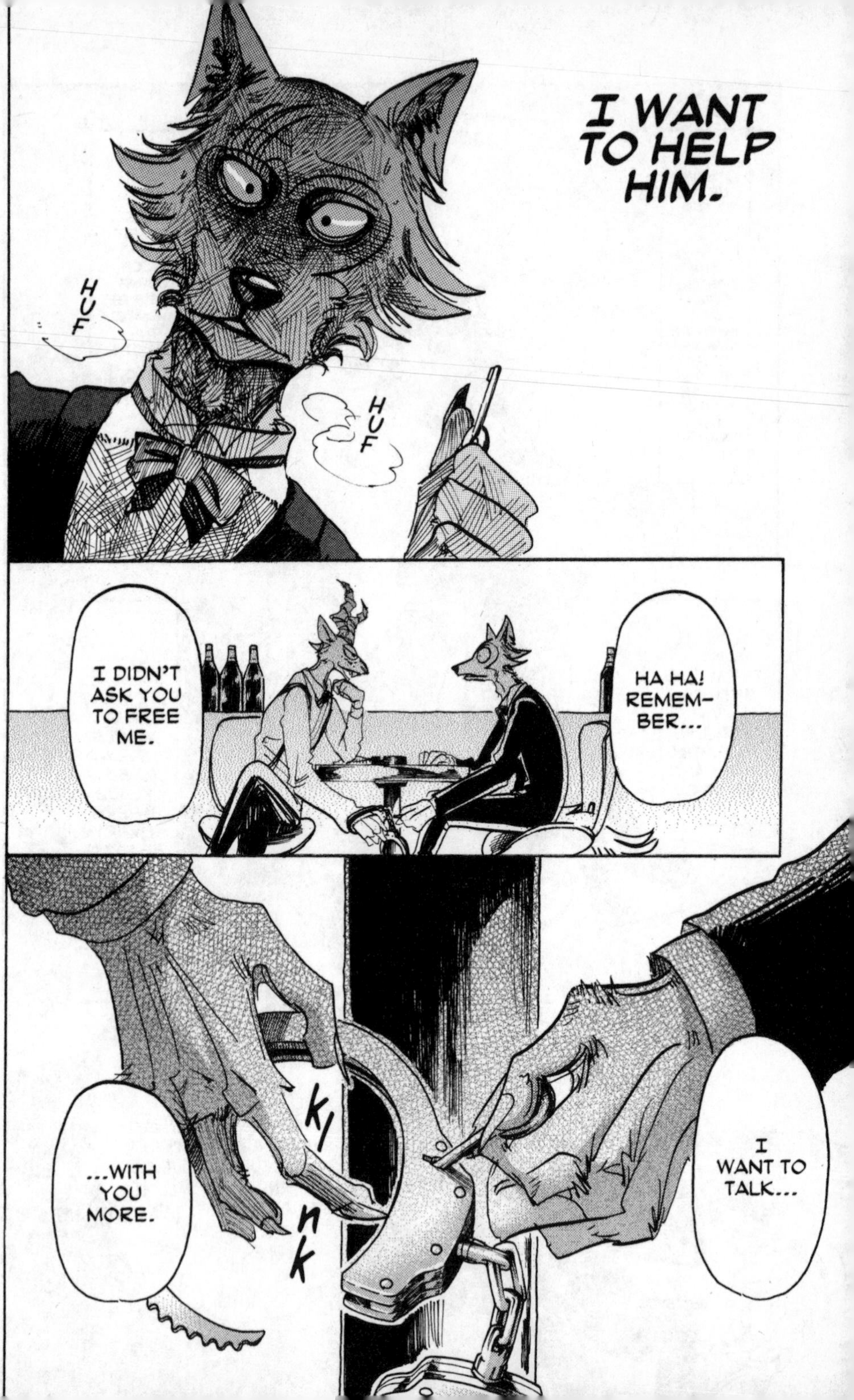
I WANT TO HELP HIM.
HUF
HUF
HA HA! REMEMBER...
I DIDN'T ASK YOU TO FREE ME.
I WANT TO TALK...
KLINK
...WITH YOU MORE.

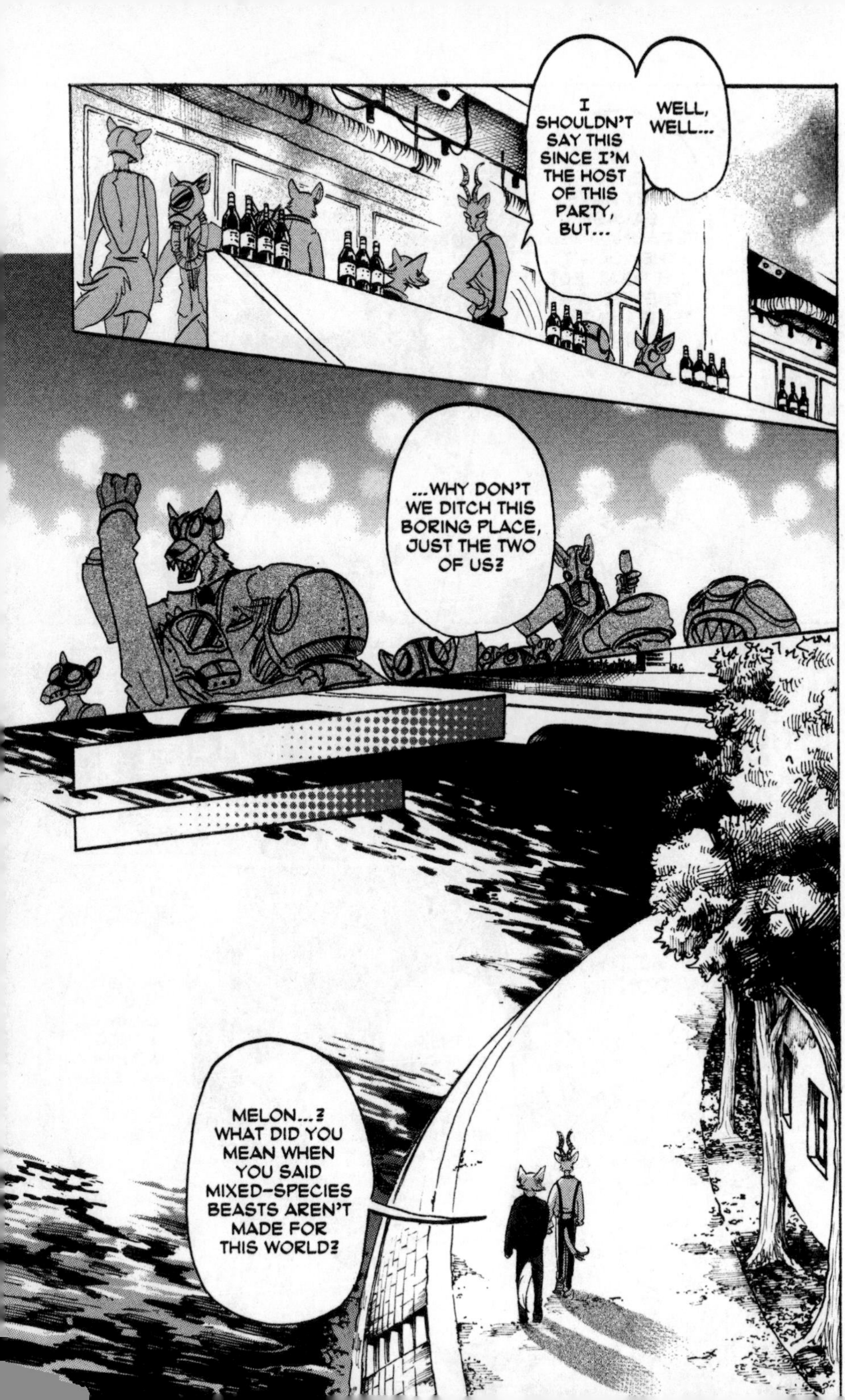
WELL, WELL...
I SHOULDN'T SAY THIS SINCE I'M THE HOST OF THIS PARTY, BUT...
...WHY DON'T WE DITCH THIS BORING PLACE, JUST THE TWO OF US?
MELON...? WHAT DID YOU MEAN WHEN YOU SAID MIXED-SPECIES BEASTS AREN'T MADE FOR THIS WORLD?

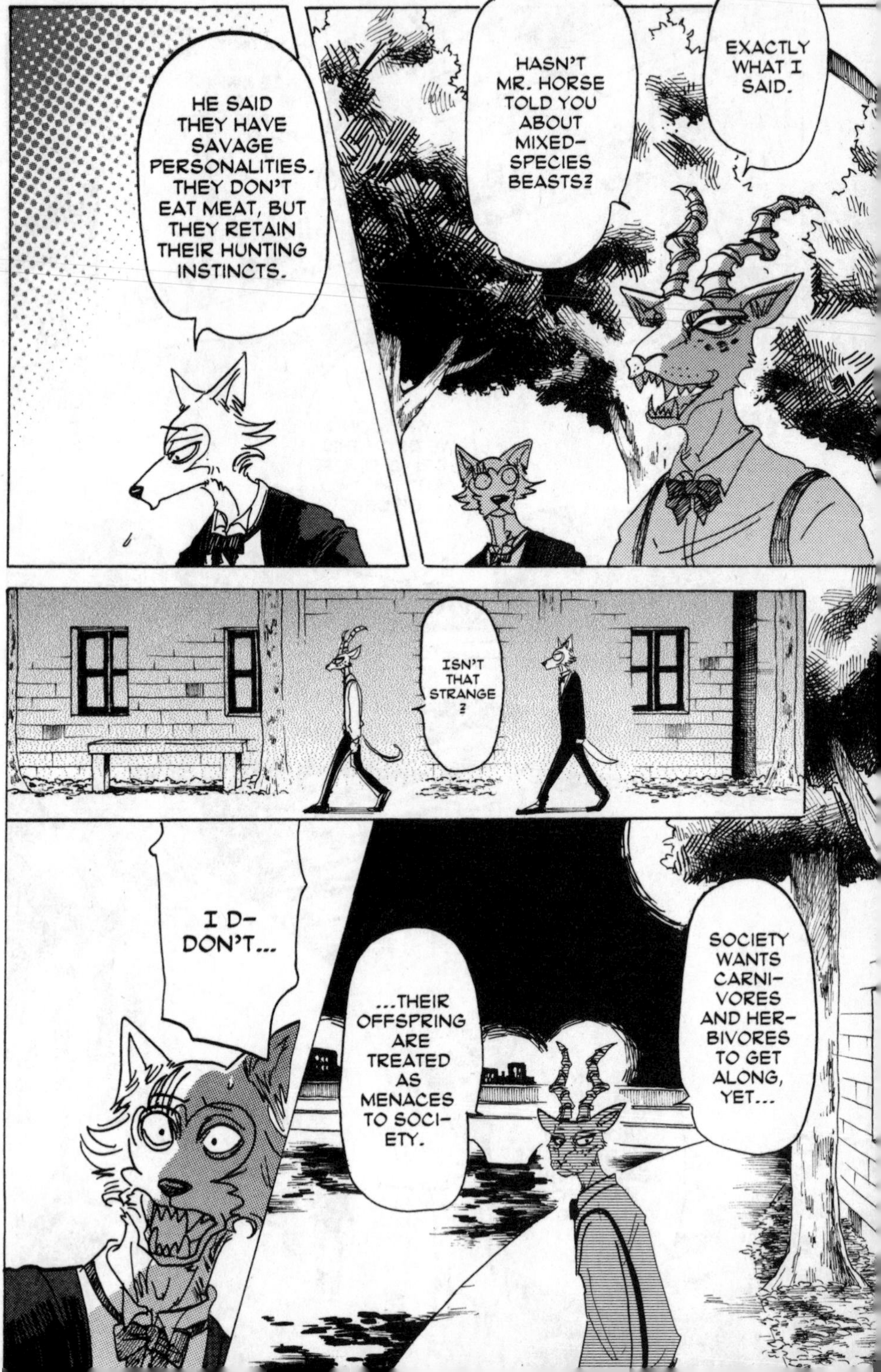

EXACTLY WHAT I SAID.
HASN'T MR. HORSE TOLD YOU ABOUT MIXED-SPECIES BEASTS?
HE SAID THEY HAVE SAVAGE PERSONALITIES. THEY DON'T EAT MEAT, BUT THEY RETAIN THEIR HUNTING INSTINCTS.
ISN'T THAT STRANGE?
SOCIETY WANTS CARNI-VORES AND HER-BIVORES TO GET ALONG, YET...
...THEIR OFFSPRING ARE TREATED AS MENACES TO SOCI-ETY.
I D-DON'T...

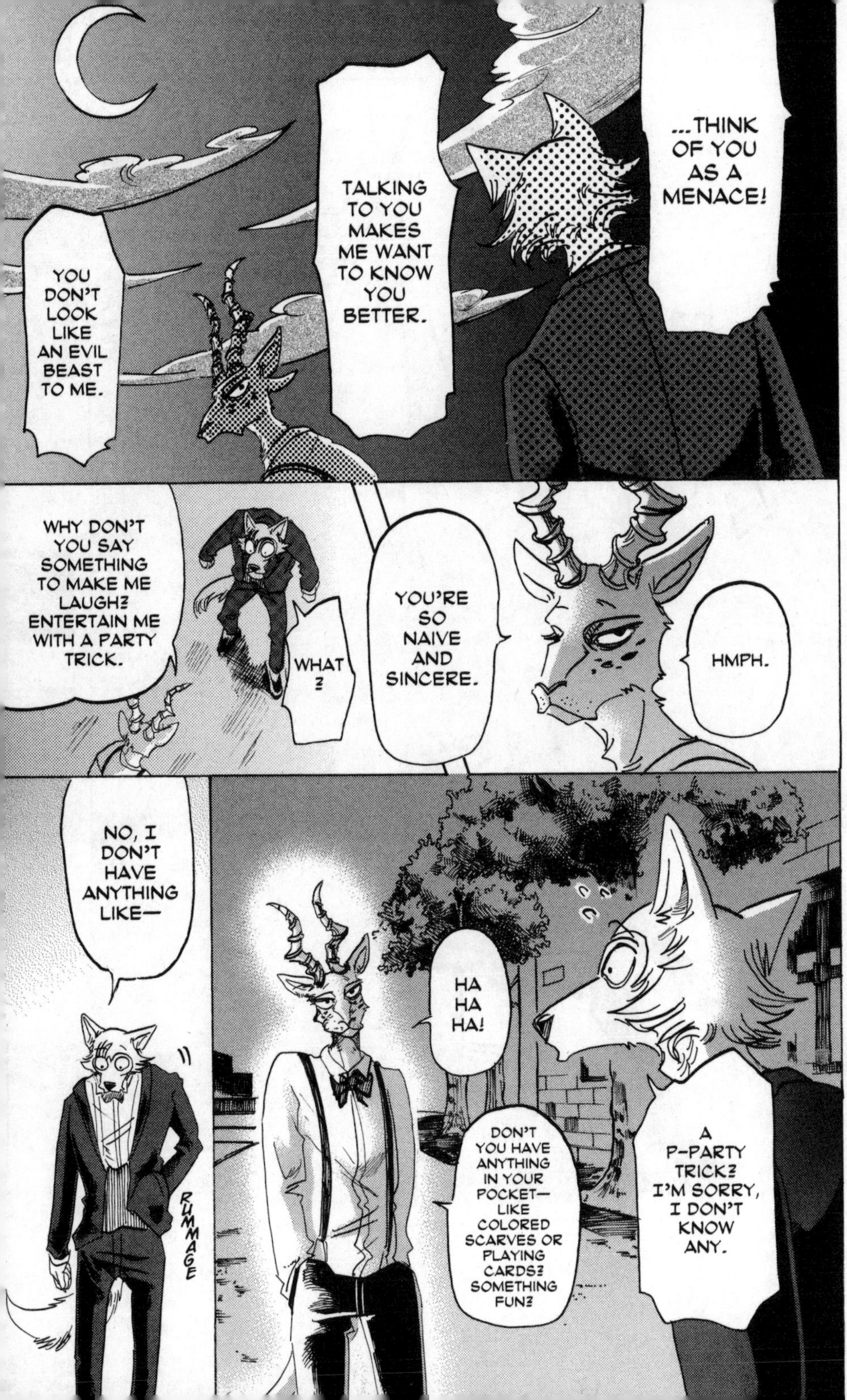
...THINK OF YOU AS A MENACE!
TALKING TO YOU MAKES ME WANT TO KNOW YOU BETTER.
YOU DON'T LOOK LIKE AN EVIL BEAST TO ME.
HMPH.
YOU'RE SO NAIVE AND SINCERE.
WHAT?
WHY DON'T YOU SAY SOMETHING TO MAKE ME LAUGH? ENTERTAIN ME WITH A PARTY TRICK.
A P-PARTY TRICK? I'M SORRY, I DON'T KNOW ANY.
HA HA HA!
DON'T YOU HAVE ANYTHING IN YOUR POCKET—LIKE COLORED SCARVES OR PLAYING CARDS? SOMETHING FUN?
NO, I DON'T HAVE ANYTHING LIKE—
RUMMAGE

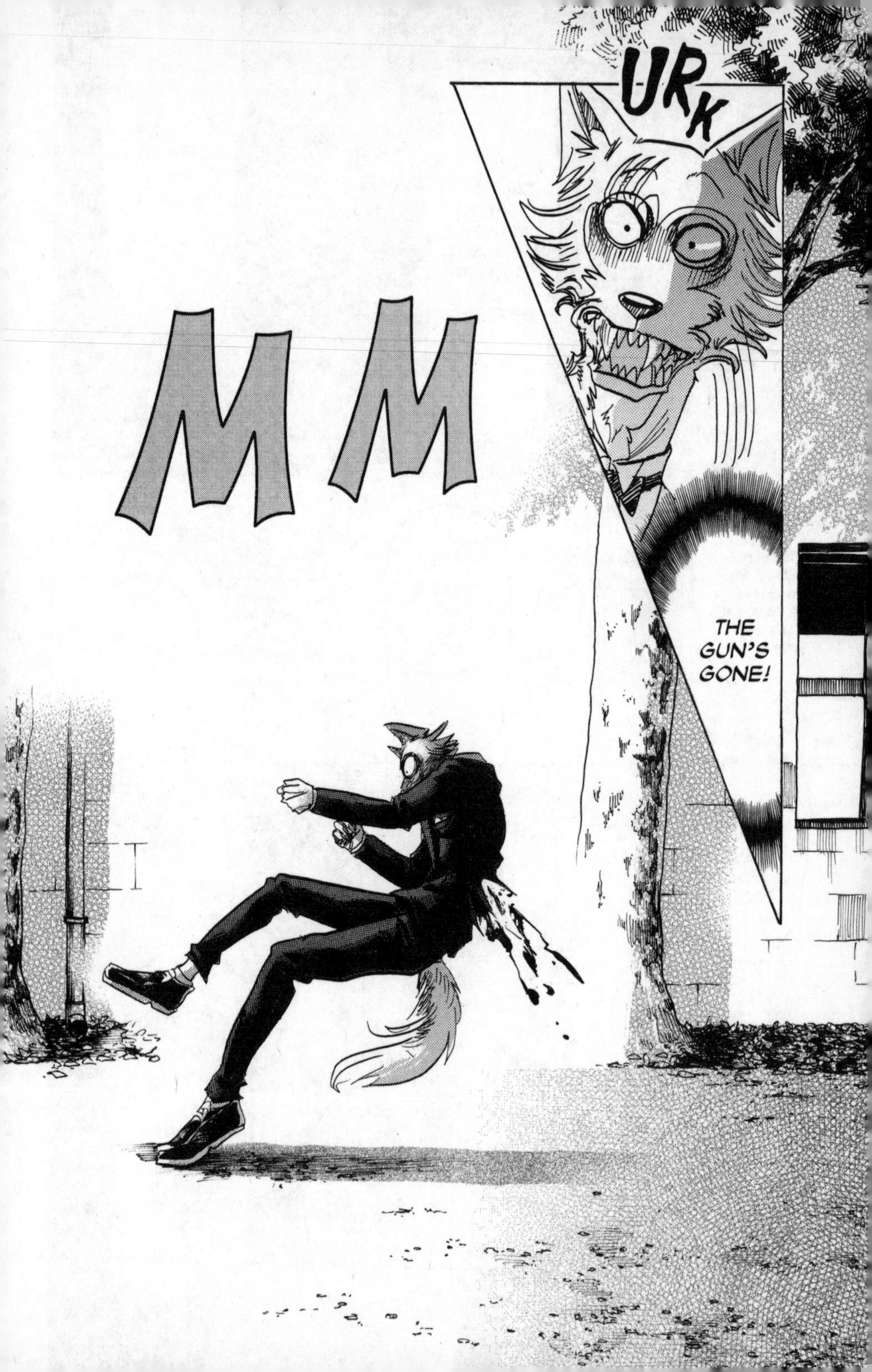
URK
THE GUN'S GONE!
MM

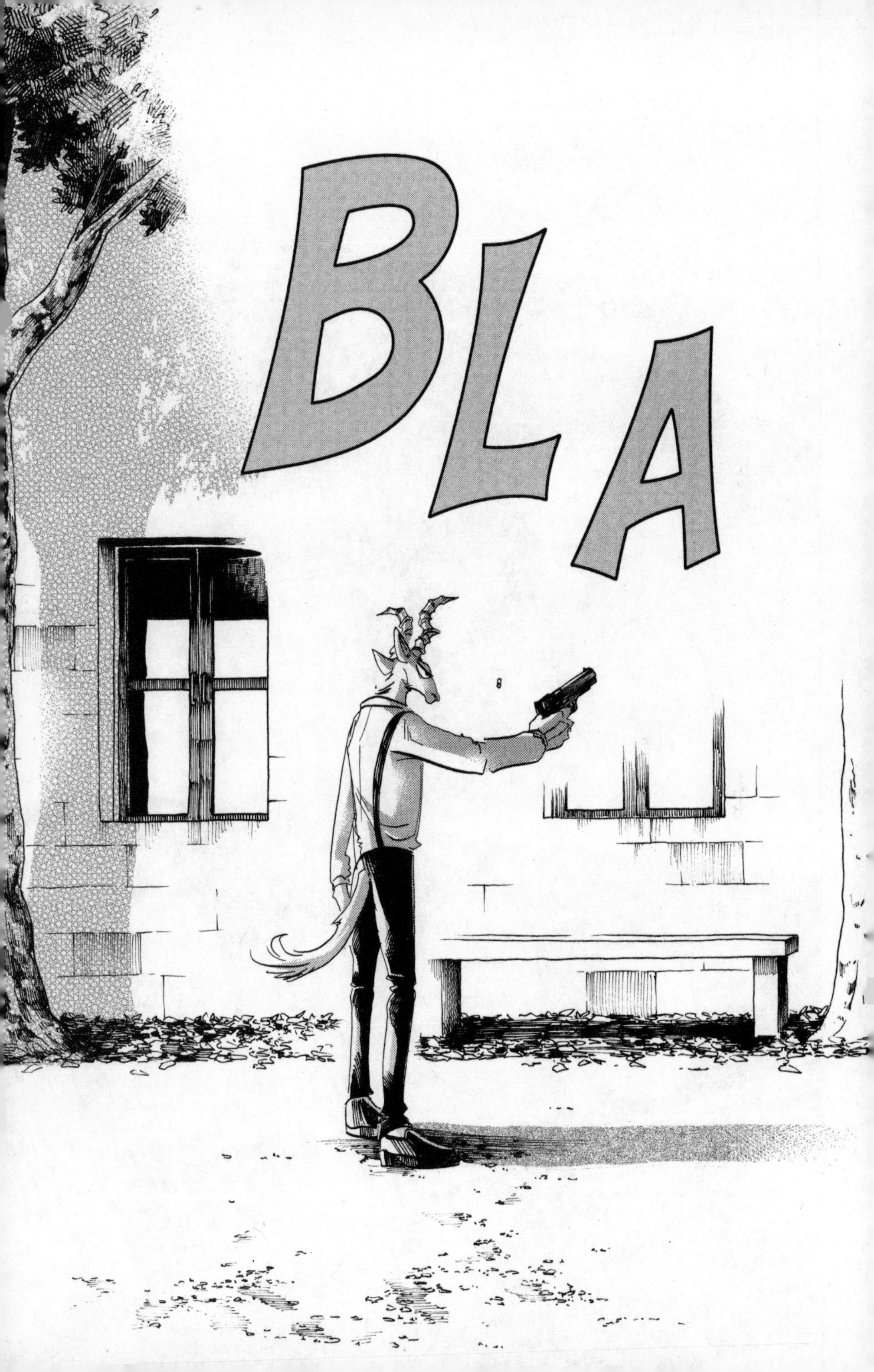
BLA

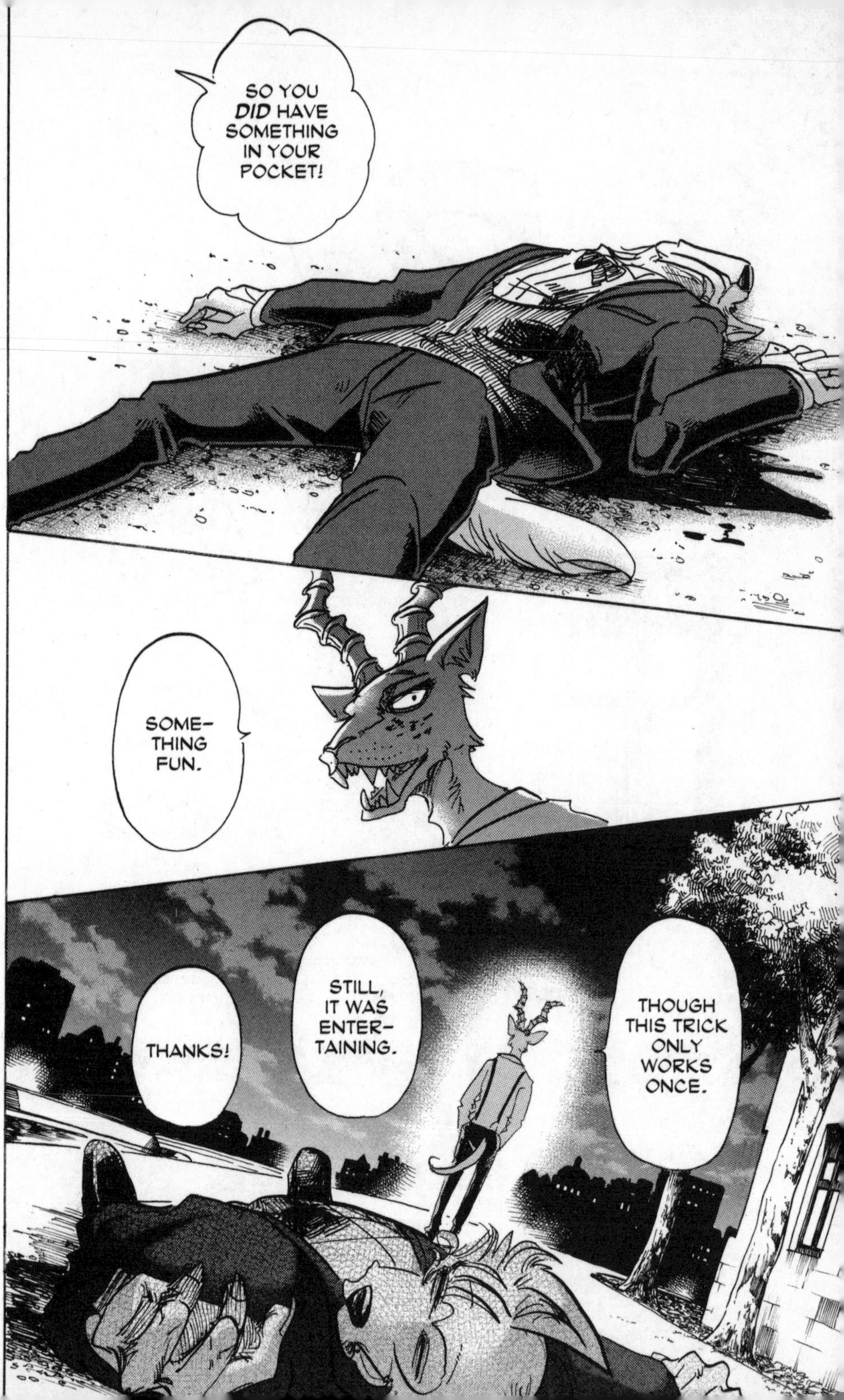
SO YOU *DID* HAVE SOMETHING IN YOUR POCKET!
SOME-THING FUN.
THOUGH THIS TRICK ONLY WORKS ONCE.
STILL, IT WAS ENTER-TAINING.
THANKS!

BEASTARS
Vol. 15

BEASTARS
Vol. 15

Chapter 130: The Lead-Gray Color of His Prosthetic Leg Occasionally Shines like a Rainbow

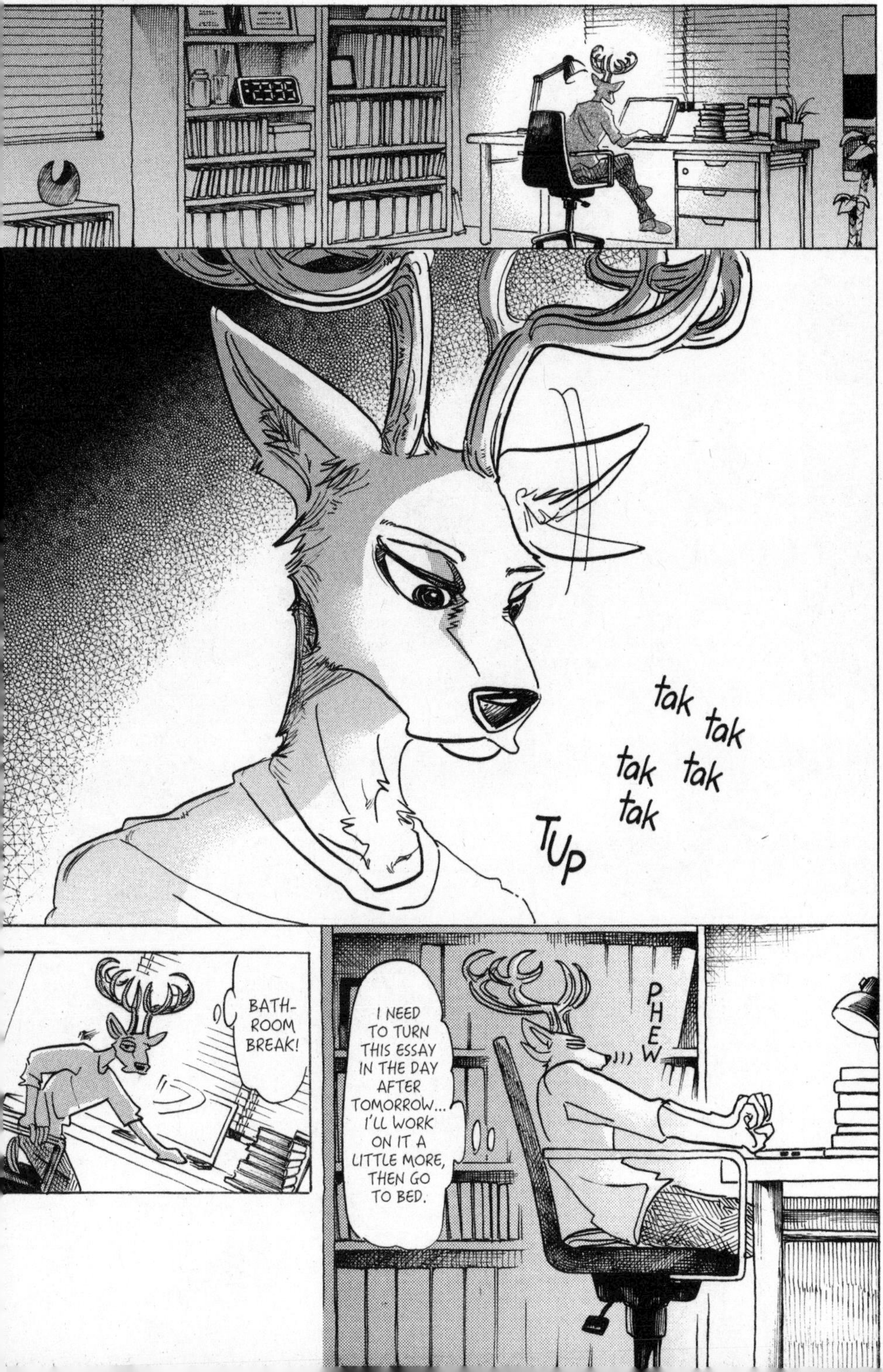
tak tak tak tak tak
TUP
PHEW
I NEED TO TURN THIS ESSAY IN THE DAY AFTER TOMORROW... I'LL WORK ON IT A LITTLE MORE, THEN GO TO BED.
BATH-ROOM BREAK!

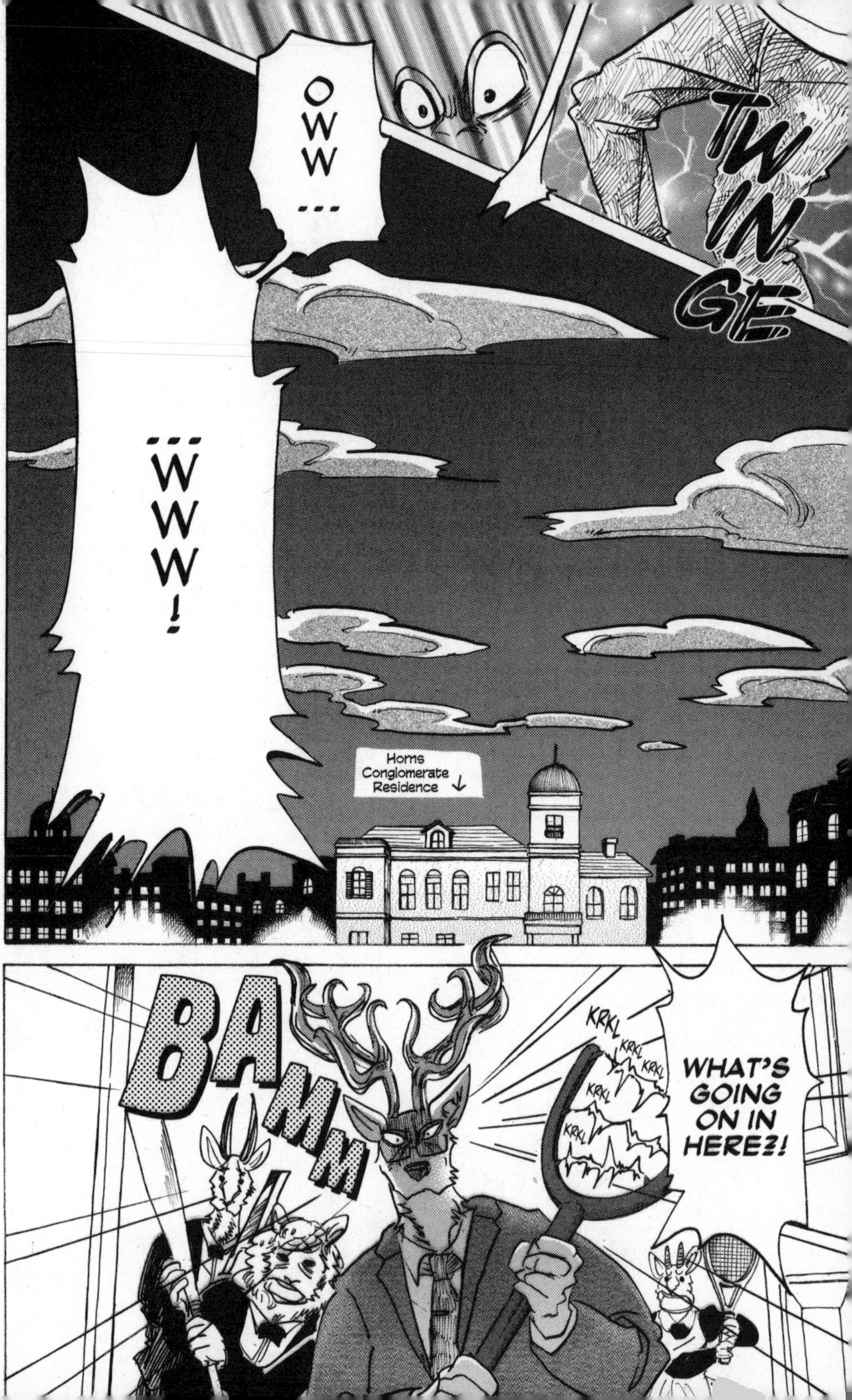
TWINGE
OWW...
...WWW!
Horns Conglomerate Residence
BAMM
KRKL KRKL KRKL KRKL KRKL
WHAT'S GOING ON IN HERE?!

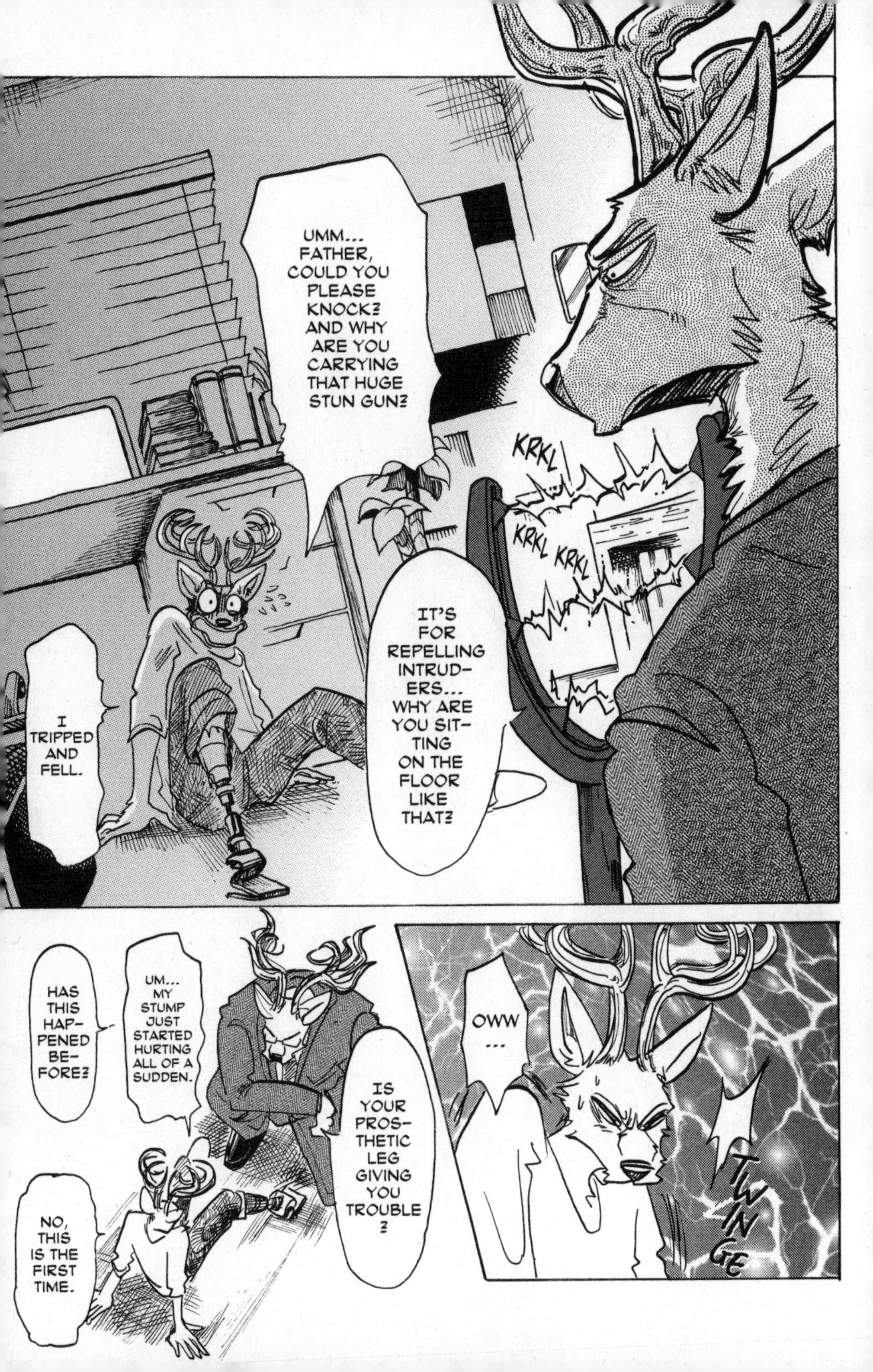
UMM... FATHER, COULD YOU PLEASE KNOCK? AND WHY ARE YOU CARRYING THAT HUGE STUN GUN?
KRKL
KRKL KRKL
IT'S FOR REPELLING INTRUDERS... WHY ARE YOU SITTING ON THE FLOOR LIKE THAT?
I TRIPPED AND FELL.
OWW...
TWINGE
IS YOUR PROSTHETIC LEG GIVING YOU TROUBLE?
UM... MY STUMP JUST STARTED HURTING ALL OF A SUDDEN.
HAS THIS HAPPENED BEFORE?
NO, THIS IS THE FIRST TIME.

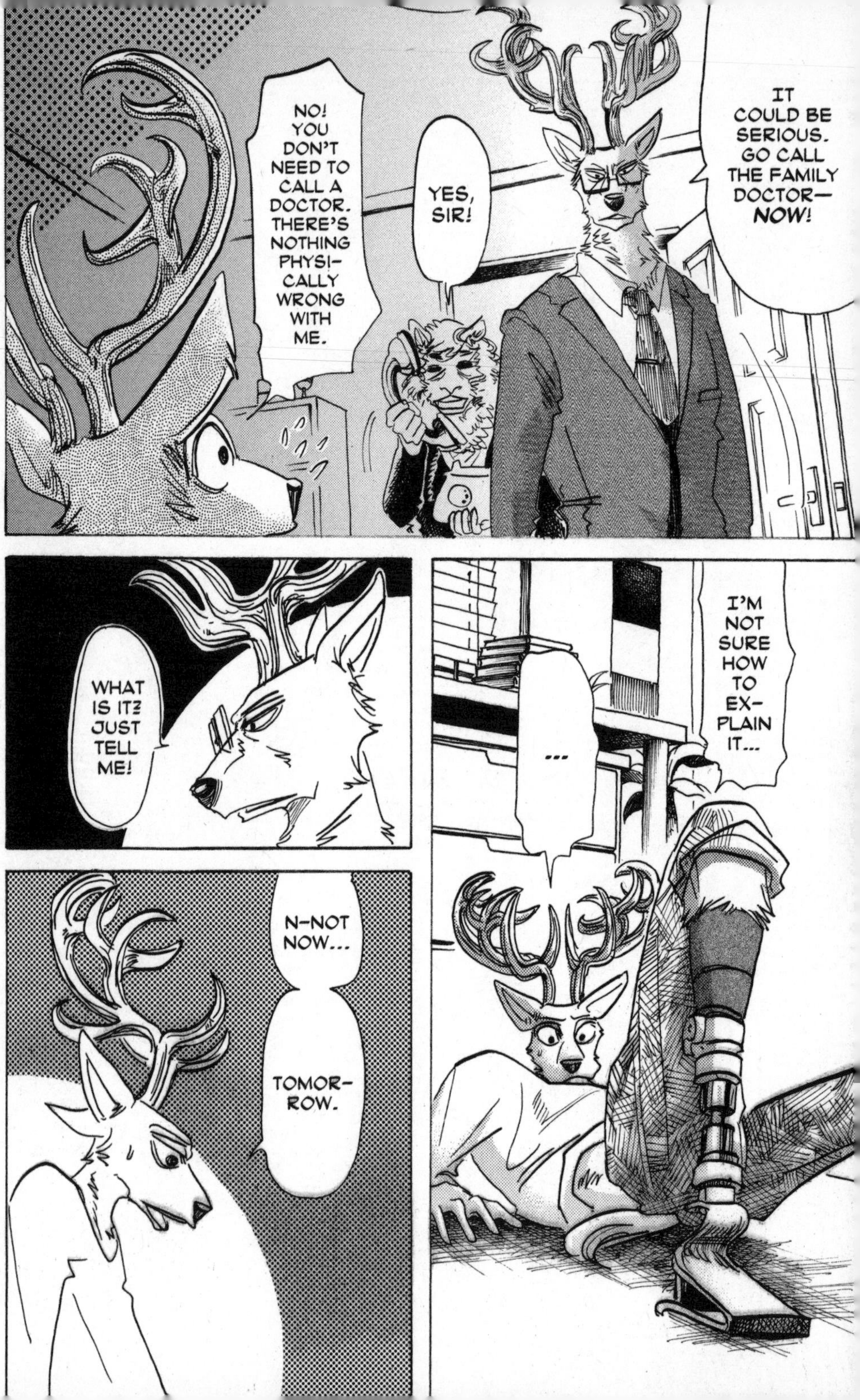
IT COULD BE SERIOUS. GO CALL THE FAMILY DOCTOR—*NOW*!
YES, SIR!
NO! YOU DON'T NEED TO CALL A DOCTOR. THERE'S NOTHING PHYSICALLY WRONG WITH ME.
I'M NOT SURE HOW TO EXPLAIN IT...
...
WHAT IS IT? JUST TELL ME!
N-NOT NOW...
TOMORROW.

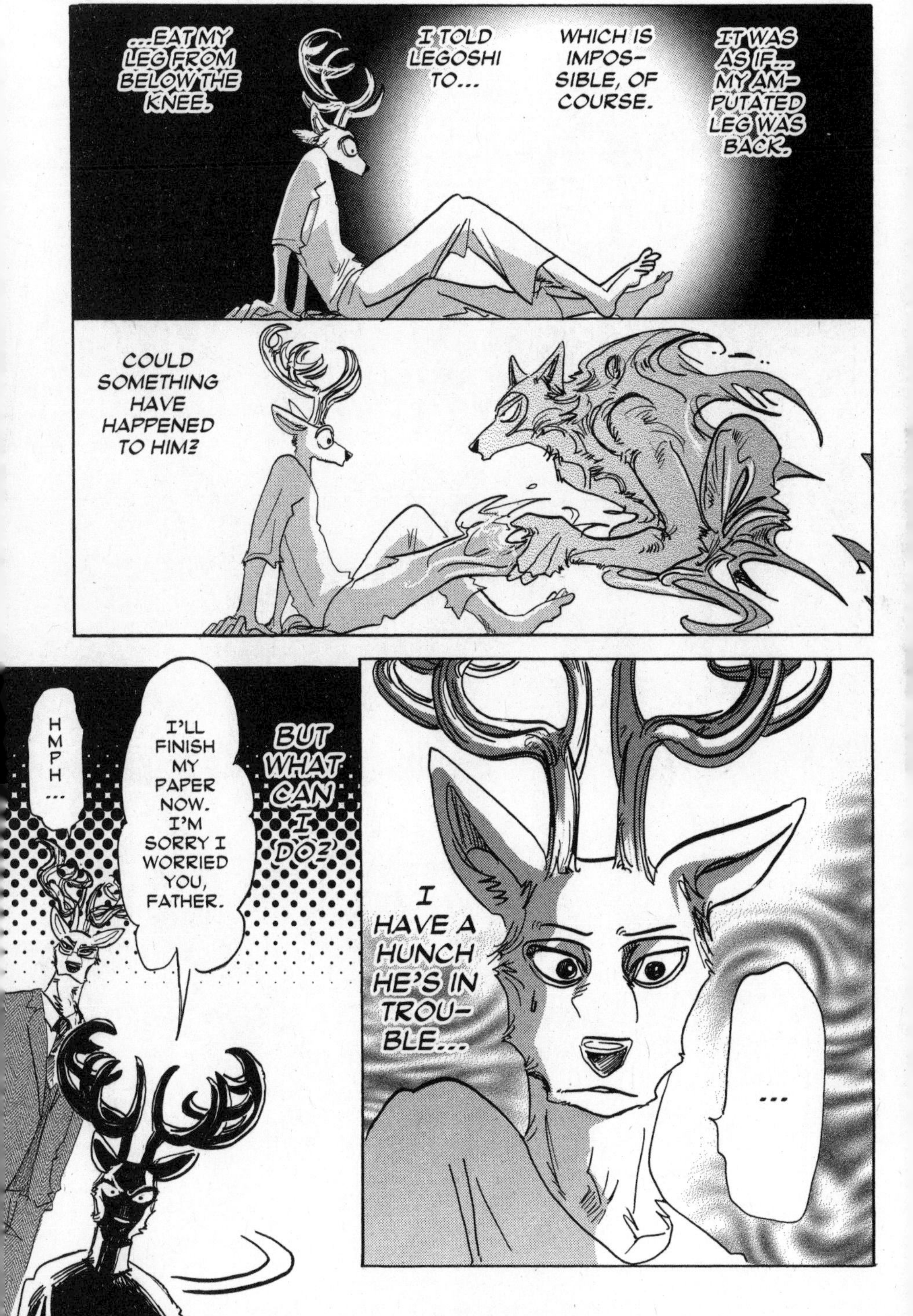
IT WAS AS IF... MY AMPUTATED LEG WAS BACK.
WHICH IS IMPOSSIBLE, OF COURSE.
I TOLD LEGOSHI TO...
...EAT MY LEG FROM BELOW THE KNEE.
COULD SOMETHING HAVE HAPPENED TO HIM?
...
I HAVE A HUNCH HE'S IN TROUBLE...
BUT WHAT CAN I DO?
I'LL FINISH MY PAPER NOW. I'M SORRY I WORRIED YOU, FATHER.
HMPH...

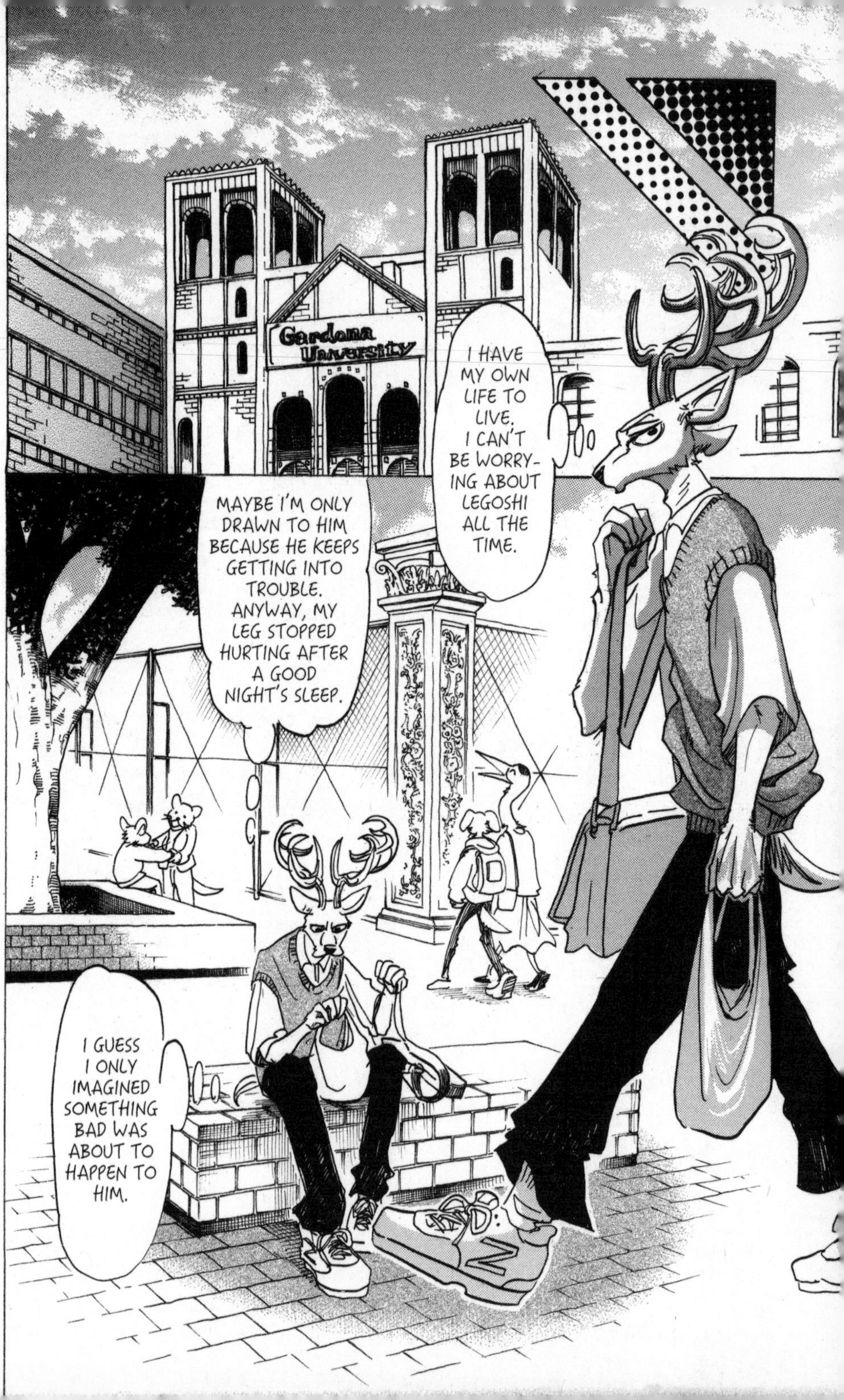
I HAVE MY OWN LIFE TO LIVE. I CAN'T BE WORRYING ABOUT LEGOSHI ALL THE TIME.
Gardona University
MAYBE I'M ONLY DRAWN TO HIM BECAUSE HE KEEPS GETTING INTO TROUBLE. ANYWAY, MY LEG STOPPED HURTING AFTER A GOOD NIGHT'S SLEEP.
I GUESS I ONLY IMAGINED SOMETHING BAD WAS ABOUT TO HAPPEN TO HIM.

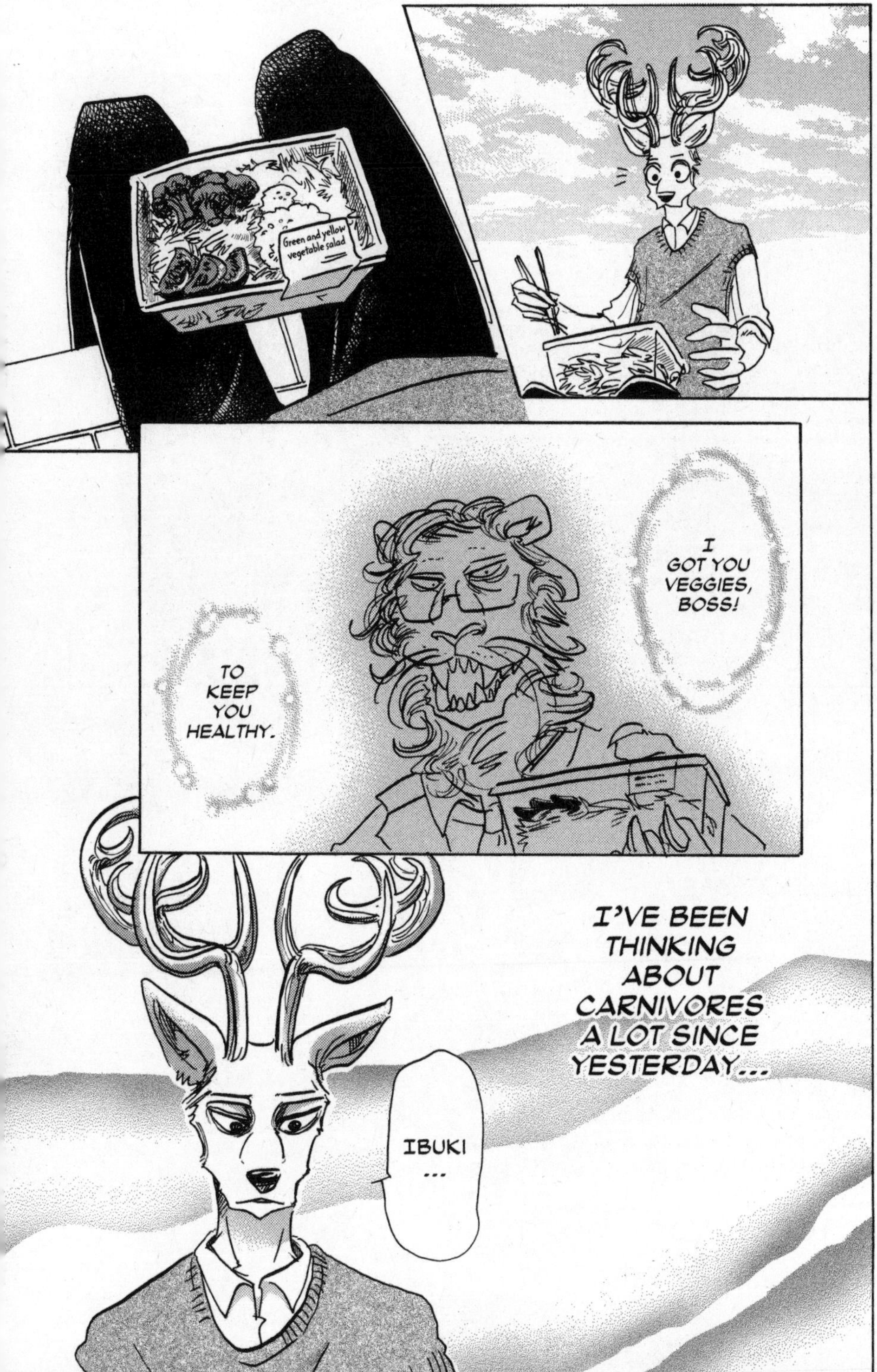
Green and yellow vegetable salad
I GOT YOU VEGGIES, BOSS!
TO KEEP YOU HEALTHY.
I'VE BEEN THINKING ABOUT CARNIVORES A LOT SINCE YESTERDAY...
IBUKI ...

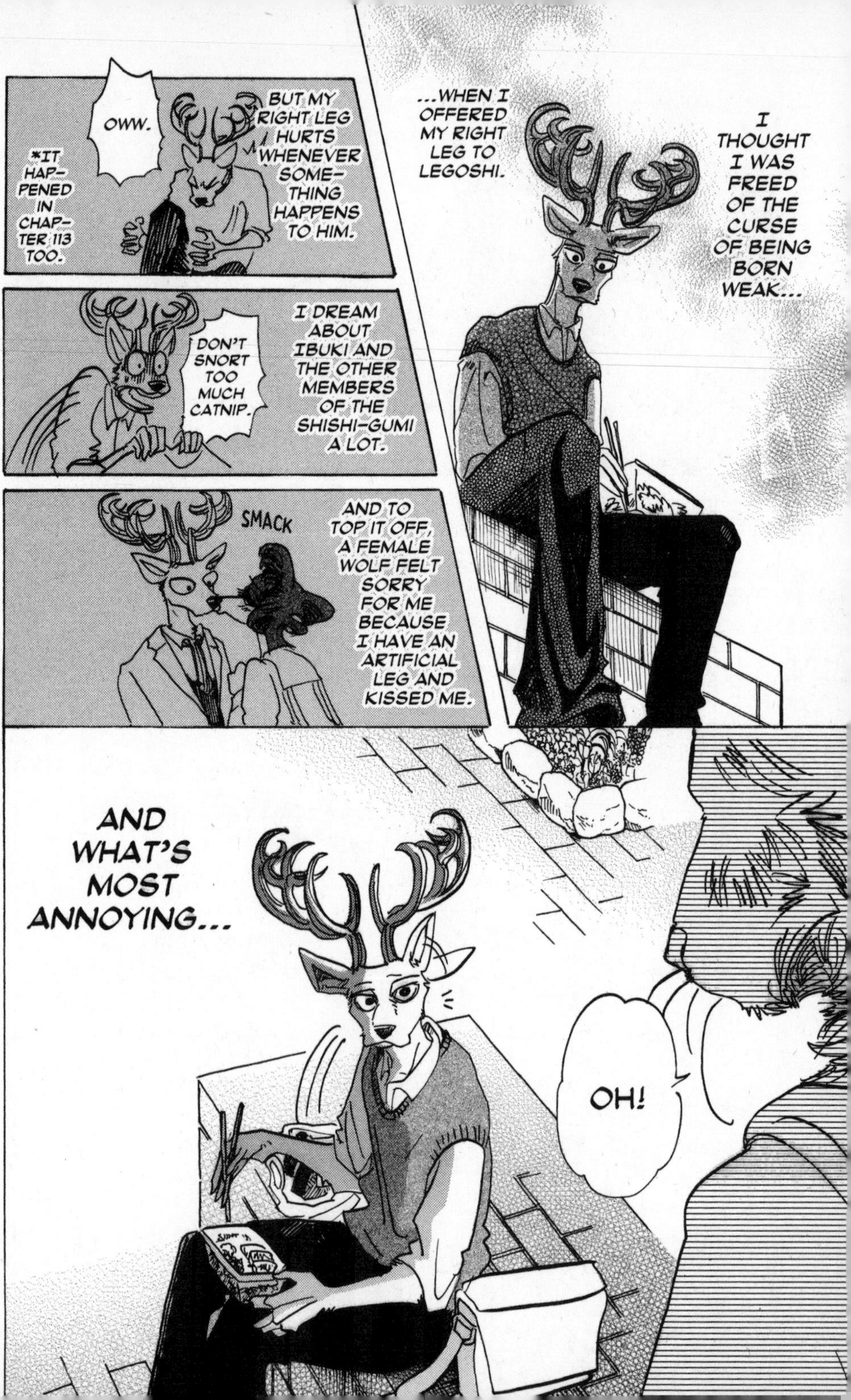
I THOUGHT I WAS FREED OF THE CURSE OF BEING BORN WEAK...
...WHEN I OFFERED MY RIGHT LEG TO LEGOSHI.
BUT MY RIGHT LEG HURTS WHENEVER SOMETHING HAPPENS TO HIM.
OWW.
*IT HAPPENED IN CHAPTER 113 TOO.
I DREAM ABOUT IBUKI AND THE OTHER MEMBERS OF THE SHISHI-GUMI A LOT.
DON'T SNORT TOO MUCH CATNIP.
AND TO TOP IT OFF, A FEMALE WOLF FELT SORRY FOR ME BECAUSE I HAVE AN ARTIFICIAL LEG AND KISSED ME.
SMACK
AND WHAT'S MOST ANNOYING...
OH!

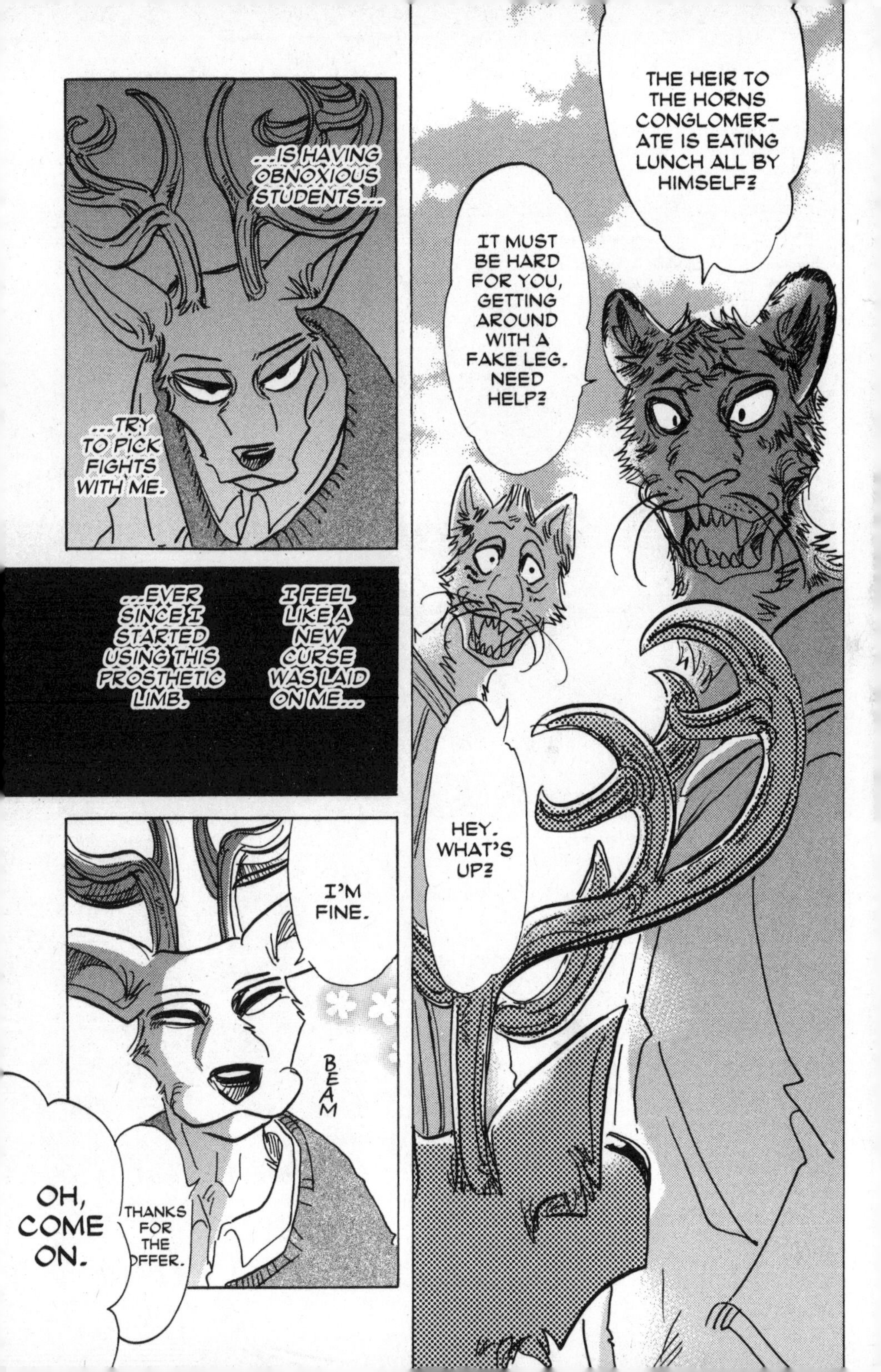
THE HEIR TO THE HORNS CONGLOMERATE IS EATING LUNCH ALL BY HIMSELF?
IT MUST BE HARD FOR YOU, GETTING AROUND WITH A FAKE LEG. NEED HELP?
HEY. WHAT'S UP?
...IS HAVING OBNOXIOUS STUDENTS...
...TRY TO PICK FIGHTS WITH ME.
I FEEL LIKE A NEW CURSE WAS LAID ON ME...
...EVER SINCE I STARTED USING THIS PROSTHETIC LIMB.
I'M FINE.
BEAM
THANKS FOR THE OFFER.
OH, COME ON.

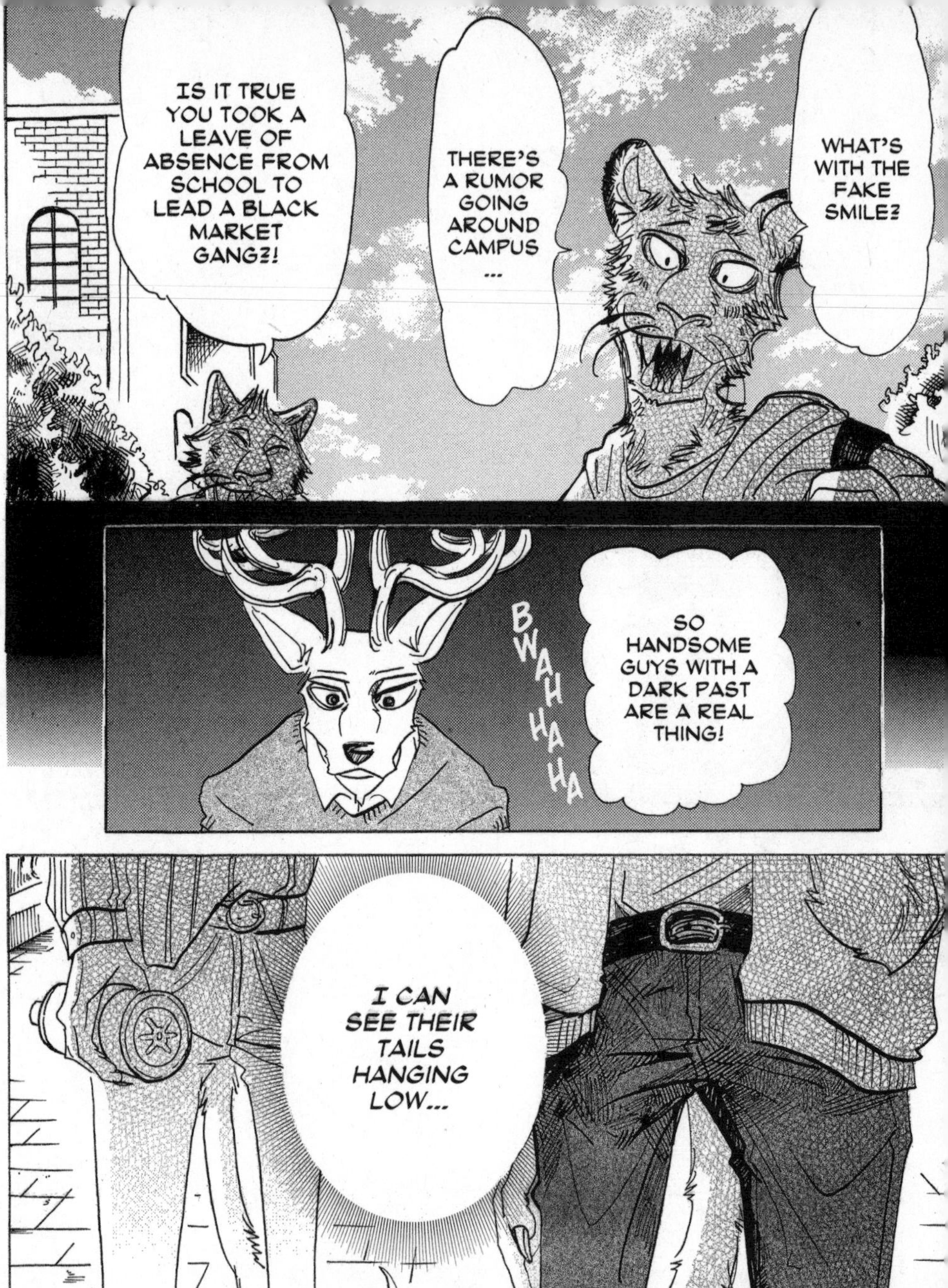
WHAT'S WITH THE FAKE SMILE?
THERE'S A RUMOR GOING AROUND CAMPUS ...
IS IT TRUE YOU TOOK A LEAVE OF ABSENCE FROM SCHOOL TO LEAD A BLACK MARKET GANG?!
SO HANDSOME GUYS WITH A DARK PAST ARE A REAL THING!
BWAHAHAHA
I CAN SEE THEIR TAILS HANGING LOW...

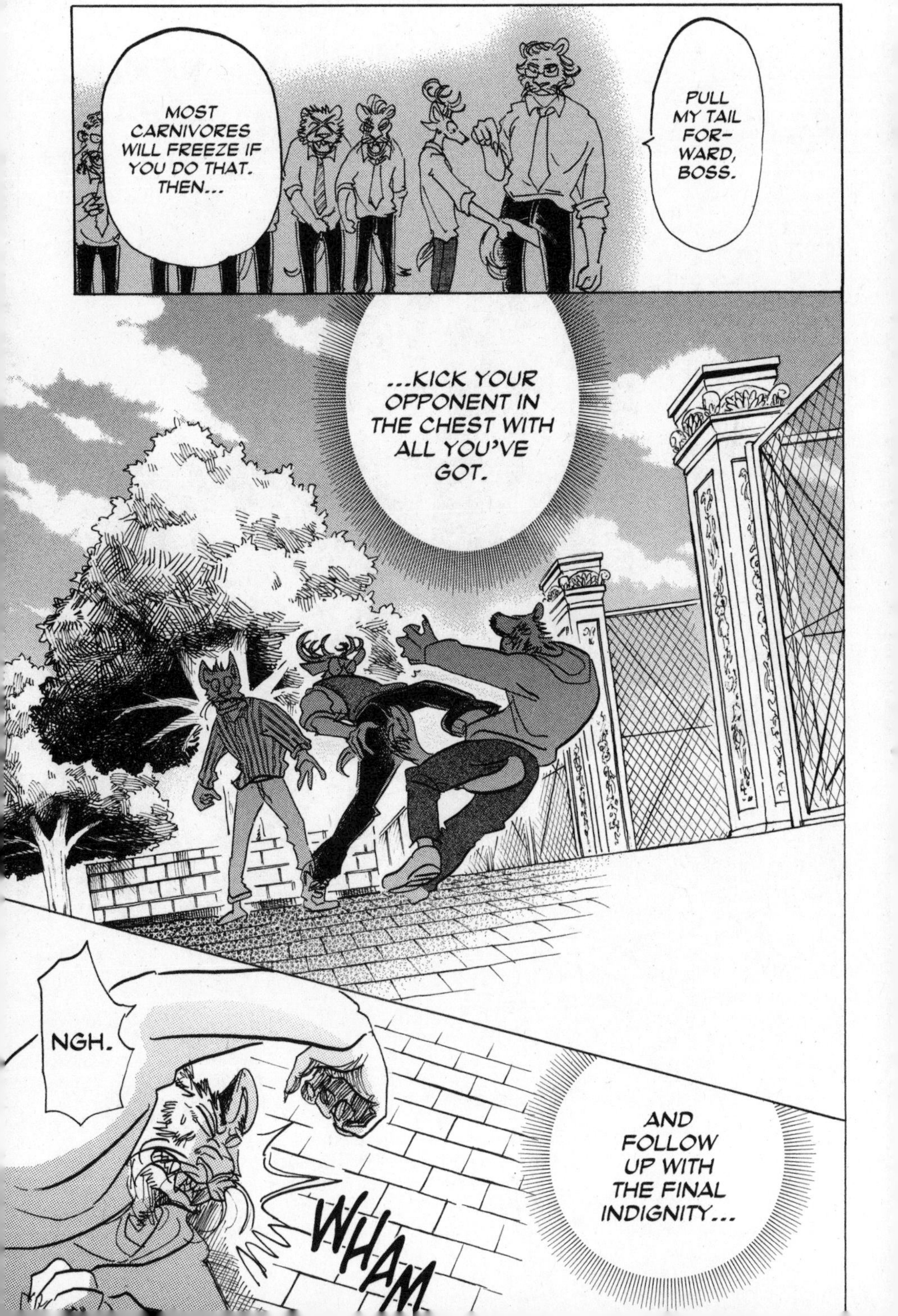
PULL MY TAIL FOR-WARD, BOSS.
MOST CARNIVORES WILL FREEZE IF YOU DO THAT. THEN...
...KICK YOUR OPPONENT IN THE CHEST WITH ALL YOU'VE GOT.
AND FOLLOW UP WITH THE FINAL INDIGNITY...
NGH.
WHAM

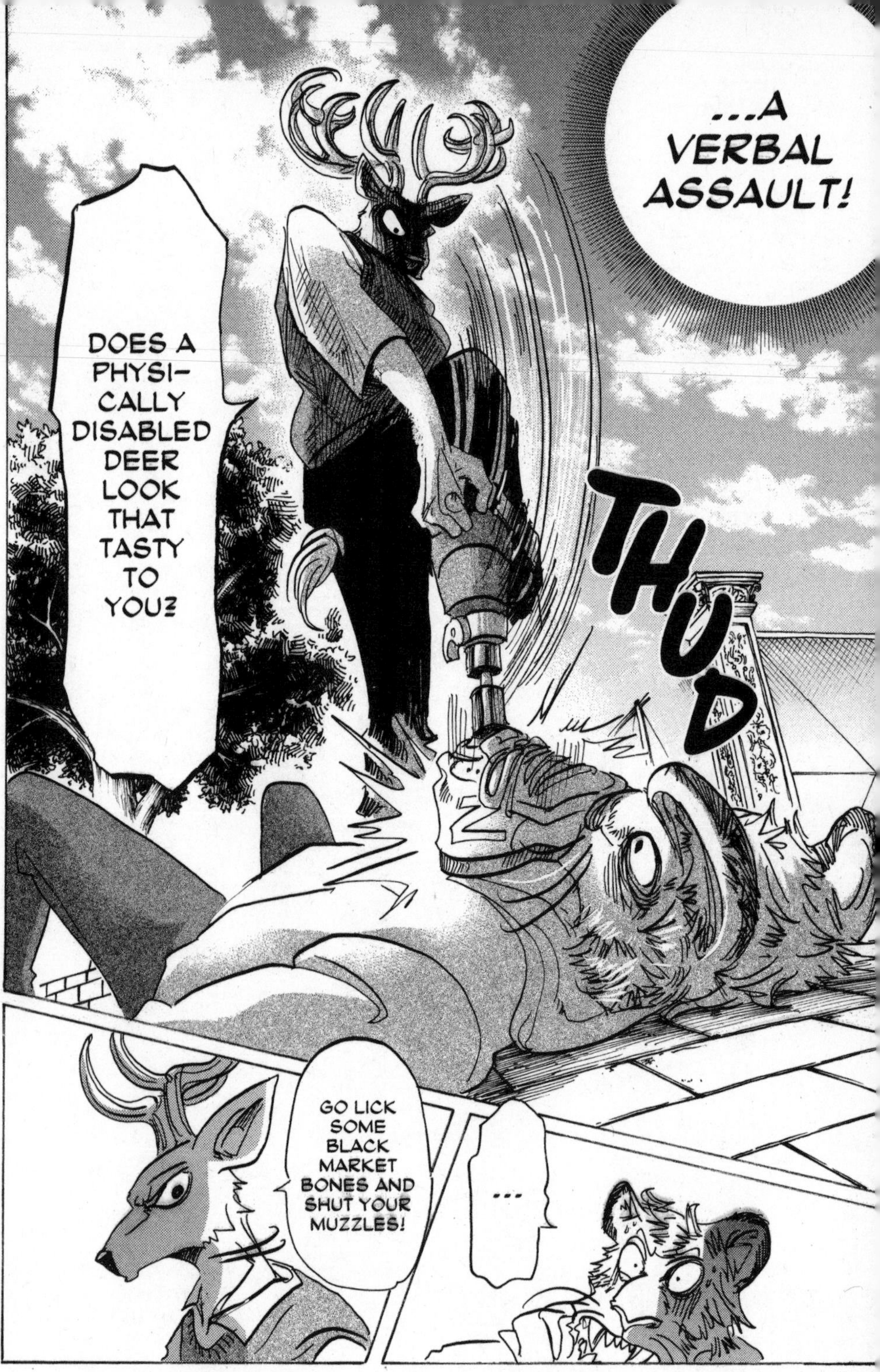
...A VERBAL ASSAULT!
DOES A PHYSICALLY DISABLED DEER LOOK THAT TASTY TO YOU?
THUD
...
GO LICK SOME BLACK MARKET BONES AND SHUT YOUR MUZZLES!

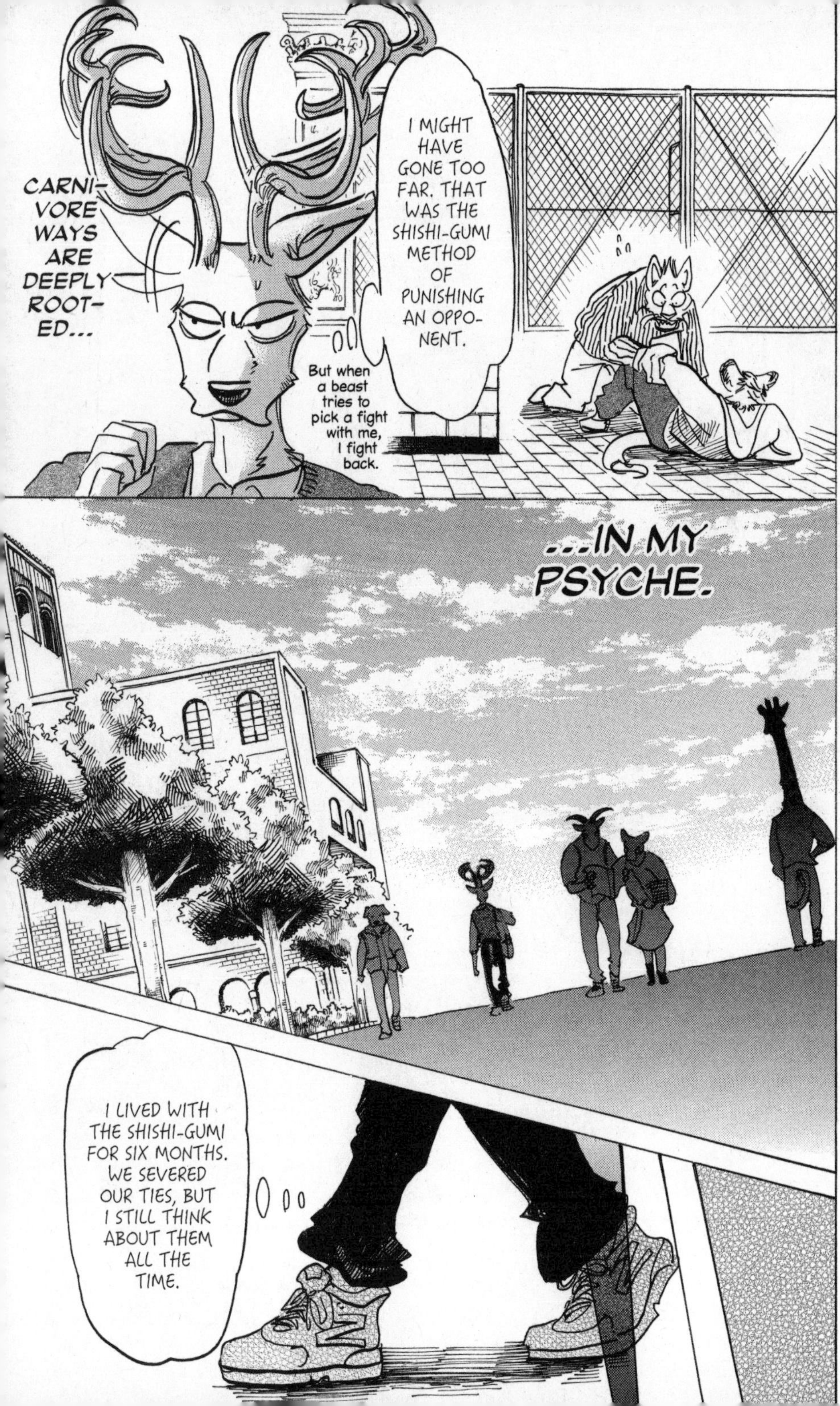
I MIGHT HAVE GONE TOO FAR. THAT WAS THE SHISHI-GUMI METHOD OF PUNISHING AN OPPO-NENT.
But when a beast tries to pick a fight with me, I fight back.
CARNI-VORE WAYS ARE DEEPLY ROOT-ED...
...IN MY PSYCHE.
I LIVED WITH THE SHISHI-GUMI FOR SIX MONTHS. WE SEVERED OUR TIES, BUT I STILL THINK ABOUT THEM ALL THE TIME.

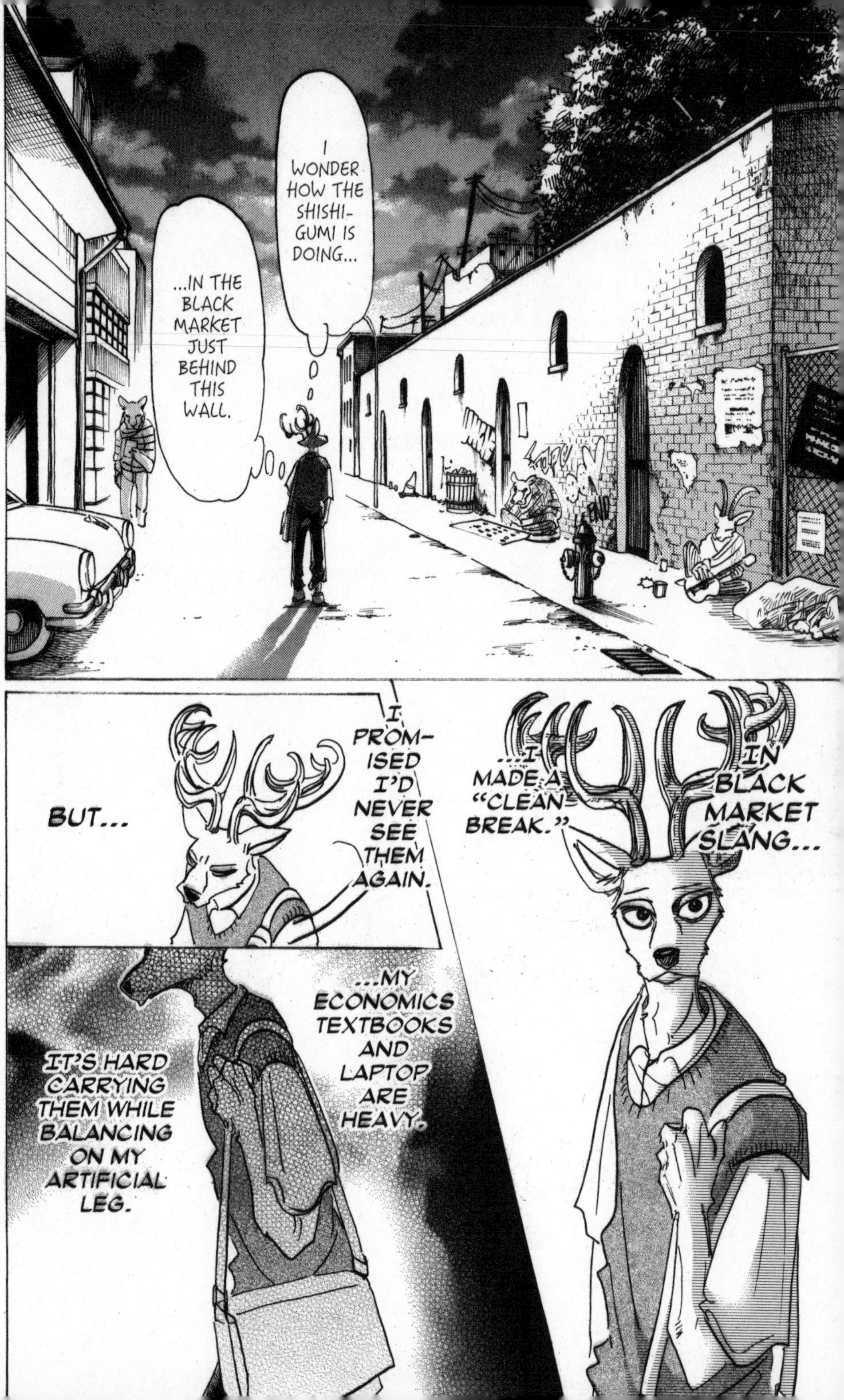
I WONDER HOW THE SHISHI-GUMI IS DOING...
...IN THE BLACK MARKET JUST BEHIND THIS WALL.
IN BLACK MARKET SLANG...
...I MADE A "CLEAN BREAK."
I PROMISED I'D NEVER SEE THEM AGAIN.
BUT...
...MY ECONOMICS TEXTBOOKS AND LAPTOP ARE HEAVY.
IT'S HARD CARRYING THEM WHILE BALANCING ON MY ARTIFICIAL LEG.

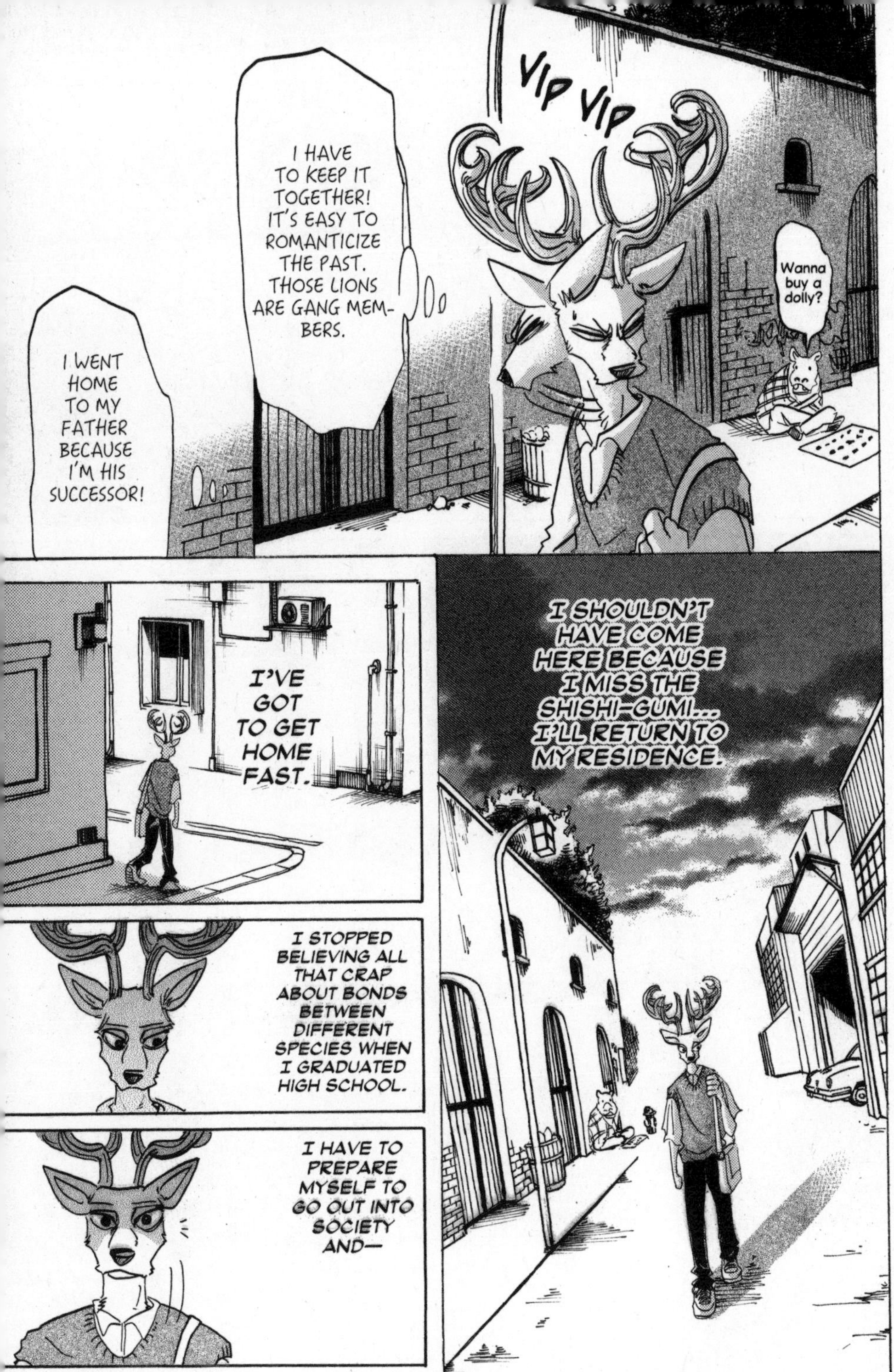
VIP VIP
Wanna buy a dolly?
I HAVE TO KEEP IT TOGETHER! IT'S EASY TO ROMANTICIZE THE PAST. THOSE LIONS ARE GANG MEMBERS.
I WENT HOME TO MY FATHER BECAUSE I'M HIS SUCCESSOR!
I SHOULDN'T HAVE COME HERE BECAUSE I MISS THE SHISHI-GUMI... I'LL RETURN TO MY RESIDENCE.
I'VE GOT TO GET HOME FAST.
I STOPPED BELIEVING ALL THAT CRAP ABOUT BONDS BETWEEN DIFFERENT SPECIES WHEN I GRADUATED HIGH SCHOOL.
I HAVE TO PREPARE MYSELF TO GO OUT INTO SOCIETY AND—

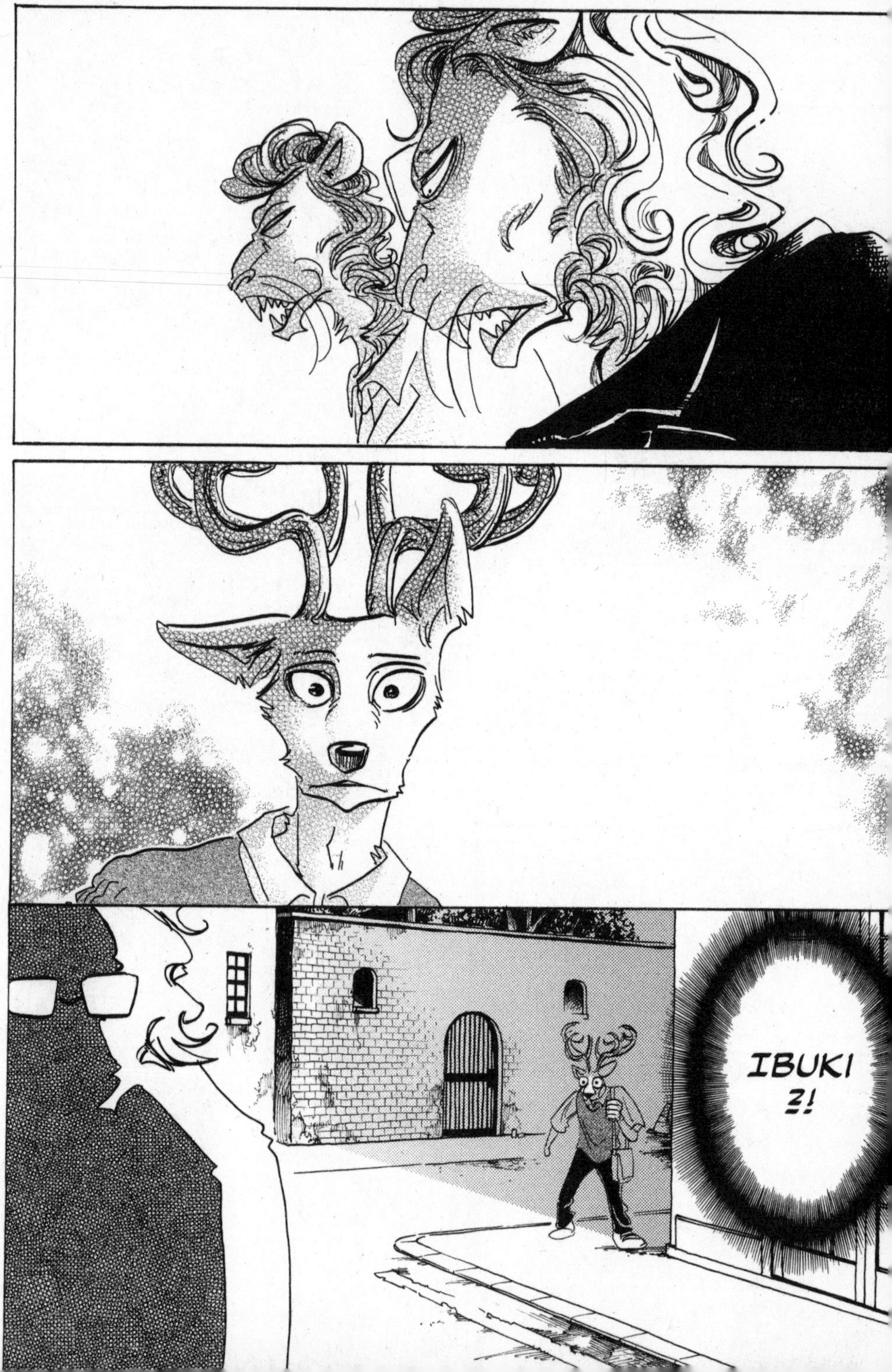
IBUKI
?!

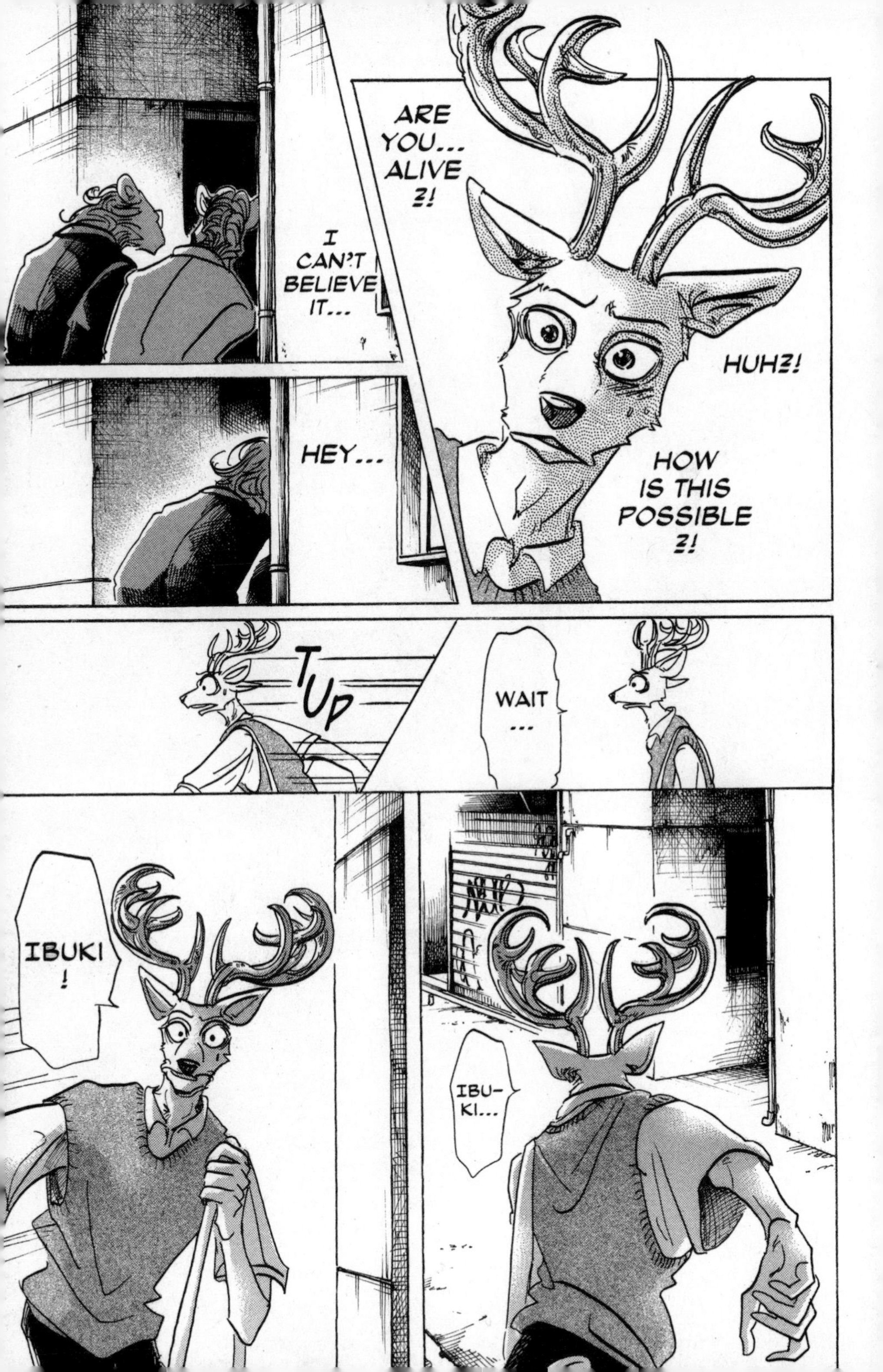
ARE YOU... ALIVE?!
HUH?!
HOW IS THIS POSSIBLE?!
I CAN'T BELIEVE IT...
HEY...
WAIT...
TUP
IBUKI...
IBUKI!

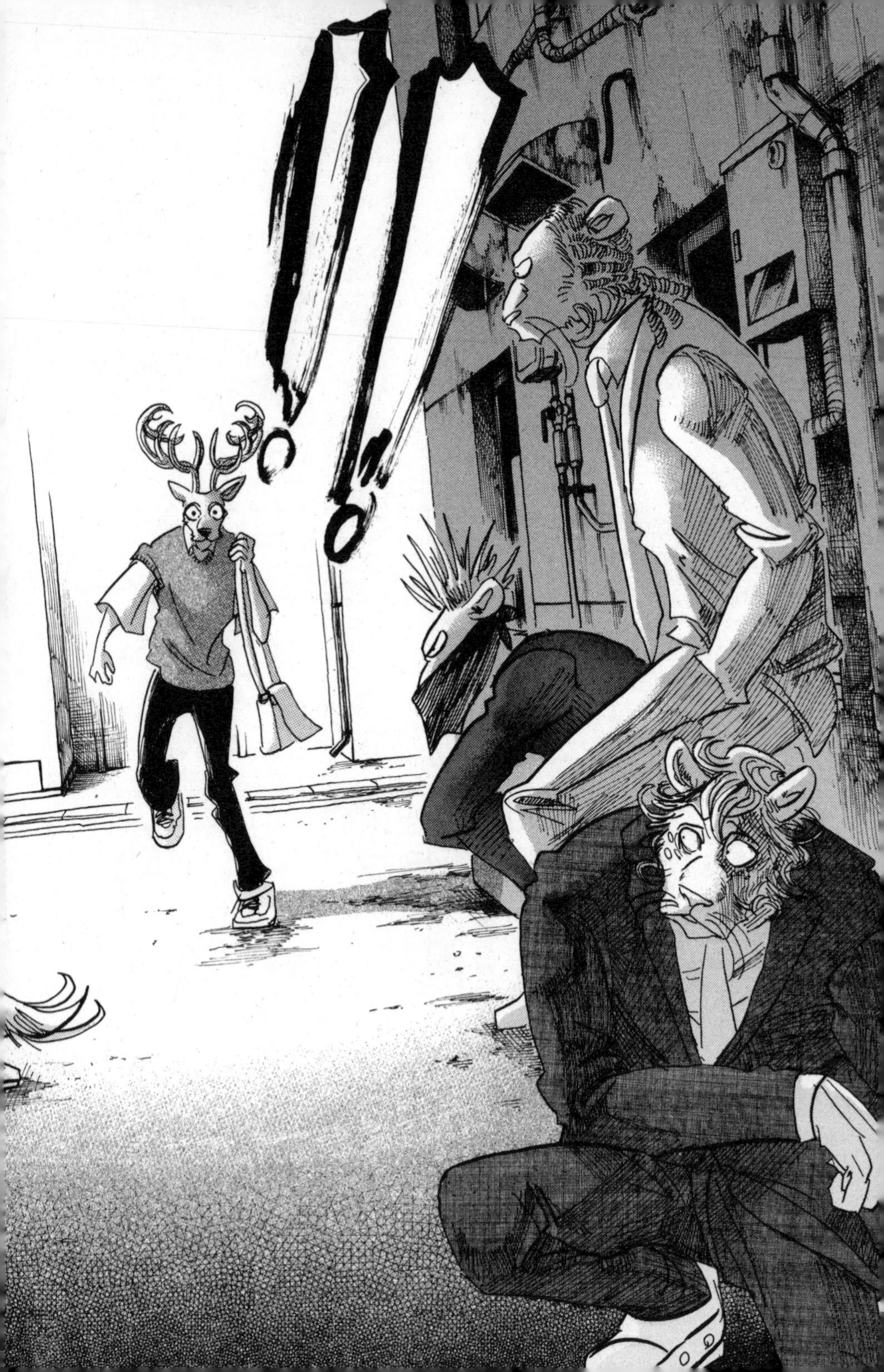
!!

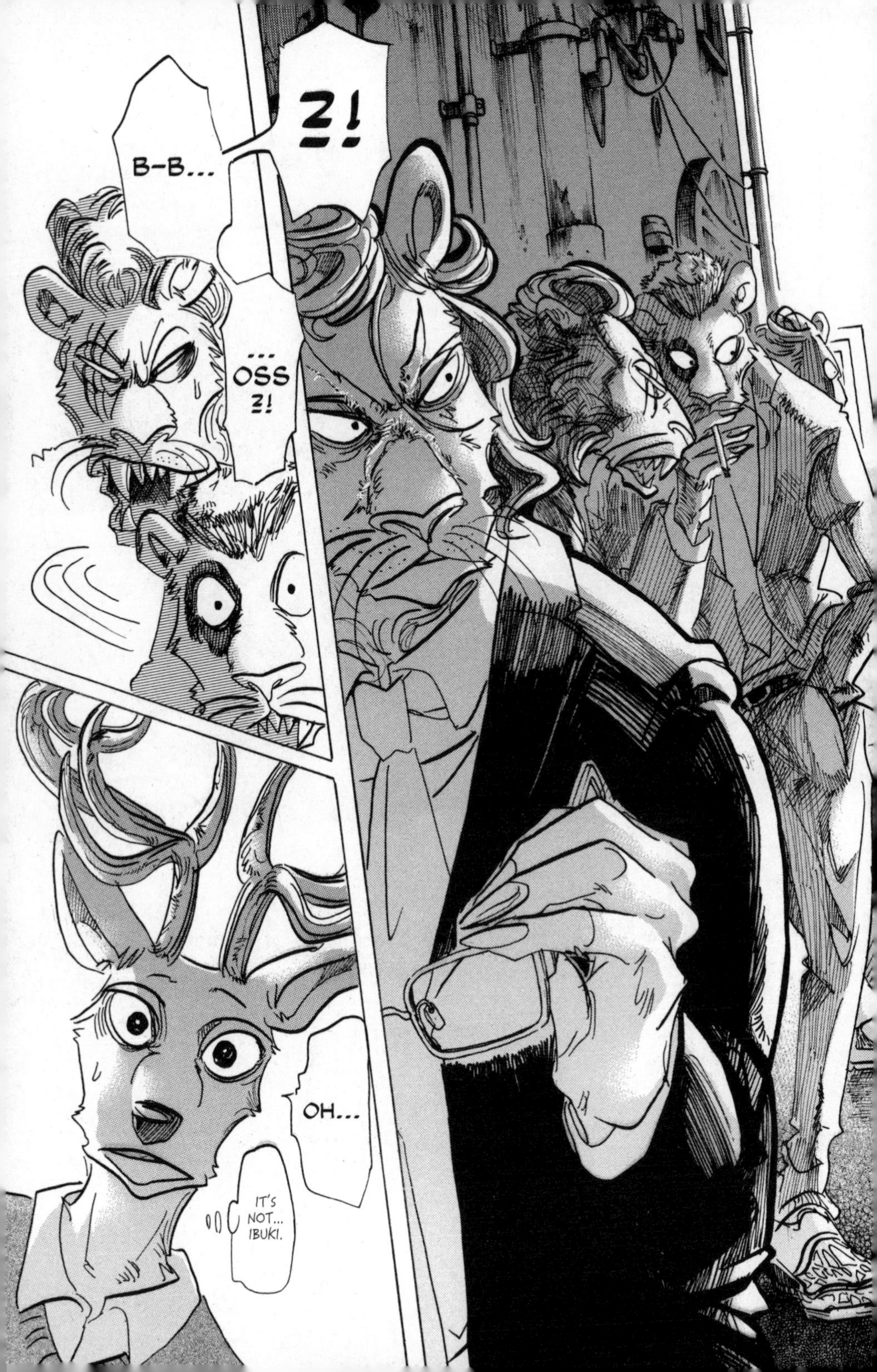
?!
B-B...
...OSS?!
OH...
IT'S NOT... IBUKI.

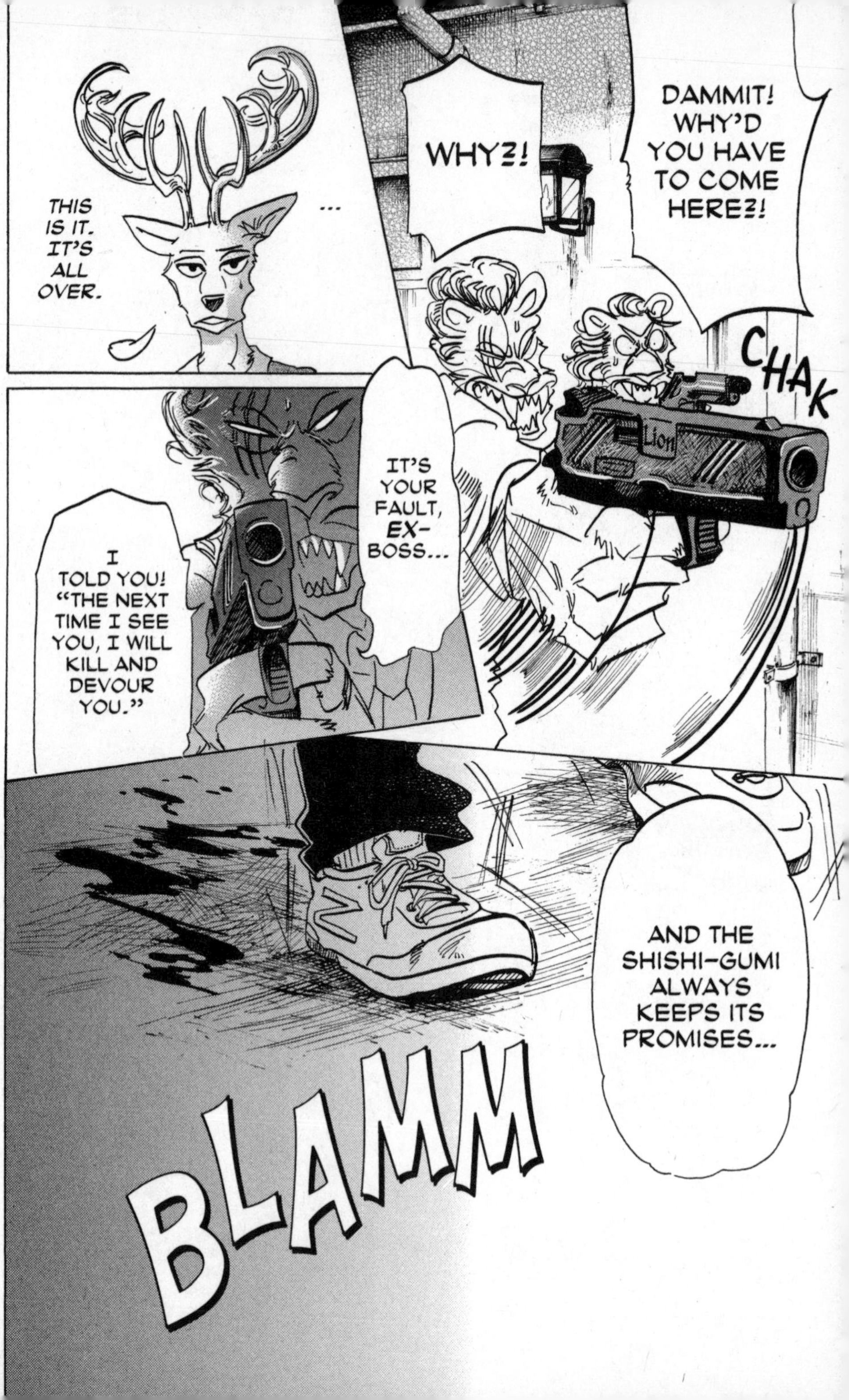
DAMMIT! WHY'D YOU HAVE TO COME HERE?!
WHY?!
CHAK
IT'S YOUR FAULT, EX-BOSS...
...
THIS IS IT. IT'S ALL OVER.
I TOLD YOU! "THE NEXT TIME I SEE YOU, I WILL KILL AND DEVOUR YOU."
AND THE SHISHI-GUMI ALWAYS KEEPS ITS PROMISES...
BLAMM

Chapter 131: Making a Catnip Flower Crown by Force

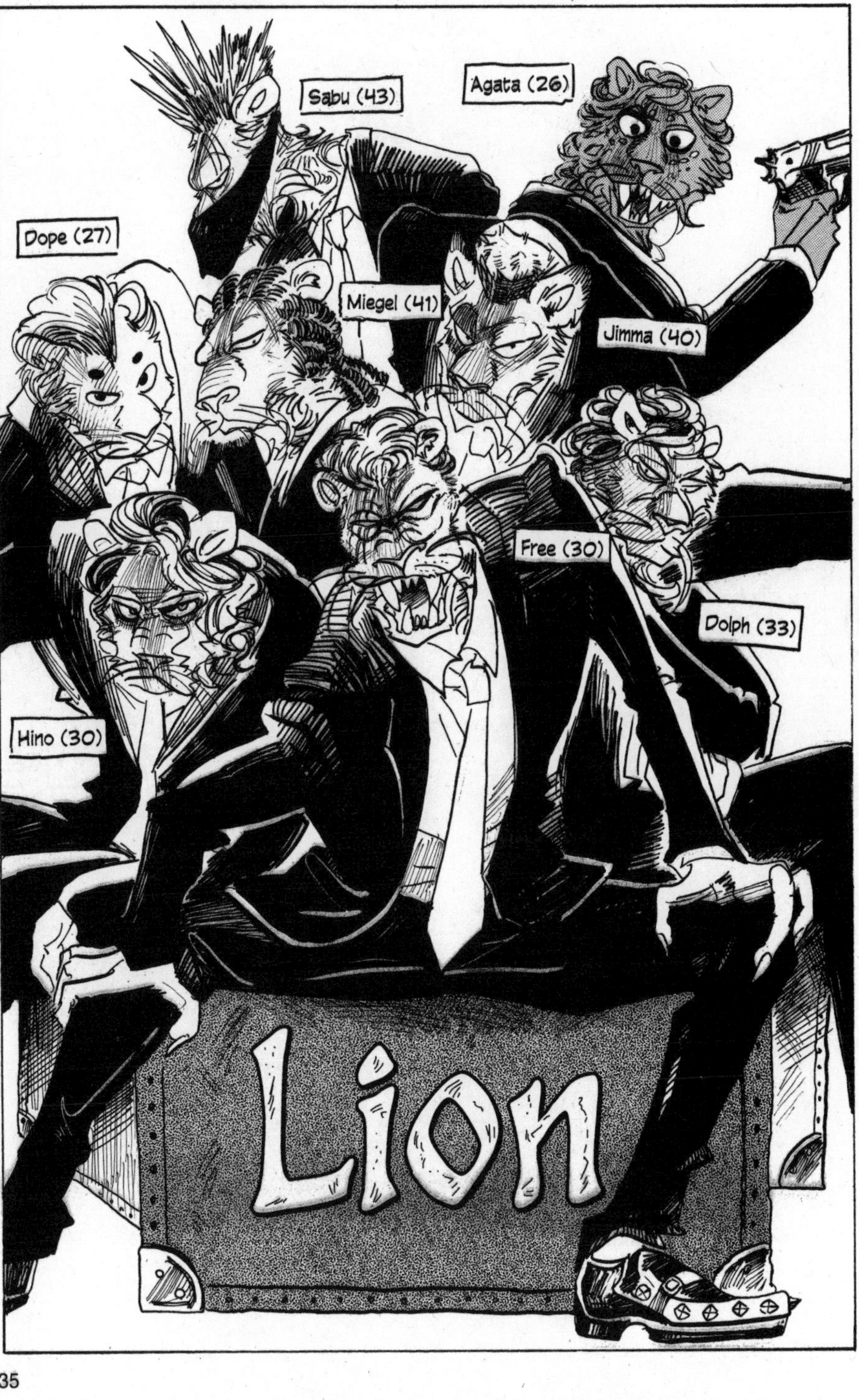

Agata (26)
Sabu (43)
Dope (27)
Miegel (41)
Jimma (40)
Free (30)
Dolph (33)
Hino (30)
Lion

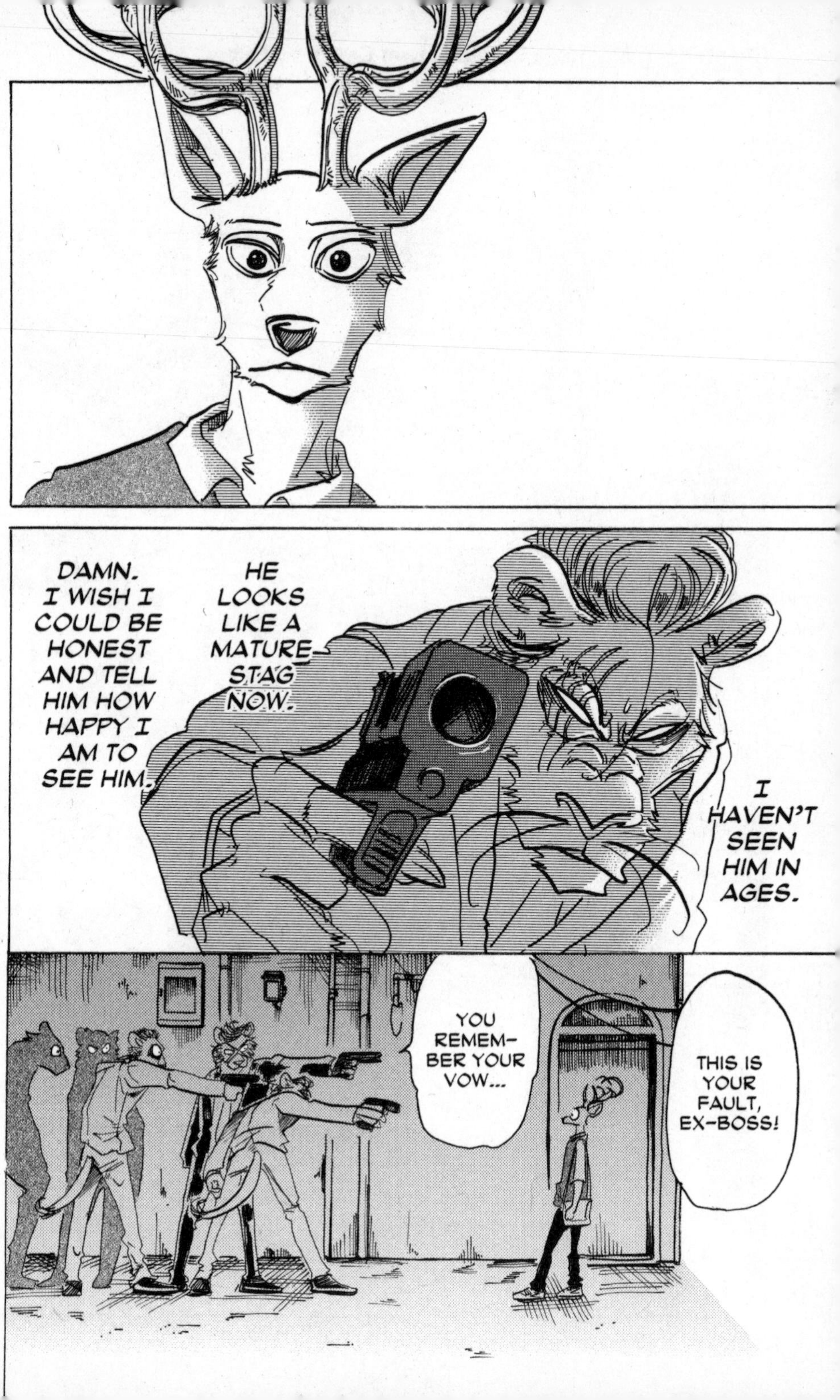
I HAVEN'T SEEN HIM IN AGES.
HE LOOKS LIKE A MATURE STAG NOW.
DAMN. I WISH I COULD BE HONEST AND TELL HIM HOW HAPPY I AM TO SEE HIM.
THIS IS YOUR FAULT, EX-BOSS!
YOU REMEMBER YOUR VOW...

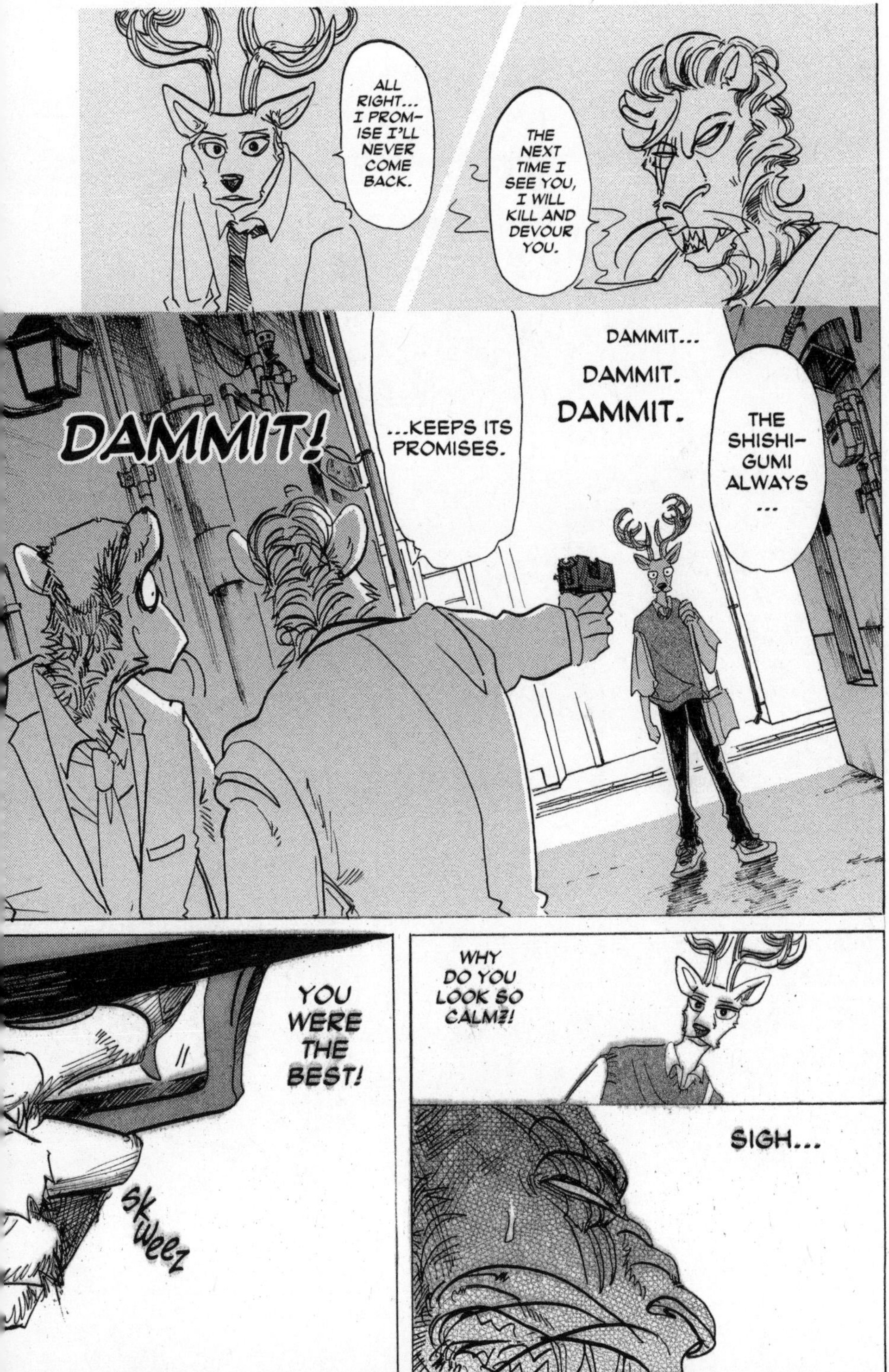
THE NEXT TIME I SEE YOU, I WILL KILL AND DEVOUR YOU.
ALL RIGHT... I PROMISE I'LL NEVER COME BACK.
THE SHISHI-GUMI ALWAYS ...
DAMMIT...
DAMMIT.
DAMMIT.
...KEEPS ITS PROMISES.
DAMMIT!
WHY DO YOU LOOK SO CALM?!
SIGH...
YOU WERE THE BEST!
SKWEEZ

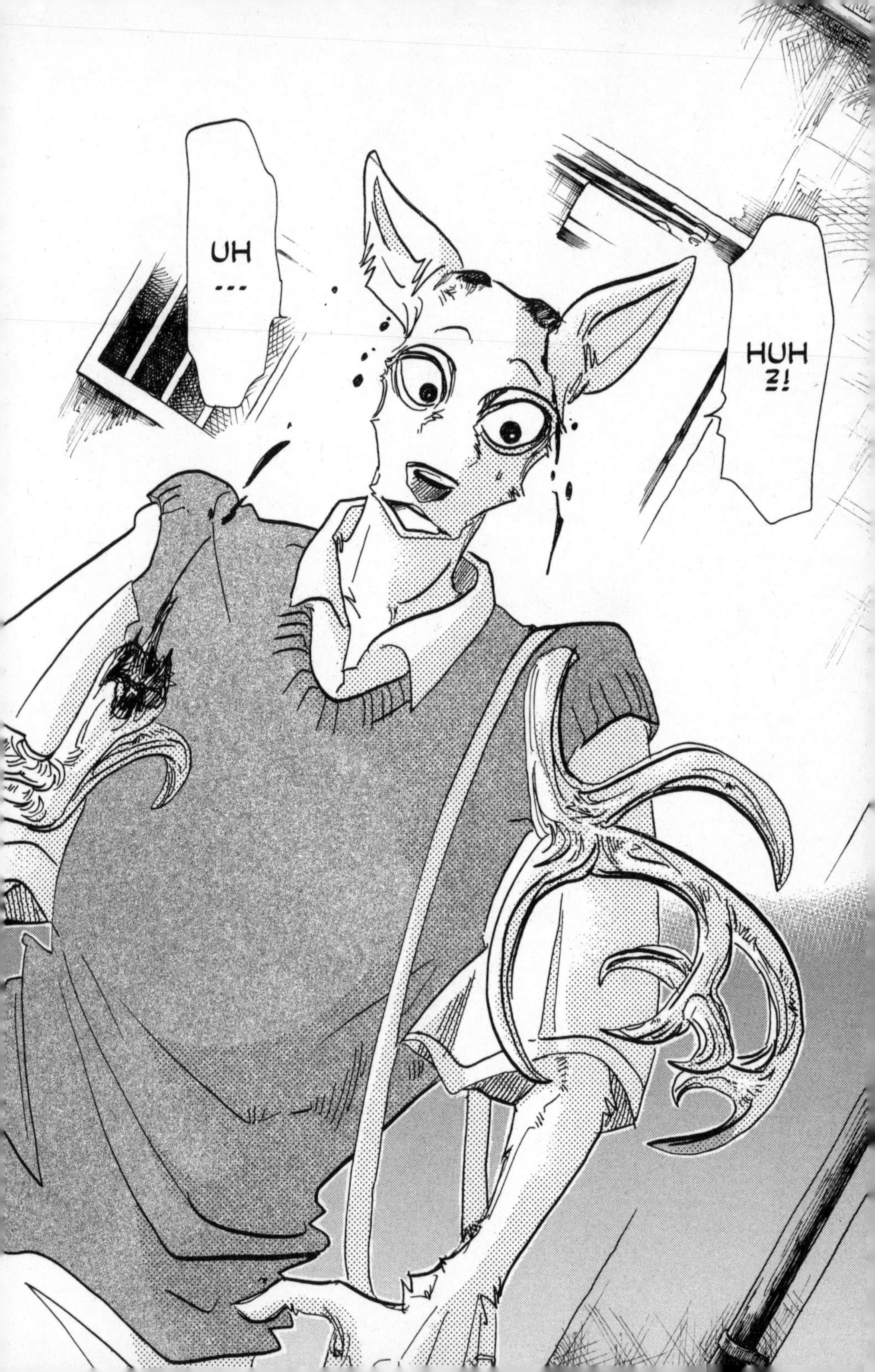
HUH ?!
UH ...

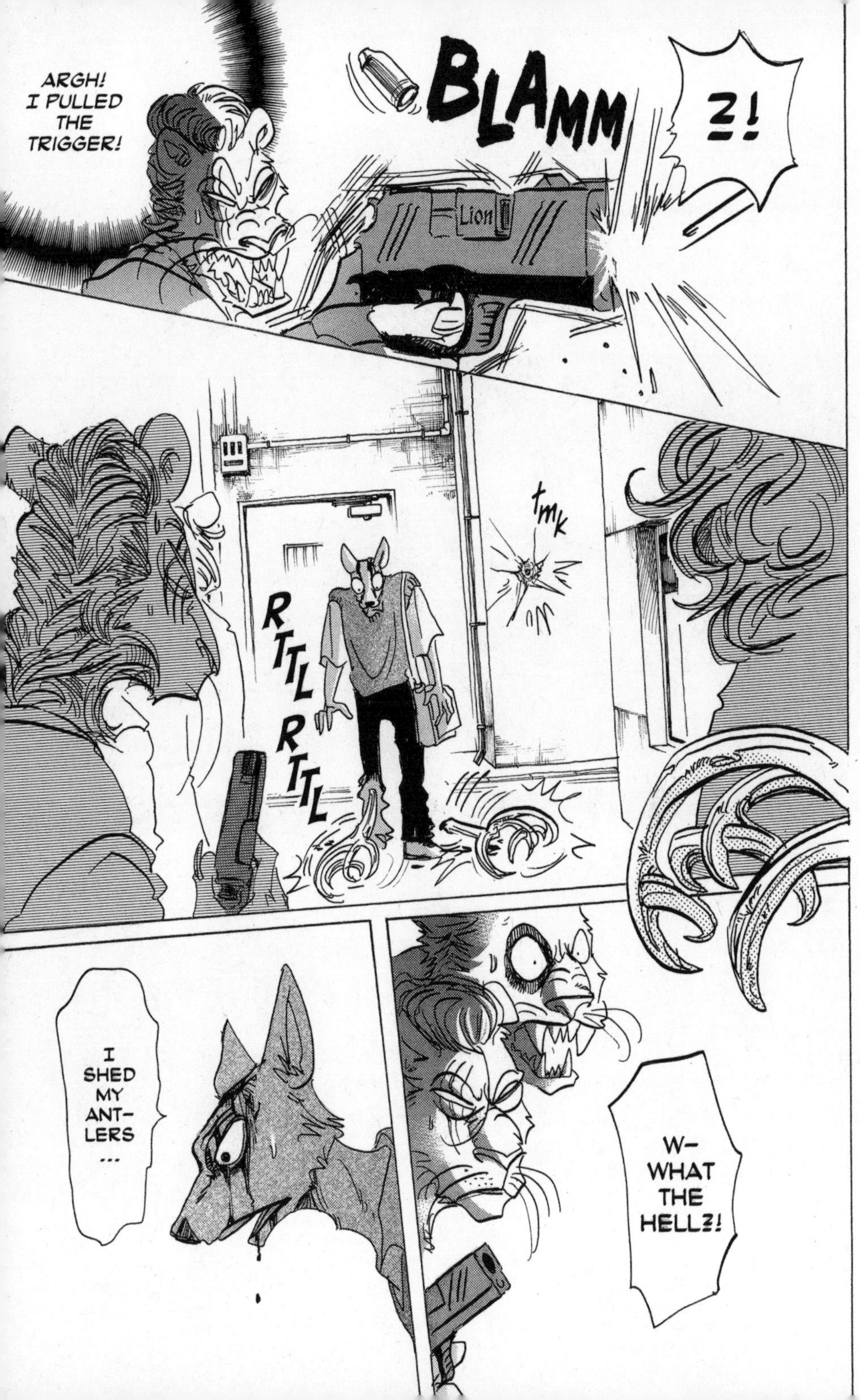
?!
BLAMM
Lion
ARGH! I PULLED THE TRIGGER!
tmk
RTTL RTTL
W-WHAT THE HELL?!
I SHED MY ANT-LERS...

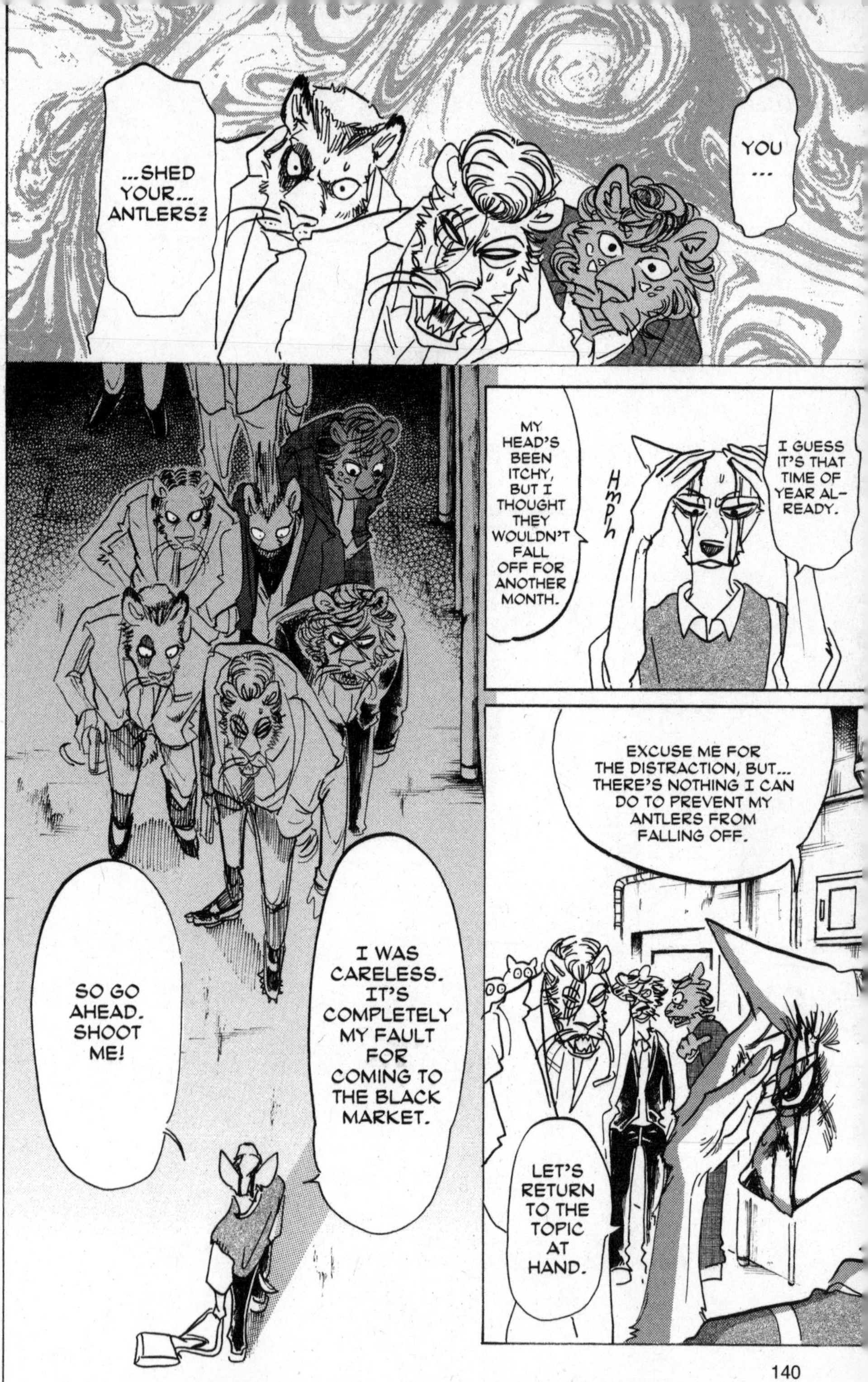
YOU ...
...SHED YOUR... ANTLERS?
I GUESS IT'S THAT TIME OF YEAR AL-READY.
Hmph
MY HEAD'S BEEN ITCHY, BUT I THOUGHT THEY WOULDN'T FALL OFF FOR ANOTHER MONTH.
EXCUSE ME FOR THE DISTRACTION, BUT... THERE'S NOTHING I CAN DO TO PREVENT MY ANTLERS FROM FALLING OFF.
LET'S RETURN TO THE TOPIC AT HAND.
I WAS CARELESS. IT'S COMPLETELY MY FAULT FOR COMING TO THE BLACK MARKET.
SO GO AHEAD. SHOOT ME!

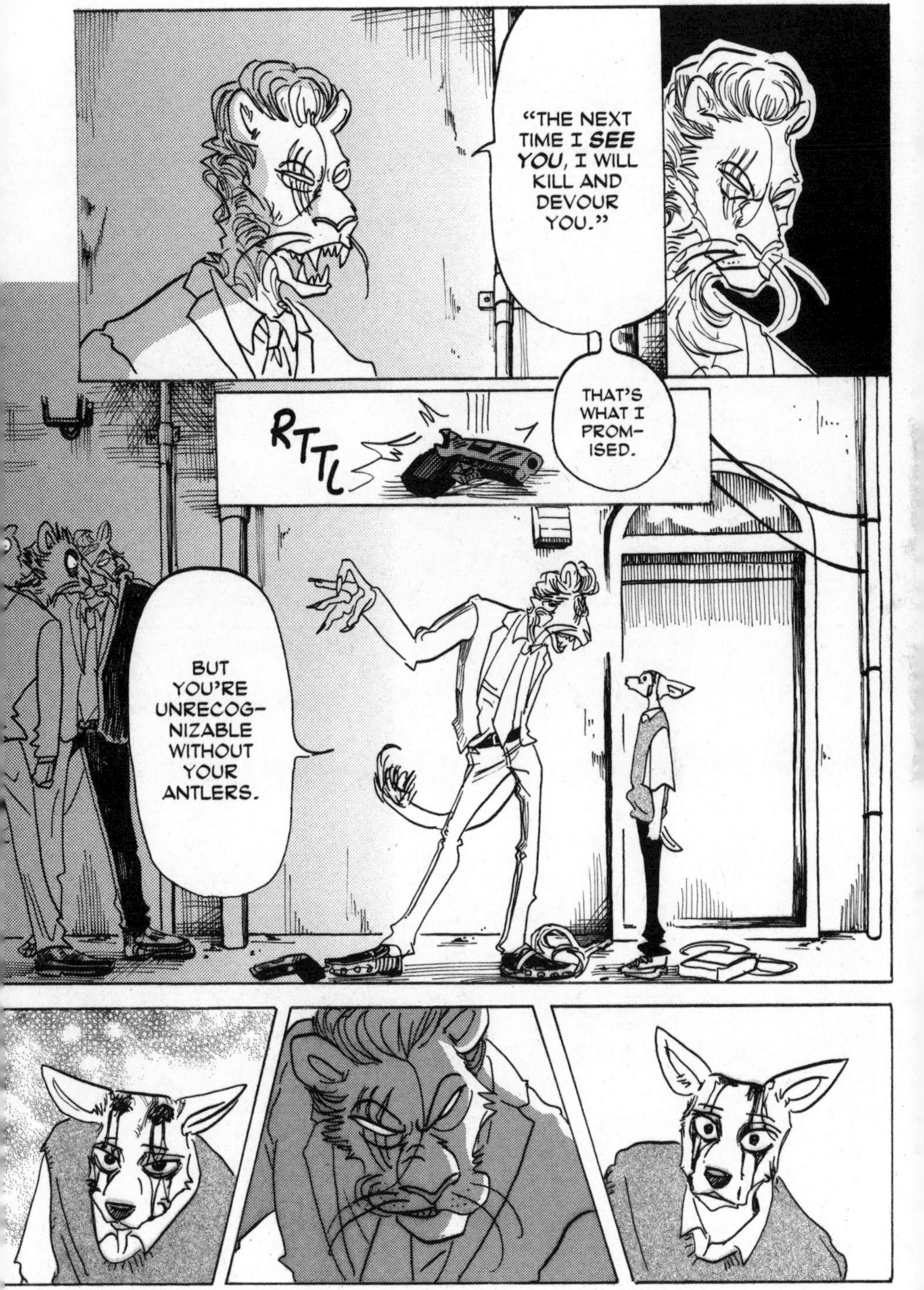
"THE NEXT TIME I SEE YOU, I WILL KILL AND DEVOUR YOU."
THAT'S WHAT I PROMISED.
RTTL
BUT YOU'RE UNRECOGNIZABLE WITHOUT YOUR ANTLERS.

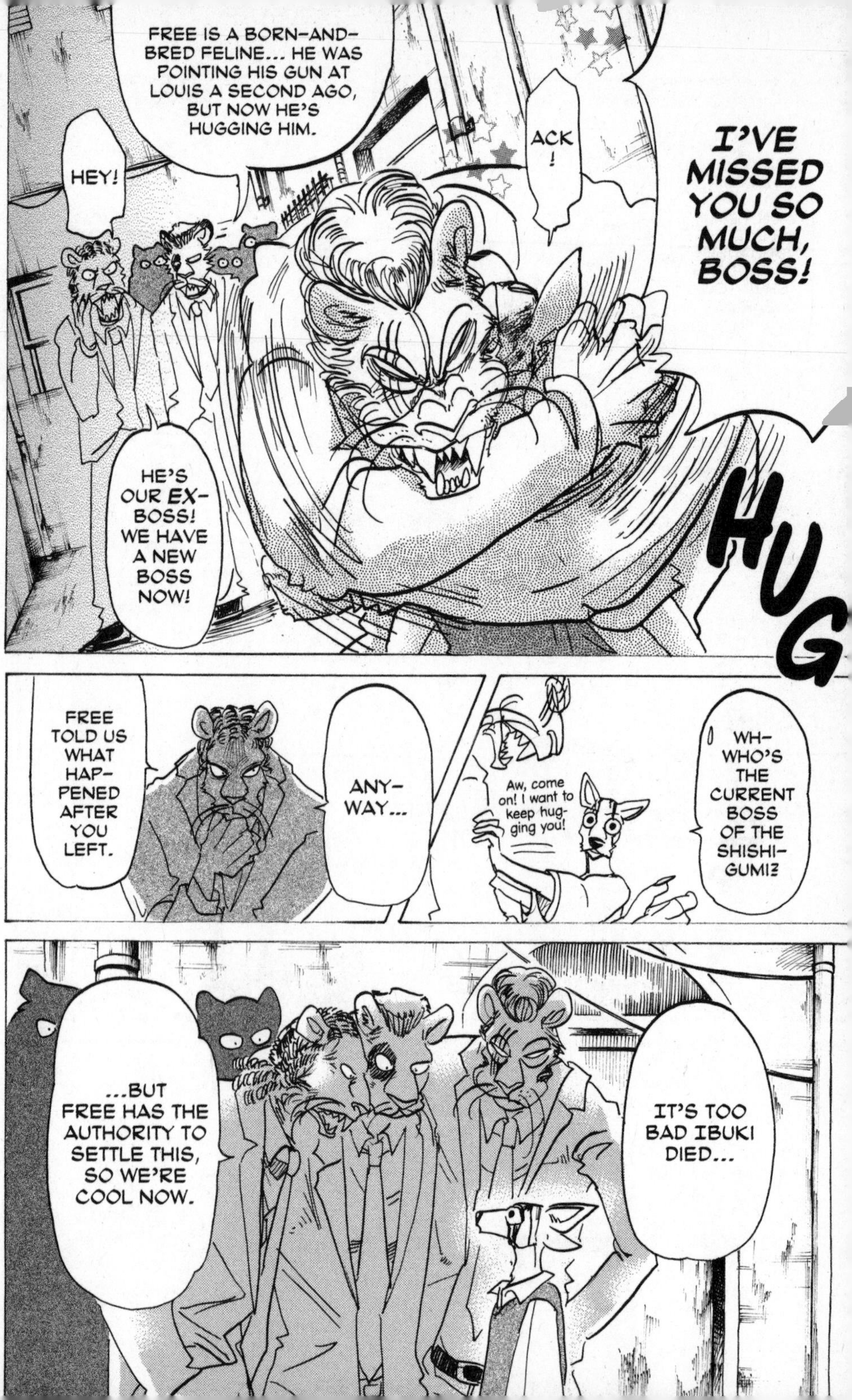
I'VE MISSED YOU SO MUCH, BOSS!
ACK!
FREE IS A BORN-AND-BRED FELINE... HE WAS POINTING HIS GUN AT LOUIS A SECOND AGO, BUT NOW HE'S HUGGING HIM.
HEY!
HUG
HE'S OUR EX-BOSS! WE HAVE A NEW BOSS NOW!
WH-WHO'S THE CURRENT BOSS OF THE SHISHI-GUMI?!
Aw, come on! I want to keep hug-ging you!
ANYWAY...
FREE TOLD US WHAT HAP-PENED AFTER YOU LEFT.
IT'S TOO BAD IBUKI DIED...
...BUT FREE HAS THE AUTHORITY TO SETTLE THIS, SO WE'RE COOL NOW.

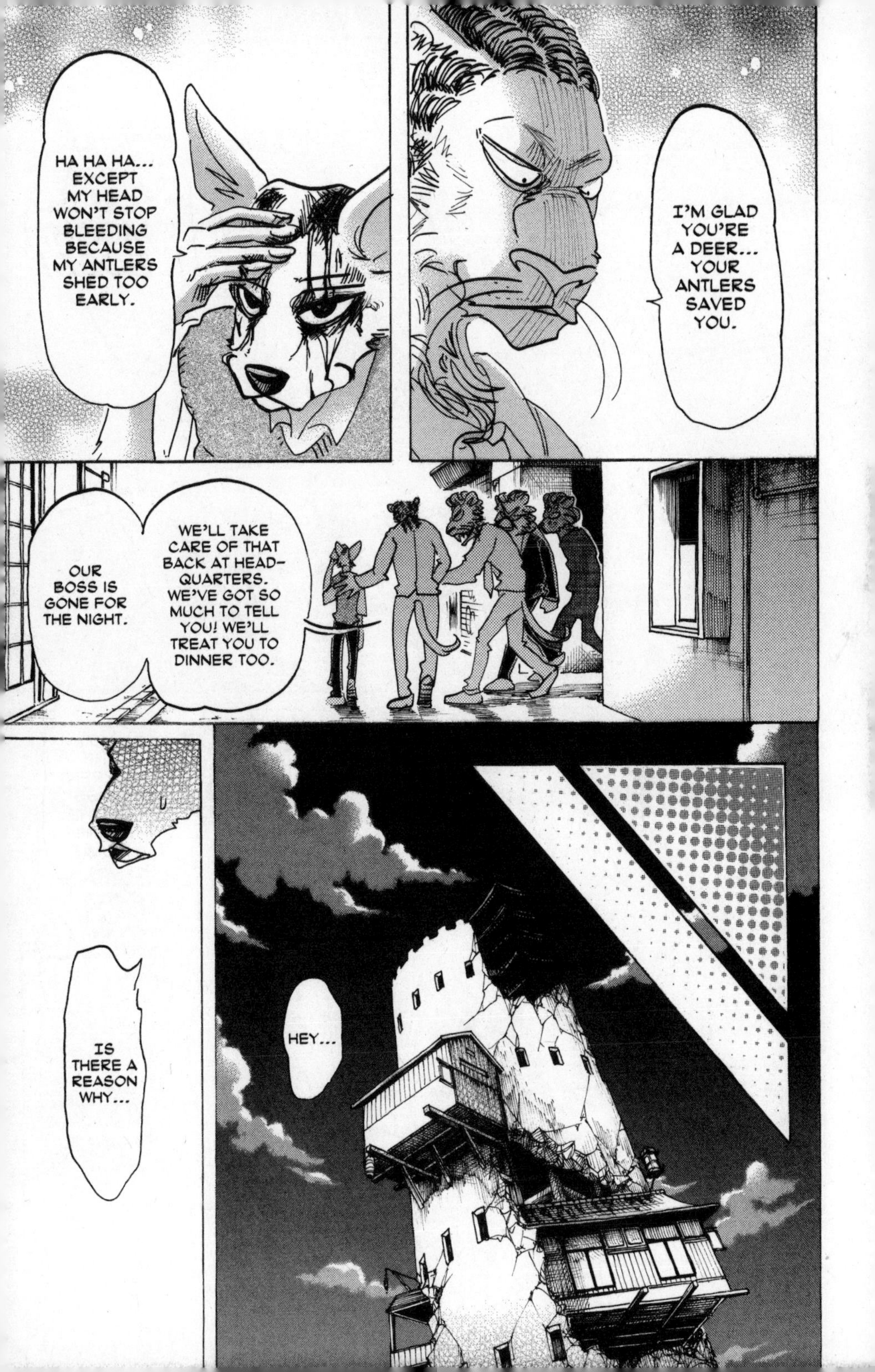
I'M GLAD YOU'RE A DEER... YOUR ANTLERS SAVED YOU.
HA HA HA... EXCEPT MY HEAD WON'T STOP BLEEDING BECAUSE MY ANTLERS SHED TOO EARLY.
WE'LL TAKE CARE OF THAT BACK AT HEAD-QUARTERS. WE'VE GOT SO MUCH TO TELL YOU! WE'LL TREAT YOU TO DINNER TOO.
OUR BOSS IS GONE FOR THE NIGHT.
HEY...
IS THERE A REASON WHY...

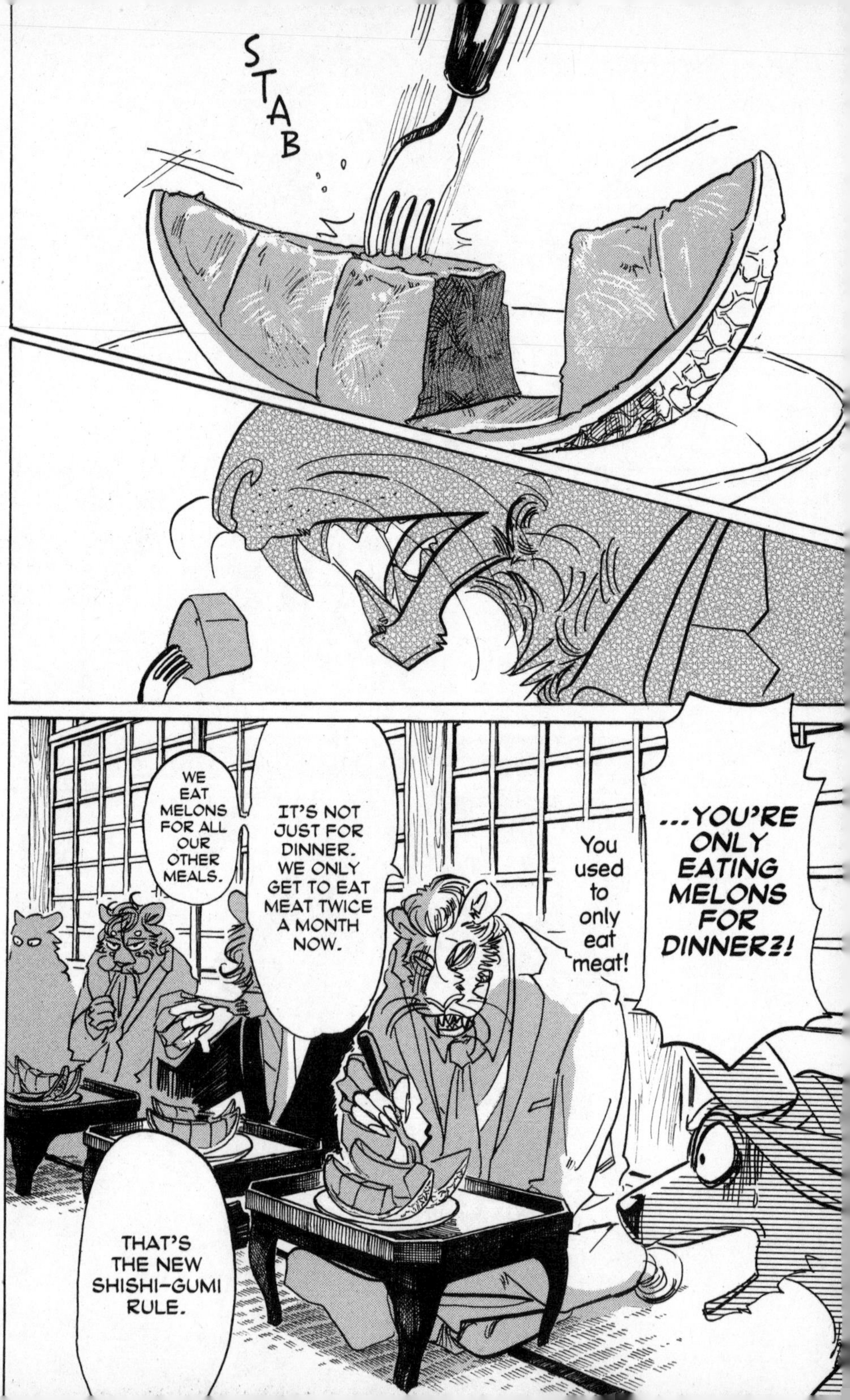
STAB
...YOU'RE ONLY EATING MELONS FOR DINNER?!
You used to only eat meat!
IT'S NOT JUST FOR DINNER. WE ONLY GET TO EAT MEAT TWICE A MONTH NOW.
WE EAT MELONS FOR ALL OUR OTHER MEALS.
THAT'S THE NEW SHISHI-GUMI RULE.

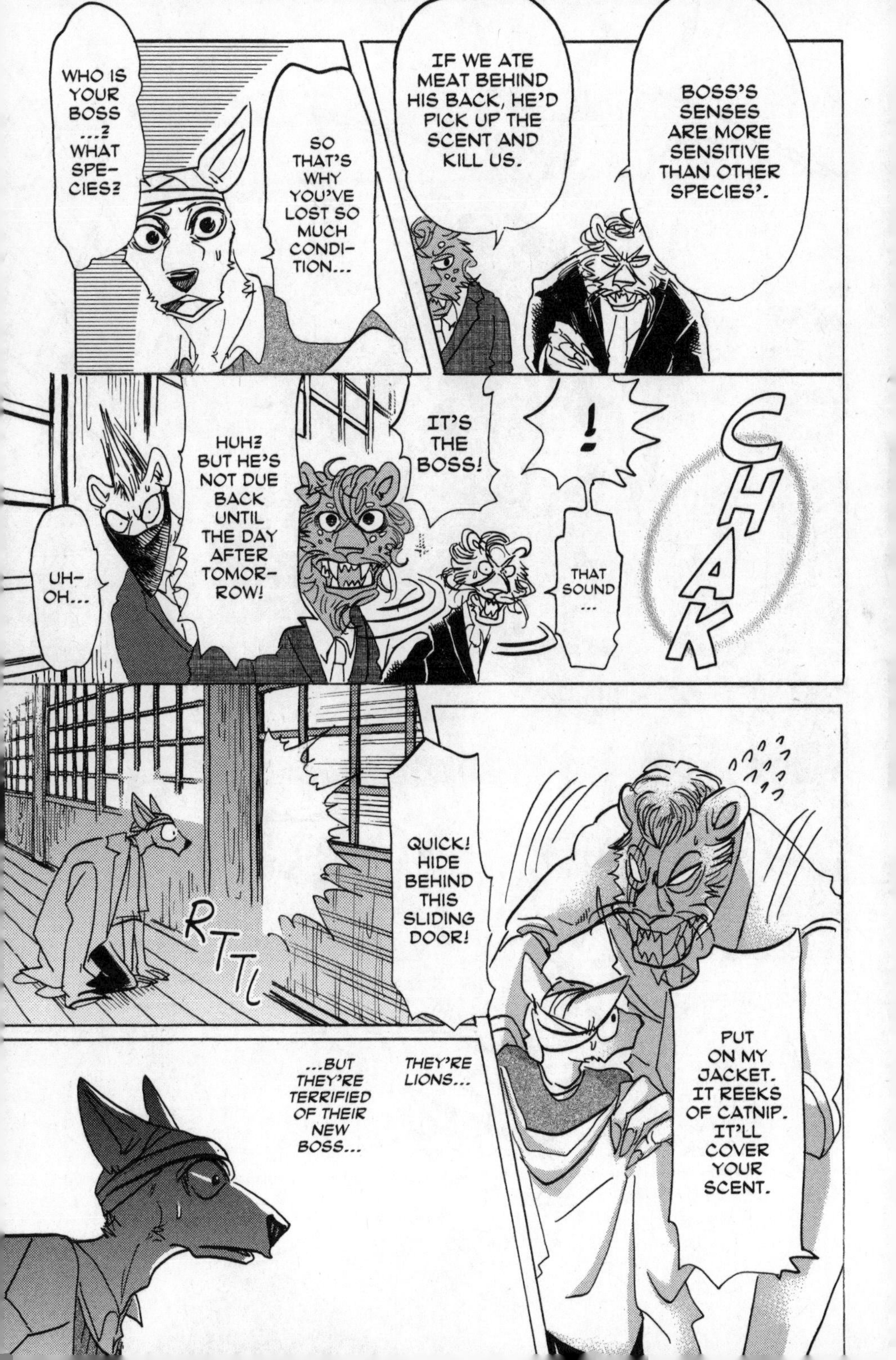
BOSS'S SENSES ARE MORE SENSITIVE THAN OTHER SPECIES'.
IF WE ATE MEAT BEHIND HIS BACK, HE'D PICK UP THE SCENT AND KILL US.
SO THAT'S WHY YOU'VE LOST SO MUCH CONDITION...
WHO IS YOUR BOSS...? WHAT SPECIES?
CHAK
!
THAT SOUND...
IT'S THE BOSS!
HUH? BUT HE'S NOT DUE BACK UNTIL THE DAY AFTER TOMORROW!
UH-OH...
QUICK! HIDE BEHIND THIS SLIDING DOOR!
PUT ON MY JACKET. IT REEKS OF CATNIP. IT'LL COVER YOUR SCENT.
RTTL
THEY'RE LIONS...
...BUT THEY'RE TERRIFIED OF THEIR NEW BOSS...

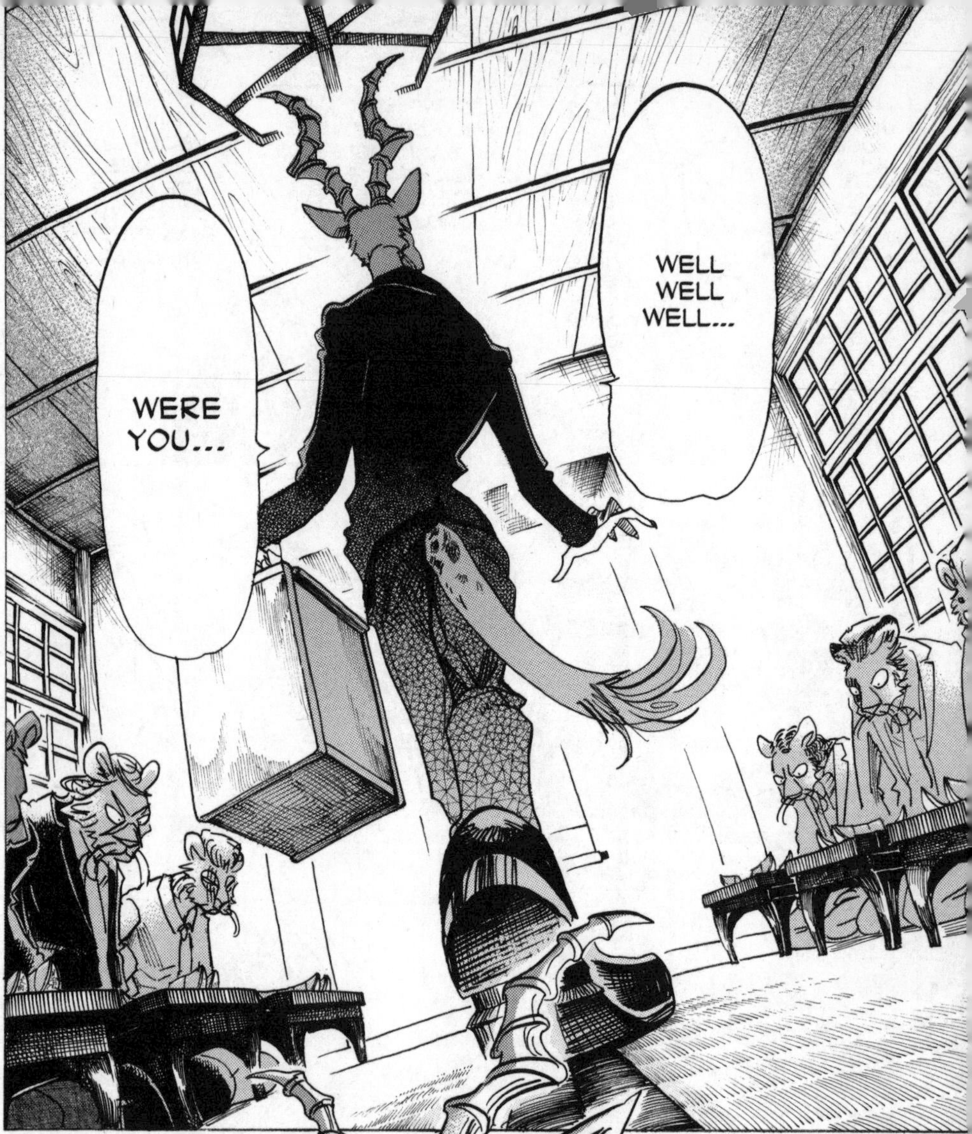
WELL WELL WELL...
WERE YOU...
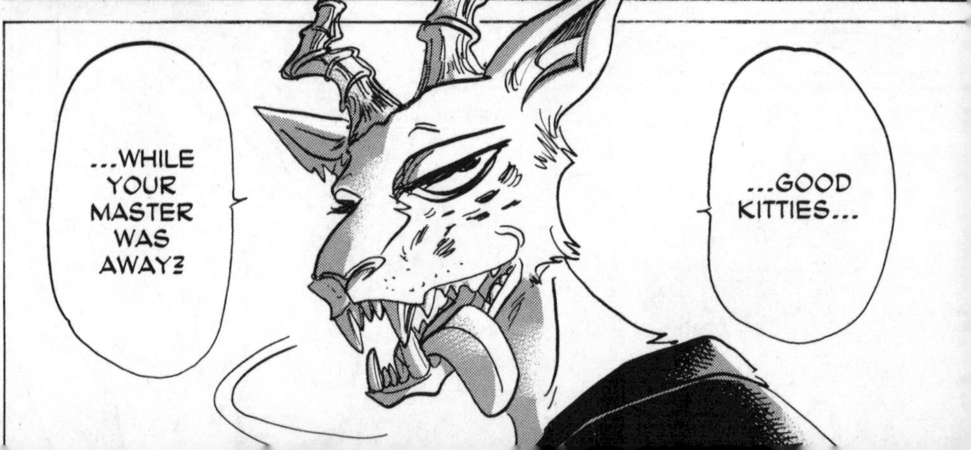
...GOOD KITTIES...
...WHILE YOUR MASTER WAS AWAY?

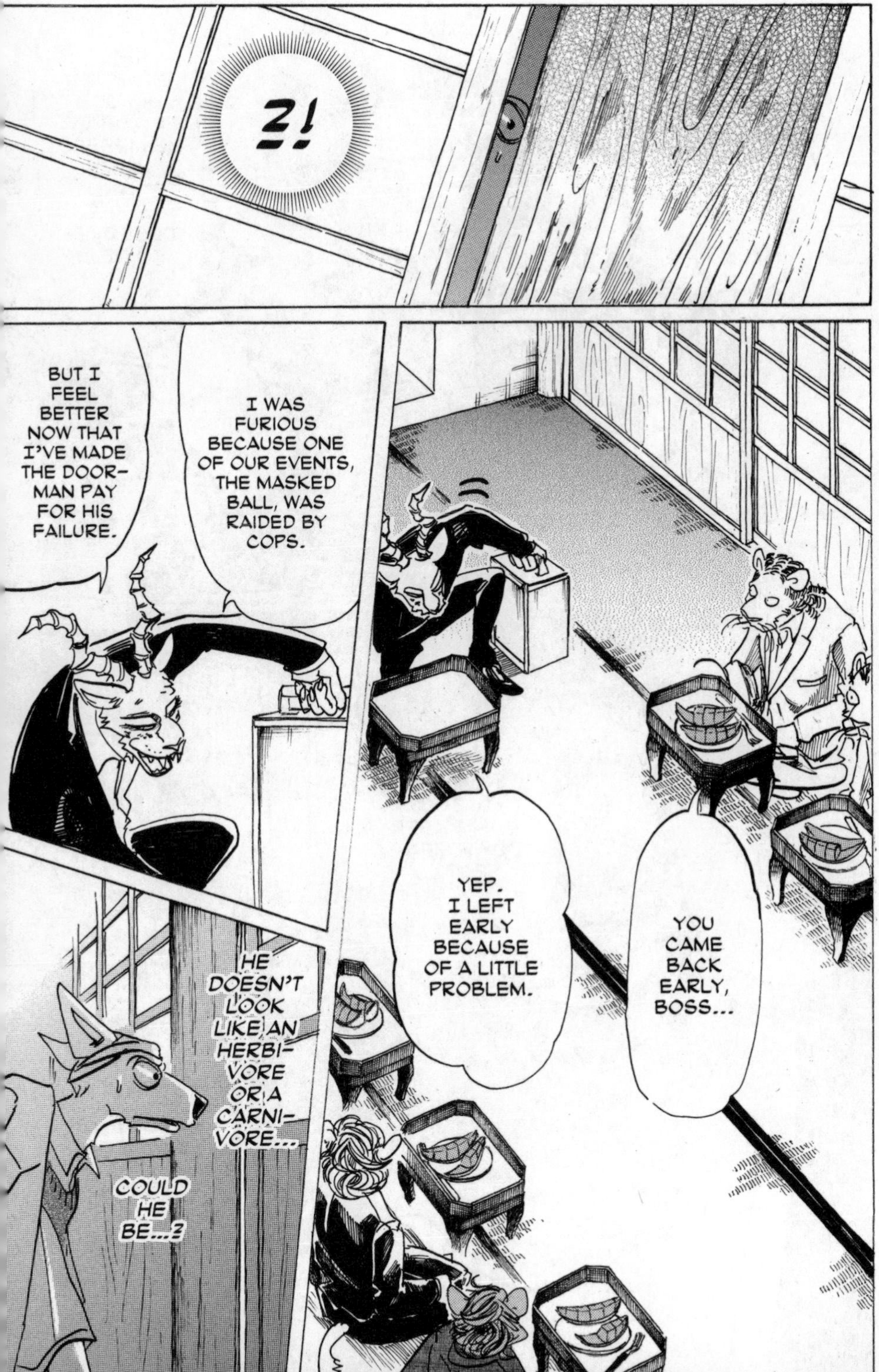
?!
YOU CAME BACK EARLY, BOSS...
YEP. I LEFT EARLY BECAUSE OF A LITTLE PROBLEM.
I WAS FURIOUS BECAUSE ONE OF OUR EVENTS, THE MASKED BALL, WAS RAIDED BY COPS.
BUT I FEEL BETTER NOW THAT I'VE MADE THE DOOR-MAN PAY FOR HIS FAILURE.
HE DOESN'T LOOK LIKE AN HERBI-VORE OR A CARNI-VORE...
COULD HE BE...?

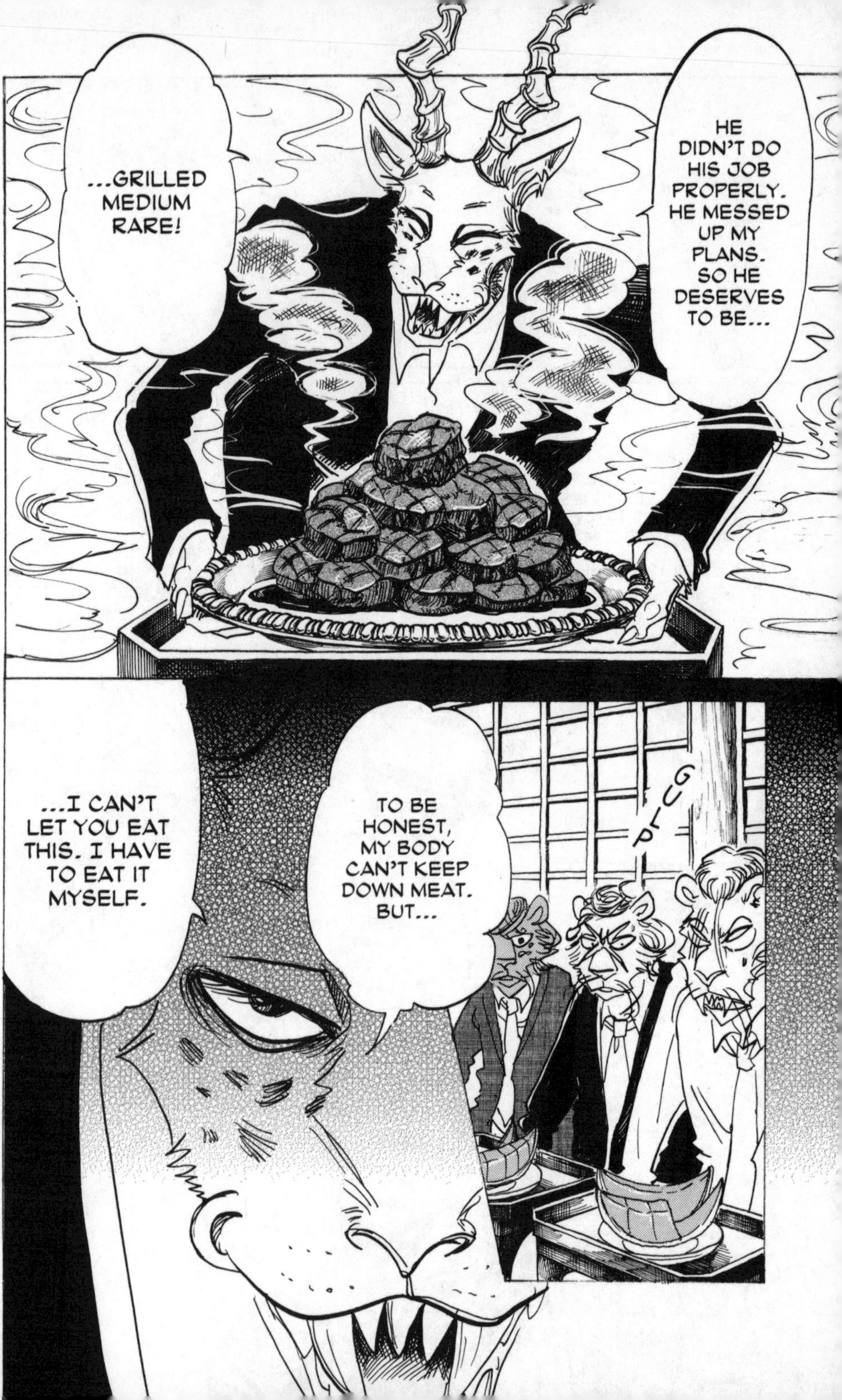
HE DIDN'T DO HIS JOB PROPERLY. HE MESSED UP MY PLANS. SO HE DESERVES TO BE...
...GRILLED MEDIUM RARE!
GULP
TO BE HONEST, MY BODY CAN'T KEEP DOWN MEAT. BUT...
...I CAN'T LET YOU EAT THIS. I HAVE TO EAT IT MYSELF.

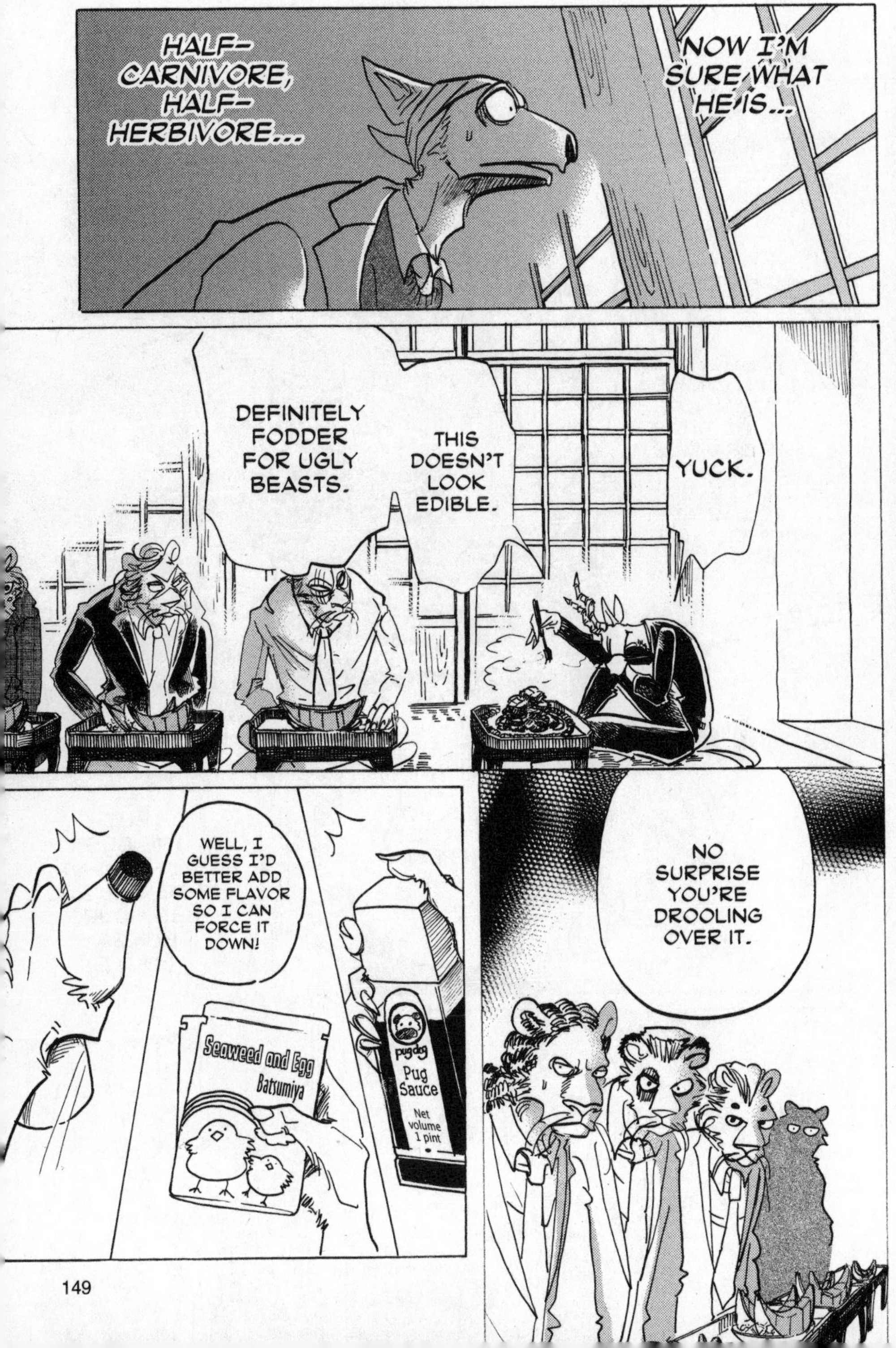
NOW I'M SURE WHAT HE IS...
HALF-CARNIVORE, HALF-HERBIVORE...
YUCK.
THIS DOESN'T LOOK EDIBLE.
DEFINITELY FODDER FOR UGLY BEASTS.
NO SURPRISE YOU'RE DROOLING OVER IT.
pugdog
Pug Sauce
Net volume 1 pint
WELL, I GUESS I'D BETTER ADD SOME FLAVOR SO I CAN FORCE IT DOWN!
Seaweed and Egg
Batsumiya

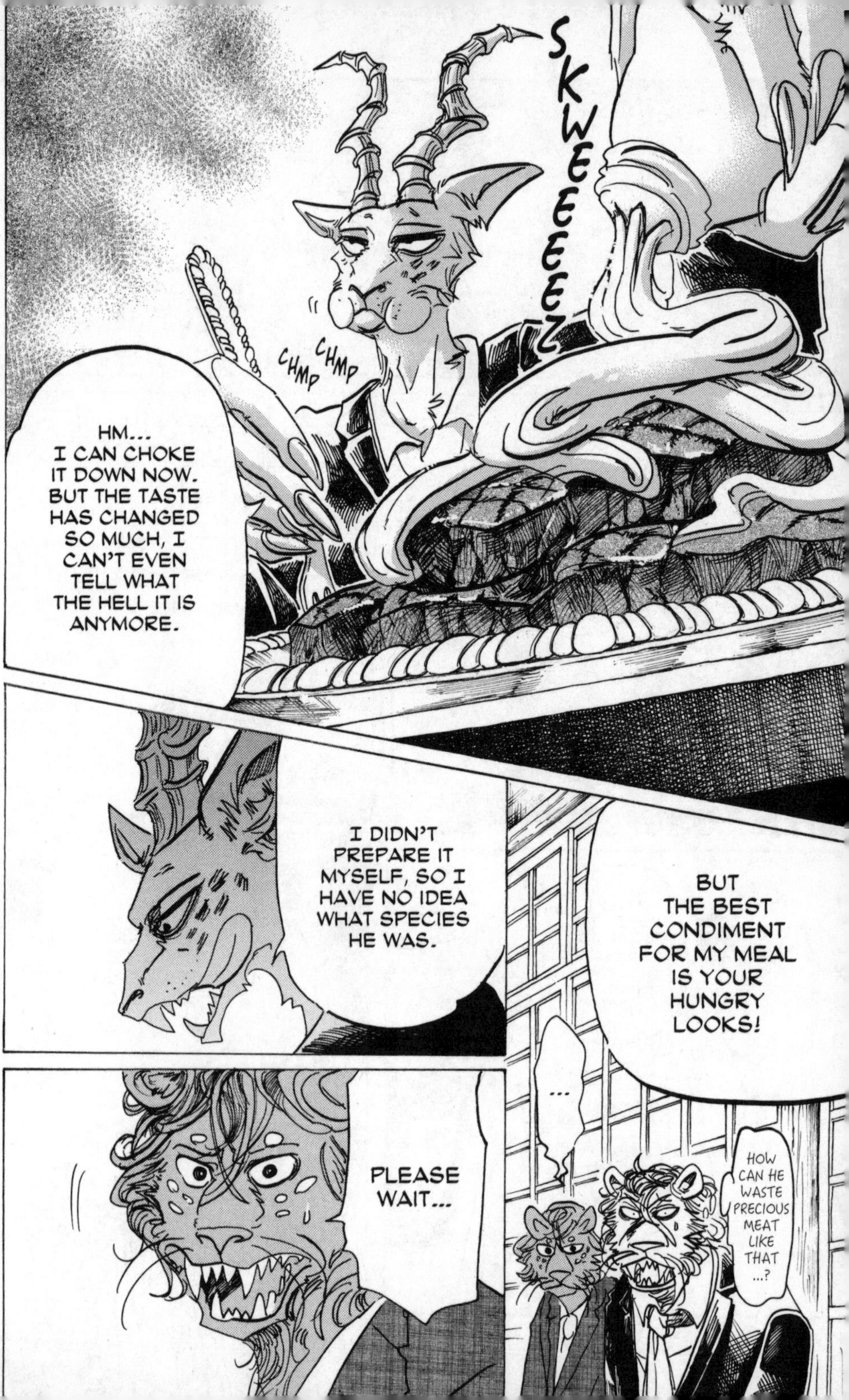
SKWEEEEEZ
CHMP CHMP
HM... I CAN CHOKE IT DOWN NOW. BUT THE TASTE HAS CHANGED SO MUCH, I CAN'T EVEN TELL WHAT THE HELL IT IS ANYMORE.
I DIDN'T PREPARE IT MYSELF, SO I HAVE NO IDEA WHAT SPECIES HE WAS.
BUT THE BEST CONDIMENT FOR MY MEAL IS YOUR HUNGRY LOOKS!
...
HOW CAN HE WASTE PRECIOUS MEAT LIKE THAT ...?
PLEASE WAIT...

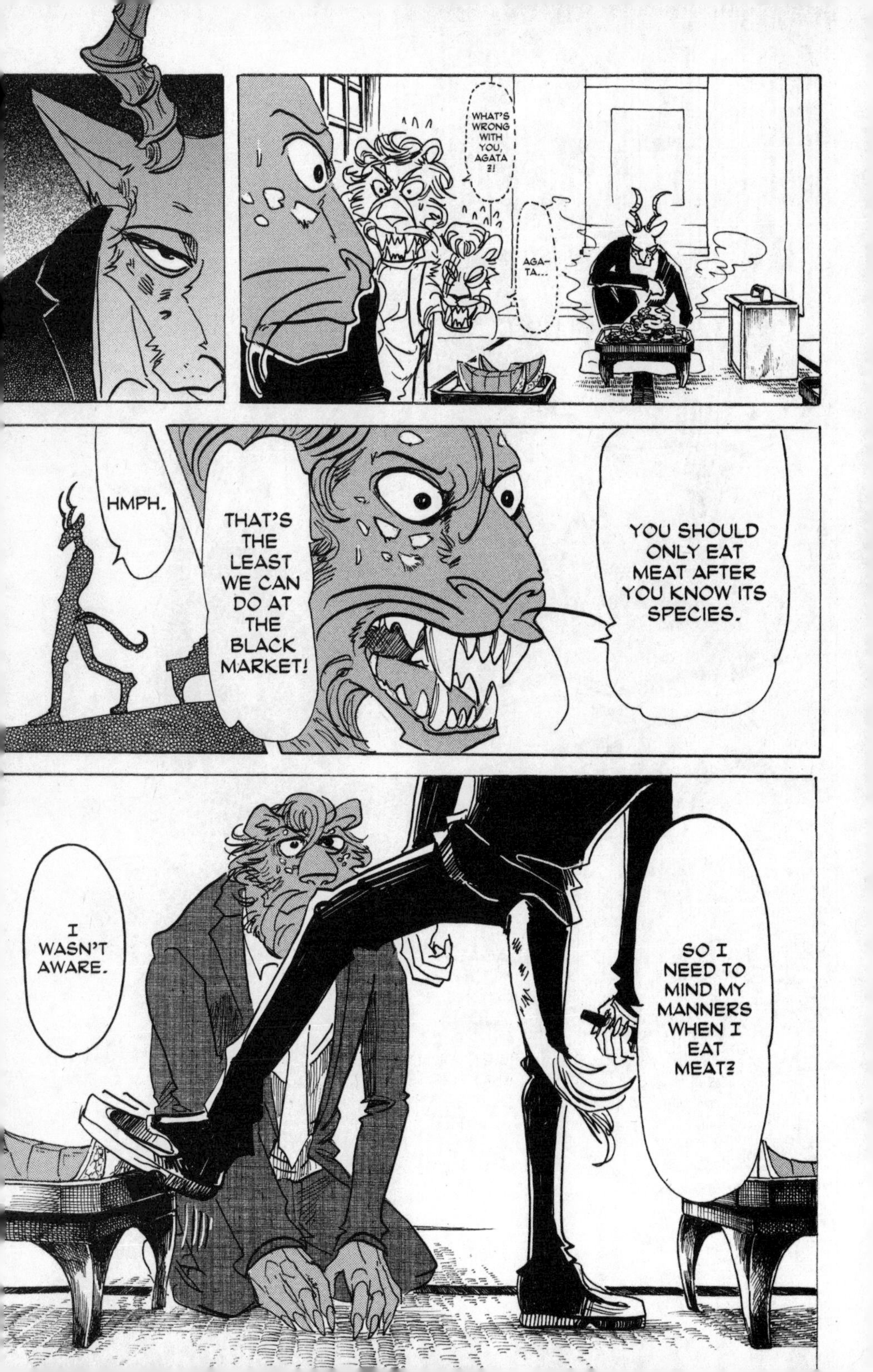
AGATA...
WHAT'S WRONG WITH YOU, AGATA?!
YOU SHOULD ONLY EAT MEAT AFTER YOU KNOW ITS SPECIES.
THAT'S THE LEAST WE CAN DO AT THE BLACK MARKET!
HMPH.
SO I NEED TO MIND MY MANNERS WHEN I EAT MEAT?
I WASN'T AWARE.

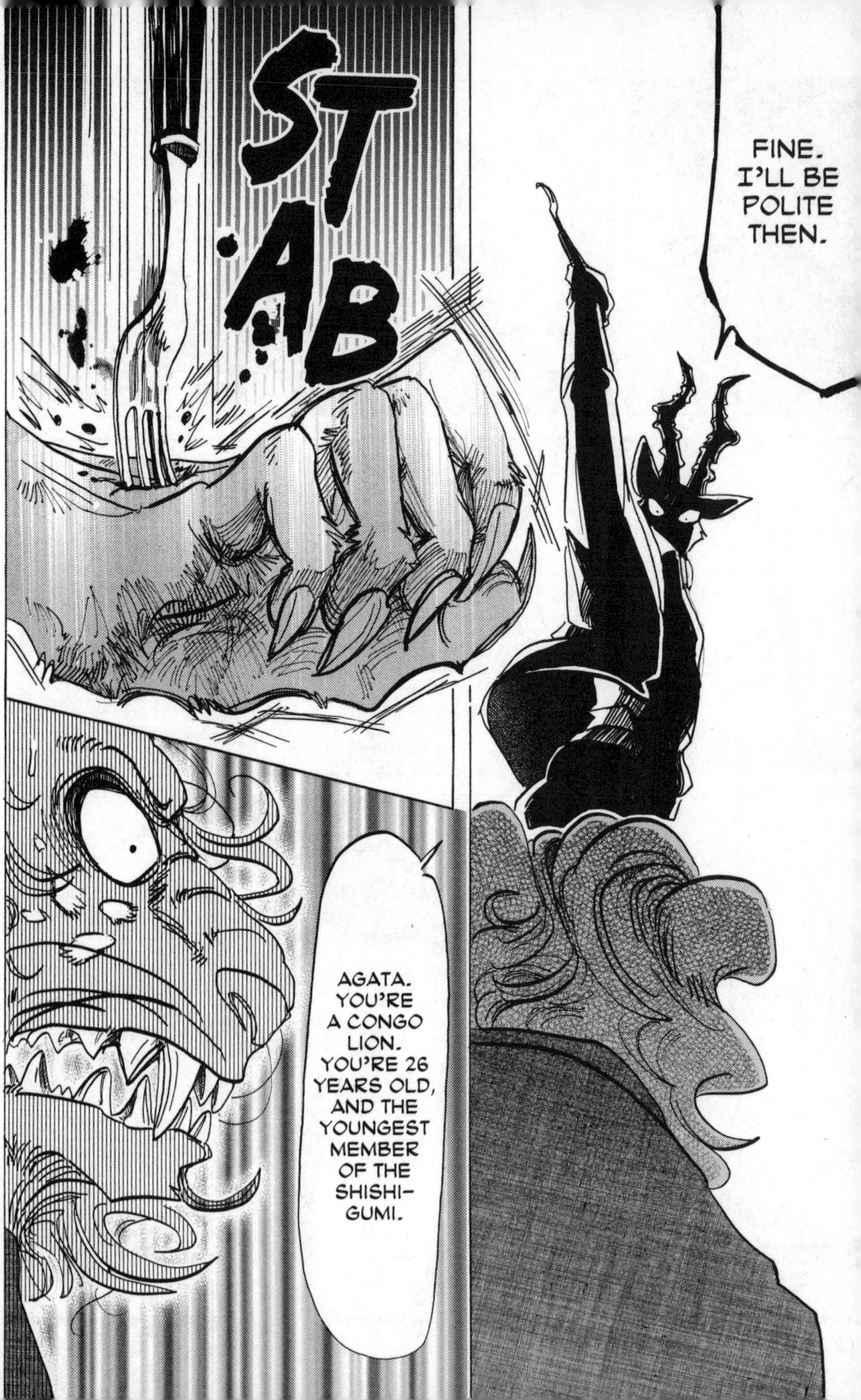
FINE. I'LL BE POLITE THEN.
STAB
AGATA. YOU'RE A CONGO LION. YOU'RE 26 YEARS OLD, AND THE YOUNGEST MEMBER OF THE SHISHI-GUMI.

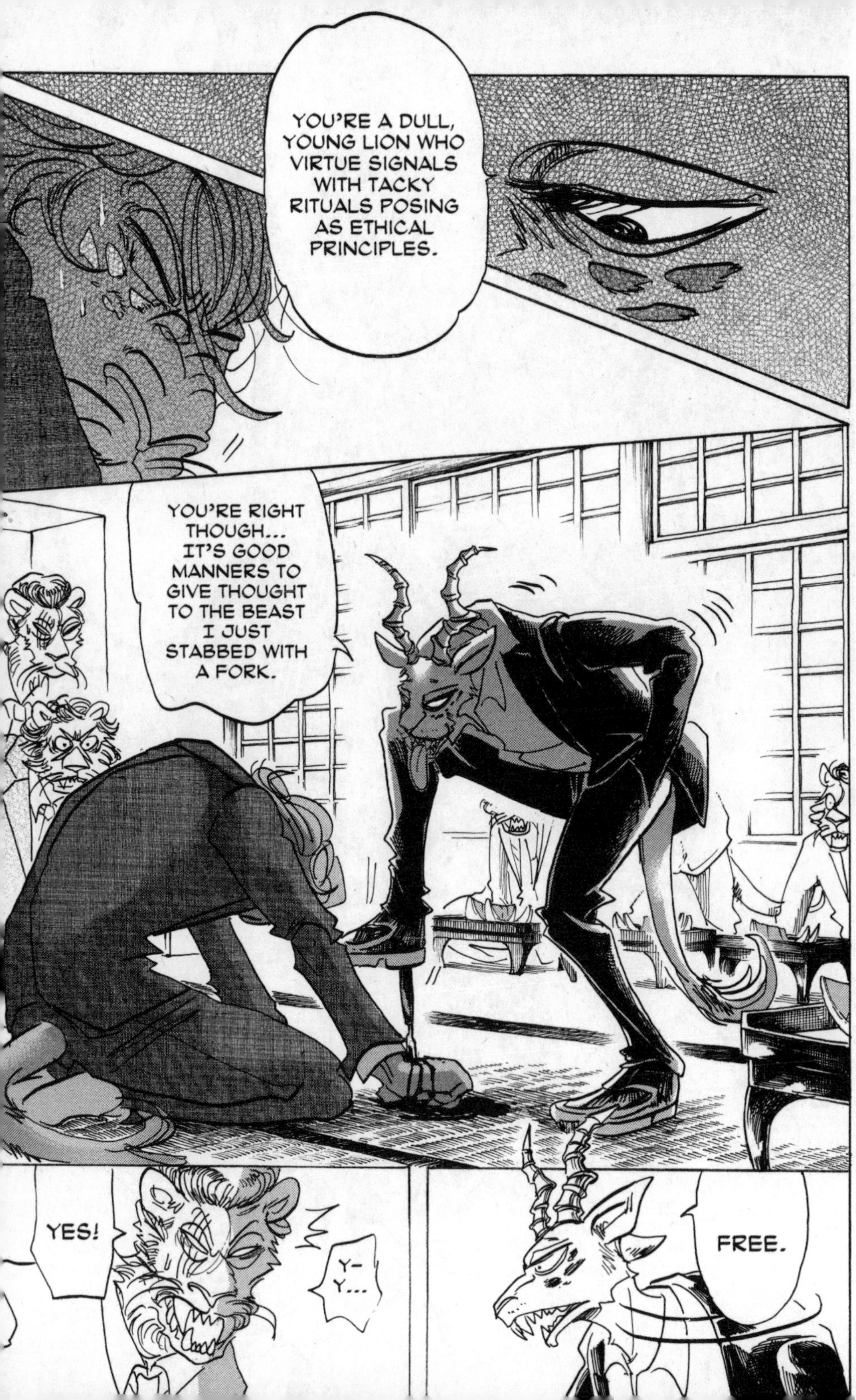
YOU'RE A DULL, YOUNG LION WHO VIRTUE SIGNALS WITH TACKY RITUALS POSING AS ETHICAL PRINCIPLES.
YOU'RE RIGHT THOUGH... IT'S GOOD MANNERS TO GIVE THOUGHT TO THE BEAST I JUST STABBED WITH A FORK.
FREE.
Y– Y...
YES!

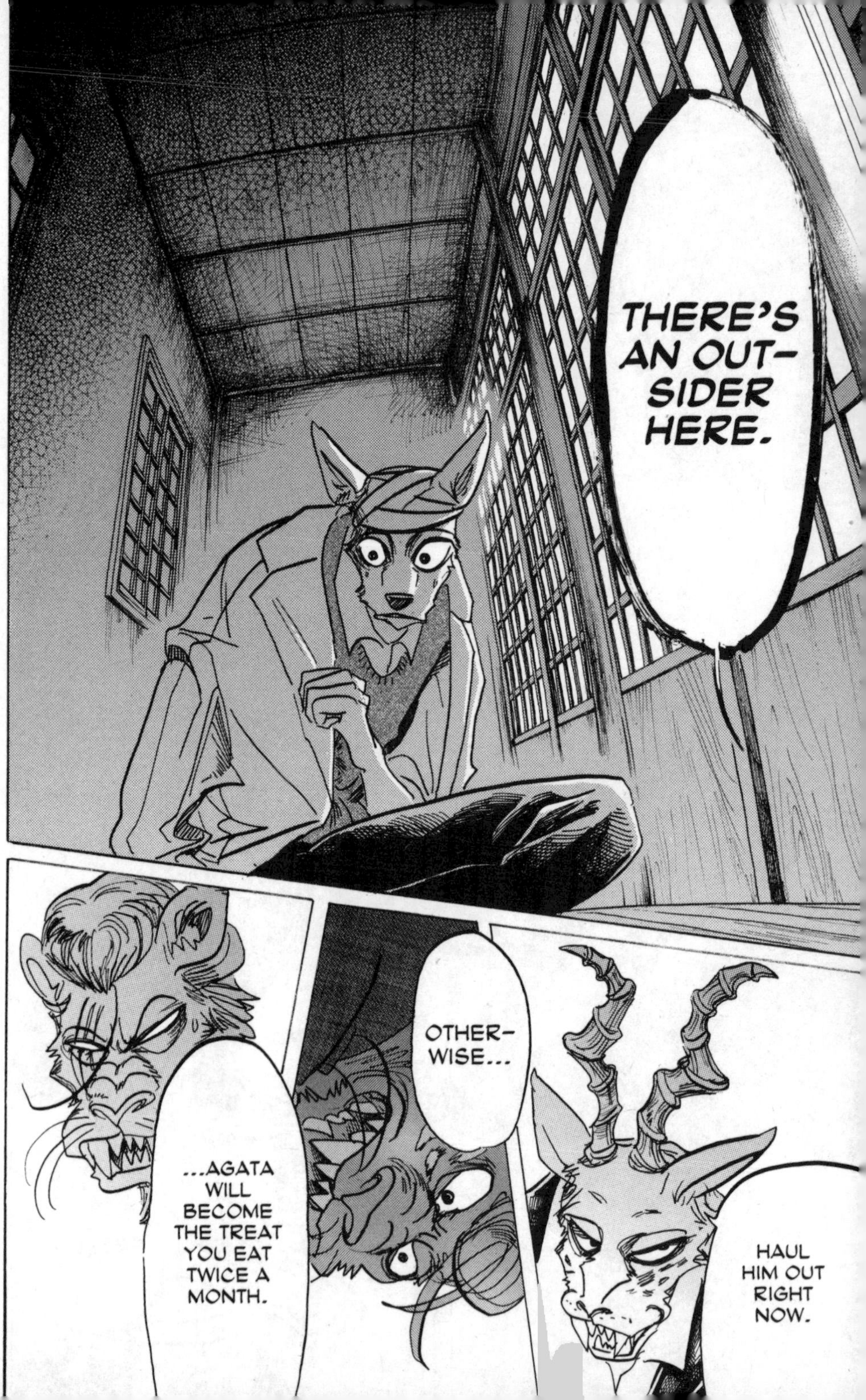
THERE'S AN OUT-SIDER HERE.
HAUL HIM OUT RIGHT NOW.
OTHER-WISE...
...AGATA WILL BECOME THE TREAT YOU EAT TWICE A MONTH.

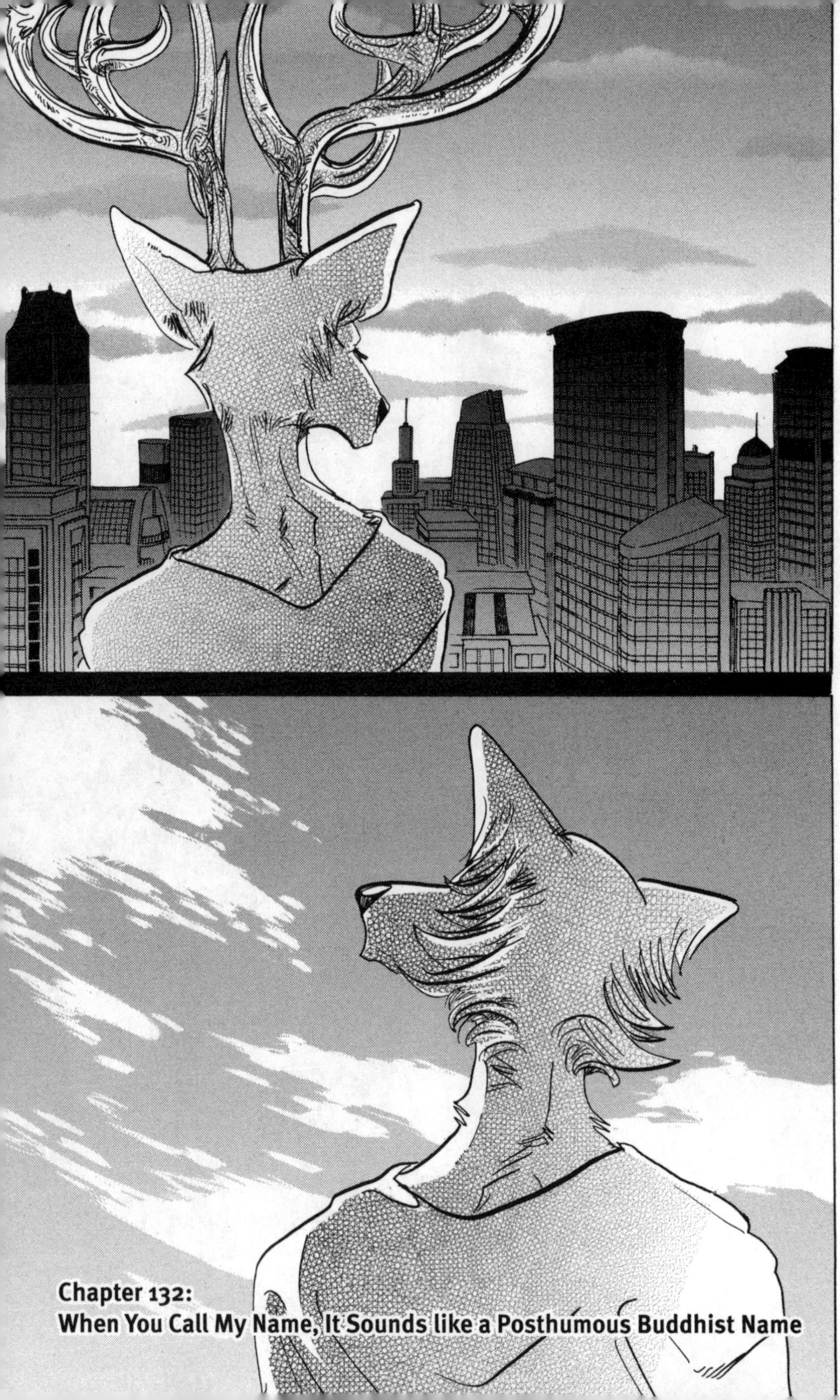

Chapter 132:
When You Call My Name, It Sounds like a Posthumous Buddhist Name

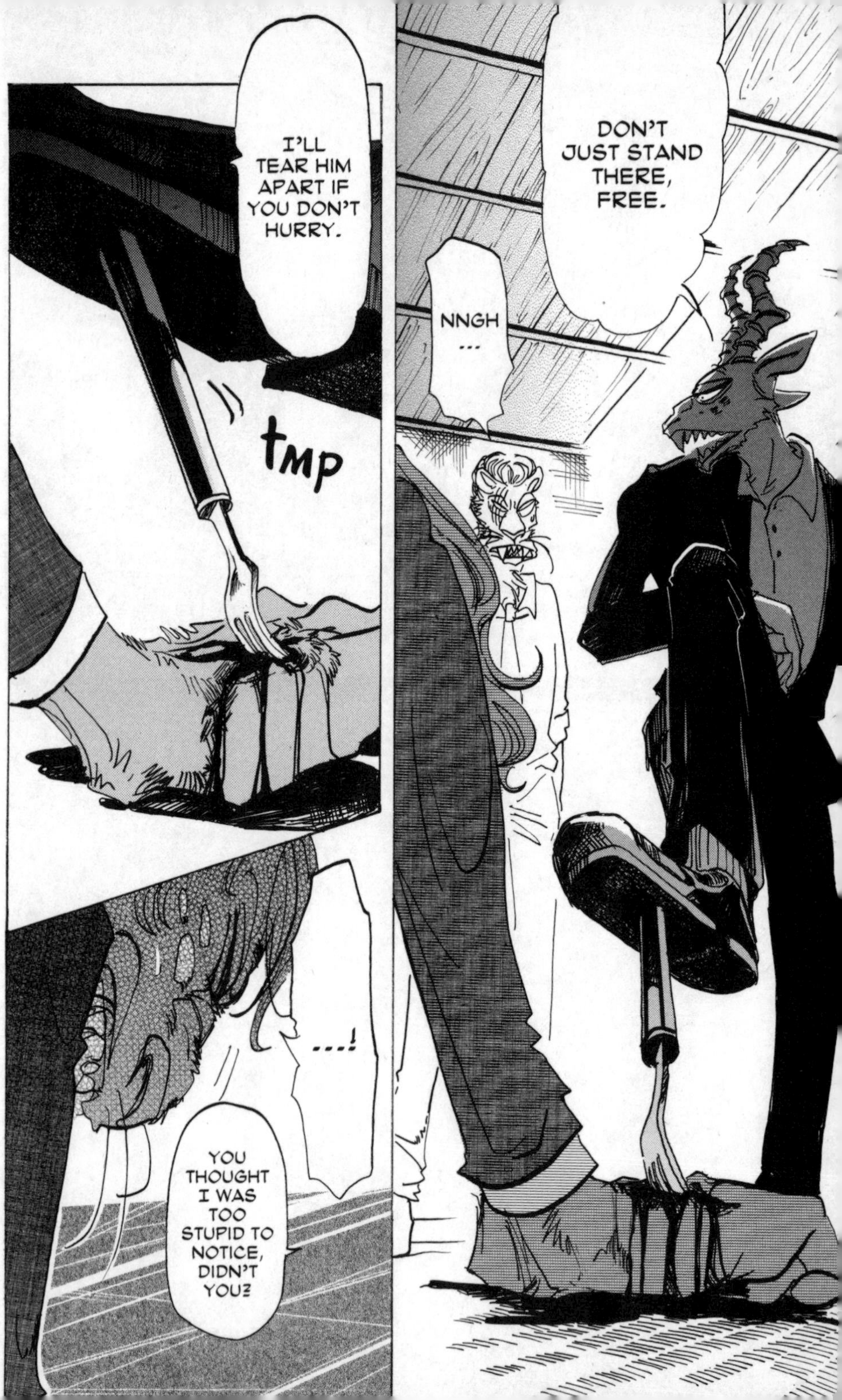
DON'T JUST STAND THERE, FREE.
NNGH ...
I'LL TEAR HIM APART IF YOU DON'T HURRY.
tmp
...!
YOU THOUGHT I WAS TOO STUPID TO NOTICE, DIDN'T YOU?

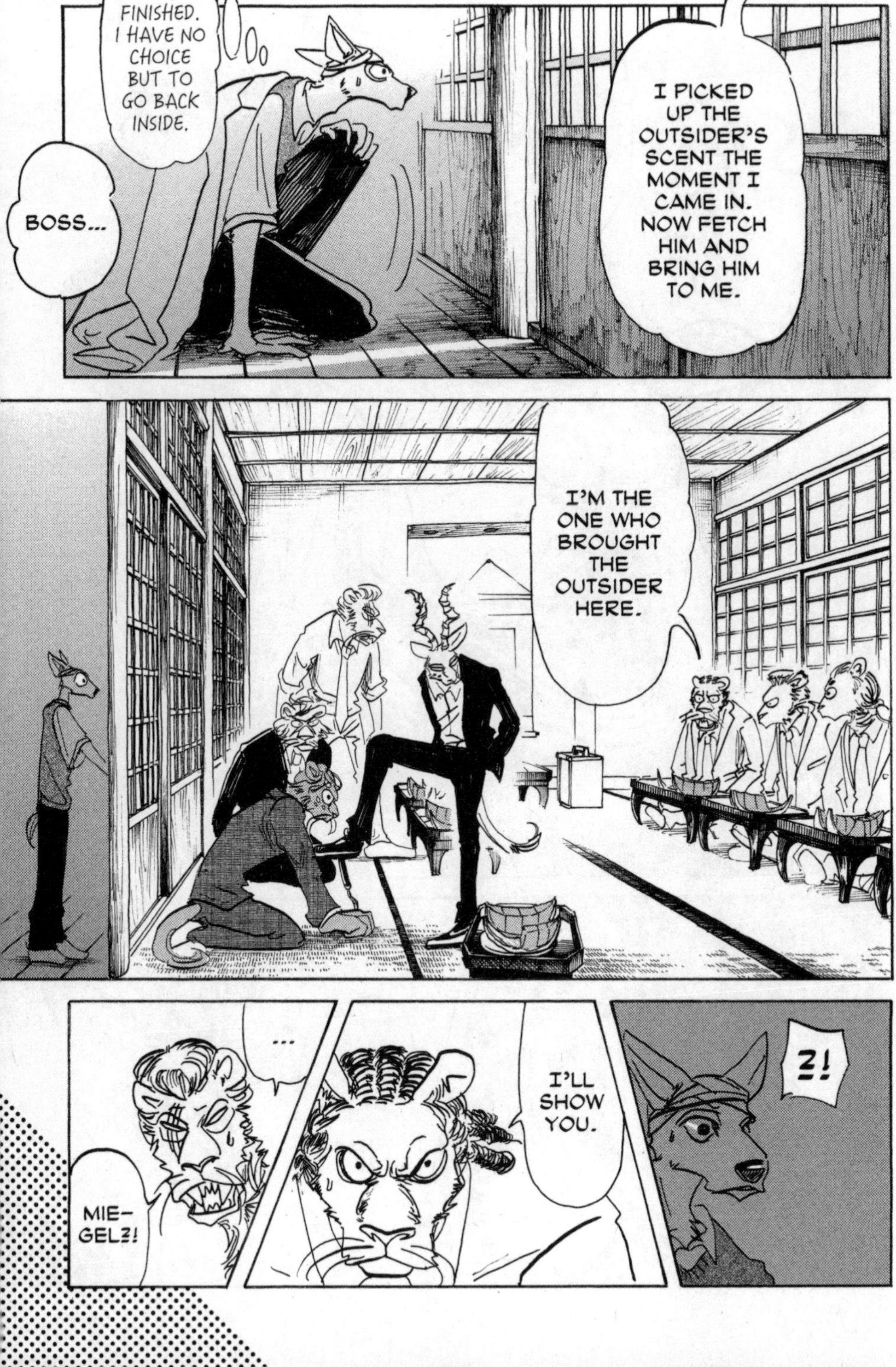
I PICKED UP THE OUTSIDER'S SCENT THE MOMENT I CAME IN. NOW FETCH HIM AND BRING HIM TO ME.
I'M FINISHED. I HAVE NO CHOICE BUT TO GO BACK INSIDE.
BOSS...
I'M THE ONE WHO BROUGHT THE OUTSIDER HERE.
Z!
I'LL SHOW YOU.
...
MIE-GELZ!

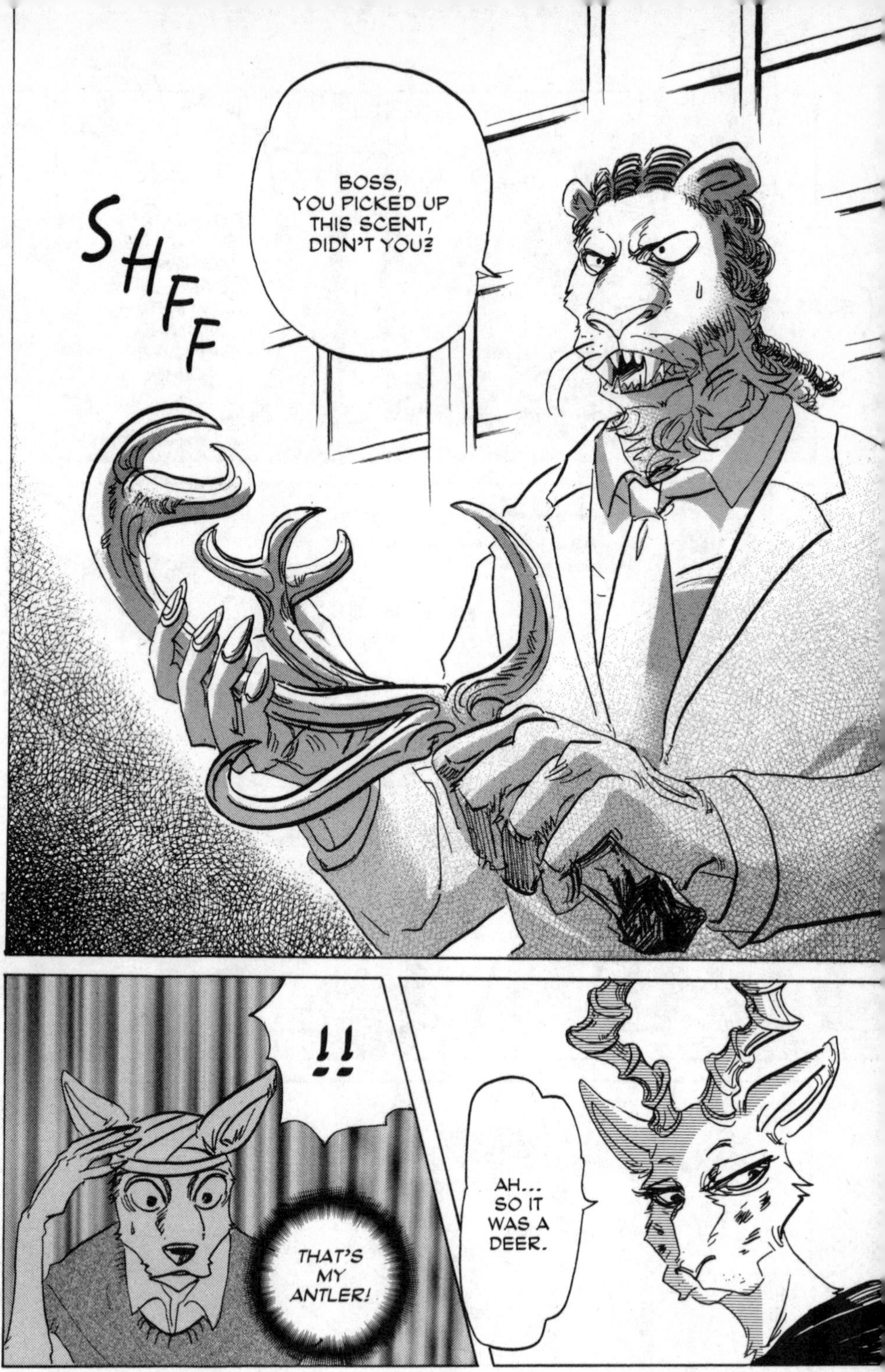
BOSS, YOU PICKED UP THIS SCENT, DIDN'T YOU?
SHFF
AH... SO IT WAS A DEER.
!!
THAT'S MY ANTLER!

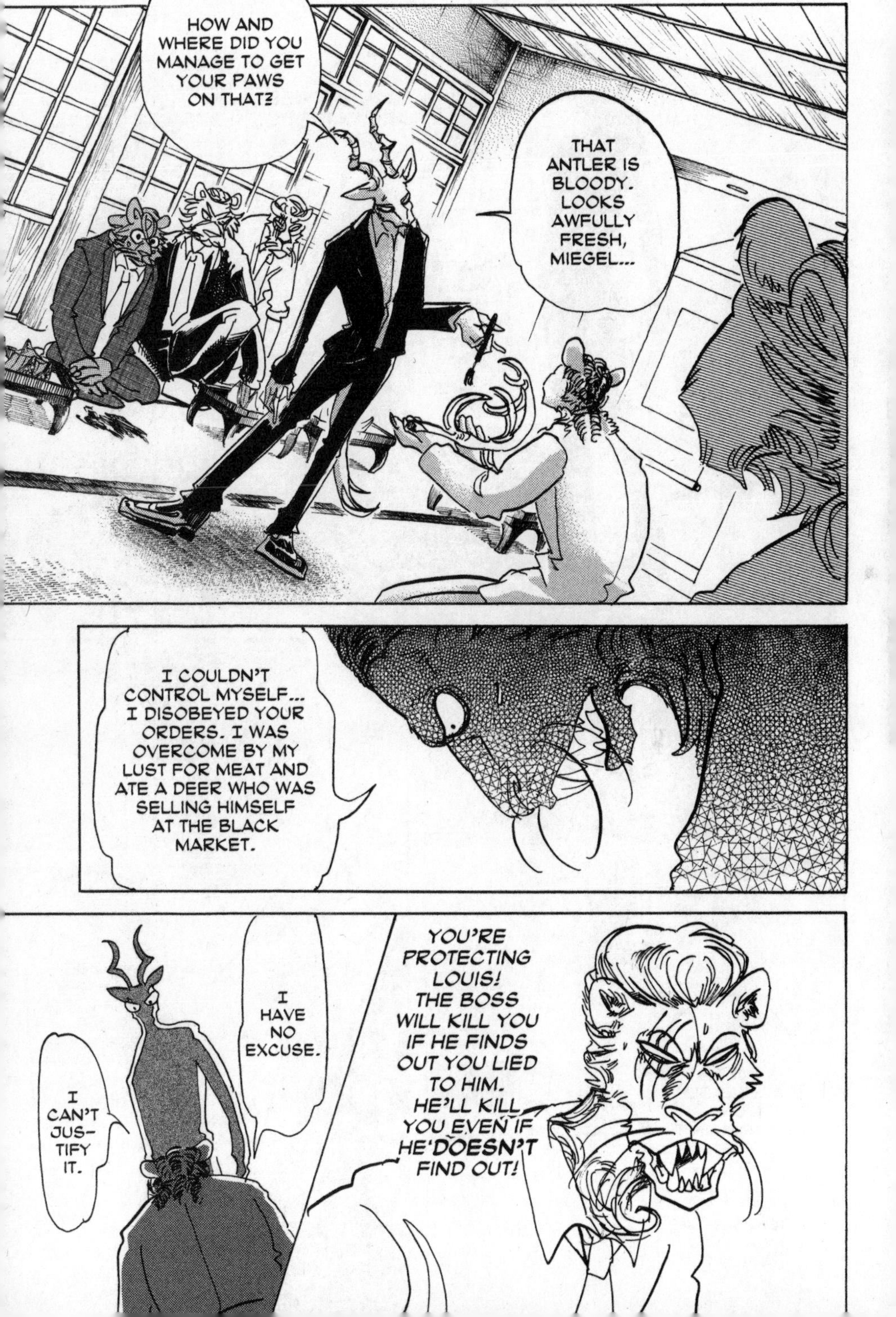
THAT ANTLER IS BLOODY. LOOKS AWFULLY FRESH, MIEGEL...
HOW AND WHERE DID YOU MANAGE TO GET YOUR PAWS ON THAT?
I COULDN'T CONTROL MYSELF... I DISOBEYED YOUR ORDERS. I WAS OVERCOME BY MY LUST FOR MEAT AND ATE A DEER WHO WAS SELLING HIMSELF AT THE BLACK MARKET.
YOU'RE PROTECTING LOUIS! THE BOSS WILL KILL YOU IF HE FINDS OUT YOU LIED TO HIM. HE'LL KILL YOU EVEN IF HE *DOESN'T* FIND OUT!
I HAVE NO EXCUSE.
I CAN'T JUS-TIFY IT.

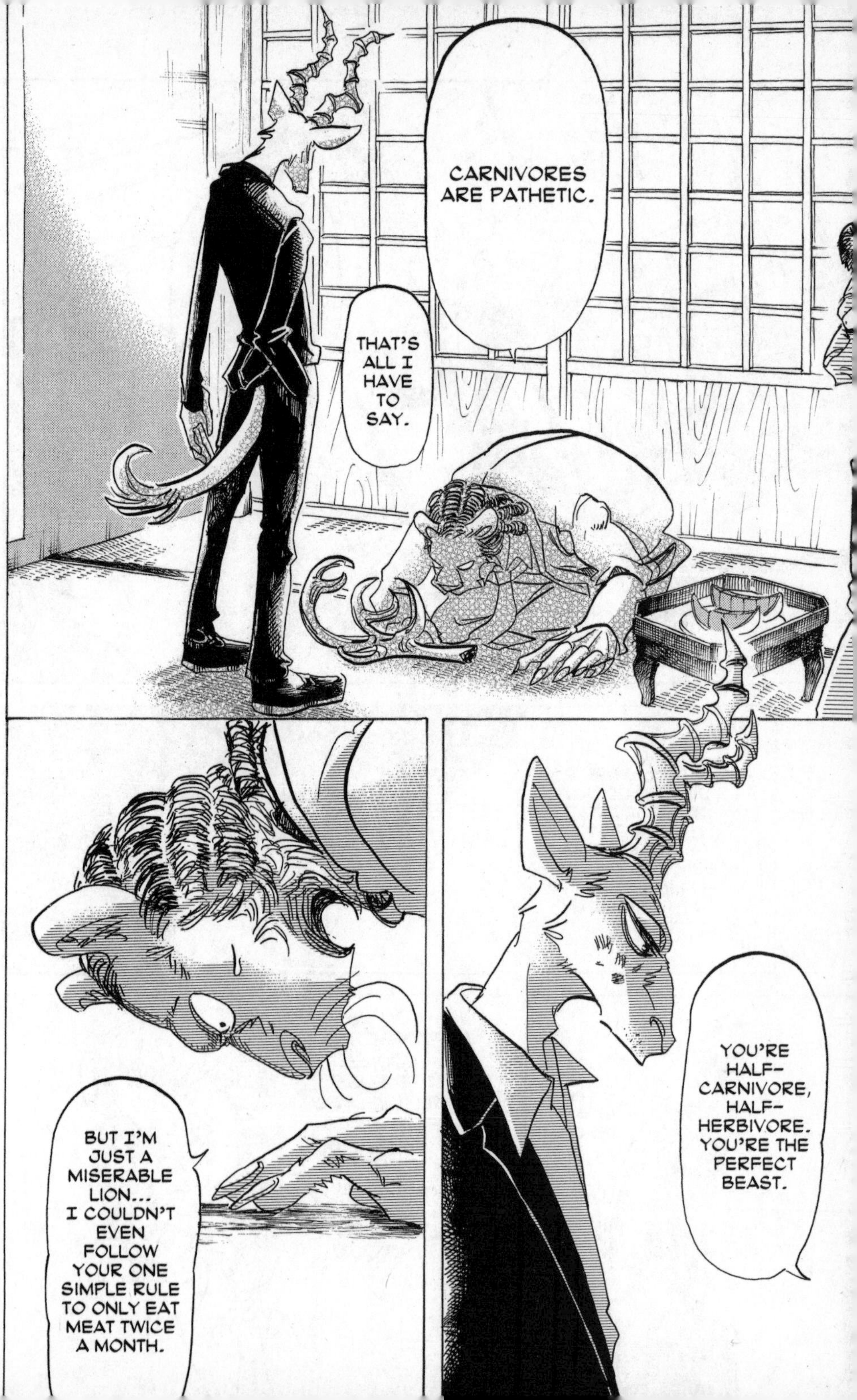
CARNIVORES ARE PATHETIC.
THAT'S ALL I HAVE TO SAY.
YOU'RE HALF-CARNIVORE, HALF-HERBIVORE. YOU'RE THE PERFECT BEAST.
BUT I'M JUST A MISERABLE LION... I COULDN'T EVEN FOLLOW YOUR ONE SIMPLE RULE TO ONLY EAT MEAT TWICE A MONTH.

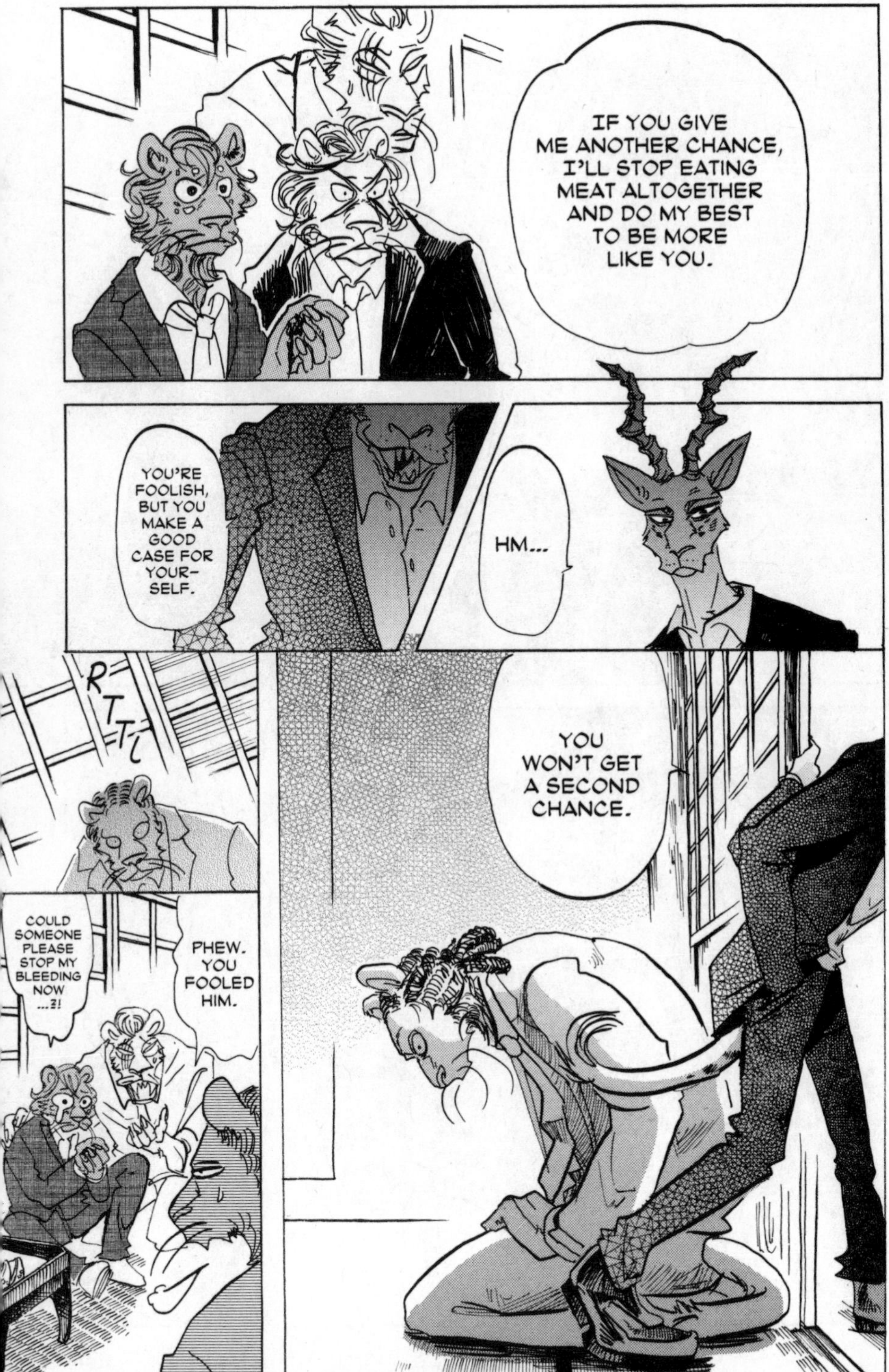
IF YOU GIVE ME ANOTHER CHANCE, I'LL STOP EATING MEAT ALTOGETHER AND DO MY BEST TO BE MORE LIKE YOU.
HM...
YOU'RE FOOLISH, BUT YOU MAKE A GOOD CASE FOR YOUR-SELF.
YOU WON'T GET A SECOND CHANCE.
RTTL
PHEW. YOU FOOLED HIM.
COULD SOMEONE PLEASE STOP MY BLEEDING NOW ...?!

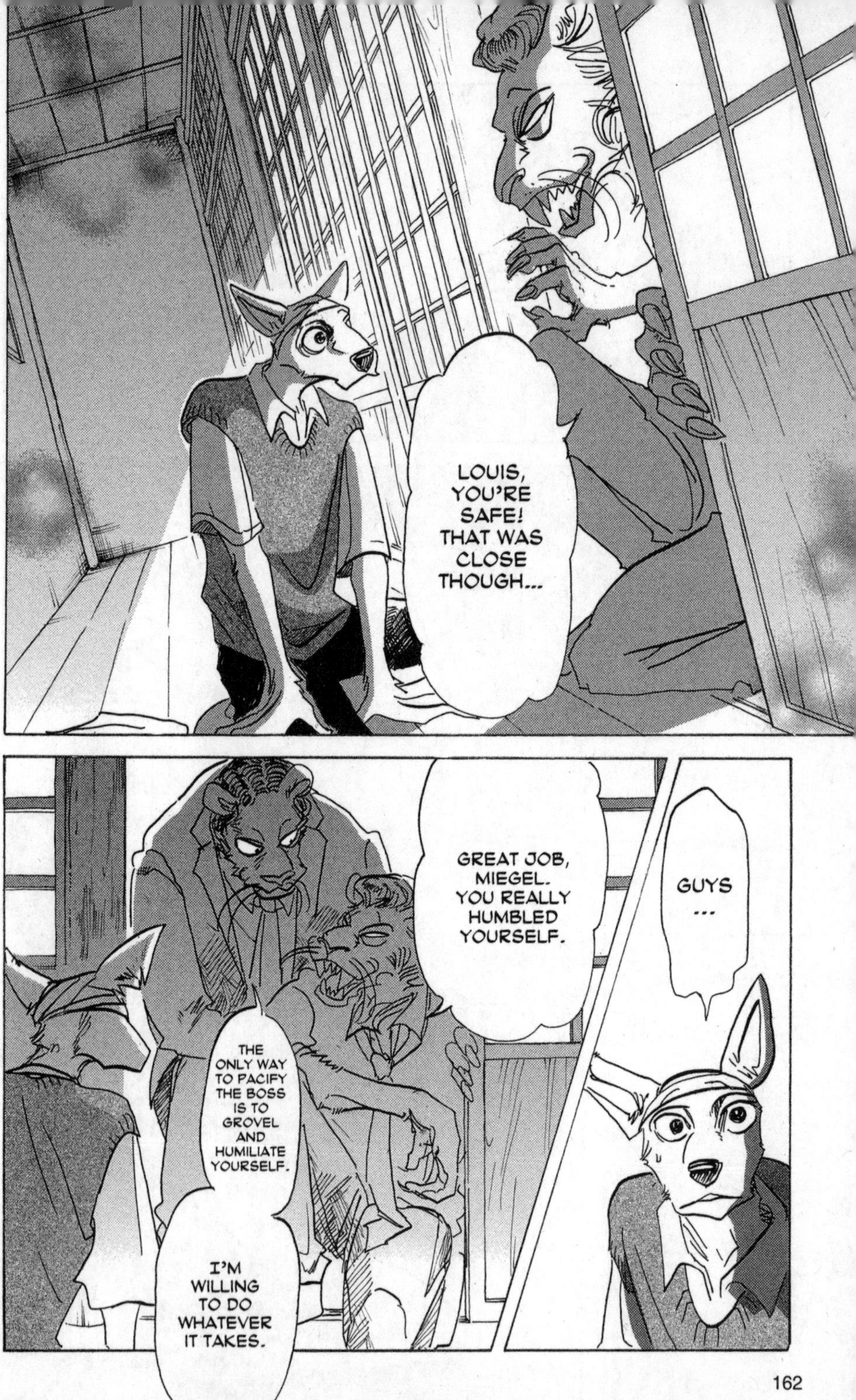
LOUIS, YOU'RE SAFE! THAT WAS CLOSE THOUGH...
GUYS ...
GREAT JOB, MIEGEL. YOU REALLY HUMBLED YOURSELF.
THE ONLY WAY TO PACIFY THE BOSS IS TO GROVEL AND HUMILIATE YOURSELF.
I'M WILLING TO DO WHATEVER IT TAKES.

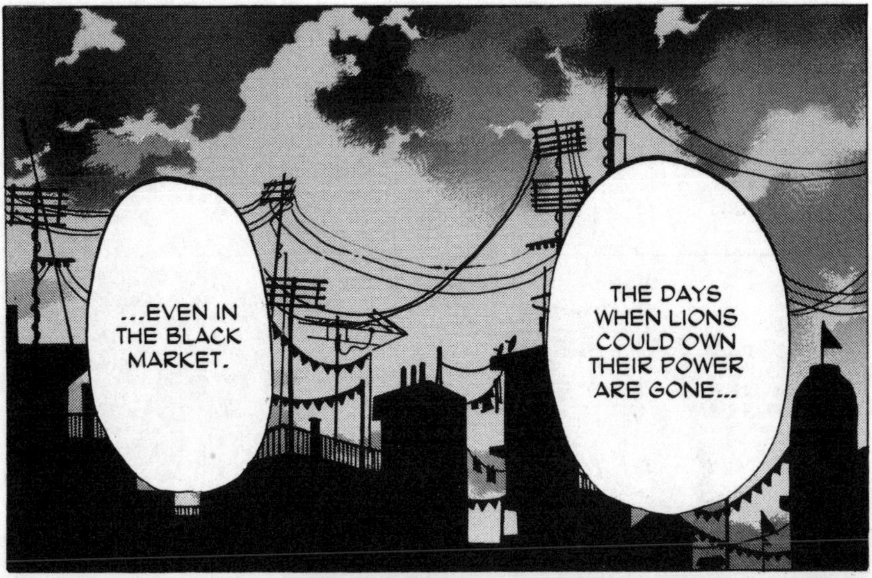
THE DAYS WHEN LIONS COULD OWN THEIR POWER ARE GONE...
...EVEN IN THE BLACK MARKET.

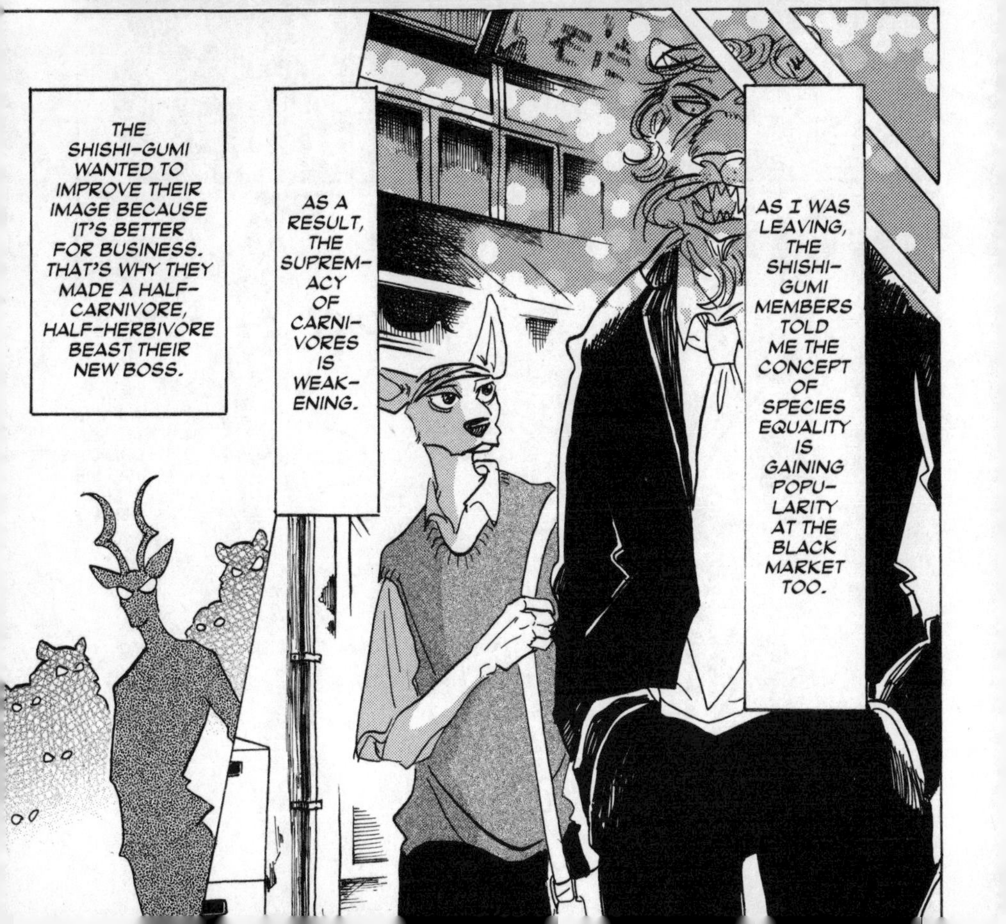
AS I WAS LEAVING, THE SHISHI-GUMI MEMBERS TOLD ME THE CONCEPT OF SPECIES EQUALITY IS GAINING POPU-LARITY AT THE BLACK MARKET TOO.
AS A RESULT, THE SUPREM-ACY OF CARNI-VORES IS WEAK-ENING.
THE SHISHI-GUMI WANTED TO IMPROVE THEIR IMAGE BECAUSE IT'S BETTER FOR BUSINESS. THAT'S WHY THEY MADE A HALF-CARNIVORE, HALF-HERBIVORE BEAST THEIR NEW BOSS.

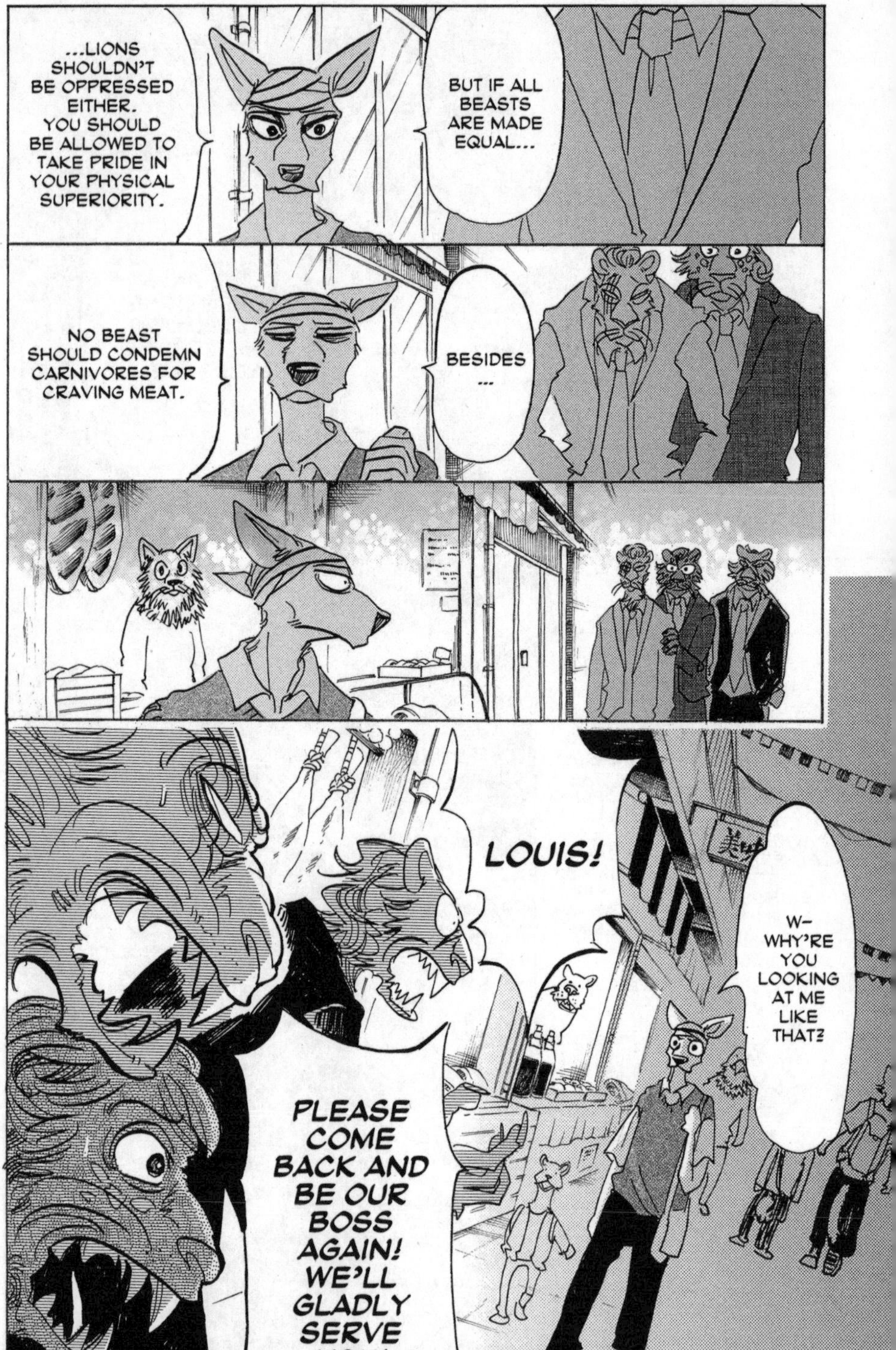
BUT IF ALL BEASTS ARE MADE EQUAL...
...LIONS SHOULDN'T BE OPPRESSED EITHER. YOU SHOULD BE ALLOWED TO TAKE PRIDE IN YOUR PHYSICAL SUPERIORITY.
BESIDES ...
NO BEAST SHOULD CONDEMN CARNIVORES FOR CRAVING MEAT.
W-WHY'RE YOU LOOKING AT ME LIKE THAT?
LOUIS!
PLEASE COME BACK AND BE OUR BOSS AGAIN! WE'LL GLADLY SERVE YOU!

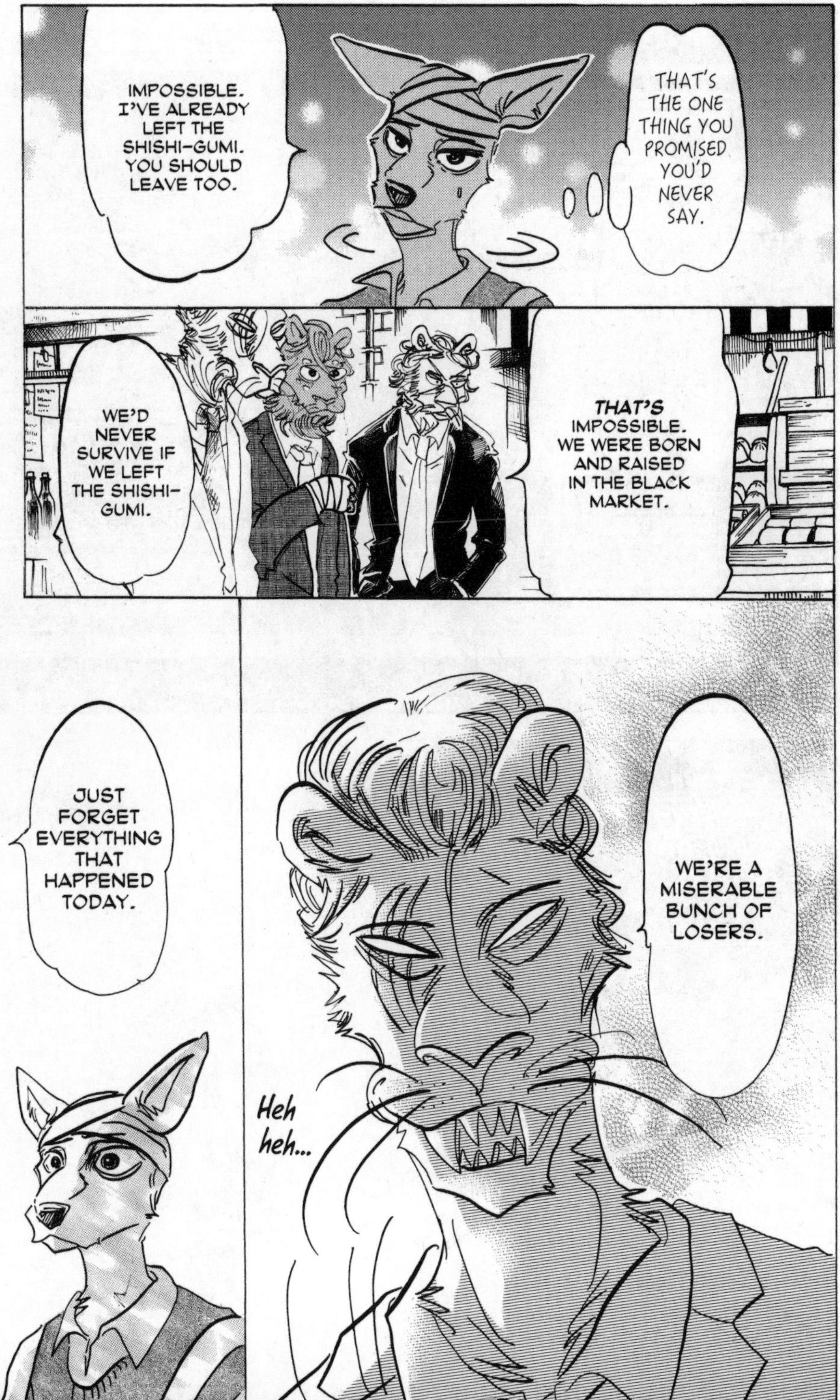
THAT'S THE ONE THING YOU PROMISED YOU'D NEVER SAY.
IMPOSSIBLE. I'VE ALREADY LEFT THE SHISHI-GUMI. YOU SHOULD LEAVE TOO.
THAT'S IMPOSSIBLE. WE WERE BORN AND RAISED IN THE BLACK MARKET.
WE'D NEVER SURVIVE IF WE LEFT THE SHISHI-GUMI.
WE'RE A MISERABLE BUNCH OF LOSERS.
Heh heh...
JUST FORGET EVERYTHING THAT HAPPENED TODAY.

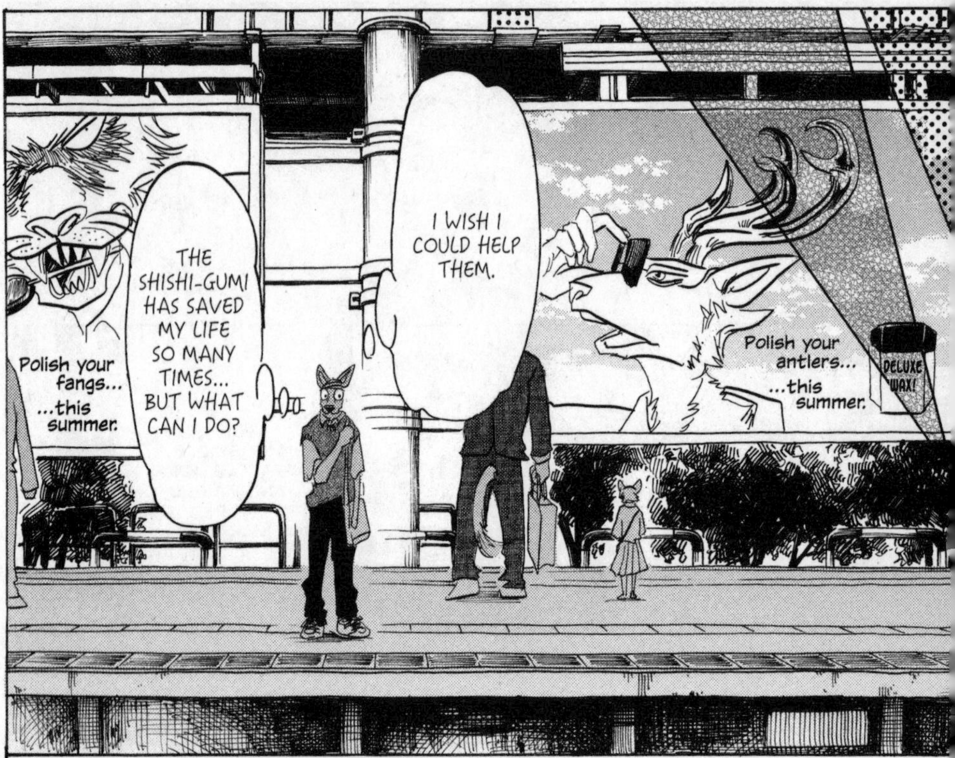
Polish your antlers... ...this summer.
DELUXE WAX!
I WISH I COULD HELP THEM.
THE SHISHI-GUMI HAS SAVED MY LIFE SO MANY TIMES... BUT WHAT CAN I DO?
Polish your fangs... ...this summer.
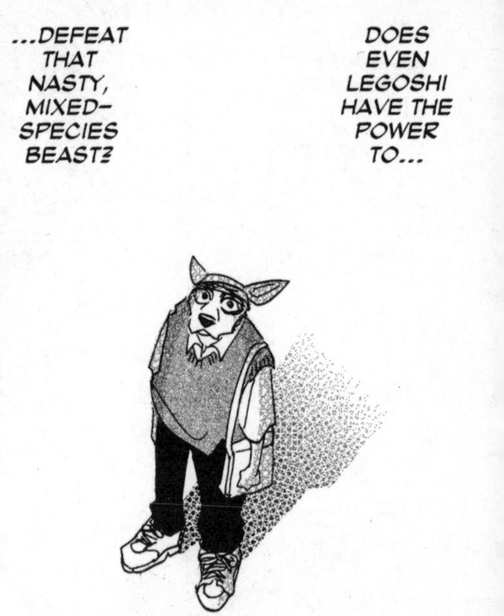
DOES EVEN LEGOSHI HAVE THE POWER TO...
...DEFEAT THAT NASTY, MIXED-SPECIES BEAST?
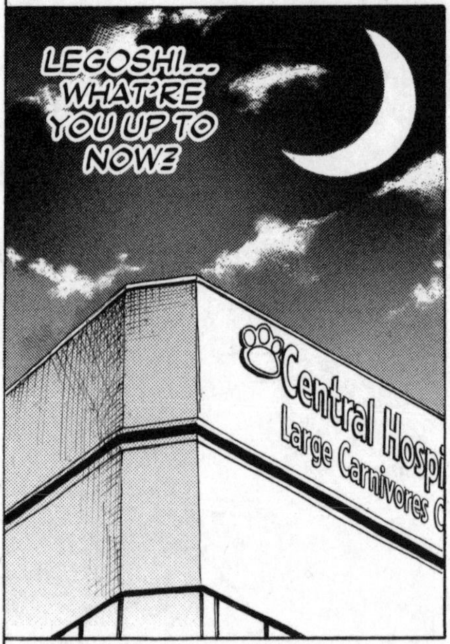
LEGOSHI... WHAT'RE YOU UP TO NOW?
Central Hospi
Large Carnivores C

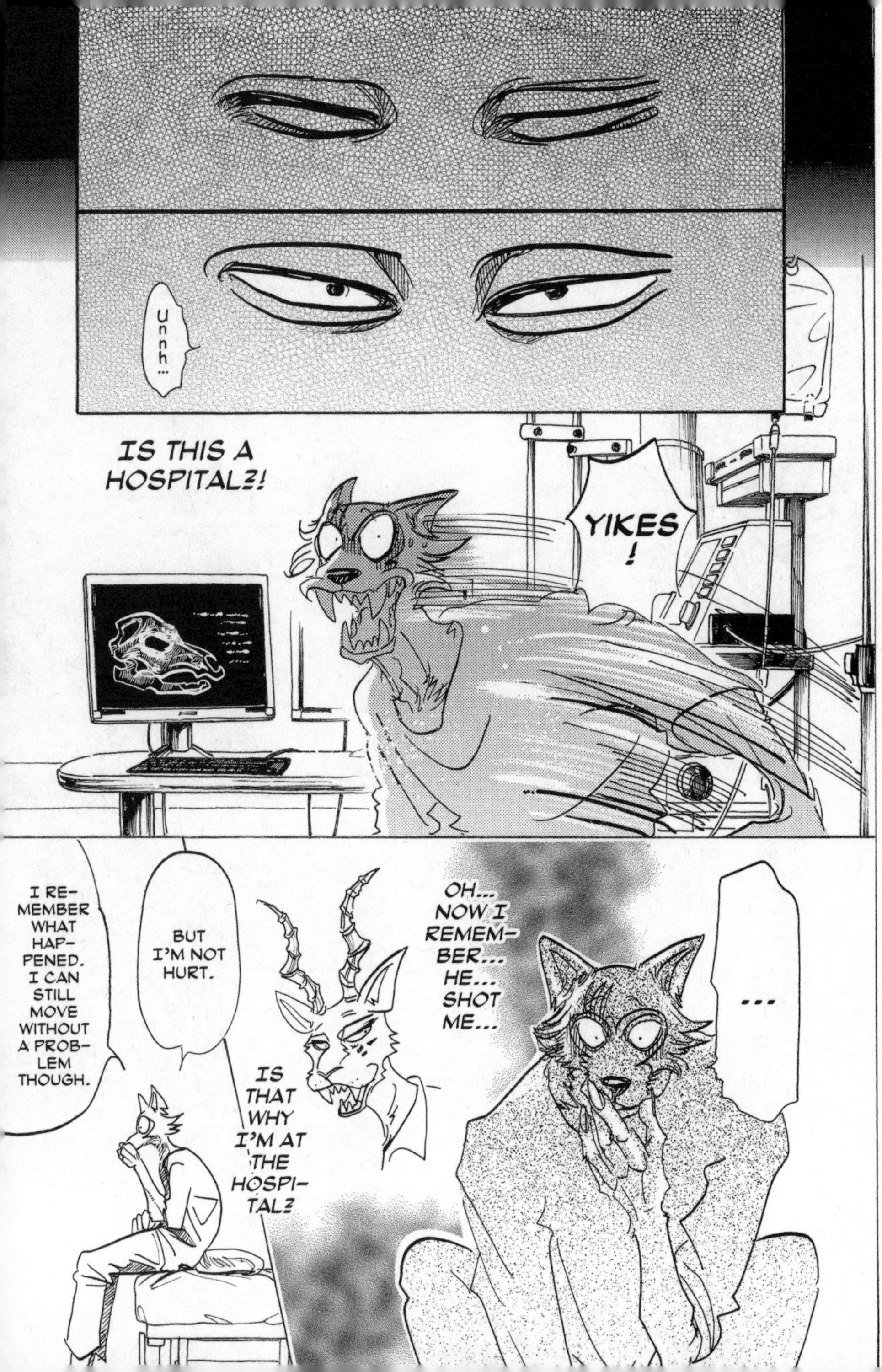
Unnh...
YIKES!
IS THIS A HOSPITAL?!
...
OH... NOW I REMEMBER... HE... SHOT ME...
IS THAT WHY I'M AT THE HOSPITAL?
BUT I'M NOT HURT.
I REMEMBER WHAT HAPPENED. I CAN STILL MOVE WITHOUT A PROBLEM THOUGH.

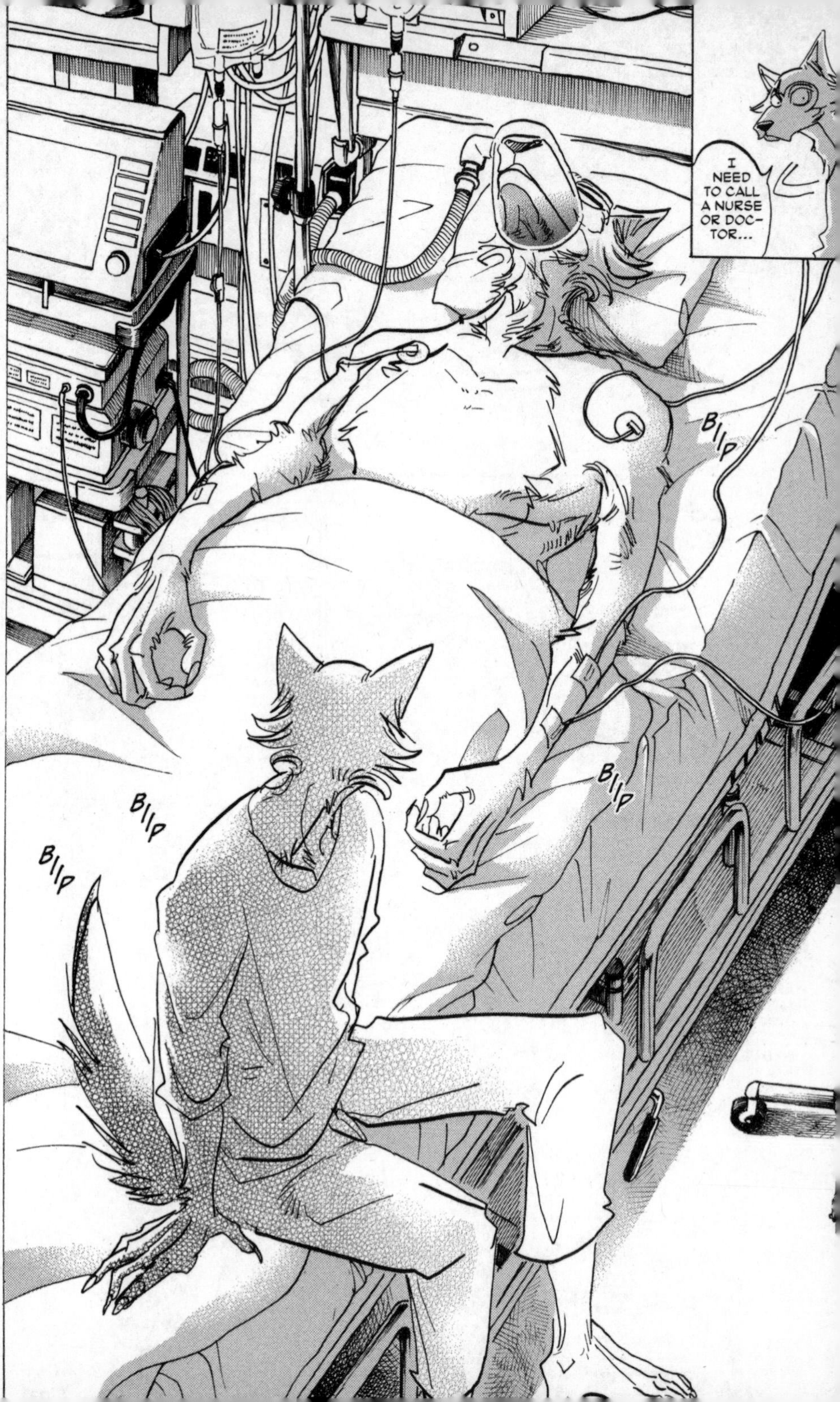
I NEED TO CALL A NURSE OR DOCTOR...
BLIP
BLIP
BLIP
BLIP

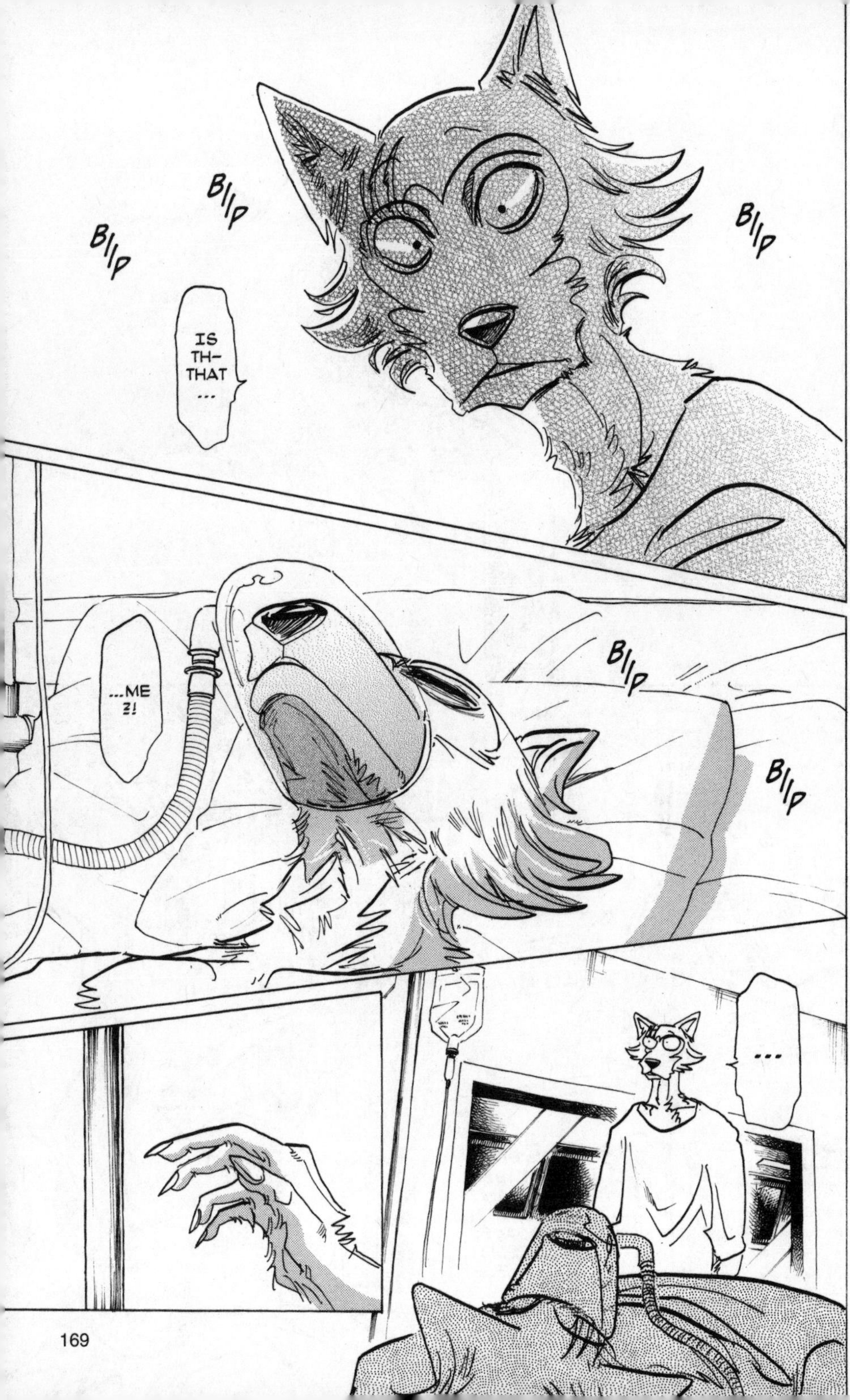
BLIP
BLIP
BLIP
IS TH-THAT ...
BLIP
BLIP
...ME ?!
...

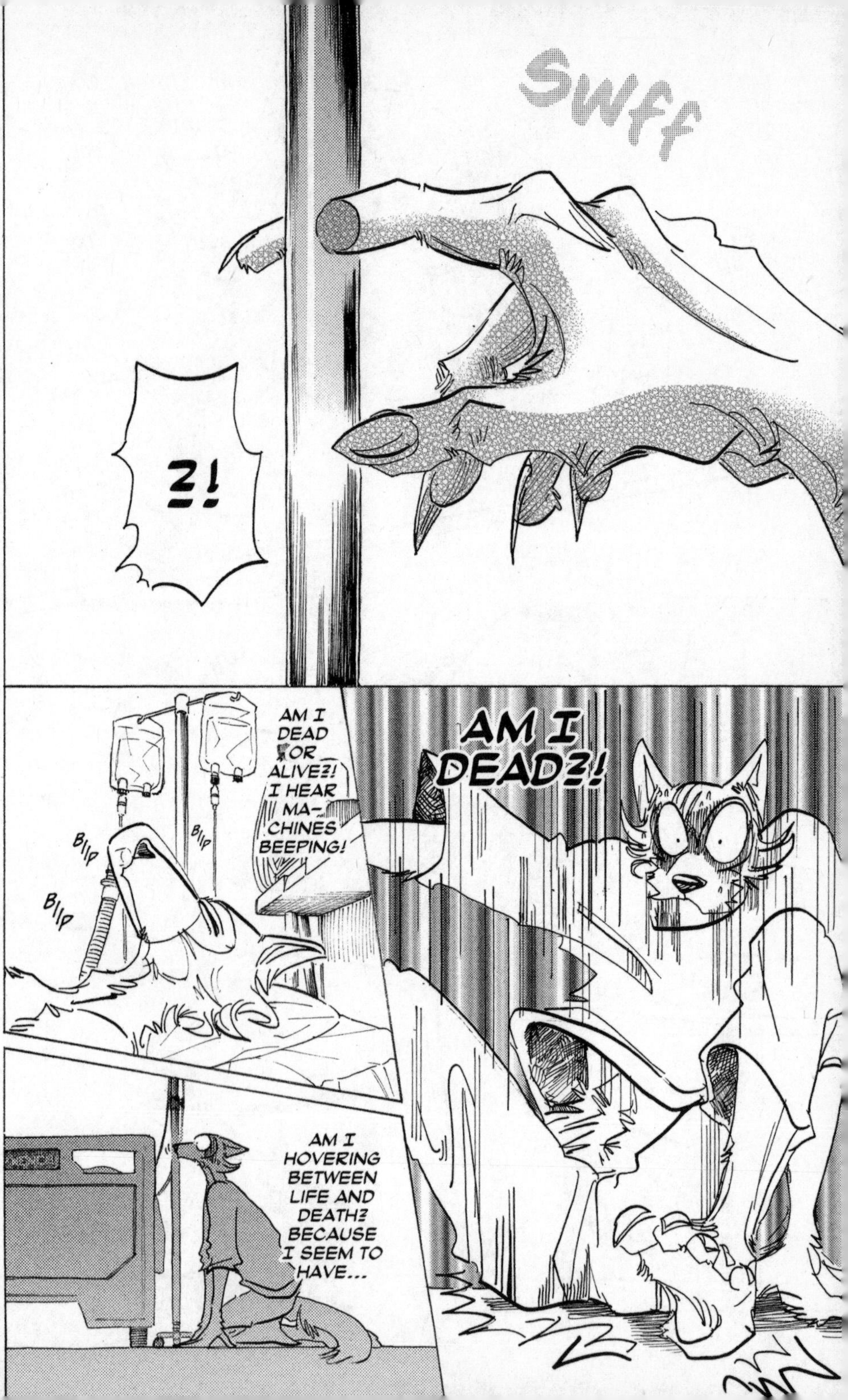
SWFF
?!
AM I DEAD?!
AM I DEAD OR ALIVE?! I HEAR MA-CHINES BEEPING!
AM I HOVERING BETWEEN LIFE AND DEATH? BECAUSE I SEEM TO HAVE...

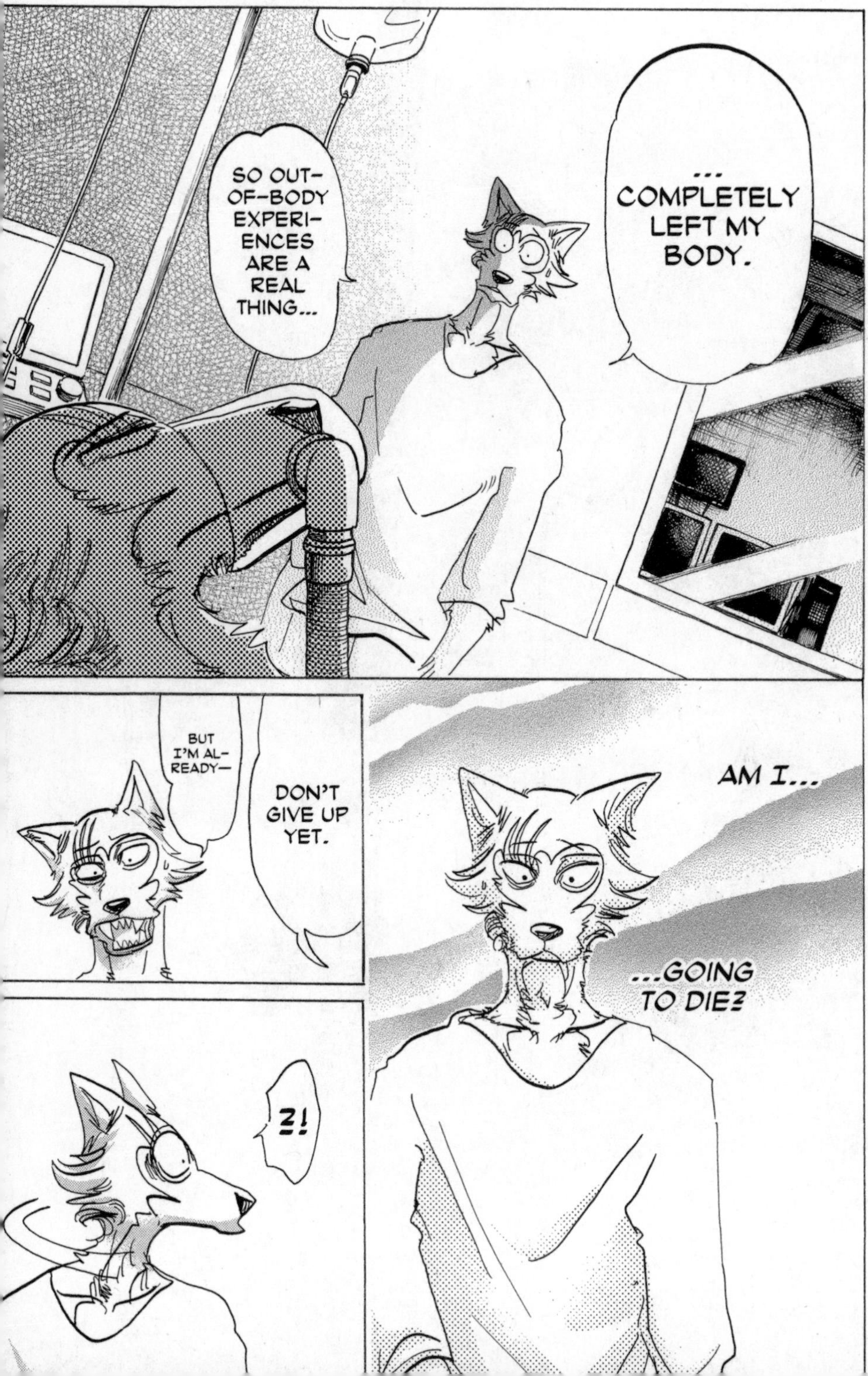
... COMPLETELY LEFT MY BODY.
SO OUT-OF-BODY EXPERIENCES ARE A REAL THING...
AM I...
...GOING TO DIE?
DON'T GIVE UP YET.
BUT I'M ALREADY—
?!

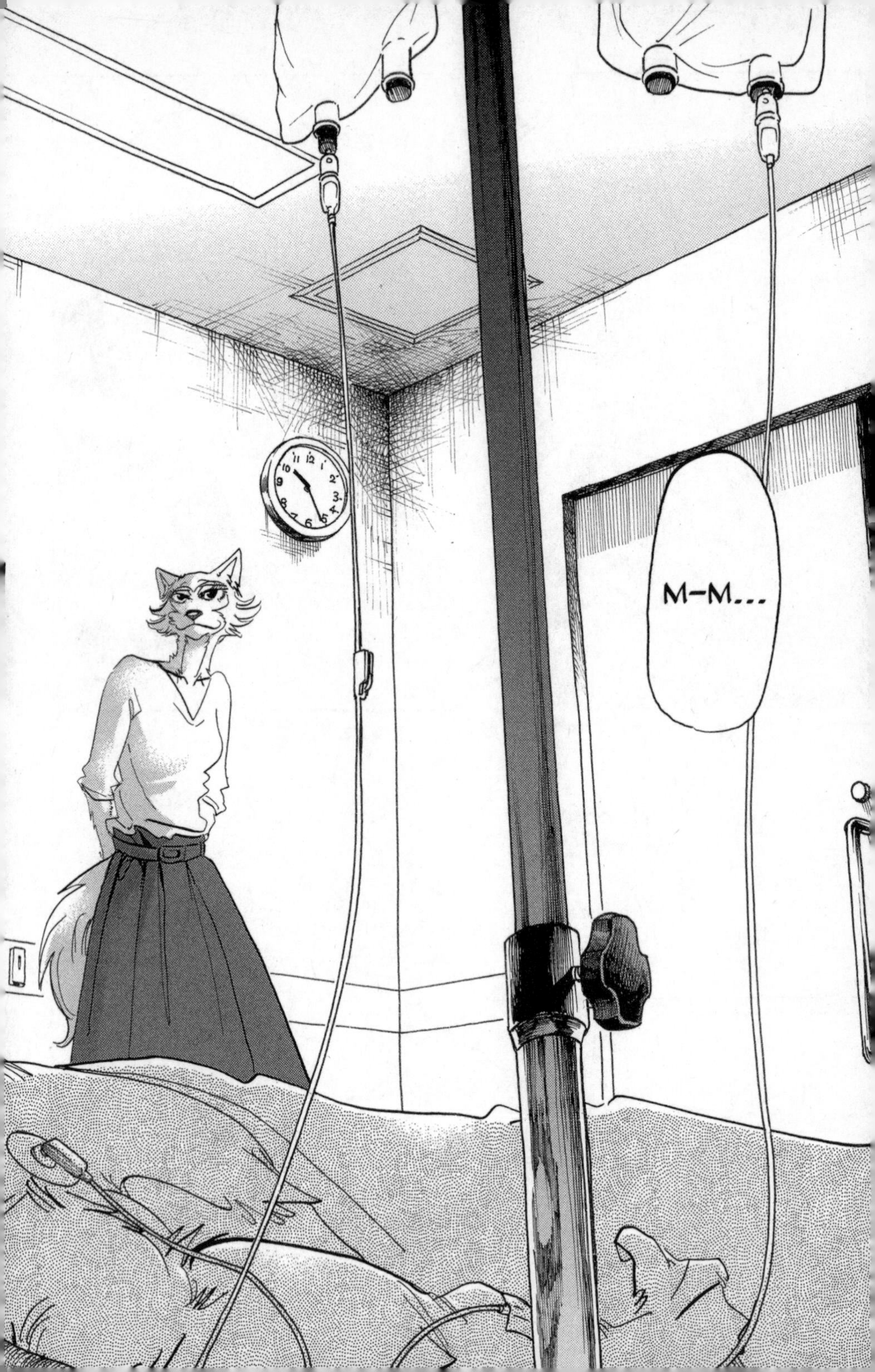
M-M...

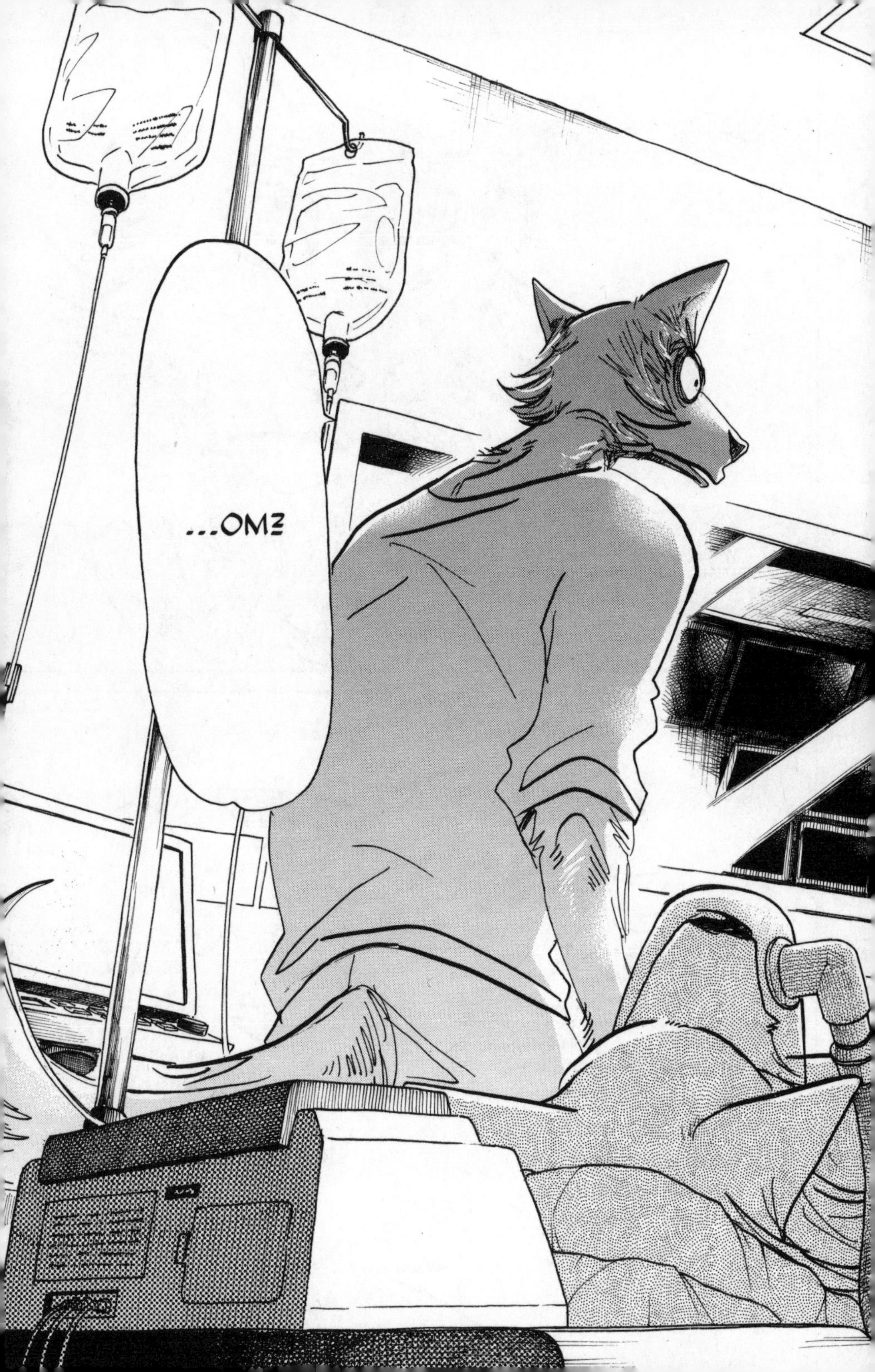
...OM3

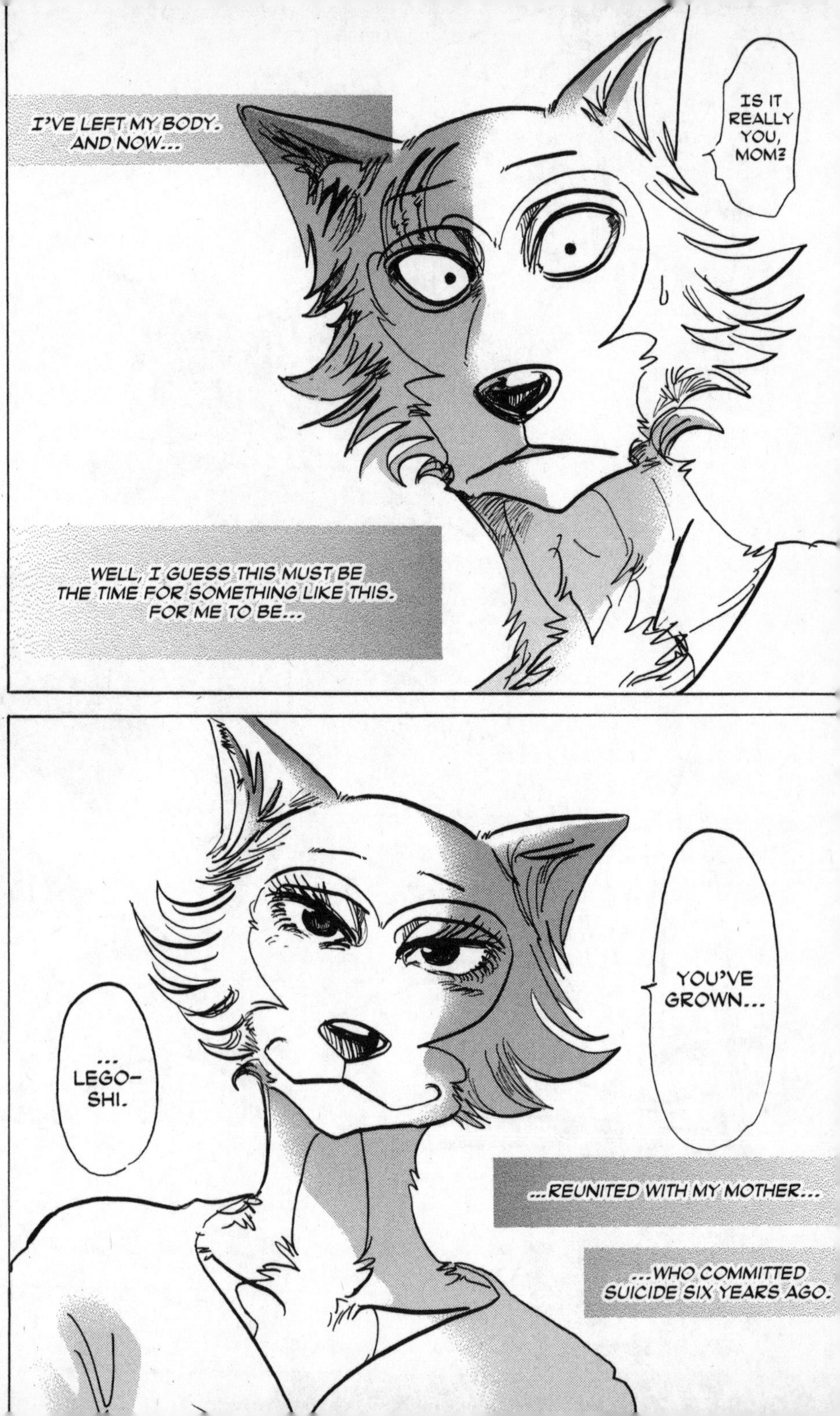
IS IT REALLY YOU, MOM?
I'VE LEFT MY BODY. AND NOW...
WELL, I GUESS THIS MUST BE THE TIME FOR SOMETHING LIKE THIS. FOR ME TO BE...
YOU'VE GROWN...
...LEGO-SHI.
...REUNITED WITH MY MOTHER...
...WHO COMMITTED SUICIDE SIX YEARS AGO.

Chapter 133: The Beach Gets Swallowed Up when the Tide Comes In

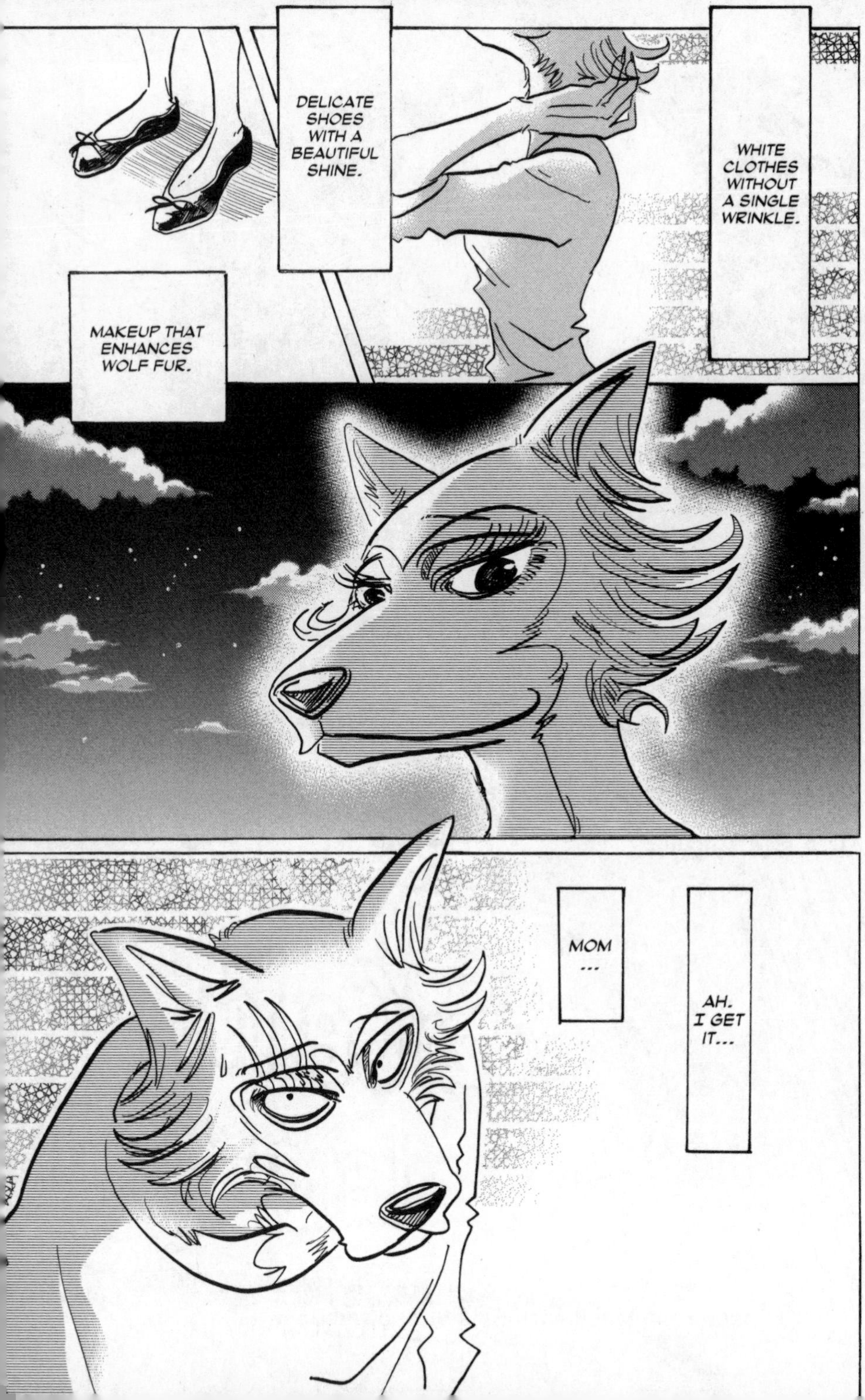
WHITE CLOTHES WITHOUT A SINGLE WRINKLE.
DELICATE SHOES WITH A BEAUTIFUL SHINE.
MAKEUP THAT ENHANCES WOLF FUR.
AH. I GET IT...
MOM ...

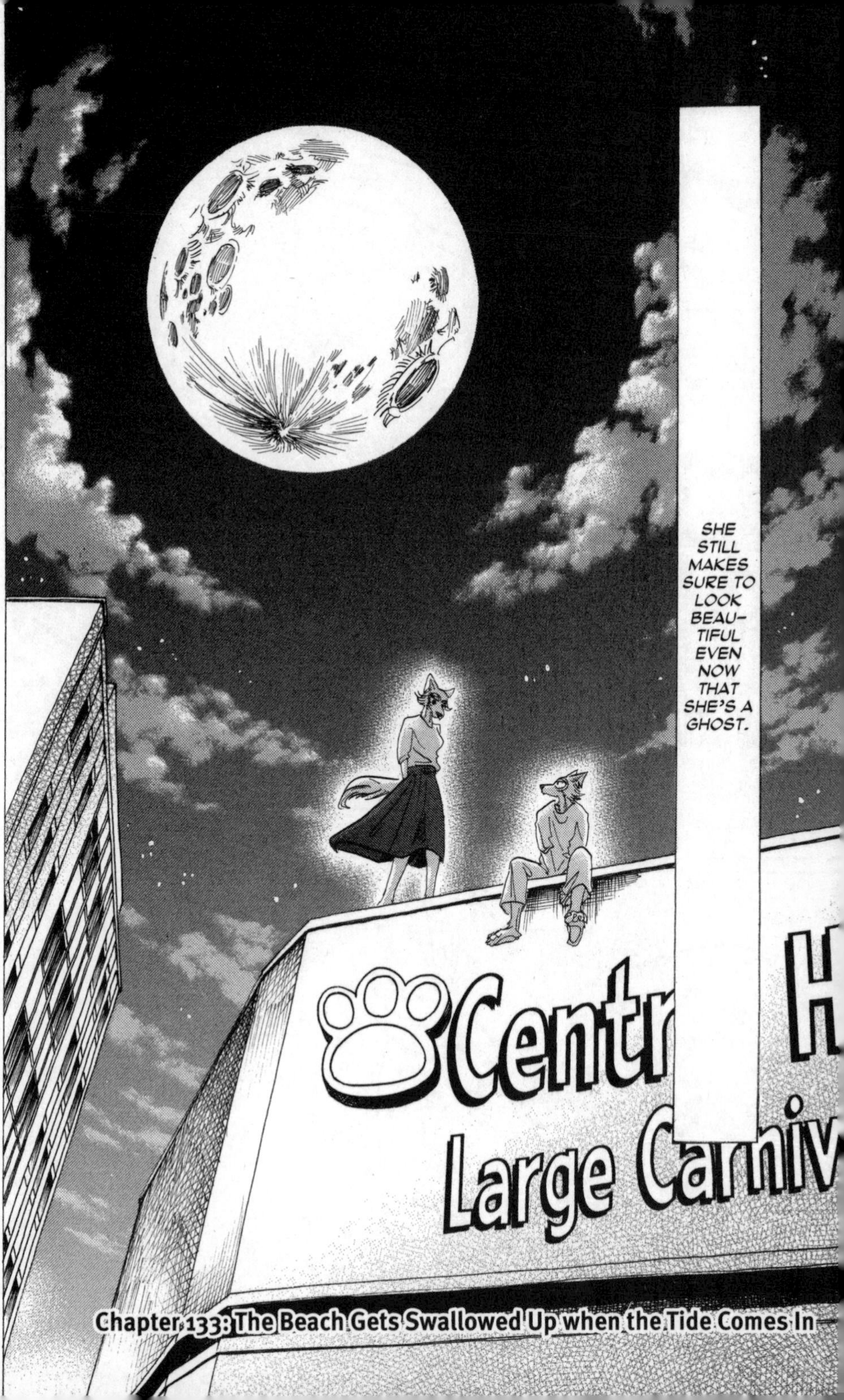
SHE STILL MAKES SURE TO LOOK BEAUTIFUL EVEN NOW THAT SHE'S A GHOST.
Centr H
Large Carniv
Chapter 133: The Beach Gets Swallowed Up when the Tide Comes In

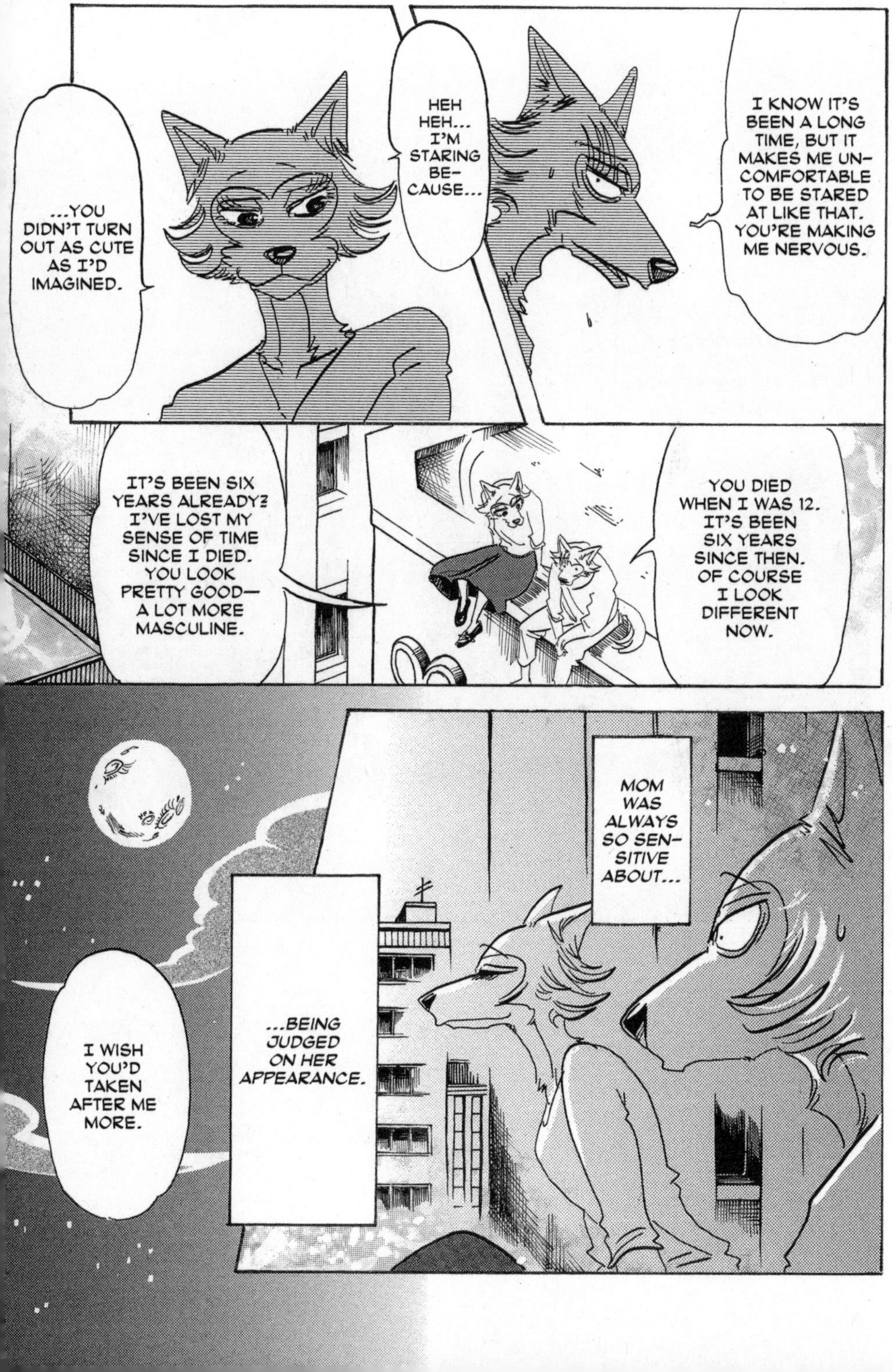
I KNOW IT'S BEEN A LONG TIME, BUT IT MAKES ME UN-COMFORTABLE TO BE STARED AT LIKE THAT. YOU'RE MAKING ME NERVOUS.
HEH HEH... I'M STARING BE-CAUSE...
...YOU DIDN'T TURN OUT AS CUTE AS I'D IMAGINED.
YOU DIED WHEN I WAS 12. IT'S BEEN SIX YEARS SINCE THEN. OF COURSE I LOOK DIFFERENT NOW.
IT'S BEEN SIX YEARS ALREADY? I'VE LOST MY SENSE OF TIME SINCE I DIED. YOU LOOK PRETTY GOOD— A LOT MORE MASCULINE.
MOM WAS ALWAYS SO SEN-SITIVE ABOUT...
...BEING JUDGED ON HER APPEARANCE.
I WISH YOU'D TAKEN AFTER ME MORE.

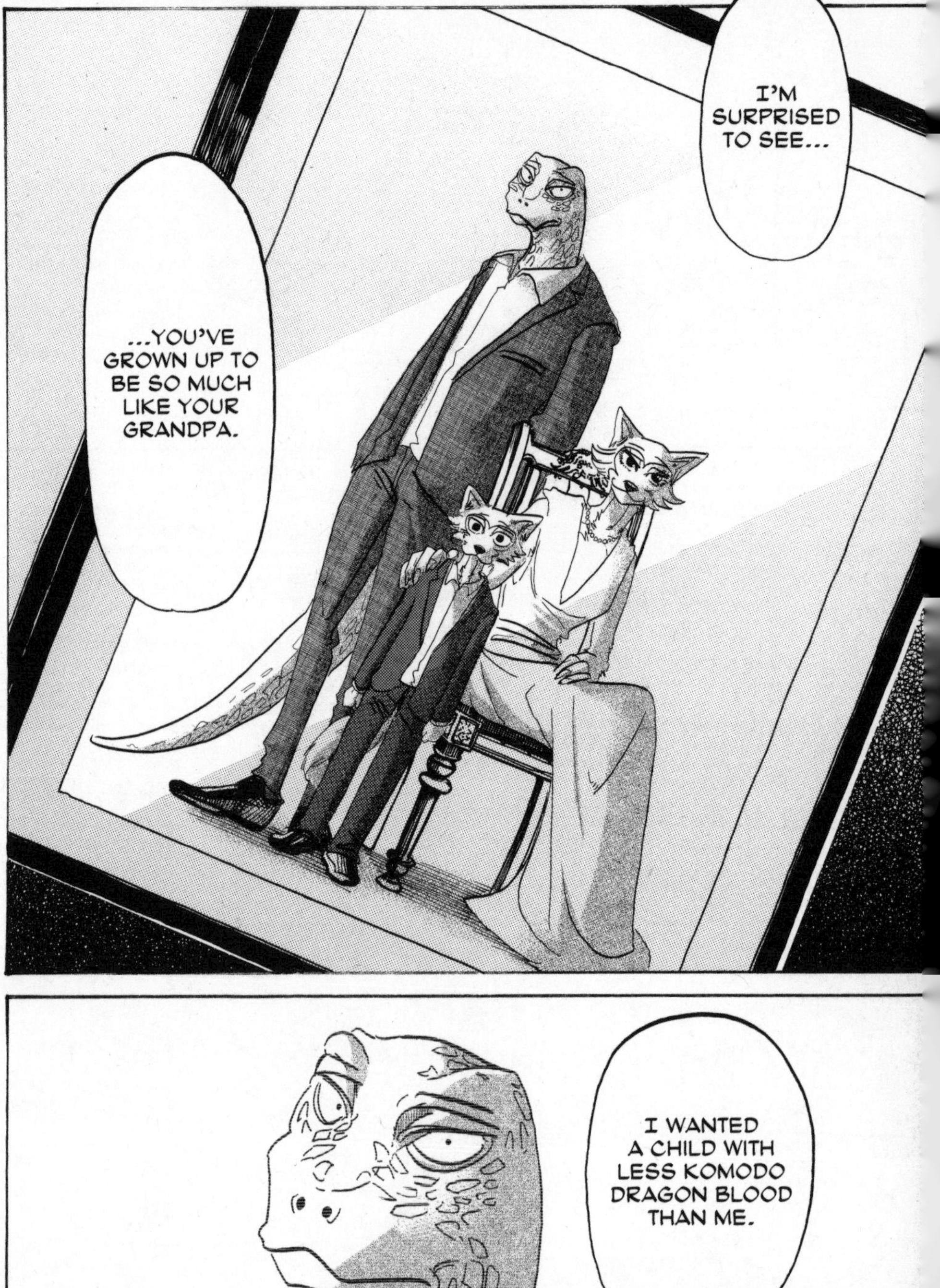
I'M SURPRISED TO SEE...
...YOU'VE GROWN UP TO BE SO MUCH LIKE YOUR GRANDPA.
I WANTED A CHILD WITH LESS KOMODO DRAGON BLOOD THAN ME.

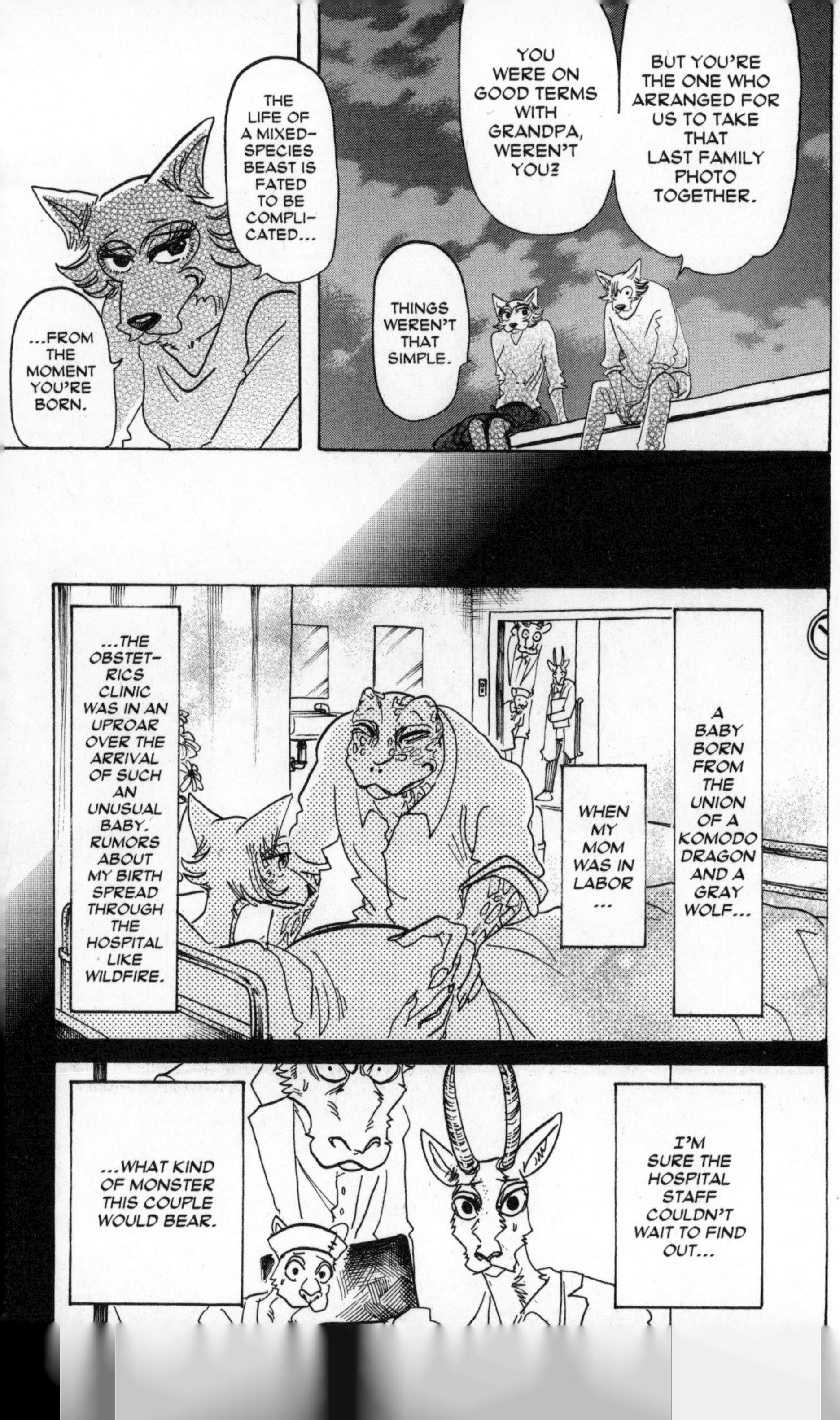
BUT YOU'RE THE ONE WHO ARRANGED FOR US TO TAKE THAT LAST FAMILY PHOTO TOGETHER.
YOU WERE ON GOOD TERMS WITH GRANDPA, WEREN'T YOU?
THINGS WEREN'T THAT SIMPLE.
THE LIFE OF A MIXED-SPECIES BEAST IS FATED TO BE COMPLICATED...
...FROM THE MOMENT YOU'RE BORN.
A BABY BORN FROM THE UNION OF A KOMODO DRAGON AND A GRAY WOLF...
WHEN MY MOM WAS IN LABOR...
...THE OBSTETRICS CLINIC WAS IN AN UPROAR OVER THE ARRIVAL OF SUCH AN UNUSUAL BABY. RUMORS ABOUT MY BIRTH SPREAD THROUGH THE HOSPITAL LIKE WILDFIRE.
I'M SURE THE HOSPITAL STAFF COULDN'T WAIT TO FIND OUT...
...WHAT KIND OF MONSTER THIS COUPLE WOULD BEAR.

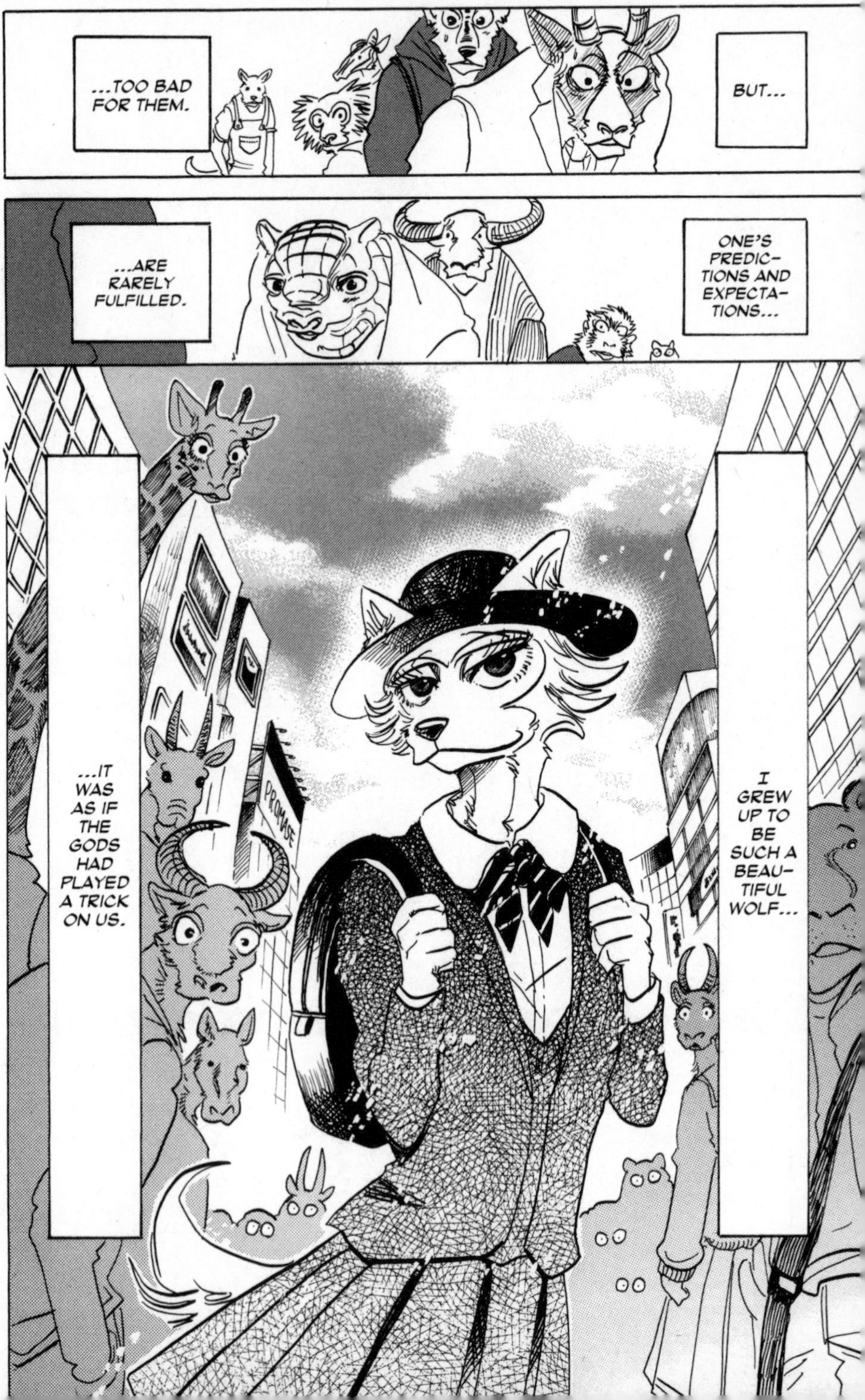
BUT...
...TOO BAD FOR THEM.
ONE'S PREDIC-TIONS AND EXPECTA-TIONS...
...ARE RARELY FULFILLED.
I GREW UP TO BE SUCH A BEAU-TIFUL WOLF...
...IT WAS AS IF THE GODS HAD PLAYED A TRICK ON US.

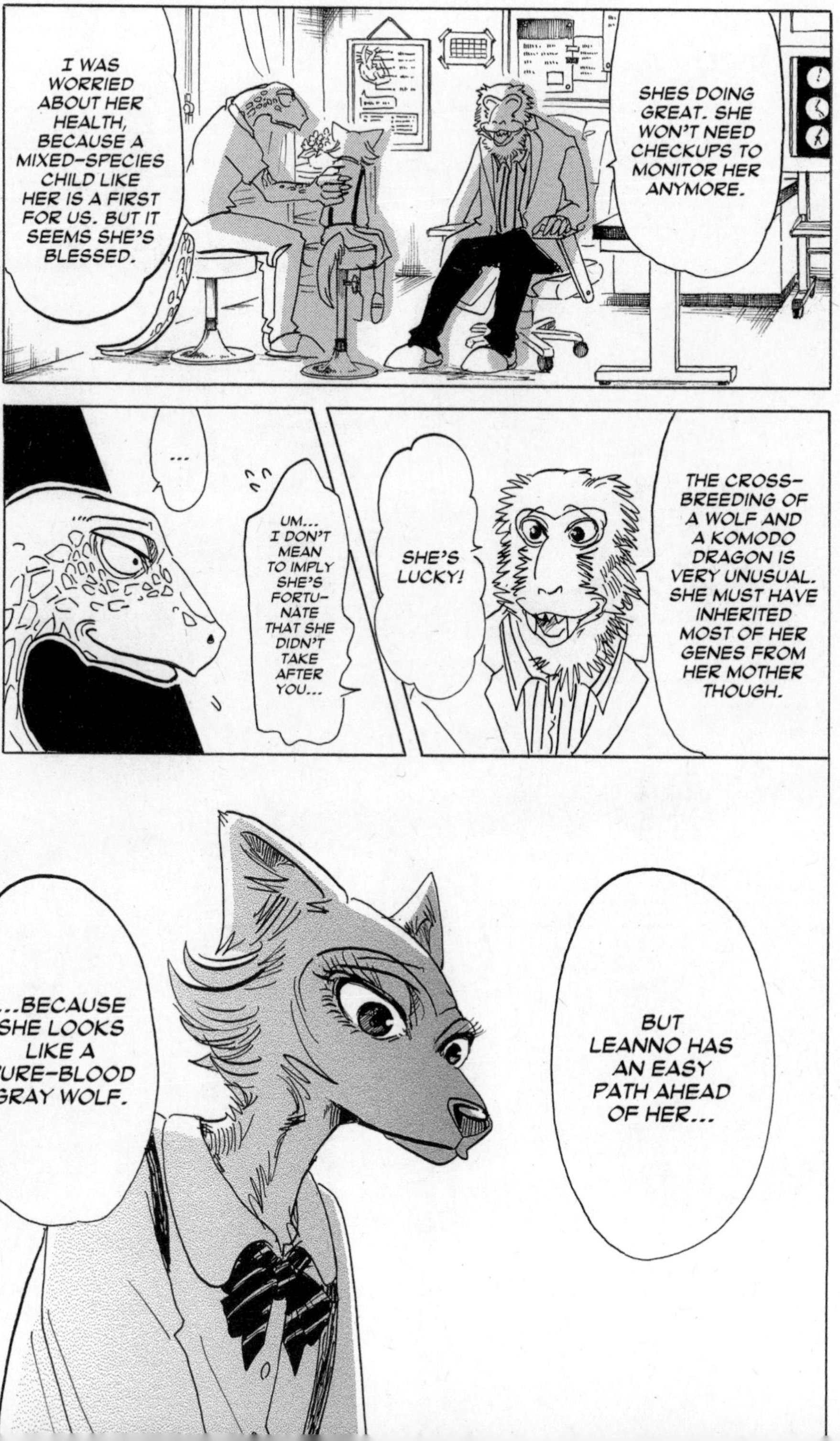
SHES DOING GREAT. SHE WON'T NEED CHECKUPS TO MONITOR HER ANYMORE.
I WAS WORRIED ABOUT HER HEALTH, BECAUSE A MIXED-SPECIES CHILD LIKE HER IS A FIRST FOR US. BUT IT SEEMS SHE'S BLESSED.
THE CROSS-BREEDING OF A WOLF AND A KOMODO DRAGON IS VERY UNUSUAL. SHE MUST HAVE INHERITED MOST OF HER GENES FROM HER MOTHER THOUGH.
SHE'S LUCKY!
...
UM... I DON'T MEAN TO IMPLY SHE'S FORTU-NATE THAT SHE DIDN'T TAKE AFTER YOU...
BUT LEANNO HAS AN EASY PATH AHEAD OF HER...
...BECAUSE SHE LOOKS LIKE A PURE-BLOOD GRAY WOLF.

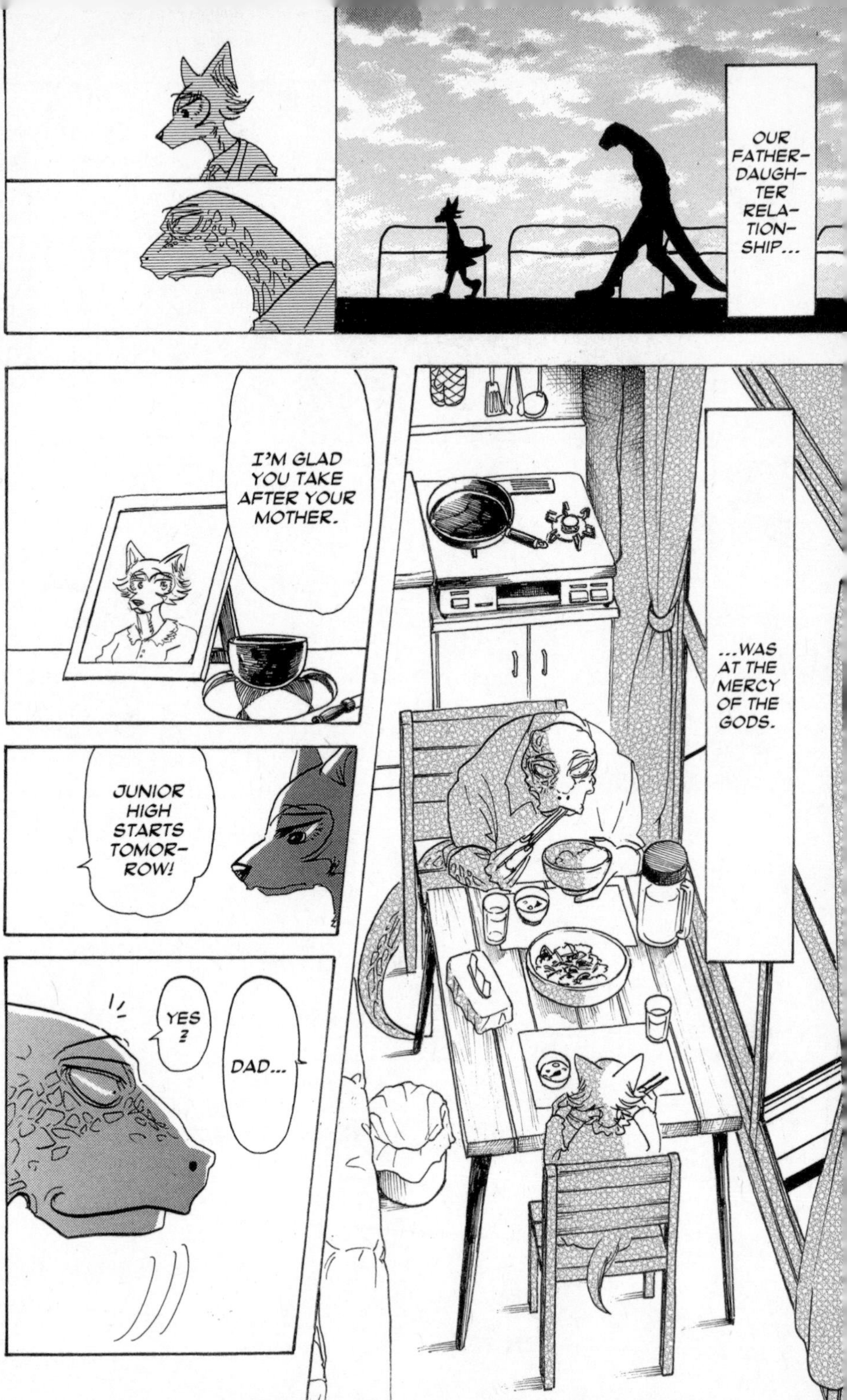
OUR FATHER-DAUGHTER RELATIONSHIP...
...WAS AT THE MERCY OF THE GODS.
I'M GLAD YOU TAKE AFTER YOUR MOTHER.
JUNIOR HIGH STARTS TOMORROW!
DAD...
YES?

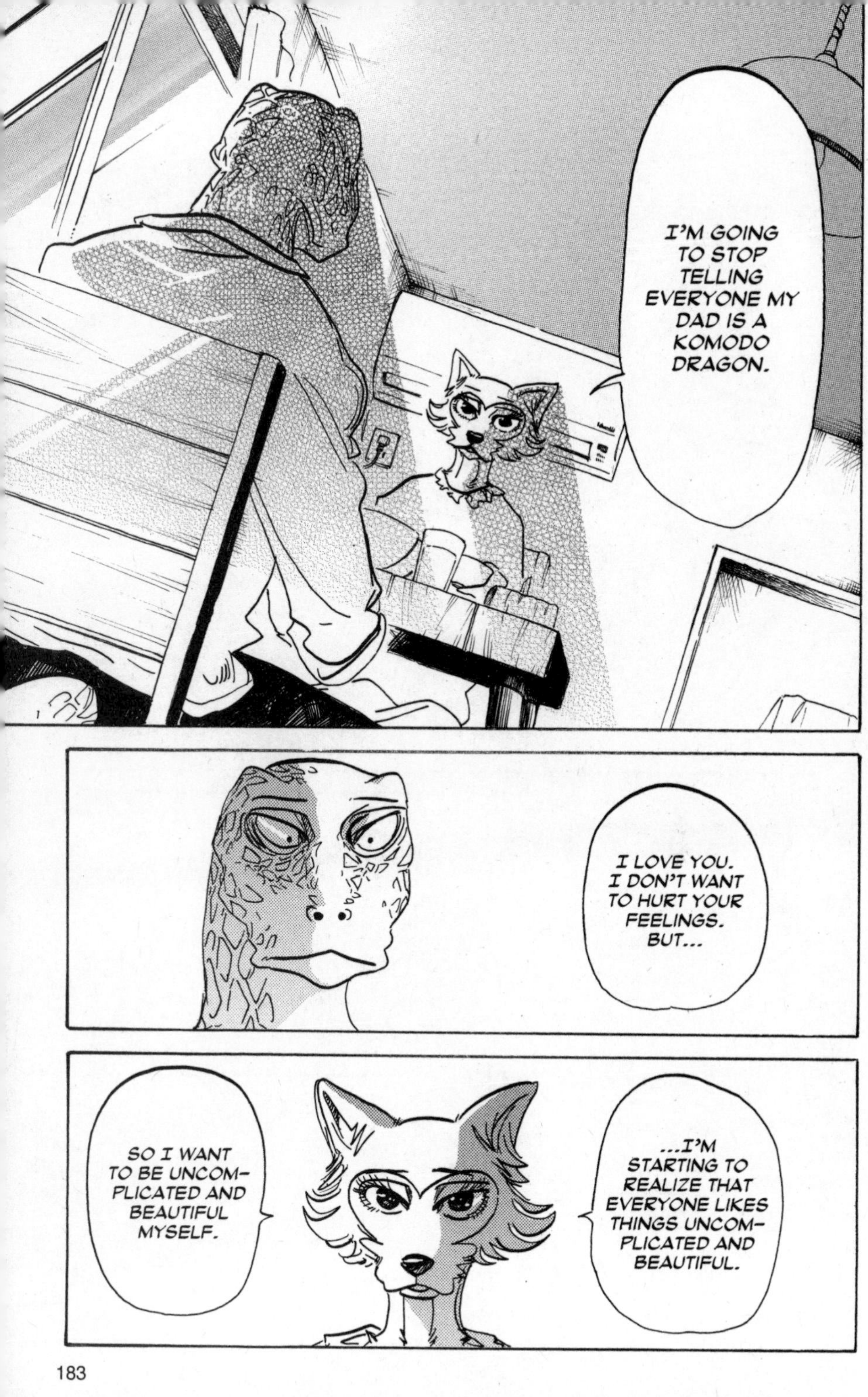
I'M GOING TO STOP TELLING EVERYONE MY DAD IS A KOMODO DRAGON.
I LOVE YOU. I DON'T WANT TO HURT YOUR FEELINGS. BUT...
...I'M STARTING TO REALIZE THAT EVERYONE LIKES THINGS UNCOM-PLICATED AND BEAUTIFUL.
SO I WANT TO BE UNCOM-PLICATED AND BEAUTIFUL MYSELF.

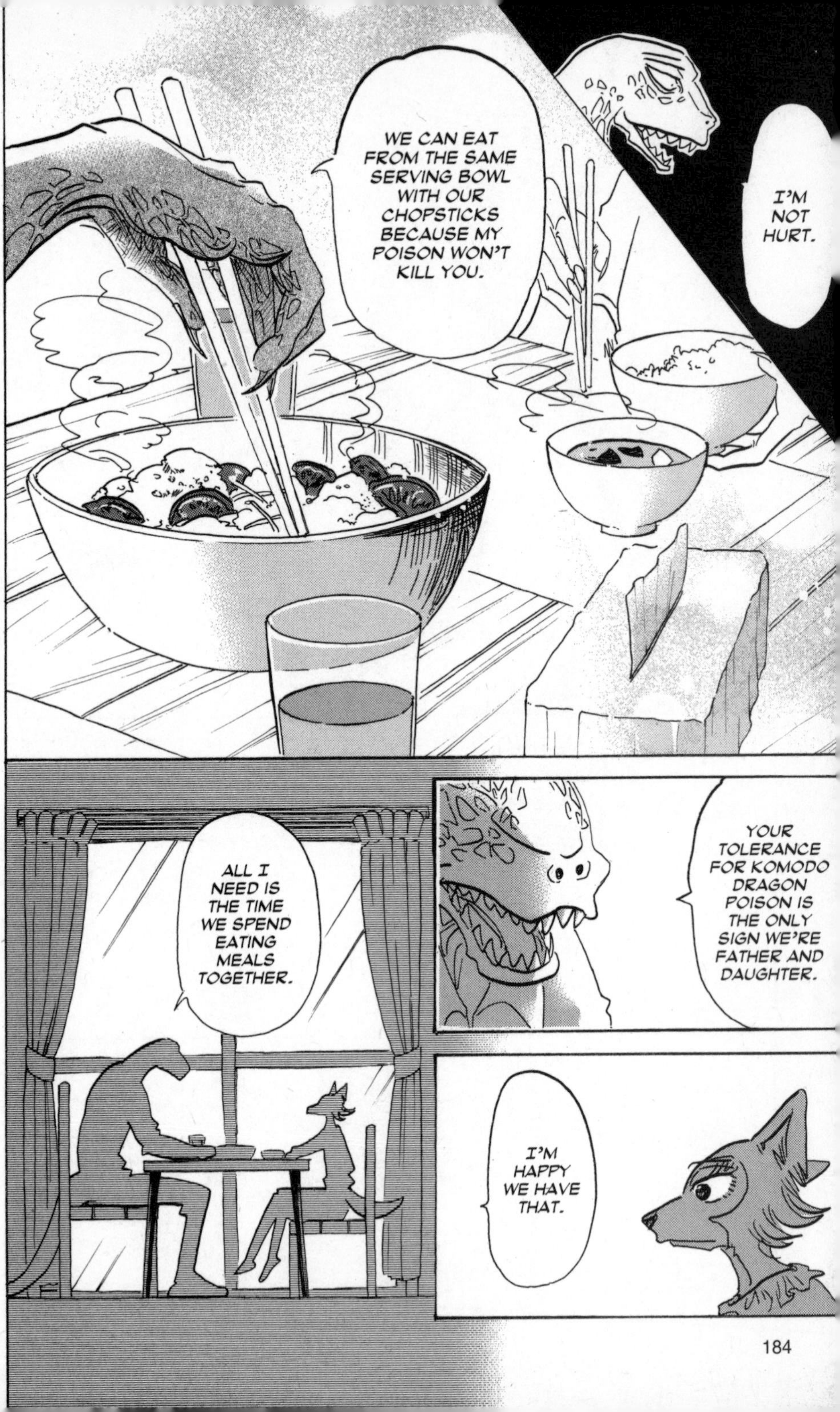
I'M NOT HURT.
WE CAN EAT FROM THE SAME SERVING BOWL WITH OUR CHOPSTICKS BECAUSE MY POISON WON'T KILL YOU.
YOUR TOLERANCE FOR KOMODO DRAGON POISON IS THE ONLY SIGN WE'RE FATHER AND DAUGHTER.
I'M HAPPY WE HAVE THAT.
ALL I NEED IS THE TIME WE SPEND EATING MEALS TOGETHER.

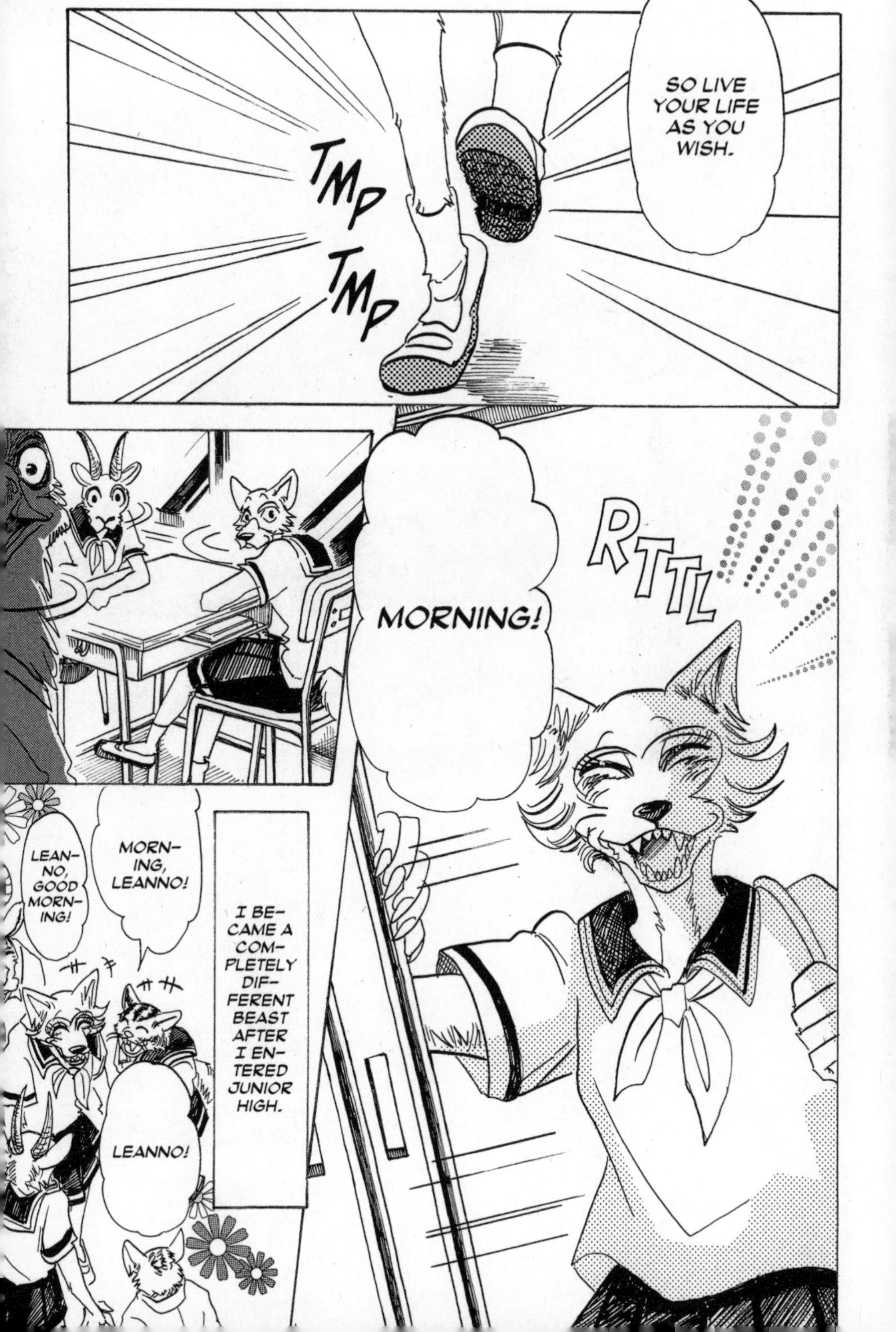
SO LIVE YOUR LIFE AS YOU WISH.
TMP TMP
RTTL
MORNING!
I BECAME A COMPLETELY DIFFERENT BEAST AFTER I ENTERED JUNIOR HIGH.
MORNING, LEANNO!
LEANNO, GOOD MORNING!
LEANNO!

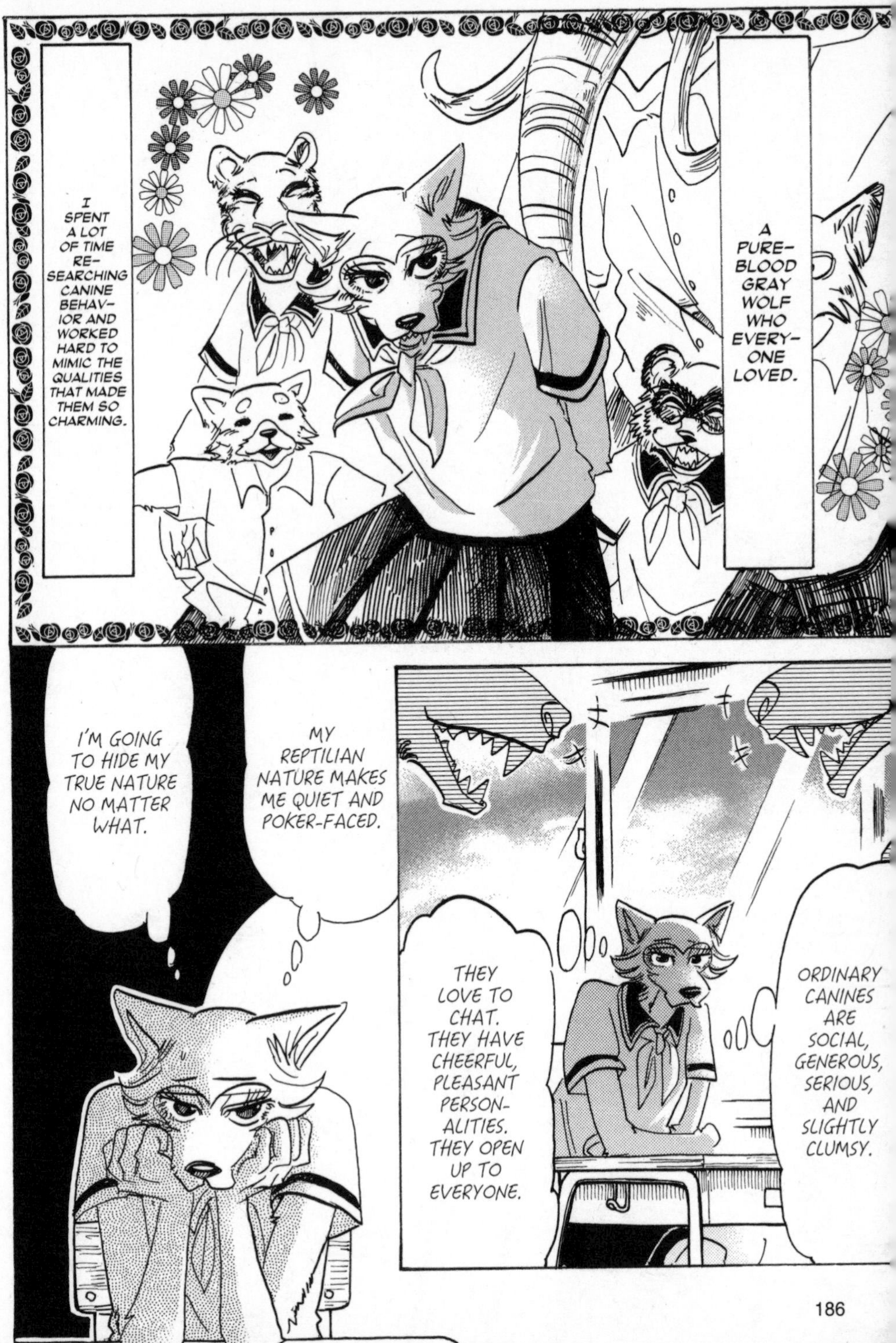
A PURE-BLOOD GRAY WOLF WHO EVERYONE LOVED.
I SPENT A LOT OF TIME RESEARCHING CANINE BEHAVIOR AND WORKED HARD TO MIMIC THE QUALITIES THAT MADE THEM SO CHARMING.
ORDINARY CANINES ARE SOCIAL, GENEROUS, SERIOUS, AND SLIGHTLY CLUMSY.
THEY LOVE TO CHAT. THEY HAVE CHEERFUL, PLEASANT PERSONALITIES. THEY OPEN UP TO EVERYONE.
MY REPTILIAN NATURE MAKES ME QUIET AND POKER-FACED.
I'M GOING TO HIDE MY TRUE NATURE NO MATTER WHAT.

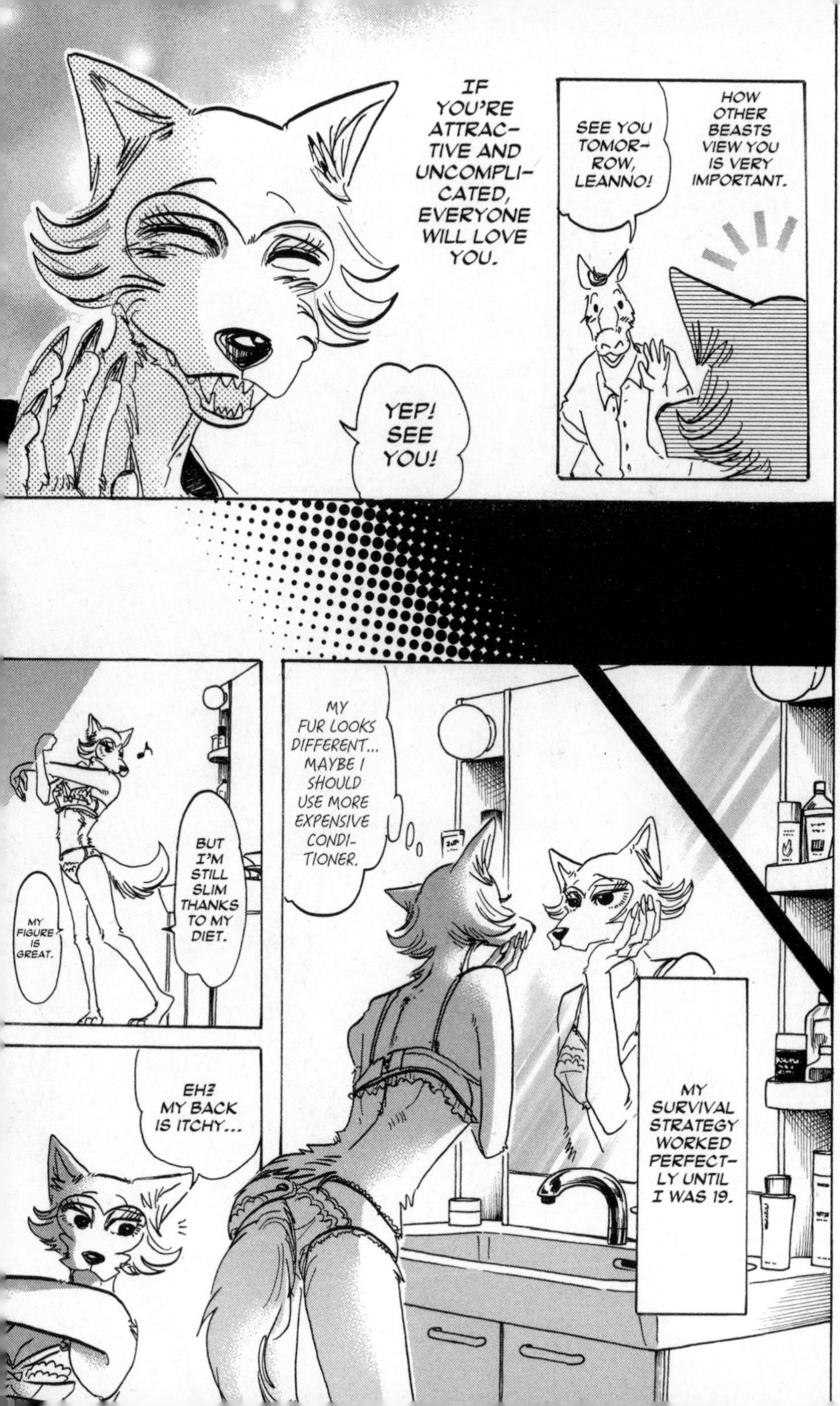
HOW OTHER BEASTS VIEW YOU IS VERY IMPORTANT.
SEE YOU TOMORROW, LEANNO!
IF YOU'RE ATTRACTIVE AND UNCOMPLICATED, EVERYONE WILL LOVE YOU.
YEP! SEE YOU!
MY FUR LOOKS DIFFERENT... MAYBE I SHOULD USE MORE EXPENSIVE CONDITIONER.
MY SURVIVAL STRATEGY WORKED PERFECTLY UNTIL I WAS 19.
BUT I'M STILL SLIM THANKS TO MY DIET.
MY FIGURE IS GREAT.
EH? MY BACK IS ITCHY...

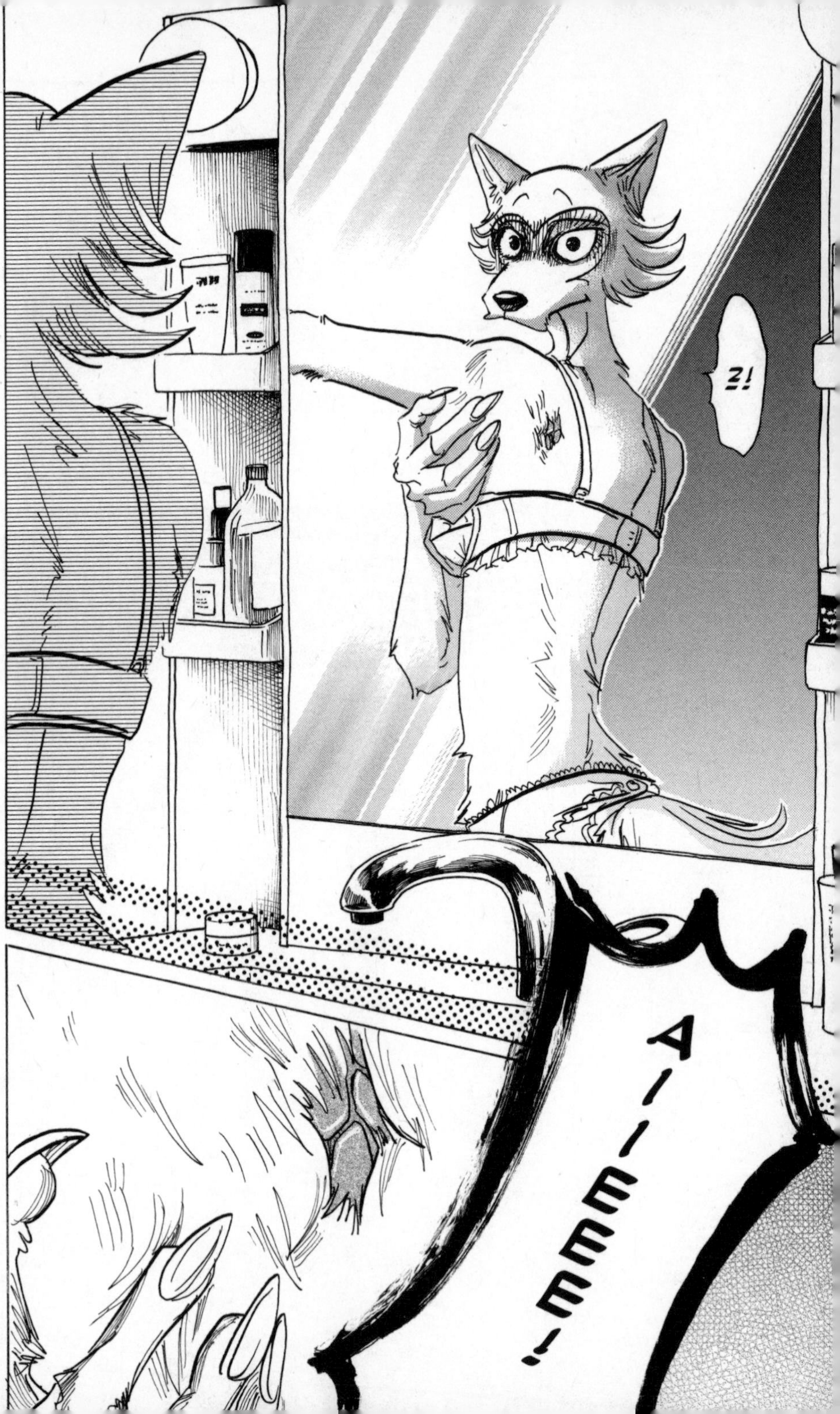
?!
AIIEEEE!

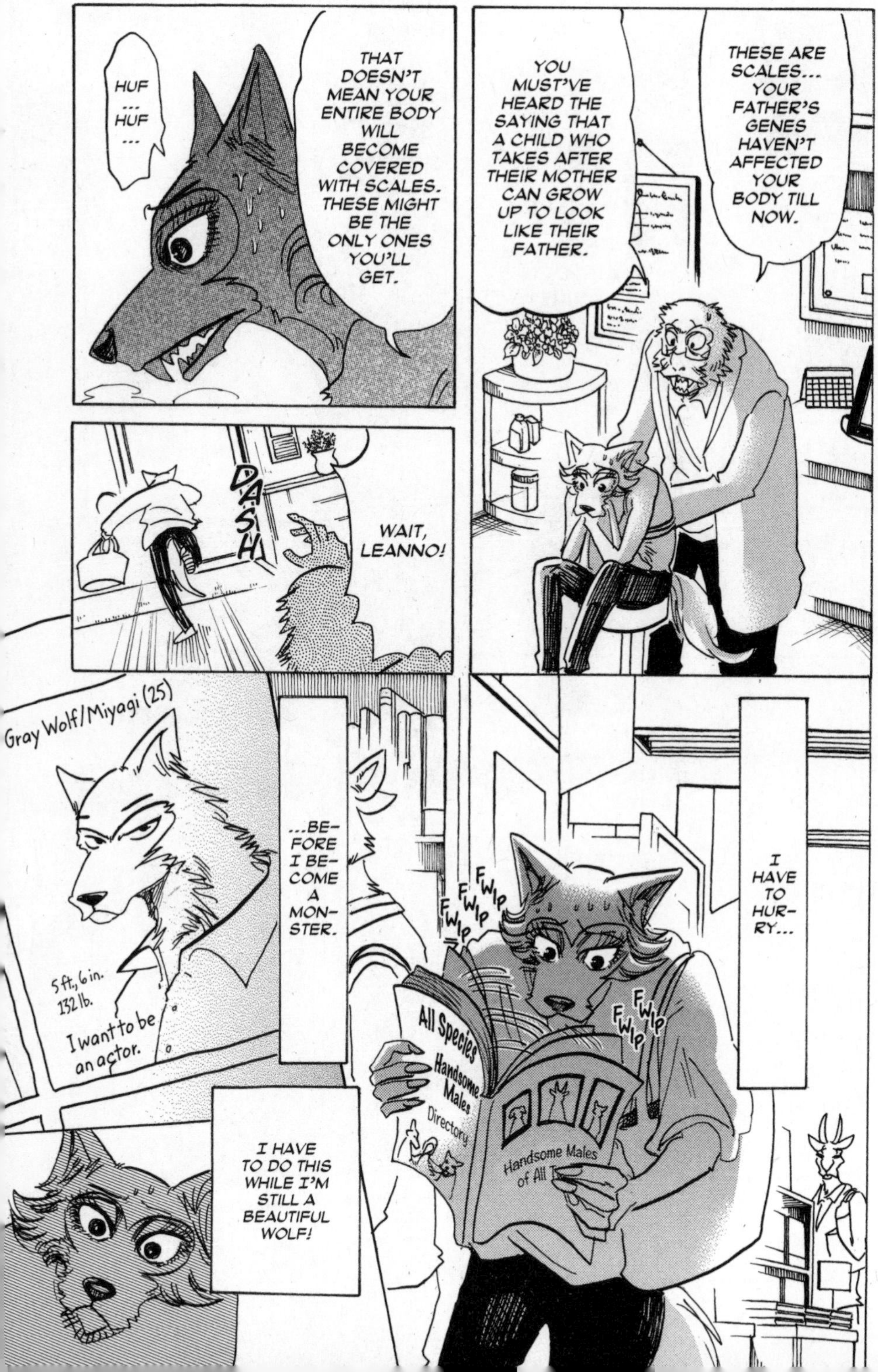
THESE ARE SCALES... YOUR FATHER'S GENES HAVEN'T AFFECTED YOUR BODY TILL NOW.
YOU MUST'VE HEARD THE SAYING THAT A CHILD WHO TAKES AFTER THEIR MOTHER CAN GROW UP TO LOOK LIKE THEIR FATHER.
THAT DOESN'T MEAN YOUR ENTIRE BODY WILL BECOME COVERED WITH SCALES. THESE MIGHT BE THE ONLY ONES YOU'LL GET.
HUF... HUF...
WAIT, LEANNO!
DASH
I HAVE TO HURRY...
FWIP FWIP
FWIP FWIP FWIP
All Species Handsome Males Directory
Handsome Males
...BEFORE I BECOME A MONSTER.
Gray Wolf/Miyagi (25)
5 ft., 6 in. 132 lb.
I want to be an actor.
I HAVE TO DO THIS WHILE I'M STILL A BEAUTIFUL WOLF!

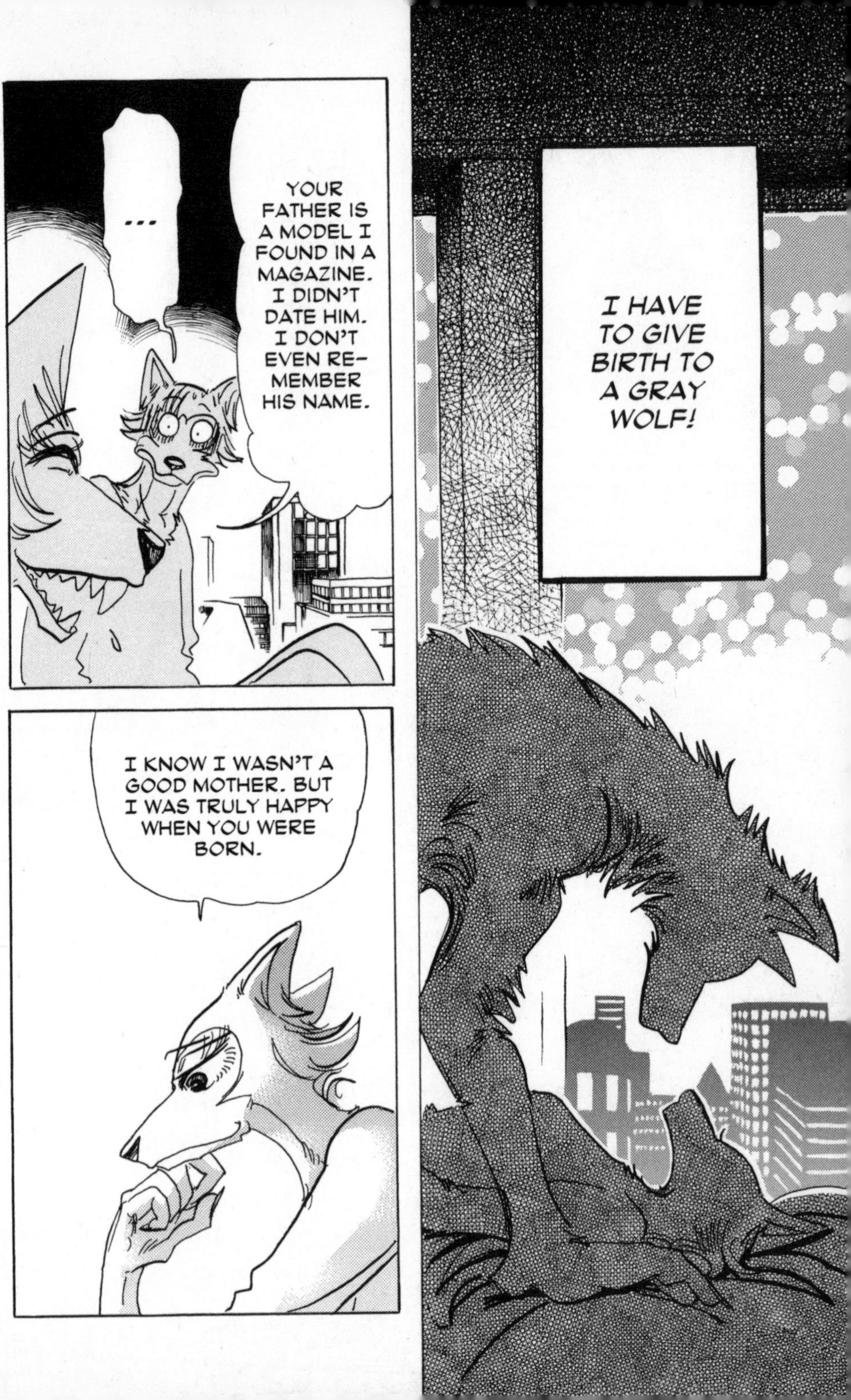
I HAVE TO GIVE BIRTH TO A GRAY WOLF!
YOUR FATHER IS A MODEL I FOUND IN A MAGAZINE. I DIDN'T DATE HIM. I DON'T EVEN REMEMBER HIS NAME.
...
I KNOW I WASN'T A GOOD MOTHER. BUT I WAS TRULY HAPPY WHEN YOU WERE BORN.

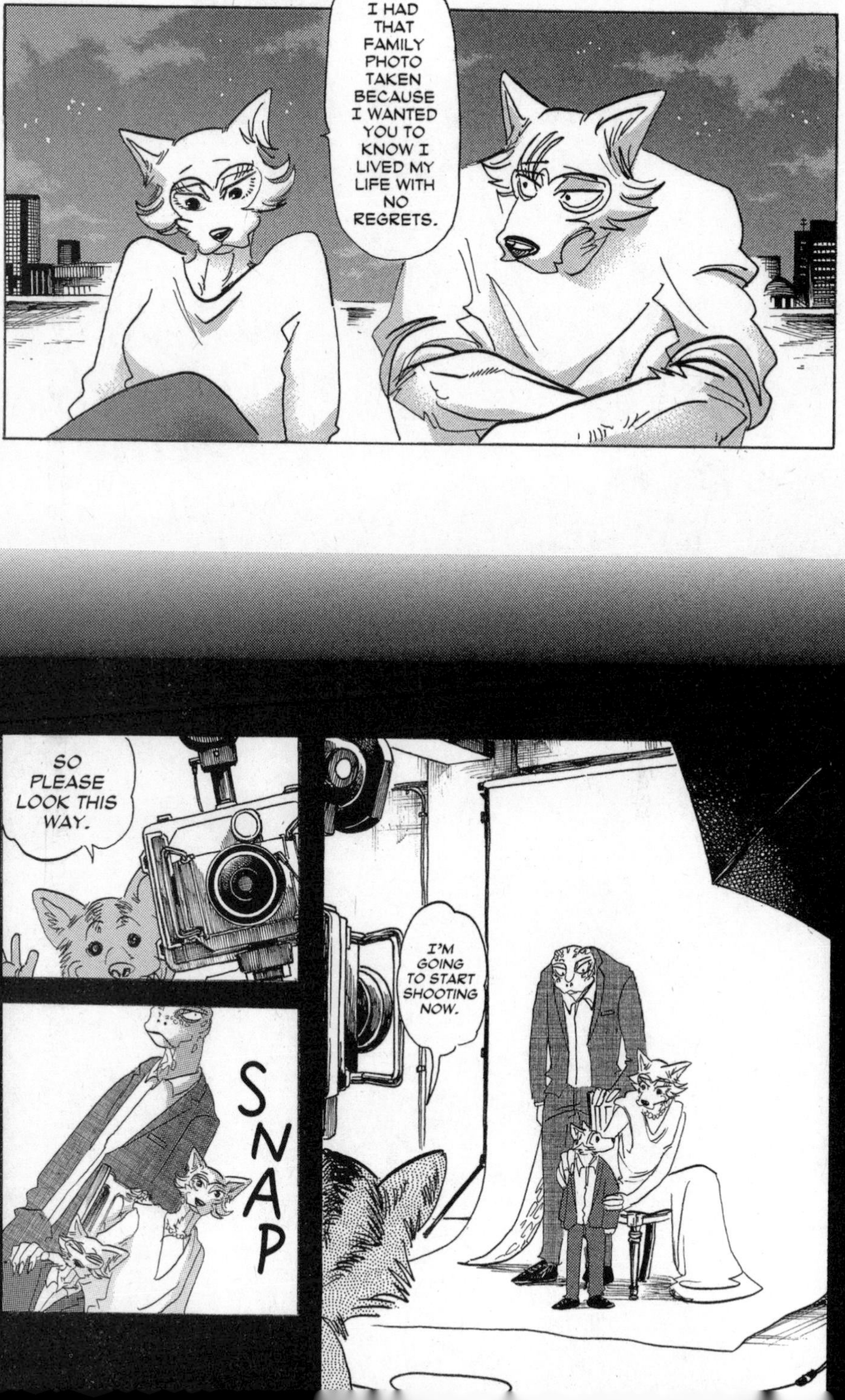
I HAD THAT FAMILY PHOTO TAKEN BECAUSE I WANTED YOU TO KNOW I LIVED MY LIFE WITH NO REGRETS.
I'M GOING TO START SHOOTING NOW.
SO PLEASE LOOK THIS WAY.
SNAP

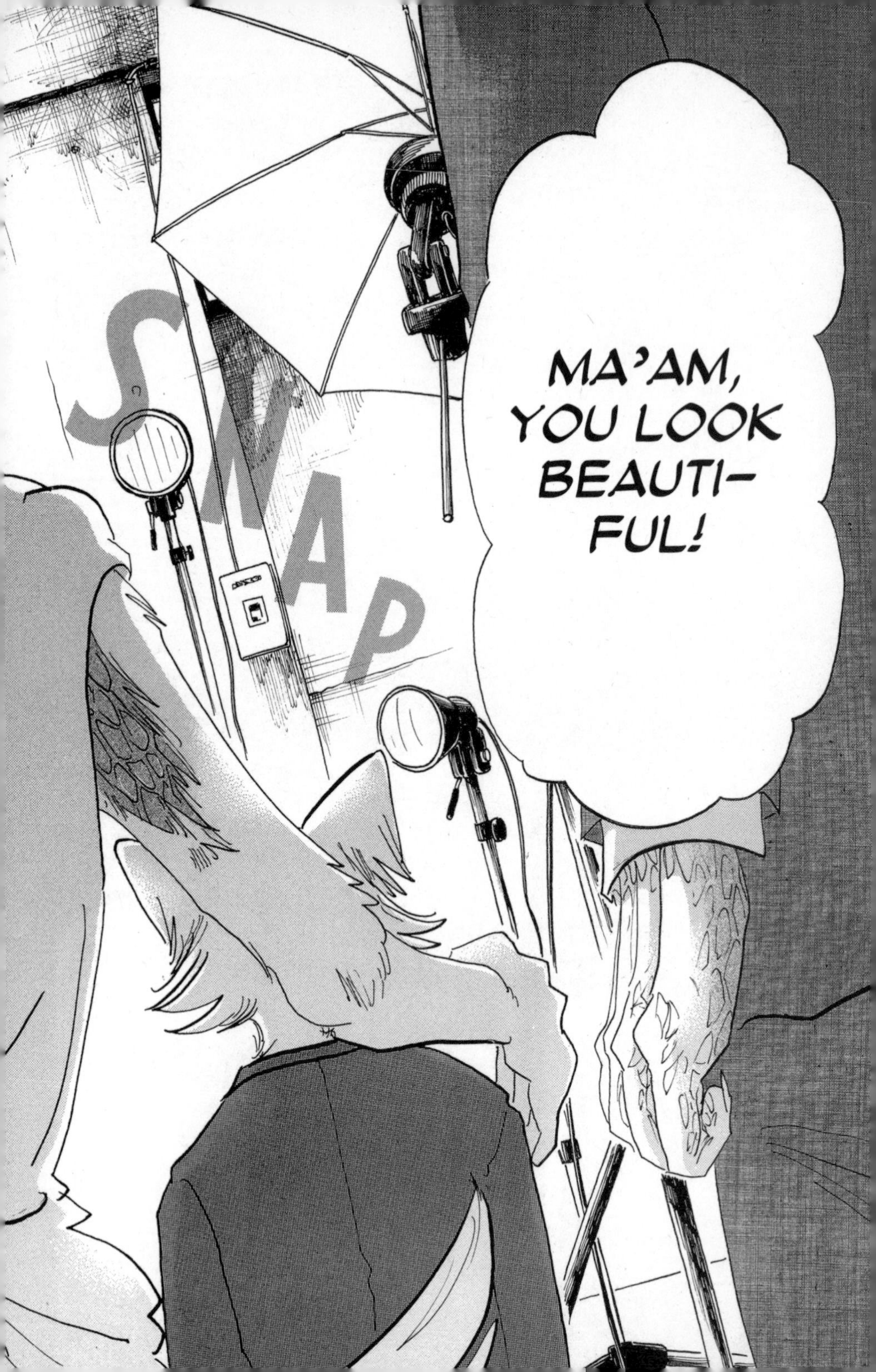
SNAP
MA'AM, YOU LOOK BEAUTI-FUL!

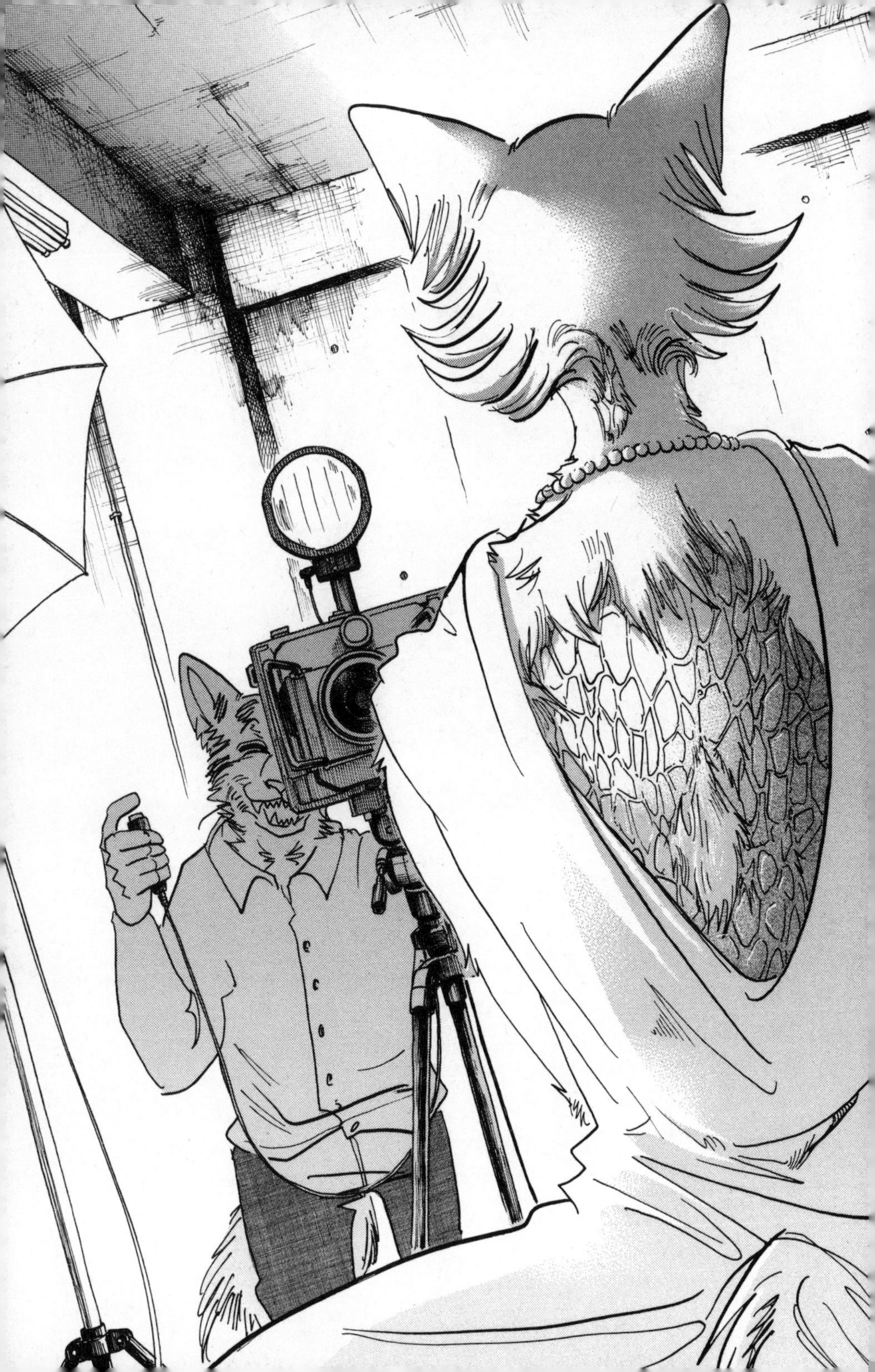

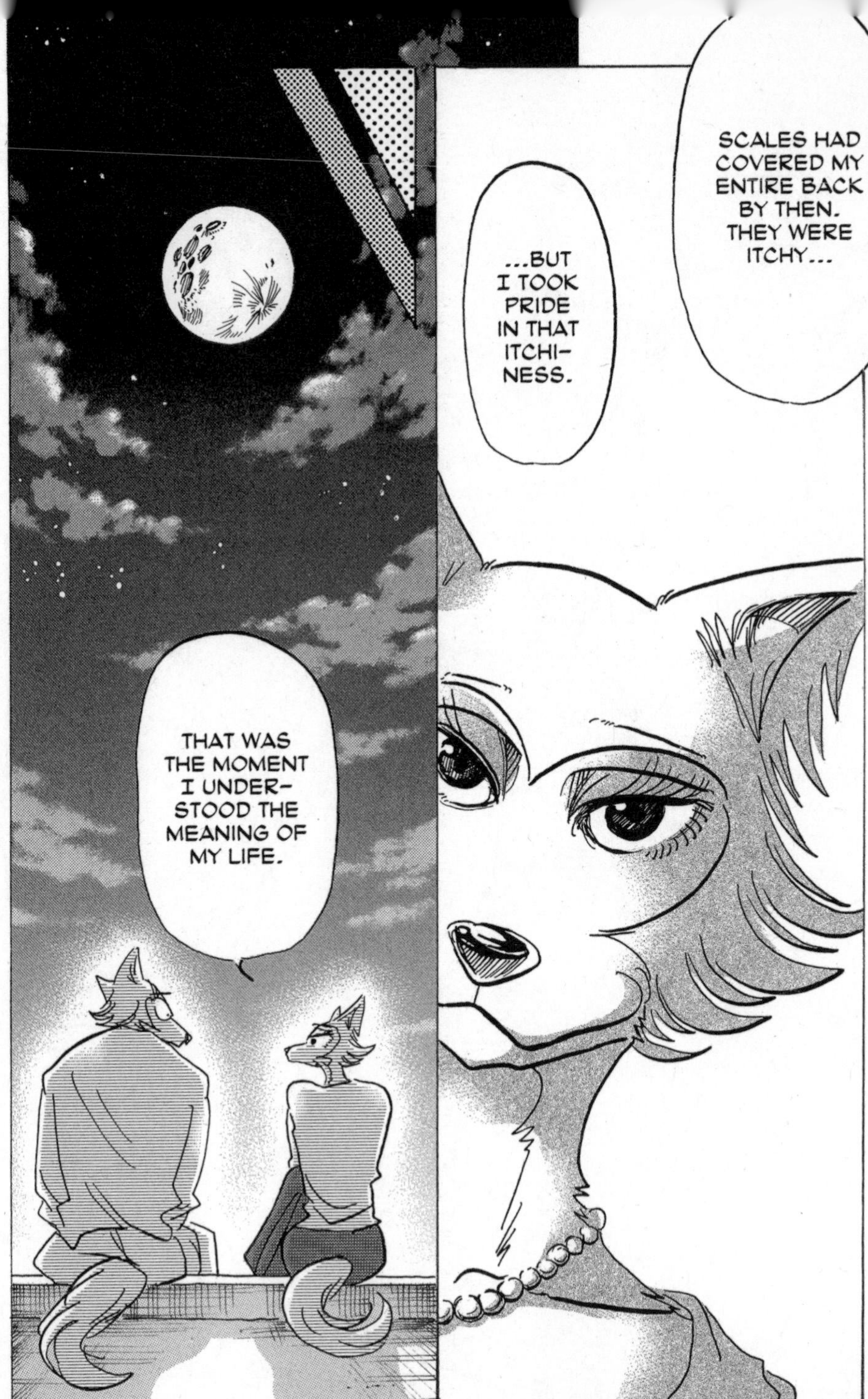
SCALES HAD COVERED MY ENTIRE BACK BY THEN. THEY WERE ITCHY...
...BUT I TOOK PRIDE IN THAT ITCHI-NESS.
THAT WAS THE MOMENT I UNDER-STOOD THE MEANING OF MY LIFE.

END OF BEASTARS VOL. 15

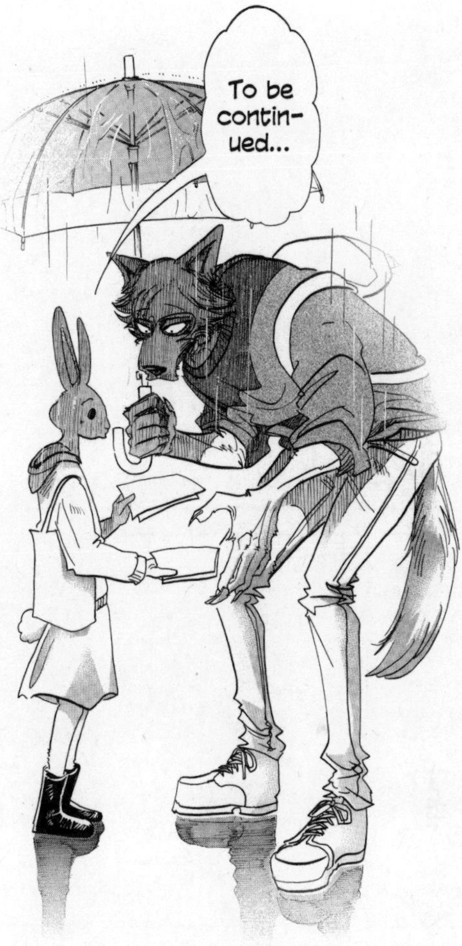
To be contin-ued...

Please read this after you finish reading chapter 133.

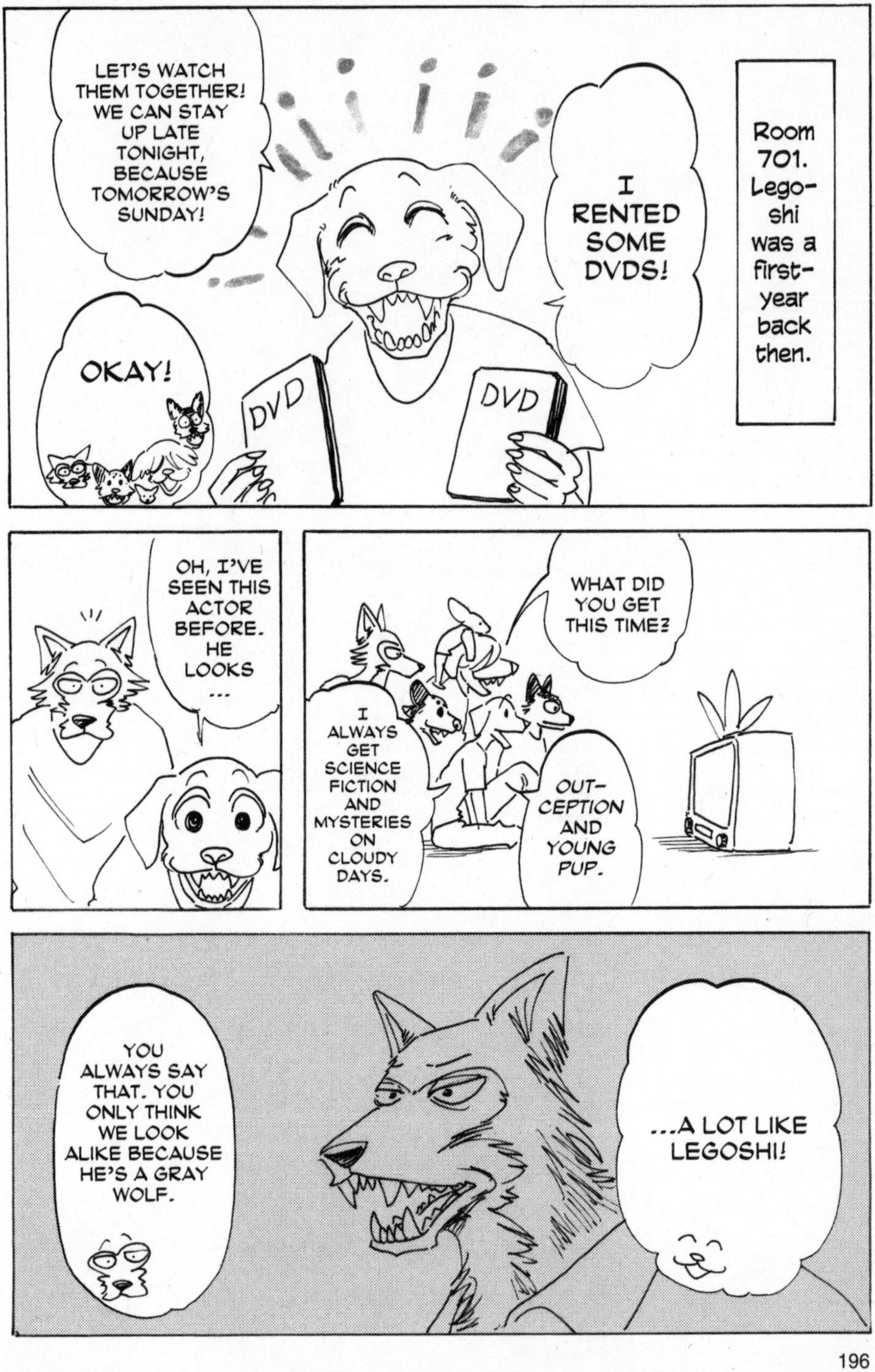

Room 701. Lego-shi was a first-year back then.
I RENTED SOME DVDS!
LET'S WATCH THEM TOGETHER! WE CAN STAY UP LATE TONIGHT, BECAUSE TOMORROW'S SUNDAY!
DVD
DVD
OKAY!
WHAT DID YOU GET THIS TIME?
OUT-CEPTION AND YOUNG PUP.
I ALWAYS GET SCIENCE FICTION AND MYSTERIES ON CLOUDY DAYS.
OH, I'VE SEEN THIS ACTOR BEFORE. HE LOOKS ...
...A LOT LIKE LEGOSHI!
YOU ALWAYS SAY THAT. YOU ONLY THINK WE LOOK ALIKE BECAUSE HE'S A GRAY WOLF.

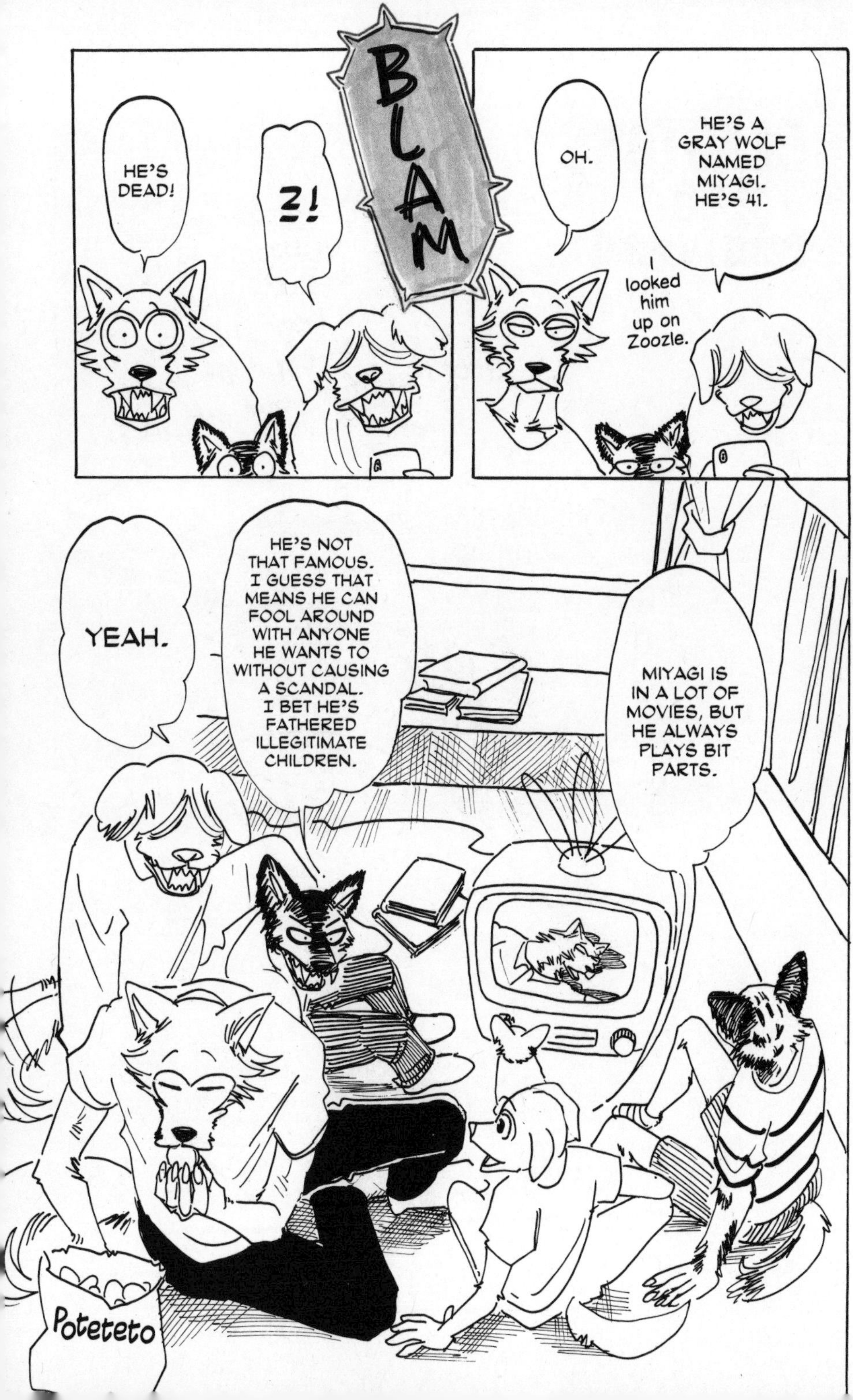
HE'S A GRAY WOLF NAMED MIYAGI. HE'S 41.
OH.
I looked him up on Zoozle.
BLAM
?!
HE'S DEAD!
MIYAGI IS IN A LOT OF MOVIES, BUT HE ALWAYS PLAYS BIT PARTS.
HE'S NOT THAT FAMOUS. I GUESS THAT MEANS HE CAN FOOL AROUND WITH ANYONE HE WANTS TO WITHOUT CAUSING A SCANDAL. I BET HE'S FATHERED ILLEGITIMATE CHILDREN.
YEAH.
Poteteto

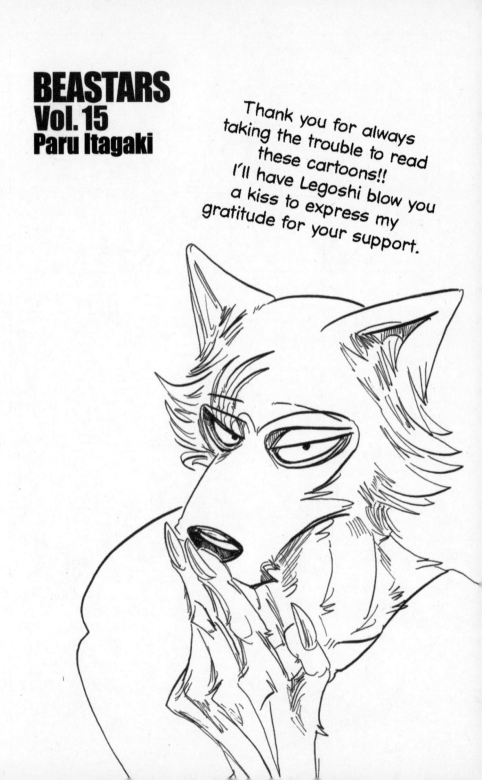

BEASTARS
Vol. 15
Paru Itagaki

Thank you for always taking the trouble to read these cartoons!! I'll have Legoshi blow you a kiss to express my gratitude for your support.

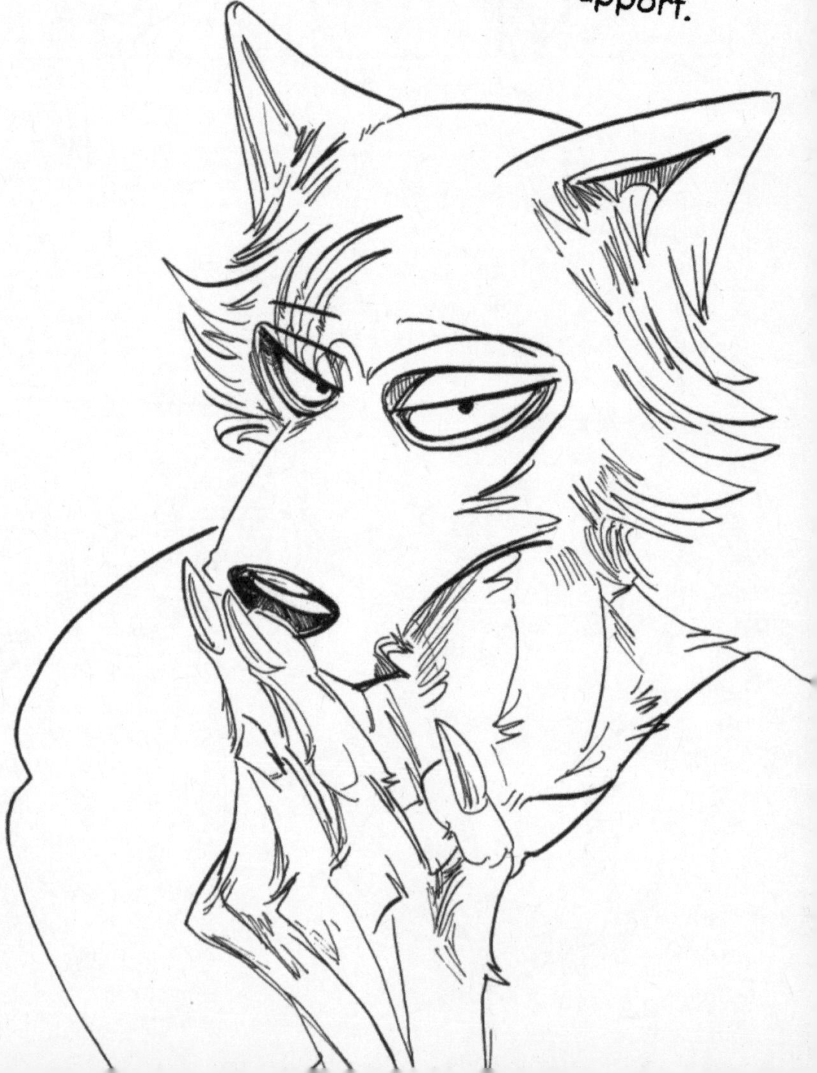

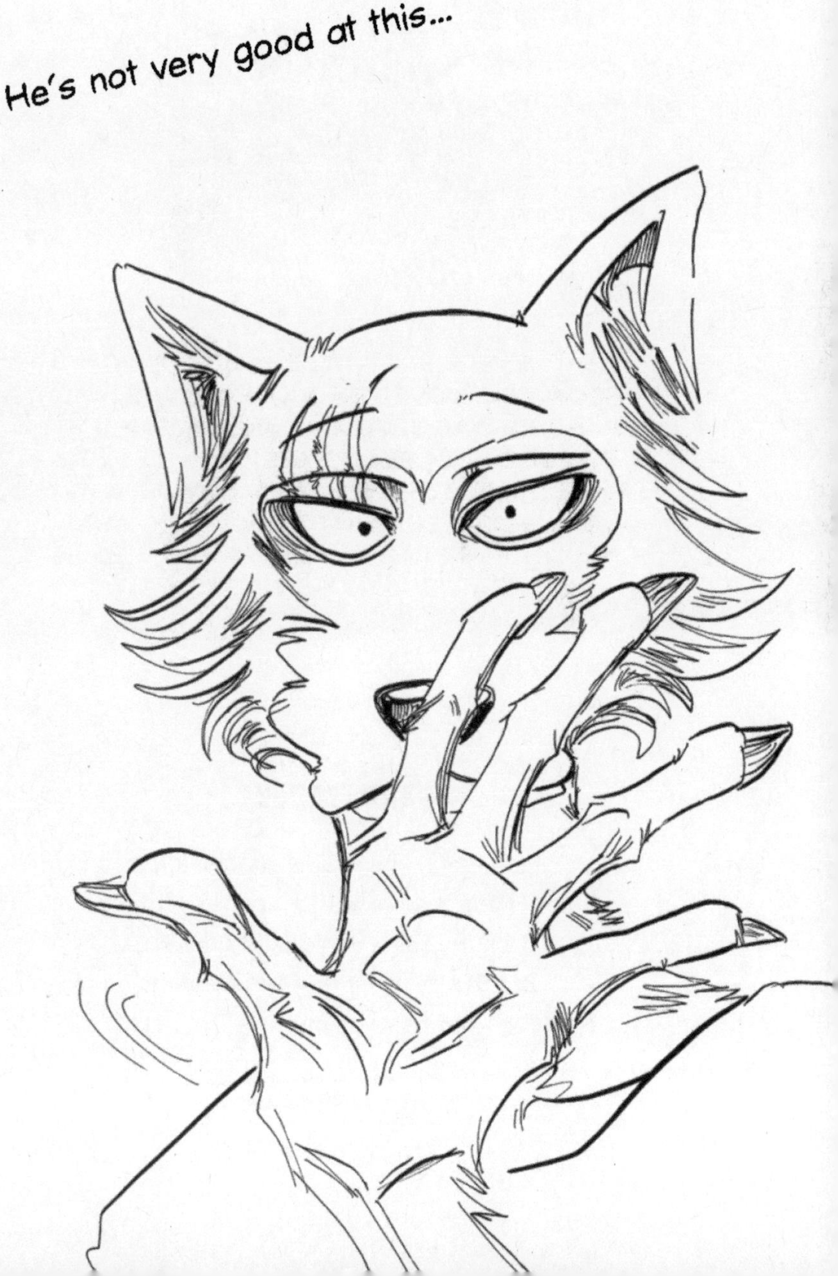
He's not very good at this...

I WAS VERY BUSY THE SUMMER OF 2019
BECAUSE I MOVED INTO A NEW PLACE, AND
BEASTARS WAS BECOMING AN ANIME! HERE'S
SOMETHING I NEED TO KEEP IN MIND EVEN
WHEN I'M BUSY—THE *BEASTARS* WORLD WILL
LIVE ON FOREVER. WHAT I FOCUS ON, WHAT I
DRAW...THESE ARE MY RESPONSIBILITIES AS
THE CREATOR AND CEO OF THIS WORLD.

PARU ITAGAKI

Paru Itagaki began her professional
career as a manga author in 2016 with the
short story collection **BEAST COMPLEX**.
BEASTARS is her first serialization.
BEASTARS has won multiple awards in
Japan, including the prestigious 2018
Manga Taisho Award.

BEASTARS

VOL. 15
VIZ Signature Edition

Story & Art by
Paru Itagaki

Translation/Tomo Kimura
English Adaptation/Annette Roman
Touch-Up Art & Lettering/Susan Daigle-Leach
Cover & Interior Design/Yukiko Whitley
Editor/Annette Roman

Published by VIZ Media, LLC
P.O. Box 77010
San Francisco, CA 94107

10 9 8 7 6 5 4 3 2 1
First printing, November 2021

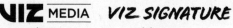

VIZ MEDIA   VIZ SIGNATURE
viz.com   vizsignature.com

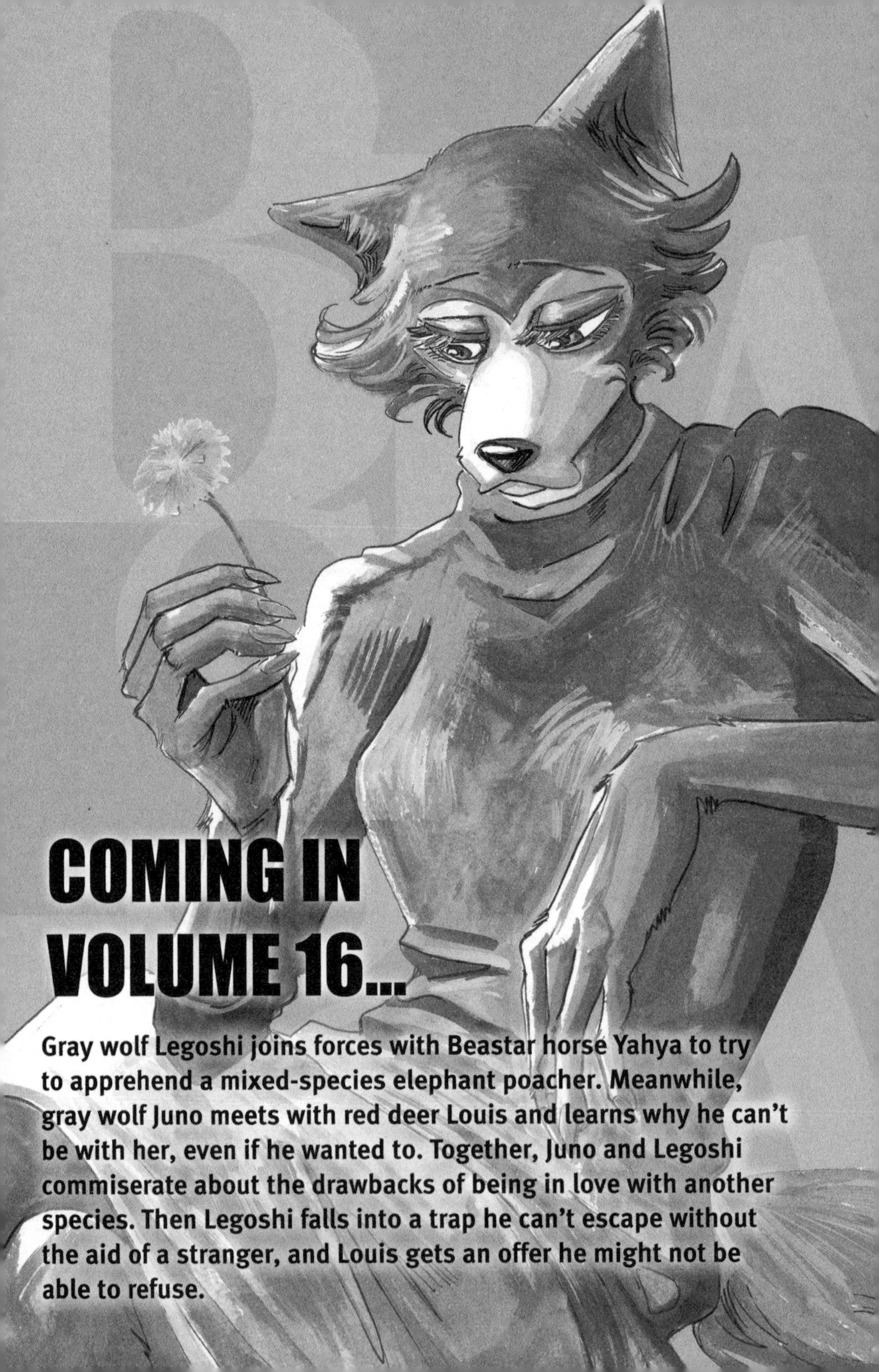

COMING IN VOLUME 16...

Gray wolf Legoshi joins forces with Beastar horse Yahya to try to apprehend a mixed-species elephant poacher. Meanwhile, gray wolf Juno meets with red deer Louis and learns why he can't be with her, even if he wanted to. Together, Juno and Legoshi commiserate about the drawbacks of being in love with another species. Then Legoshi falls into a trap he can't escape without the aid of a stranger, and Louis gets an offer he might not be able to refuse.

Six short stories that set the scene
for the best-selling *BEASTARS* series!

BEAST COMPLEX

Story and Art by **Paru Itagaki**

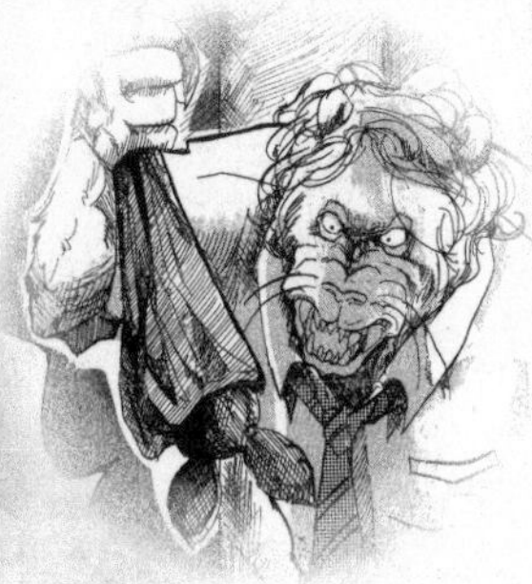

I n these six stories from the creator of the Eisner-nominated, best-selling series BEASTARS, a menagerie of carnivores and herbivores grapple with conflicts based on their differences and—sometimes—find common ground.

The Way of the House Husband

It's a day in the life of your average househusband—if your average househusband is the legendary yakuza "the Immortal Dragon"!

Story and Art by
Kousuke Oono

A former yakuza legend leaves it all behind to become your everyday househusband. But it's not easy to walk away from the gangster life, and what should be mundane household tasks are anything but!

CHILDREN OF THE WHALES

In this postapocalyptic fantasy, a sea of sand swallows everything but the past.

In an endless sea of sand drifts the Mud Whale, a floating island city of clay and magic. In its chambers a small community clings to survival, cut off from its own history by the shadows of the past.

Sweet Blue Flowers

One of the most highly regarded works of yuri!

Story and Art by **Takako Shimura**

Akira Okudaira is starting high school and is ready for exciting new experiences. And on the first day of school, she runs into her best friend from kindergarten at the train station! Now Akira and Fumi have the chance to rekindle their friendship, but life has gotten a lot more complicated since they were kids…

Collect the series!

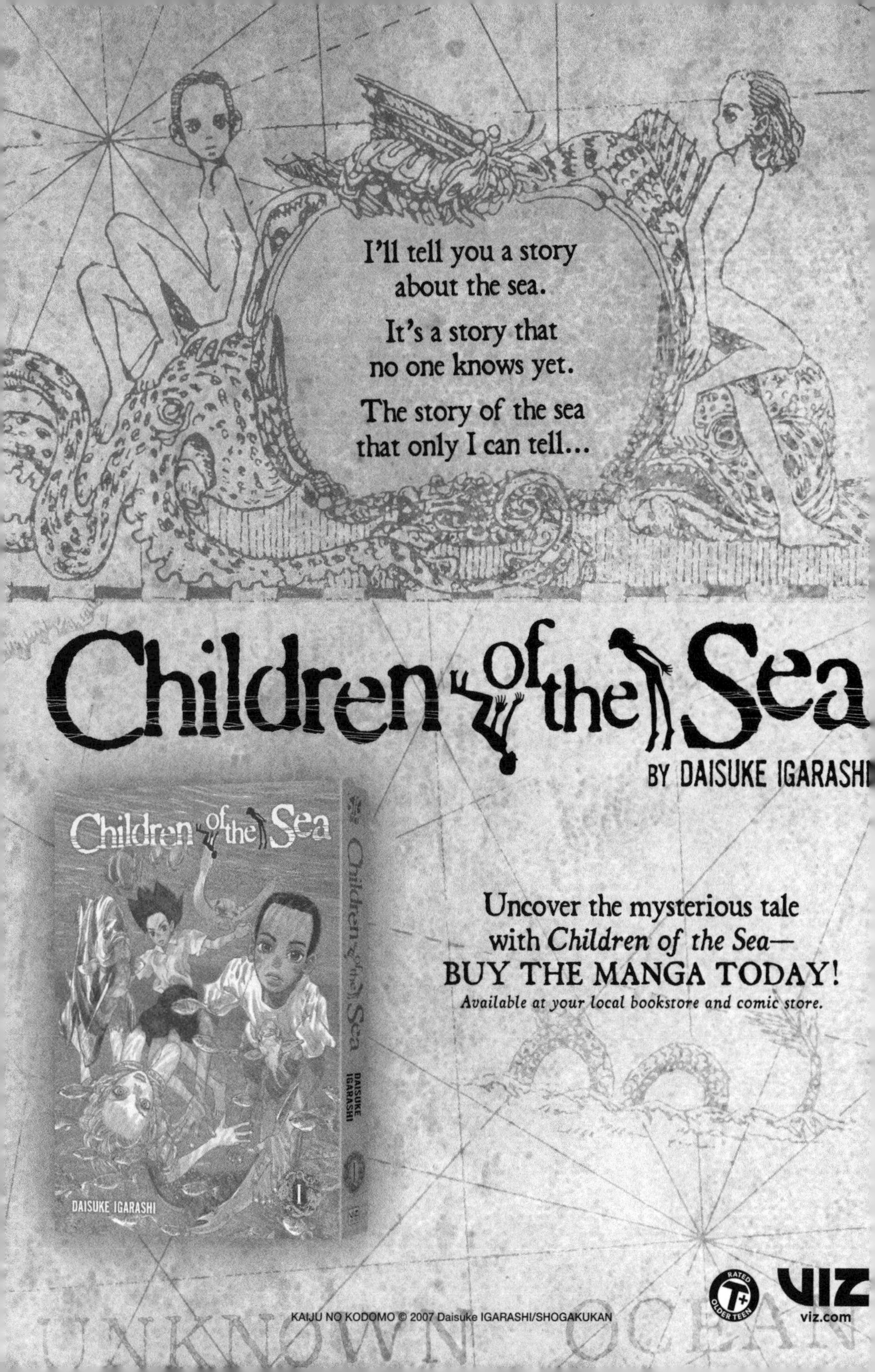
I'll tell you a story
about the sea.
It's a story that
no one knows yet.
The story of the sea
that only I can tell...
Children of the Sea
BY DAISUKE IGARASHI
Children of the Sea
DAISUKE IGARASHI
1
Uncover the mysterious tale
with Children of the Sea—
BUY THE MANGA TODAY!
Available at your local bookstore and comic store.
RATED T+ OLDER TEEN
VIZ
viz.com
KAIJU NO KODOMO © 2007 Daisuke IGARASHI/SHOGAKUKAN
UNKNOWN OCEAN

This is the last page.

BEASTARS reads from right to left to preserve the orientation of the original Japanese artwork.